IRELAND, AUSTRALIA AND NEW ZEALAND

History, Politics and Culture

Editors
**Laurence M. Geary
and Andrew J. McCarthy**
University College Cork

IRISH ACADEMIC PRESS
DUBLIN • PORTLAND, OR

First published in 2008 by Irish Academic Press

44, Northumberland Road,	920 NE 58th Avenue, Suite 300
Ballsbridge,	Portland, Oregon
Dublin 4, Ireland	97213-3786

www.iap.ie

British Library Cataloguing in Publication Data
An entry can be found on request

ISBN 978 0 7165 2861 6 (cloth)
ISBN 978 0 7165 2862 3 (paper)

Library of Congress Cataloging-in-Publication Data
An entry can be found on request

Typeset in 10/12pt Caslon 540 by FiSH Books, Enfield, Middx.
Printed by Biddles Ltd., King's Lynn, Norfolk

Contents

Abbreviations

AAP	Australian Associated Press
ALP	Australian Labor Party
ALUI	Australian League for an Undivided Ireland
BL	British Library
BNA	British National Archives
DLP	Democratic Labor Party
D/T	Department of An Taoiseach
EOKA	National Organization of Cypriot Fighters
GDP	Gross Domestic Product
INA	Irish National Association
IRA	Irish Republican Army
NAI	National Archives of Ireland
NLI	National Library of Ireland
NLA	National Library of Australia
RSSILA	Returned Sailors' and Soldiers' Imperial League of Australia
RUC	Royal Ulster Constabulary
TD	Teachta Dála
UCDA	University College Dublin Archives

List of Tables

List of Figures

Notes on Contributors

Ciara Breathnach is a lecturer in the Department of History, University of Limerick. She is the author of *The Congested Districts Board of Ireland, 1891–1923* (2005), *Framing the West: Images of Rural Ireland, 1891–1920* (ed. 2007), and *Portraying Irish Travellers* (ed. with Aoife Bhreatnach, 2006).

Malcolm Campbell is Associate Professor of History, University of Auckland, where he teaches Australian and Irish history. His current project is a history of the Irish in the Pacific World from 1760 to 1945.

Richard P. Davis is Professor Emeritus of History, University of Tasmania. He is the author of several books and articles on Irish and Australian history.

Frances Devlin-Glass is Associate Professor in the School of Communication and Creative Arts, Deakin University (Melbourne). She teaches Literary Studies, and is currently working on an Australian Research Council-funded project to investigate new definitions of the sacred in Australian literature. She has been the director of Bloomsday in Melbourne since 1994.

Tony Earls is a practising lawyer in Sydney. He is an active researcher, writer and presenter on aspects of Irish and Australian legal history. His current research interest is directed at the legal and cultural backgrounds of nineteenth-century Irish-Australian lawyers.

Lyndon Fraser is a senior lecturer in the School of Anthropology and Sociology, University of Canterbury. He is author of *To Tara via Holyhead: Irish Catholic Immigrants in Nineteenth-Century Christchurch* (1997), *A Distant Shore: Irish Migration and New Zealand Settlement* (ed. 2000), and *Castles of Gold: A History of New Zealand's West Coast Irish* (2007).

Laurence M. Geary lectures in history at University College Cork, and is the author of *Medicine and Charity in Ireland, 1718–1851* (2004).

David Grant is a part-time research student at the Open University, Milton Keynes, UK. He is currently researching aspects of W. Vincent Wallace's life and work, including his best-known opera, *Maritana* (1845).

Michael Hopkinson is reader in History at the University of Stirling. He is the author of *Green Against Green. The Irish Civil War* (1988) and *The Irish War of Independence* (2002), and has edited Frank Henderson's *Easter Rising* (1998) and *The Last Days of Dublin Castle: The Diaries of Mark Sturgis* (1999).

Jeff Kildea is a barrister, author and part-time lecturer at the University of New South Wales. He has taught Australian and Irish history to under-graduates and continuing education students. He has written books and articles and presented papers both in Australia and Ireland on Irish and Irish-Australian history.

Carla King is a lecturer in Modern History at St Patrick's College, Drumcondra, Dublin. Her eight-volume edition, *Michael Davitt: Collected Writings 1868–1906*, was published in 2001. She is working on a bio-graphy of the later life of Michael Davitt.

Peter Kuch is Eamon Cleary Professor of Irish Studies, University of Otago, Dunedin. He is the New Zealand and Australian representative on the inter-national organising committee of the Irish Theatrical Diaspora project, a multi-national research initiative charting the performance history of Irish theatre in provincial Ireland, UK, USA, Canada, New Zealand and Australia.

Andrew J. McCarthy is a lecturer in the Department of History, University College Cork, and has a number of publications on twentieth-century Irish history.

Ruán O'Donnell is a senior lecturer in History and Head of Department, University of Limerick. He is the author of several books and is currently working on a history of the IRA 'border campaign' of 1956–62 and a number of related projects.

Rory O'Dwyer lectures in the Department of History, University College Cork. He has published articles on the commemoration of the 1916 Rising, religious events in Ireland in the twentieth century, and popular culture.

Pamela O'Neill, FSA Scot, is a research fellow in the University of Melbourne's School of Historical Studies. She is series editor for the Sydney Series in Celtic Studies and (founding) president of the Australian Early Medieval Association.

Brad Patterson is director of the Irish-Scottish Studies Programme at the Stout Research Centre for New Zealand Studies, Victoria University of Wellington. His recent edited works include *Sport, Society and Culture in New Zealand* (1999) and *The Irish in New Zealand: Historical Contexts and Perspectives* (2002).

Brega Webb is a postgraduate researcher at the Moore Institute for Research in the Humanities and Social Studies, National University of Ireland, Galway.

Preface

The chapters in this volume represent a selection of the papers delivered at the fourteenth Irish–Australia conference, which was held at University College Cork in June 2005. The volume is divided into four sections: 'Ireland and the Pacific World'; 'Cultural Transmission'; 'Citizenship'; and 'Politics, War and Remembrance'.

In the opening essay, Malcolm Campbell attempts to capture the experiences of Irish people who traversed the Pacific World between 1788 and 1922. He traces the complex movements of people in the area from the west coast of the Americas through the Pacific to Australia and New Zealand during this period.

Continuing the theme of migration, Lyndon Fraser explores Irish ethnicity on the west coast of New Zealand. He focuses on the ways in which Irish men and women sustained themselves in goldfield communities, and argues that the west-coast Irish were at the forefront of colonisation and well represented in all sectors of the region's economy.

By 1869 New Zealand was in a state of economic stagnation and in the following year Julius Vogel, Treasurer of the Colonial Government, announced an ambitious scheme to develop the colony by borrowing capital abroad and spending it on public works and assisted immigration schemes. Ciara Breathnach charts the recruitment of European migrants under the assisted and nominated passage schemes and focuses on the exclusion of the Irish, more specifically the Catholic Irish, from these schemes.

The Irish Protestant experience in colonial New Zealand has been largely concealed save for the North Island settlement of Katikati, which was founded in 1875. This has been portrayed as a direct transplantation of Ulster culture to the New World, and a place where the province's culture endured. However, recent research suggests that Katikati was atypical, that the transplanted culture proved far less durable than has hitherto been believed. Brad Patterson surveys changing interpretations of the Katikati settlement since its foundation and assesses its significance in the wider historiography of Irish migration to New Zealand.

Section II of the book explores aspects of cultural transmission from Ireland to the antipodes. David Grant traces the Australian career of Irish-born violinist, pianist and composer W. Vincent Wallace, who lived in Sydney between 1835 and 1838. Wallace was probably the first major musical executant and composer to visit Australia. He established the country's first music academy, and Grant assesses his musical impact and legacy.

Brega Webb looks at the life and poetry of County Galway-born Mary Anne Kelly, who, under the pseudonym 'Eva', was one of the poets associated with the Young Ireland movement in the 1840s. In 1848 she became engaged to Kevin Izod O'Doherty, a surgeon and editor of the *Irish Tribune*. He was subsequently tried for sedition and sentenced to ten years' transportation to Van Diemen's Land. After his release, they married, and settled in Australia in 1862, where Kelly continued to write poetry. She died in straitened circumstances in Brisbane in 1910.

Peter Kuch traces the history of the 'Abbey' Irish Players' visit to Australia in 1922 to perform Lennox Robinson's *The White-Headed Boy*. After seasons in Sydney, Melbourne and Adelaide, the company embarked on an extensive tour of Queensland. Kuch examines that tour both for its own sake and in terms of the fortunes of Irish theatre in Australia in the early decades of the twentieth century.

Frances Devlin-Glass revisits one of the iconic texts of the pastoral era, Mary Durack's *Kings in Grass Castles* (first edition, 1959), in the light of subsequently published Aboriginal life-stories and *testimonii* and more recent fictional treatments of the period. Devlin-Glass explores Durack's systematic deployment of tropes of Irishness to construct pioneer heroism/victimhood, and simultaneously to generate affect for the 'underdog'. This creates a highly unstable text, which serves to deflect attention from the extent to which the enterprise of pioneering within the extensive Durack pastoral dynasty (which settled vast tracts of remote south-west Queensland and the Kimberleys and was more benign than most) was implicated in the theatre of racist cruelty on the frontier.

Pamela O'Neill's chapter investigates funerary monuments in a number of Australian cemeteries, some of which sport representations of early Irish monastic landscapes, including such features as high crosses and round towers. O'Neill suggests that the scenes are intended to represent specific locations in Ireland rather than the generic idea of Irish monasteries. She explores possible means of transmission of the images to the Australian commissioners and creators of the monuments and she evaluates relationships between the decedents and the particular landscapes which appear to be represented on their monuments.

In the volume's penultimate section, Richard Davis surveys Irish influence on Tasmania from the convict period to the present, and in the process examines the lives and impact of eminent citizens; Orange and Green rivalry; battles over education; and support for Irish independence. Some 14,000 Irish people were transported to the colony, mostly in the period of the Great Famine, but a relatively small number of free settlers had a far greater influence on Tasmania. Davis concludes by noting the change in the general Tasmanian perception of Ireland from a source of hated criminals to a model for economic development.

Larry Geary sketches the colonial career of one of Davis's free settlers, County Cork-born Roderic O'Connor, who put down dynastic roots in Van Diemen's Land in 1824. However, in Geary's chapter, Roderic plays second fiddle to his splendidly eccentric father, Roger, whose colourful career embraced Irish patriotism, banditry, pamphleteering, and antiquarianism, and it is likely that the consequences of at least some of these career choices contributed to Roderic's decision to emigrate.

Tony Earls continues the theme of eminent citizens, specifically the career of Australia's longest-serving Attorney General, John Hubert Plunkett, a protégé of Daniel O'Connell. In 1831 Plunkett was appointed to the post of Solicitor General to New South Wales, and for the next thirty years he was central to the progression of New South Wales from a penal colony to a fledgling democracy. Earls suggests that Plunkett's activities were informed by a profound belief in Irish Catholic emancipationist values, and that that ethos has been a significant influence in the development of Australian forms of equality, democracy and justice.

In the volume's final section, under the rubric 'Politics, War and Remembrance', Carla King assesses Michael Davitt's seven-month lecture tour of Australia and New Zealand in 1895, and concludes that his antipodean experiences were important in the development and radicalization of his political and social ideas. She regards his record of the tour, *Life and Progress in Australasia*, which was published in 1898, as much more than a travel book, arguing that Davitt engaged with the society he found. Among the issues that interested him most were the political systems in the colonies; the labour movement; the Irish emigrant experience; the living and working conditions of gold miners, Aborigines, and Kanakas on the sugar plantations; and the prison system.

Michael Hopkinson explores the reasons for the peace initiative undertaken by Archbishop Clune of Perth during the Irish War of Independence and analyses the reasons for its failure. He places the event in an Irish, British and Australian context, and suggests that, of the many peace efforts during the War of Independence, Clune's mission came closest to success and had major repercussions in both Rome and Western Australia.

Rory O'Dwyer assesses Éamon de Valera's only visit to the southern hemisphere, part of his 'World Anti-Partition Tour' in 1948. Frank Aiken, from whose personal papers much of these events are reconstructed, accompanied de Valera to the antipodes. O'Dwyer focuses on events and reactions in Australia and New Zealand. He analyses the response to the visit in the local media, among politicians and the Irish community in the two countries, and at home in Ireland.

Ruán O'Donnell examines Australian reaction to the revival of the IRA and Sinn Féin after 1948. Against the backdrop of visits to Australia by the political leaders of Northern Ireland and the Irish Free State, Lord Brookeborough and Éamon de Valera, O'Donnell traces the gradual eclipse of the Australian League for an Undivided Ireland (ALUI) by militant republican organisations, and analyses critically the nature of Australian newspaper reportage of Irish republican activity in Ireland.

A generation earlier, in excess of 300,000 Australians and more than 200,000 Irishmen volunteered for a war that was to become a defining event in the national history of both countries but which each has chosen to remember differently. In general, Australians revere their war dead and the Anzac tradition underpins Australian national identity, whereas in Ireland remembrance has been a contested issue, with attitudes ranging from hostility and indifference in the South, to sectarian appropriation in the North. In the volume's closing chapter, Jeff Kildea explores the memory and commemoration of the First World War in Ireland and Australia, and the role the war played in the evolving nationalism of both countries.

The editors wish to acknowledge the financial support provided by the Arts Faculty (now the College of Arts, Celtic Studies and Social Sciences), University College Cork, for the fourteenth Irish–Australia conference.

We gratefully acknowledge the financial assistance towards this publication we received from the Publications Fund of the College of Arts, Celtic Studies and Social Sciences, University College Cork, and also from the Publications Fund of the National University of Ireland.

Lisa Hyde of Irish Academic Press has been helpful and supportive, and has provided expert guidance throughout the publication process.

Laurence M. Geary
Andrew J. McCarthy

PART I

Ireland and the Pacific World

1

Irish Immigrants in the Pacific World

Malcolm Campbell

On 19 June 1767, the Royal Navy frigate HMS *Dolphin*, on a voyage of exploration in the Pacific under the command of Captain Samuel Wallis, observed through the haze land to the southwest. The sighting caused great excitement, not only because the ship's provisions were running disturbingly low after four months at sea, but because the vessel's mission appeared finally to have been fulfilled. The sailing-master, George Robertson, wrote in his journal: 'We now supposed we saw the long-wished-for Southern Continent, which has been often talked of, but never before seen by any Europeans.'[1] However, Robertson's hope that this land was Terra Australis proved to be unfounded. The *Dolphin* had sighted not the Great South Land but Tahiti, the first European expedition to do so. Initially the ship's officers maintained firm discipline as the crew explored the island and engaged in trade with its curious inhabitants. Nails proved especially alluring to the Tahitians and were bartered, initially for hogs and fruits, and, later, for sexual services. Tahitian elders' attempts to interest the ship's company in the island's women were initially thwarted when a cautious junior officer followed scrupulously his instructions and refused to permit the 'young girls' to board the ship despite the frantic pleas of the seamen.[2] Still the ship's discipline held, and men on shore leave were ordered strictly to remain in sight of the vessel. But on 6 July, while Captain Wallis suffered below decks the debilitating effects of 'bilious fevers and colics', the ship's order was finally compromised. Robertson recorded in his journal:

> At noon we returned on board and found our traders had but very indifferent success, they only brought off four pigs, a few fowls and some fruit. I was told by one of the Young Gentleman [*sic*] that a new sort of trade took up most of their attention this day, but it might more properly be called the old trade. He says a Dear Irish boy, one of our marines, was the first that begun the trade, for which he got a very severe thrashing from the Liberty men for not beginning in a more

decent manner, in some house, or at the back of some bush or tree.
Paddy's excuse was the fear of losing the Honour of having the first.[3]

Three weeks later, on 27 July, with his ship almost stripped bare of nails
and spikes, Captain Wallis finally ordered the *Dolphin* to leave Tahiti.

The arrival of the *Dolphin* in Tahiti marks a suitable starting point for
an exploration of the Irish presence in the Pacific World, the vast area
extending from the Western Americas to Australia, encompassing the
islands of the Pacific, New Zealand and also small European populations
in the Asian nations on the western rim of the Pacific. In the next century
and a half, the presence of Europeans increased markedly across this
region, ineradicably transforming landscapes, initiating a rapid decline
among the existing populations, causing profound disruption of existing
cultures, and initiating new political, economic and social structures. The
Irish were participants in all these processes, sometimes as contributors
and collaborators in the exertion of a broadly British influence across the
Pacific World, more rarely in resistance to the intrusion of colonial power.
In some situations the Irish were virtually indistinguishable from the
English, Scots or Welsh, at other times they were starkly identifiable, a
more cohesive and narrowly defined group that brought their own
particular imprint to the shaping of the Pacific World.

It is now commonplace to write and speak of the Irish presence within
the Atlantic World, a zone with a rich and well-developed historiography.
To do so acknowledges the coherence of that area, and implicitly recog-
nizes that the region was a site of a multifaceted exchange that encom-
passed the movement of Irish peoples, goods and ideas. My contention is
that, though at present little known or understood, similar trans-national
webbing spanned the Pacific World and connected its Irish peoples from
the late eighteenth century to the early twentieth century. This chapter
outlines the key lines of inquiry or nodes of study that constitute the trans-
national history of the Irish in the Pacific World.

First, who were the Irish of the Pacific World? We know with certainty
that the Irish were present as Europeans initially colonised the Pacific.
The 'Dear Irish boy', Paddy, was not the lone Irishman on the *Dolphin*:
Irish-born sailors constituted about 5 per cent of the ship's crew.[4] Others
served in Cook's voyages of exploration later in the eighteenth century.
Given their presence in the services it is hardly surprising that the Irish-
born were also present in significant numbers when the British
subsequently decided to establish a permanent presence in the Western
Pacific at Sydney Cove in 1788. From the late eighteenth century
onwards the Irish were an important fixture of Australian life, whether
serving within the various colonial administrations, the judiciary or the

clergy; or figuring among the 40,000 convicts transported from Ireland and one-fifth that number again of Irish men and women who were tried in Britain; or arriving with the tens of thousands of free immigrants who constituted so significant a proportion of the European population of pre-Federation Australia.

New Zealand presents a similar picture in respect of the Irish influence on colonial foundations. After Queen Victoria signed the royal charter to create the colony of New Zealand in November 1840, formally liberating the newest crown acquisition from New South Wales, it was a Waterford-born naval officer, William Hobson, who was appointed the first governor. Hobson received his instructions from the Secretary of State for the Colonies, Lord Normanby (Constantine Henry Phipps), who had returned only recently to London from his previous posting as Lord Lieutenant of Ireland. As Lord Lieutenant, Normanby had won the warm praise of Daniel O'Connell.[5] It seems likely that Normanby played a significant role in drafting the royal charter, which decreed that the infant colony should be divided into three provinces: New Ulster (the North Island), New Munster (the South Island) and New Leinster (Stewart Island).[6]

Though these 'Irish' provinces did not long endure, they provided a foretaste of Irish–New Zealand connections that intensified in the second half of the nineteenth century as the pace of immigration to the colony quickened. The high point for the Irish inflow was the Vogel era of the 1870s when, attracted by the colonial government's offer of assisted passages, more than 100,000 newcomers from the United Kingdom arrived to contribute to a period of rapid economic expansion. The Irish-born constituted 22.4 per cent of the intake in the decade 1871–1880, and 27.5 per cent of those who received government assistance.[7] By 1878, when the colony had a non-Maori population of 414,000, some 43,758 of the population was Irish-born, nearly 11 per cent of the total.[8] Thereafter the overall level of immigration to the colony declined. By the beginning of the twentieth century, the Irish-born constituted only 5.6 per cent of the non-Maori population.

Far away in the Americas, the Irish were also eyeing the Pacific. Some ventured westward from Valparaiso as the trans-Pacific trade in peoples and goods developed after 1800. When San Francisco supplanted its Chilean counterpart as the American gateway to the Pacific half a century later, a substantial Irish presence was soon visible there too. The Irish-born had been present in significant numbers in the small Californian population, even before the war with Mexico. However, the discovery of gold in 1848 provided the impetus for a rapid expansion in the territory's population and drew large numbers of gold-seekers, including many of Irish birth or descent, to the American West Coast.[9] The Californian population increased dramatically, rising from around 14,000 in 1848 to nearly 93,000 in 1850. Within this novel society, the Irish were strongly represented, accounting for 11 per cent of the overseas-born population.

It is not until the second half of the nineteenth century, however, that we can attempt any serious reckoning of the scale of the Irish-born presence within the Pacific World. In 1870–71, when adequate census data exist for most of the region, in the order of 300,000 Irish-born resided within the area bounded by the Western Americas and South Australia, a number equivalent to one-fifteenth of Ireland's population at that time.[10] Most lived on the periphery of the Pacific, participants in the process of explosive Anglophone expansion that cut a swathe westward from the Mississippi River to the Pacific Coast, and then to Australasia, after 1850. Its largest concentrations were in Eastern Australia, New Zealand and California, especially in the rapidly emerging cities of the new urban frontier such as San Francisco, Auckland and 'marvellous' Melbourne. Though small by comparison with the Irish-born population centred on the Atlantic, this was undoubtedly a dynamic and remarkably mobile group of immigrants, whose movements and transactions interlaced the Pacific in complex ways. A high proportion were not direct migrants from Ireland, but had moved towards and then within the Pacific world in calculated stages.

San Francisco provides a case in point. In 1852 only 7 per cent of that city's Irish-born immigrants identified their previous place of residence as having been in the British Isles. Instead, California's Irish-born arrived on the West Coast after periods of residence elsewhere, and were in the main experienced New World settlers by the time they reached the Golden State.[11] Unsurprisingly, the largest number had previously resided elsewhere in the United States. In 1852, 45 per cent of San Francisco's Irish-born population had previously lived in the east, most in either New England or the mid-Atlantic states, with smaller numbers in states adjacent to the Mississippi River or in British North America. At mid-century, two main routes existed for these migrants to travel to California. The most daunting was the overland route, and Irish settlers were prominent participants in the early parties that survived the arduous trek across the Rocky Mountains to arrive in the far west. However, in the years before the completion of the transcontinental railway, a greater number of new settlers arrived by sea. Between 1855 and 1869 three-quarters of new arrivals to San Francisco chose to sail south along the Atlantic coast and cross the isthmus at Panama before sailing north to California, a journey made simpler following the opening of the Panama railway in 1855.[12]

The other main source of Irish immigrants to California was Australasia, stark proof of the mid-nineteenth-century propensity for transpacific migration. In fact, in 1852 the number of trans-Pacific Irish residents in San Francisco was almost identical to the number who had relocated within the continental United States. Within Australasia, by far the greatest number of Irish came from Sydney, or gave Australia as a generic label for their previous place of residence. Fewer than 1 per cent of the immigrants indicated that they were previous residents of New Zealand.[13] This eastward migration of the Irish to California has attracted only limited attention from historians to date. Most of the Irish arrived as part of the group known pejoratively as the 'Sydney Ducks', gold-seekers who met an adverse reception upon arrival in San Francisco due to their purported criminality (some were undoubtedly ex-convicts) and their reputation for gambling and excessive drinking. On account of their negative image, the 'Ducks' became a particular target of San Francisco's Committee of Vigilance in 1851.[14] However, despite their reputation, the evidence suggests that immigrants from Australia were not principally young, single, reckless men. The most careful demographic study to date shows these transpacific migrants frequently arrived as family units. The average age of the men and women who disembarked in San Francisco was significantly above that of California as a whole, and the sex ratio of the group (152 males to 100 females) far more closely approximated that of the entire United States (105 in 1850) than California (1,214 in 1852). Irish immigrants arriving from Sydney in 1852 were represented across all major occupational categories, though like their English-born counterparts, most engaged in labouring work.[15]

Other Irish migrants took to the islands, again, mostly after periods of transition elsewhere. No one can be certain of the numbers, though histories of Polynesia in particular provide ample evidence of the presence of individual Irish. To the vastness of the Pacific World came the Irish-born and those of Irish descent, as beachcombers, traders, missionaries and colonial administrators; men like Peter Dillon, born in 1788 to a County Meath family, who served in the Royal Navy before achieving renown as a ship's captain, trader and ethnographer of the Pacific; or William Henry, born in Sligo in 1770, who joined the London Missionary Society and was posted with his family to the service of God in Tahiti. The 'tattooed Irishman', James O'Connell, spent time in the Caroline Islands in Micronesia before touring America as a circus performer renowned for his body art.[16] The longevity of the Irish presence, like its diversity, is not in doubt: it ran the length of Britain's colonial domination. Sir Hubert Murray (1861–1940), son of the Irish Australian pioneer Terence Aubrey Murray, was administrator of New Guinea from 1908 until shortly before the outbreak of the Second World War. A history of the Irish needs to address all these lives: men and women of Irish birth, and many of Irish descent, whose experiences took shape on the beaches where European encountered islander, on the missions, in the affluent colonial bungalows, and deeper still in the interiors of the remoter parts of the Pacific World.

The Irish presence in the Pacific extended well beyond the multi-directional movement of people. It was a site of complex exchanges of news, ideas and identities. Kevin Kenny has cautioned against the excesses of trans-national approaches to the study of the Irish, arguing that critical aspects of their experience require analysis against the backdrop of the state.[17] This is undoubtedly true, and nowhere more so than in the celebrated examples of early state intervention, the 'working men's paradises', Australia and New Zealand. Nevertheless, clear avenues of inquiry can be identified that permit exploration of the range of Irish experiences, the trans-national interactions between groups of Irish within the Pacific World, and the impact of those lives on the existing communities of that world. This is a history pertinent to Ireland and its historians but also one of wider global significance that necessarily presents its own challenges – I agree only in part when Kenny writes that the historian's job 'is to make sense of this activity [by which he meant, Irish engagement within the empire] and what it means for Irish history'.[18] The remainder of this chapter identifies several avenues of inquiry that, in addition to the establishment of demographic baselines, are critical to a study of the Irish in the Pacific World.

Historians have recently begun to look afresh at Irish participation in the creation of the British Empire. As Nicholas Canny pointed out, 'the question of whether Irish people who participated in many of Britain's imperial projects were truly committed to the cause or were some type of fifth column is one that – like the "gendering of Empire" – has been brought to the fore'.[19] Attention has been devoted most closely to the colonising role of the Irish in the Americas and Asia, but much less so to the Pacific World. In this new setting, both sides of the collaboration-resistance debate boast their advocates. It is clear that numbers of Irish were present across the Pacific World from the late eighteenth century in a variety of locations and pursuits, and that they adopted a range of complex positions in relation to the colonising process that was then occurring. In New Zealand, for example, Irish soldiers in army regiments proved critical in enforcing British control during the Maori wars, while at the same time a number of Irish deserters chose consciously to serve with Maori resisters.[20] Consideration of these developments within the framework of the Pacific World will contribute significantly to broader debates about the Irish participation in colonial expansion as well as to the national historiographies of the Pacific nations.

The transmission of news – from Ireland, and of Irish communities abroad – was another critical aspect of the lives of the Irish and their descendants within the Pacific World. Heather McNamara has written, 'in comparison to the movements of peoples, exchanges of news within the Irish Diaspora remain little studied'. Immigrants' letters are best served in the existing historical literature, while exchanges of information between the secular and Irish-Catholic press remain at best scarcely addressed.[21] However, a striking feature to emerge from reading Irish – and in particular, Roman Catholic – newspapers on either side of the Pacific is the extent of coverage of the Irish presence on the Pacific's opposite shore. Through the latter decades of the nineteenth century, San Francisco's *Monitor* carried regular and detailed descriptions of Irish (Catholic) developments in Australia, while in New Zealand and Australia there was extensive coverage of Irish-American life, drawn mainly from the *Monitor*, as well as the more widely circulating *Boston Pilot* and *Irish World*. Innovative research has commenced into these connections, including the work of Kevin Molloy on the New Zealand press and Heather McNamara's excellent study on the New Zealand *Tablet*. McNamara shows, for example, that the Dunedin-based *Tablet* was exchanged with seven Australian Catholic newspapers, including the Melbourne *Advocate*, and Sydney's *Freeman's Journal* and *Catholic Press*, as well as with nine US-based papers, including the *Monitor* and the New York-based *Irish World*. Sometimes these were exchanges based on longstanding institutional arrangements; other swaps arose from more personal connections between the editors. These proved extremely resilient arrangements, able to avoid the censorious eye of governments when the pro-nationalist content was deemed seditious. During the First World War, for example, Andrew and Matthew Organ, natives of County Cork, smuggled banned newspapers, including the *Irish World,* into Australia while sailors plying the Pacific route.[22] A central pillar of a study of the Irish in the Pacific World is to examine the transmission of Irish news and newspapers across the Pacific and explore the role of these exchanges in the creation and maintenance of diasporic identities.

Religious connections constitute another line of inquiry. Intimate connections have long been recognized to exist between the Roman Catholic Church in New Zealand and Australia, but wider ties, relationships and activities across the Pacific World have received much more limited attention. Tantalising evidence suggests that in the nineteenth and early twentieth centuries these connections were extensive, from the westward mission of the globetrotting Fr Patrick Hennebury, reputedly the most widely travelled Irishman of his era, to Archbishop Daniel Mannix's passage to San Francisco at the commencement of his 1920 overseas tour.[23] However, the connections were wider than the Catholic Church, and linked distant Protestant Irish populations. From the appearance of the revivalist

William 'California' Taylor in Victoria in the mid-1860s, the arrival of trans-Pacific evangelical preachers in Australia became increasingly common, and their messages seem to have been favourably received by the sizeable crowds who attended their meetings.[24] Among these visitors were a number of Irishmen, including the Revd George Grubb, whose style prompted Stuart Piggin to observe recently, 'Australian evangelism owes much both in tone and in potency to Irish Protestants'.[25]

Nationalism constitutes another critical linkage. Where Irish nationalism in the Atlantic World has been extensively examined, the presence, intensity and functionality of Irish organisations in the Pacific world have not received similar attention. This is true even though, in the western United States, New Zealand and Australia, the cause of Irish nationhood also provoked (at different times, and in varying degrees) estrangement between the Irish and the host society, as well as profound division among the Irish themselves.[26] Many links can be identified spanning the Pacific World. In the 1880s the Redmond brothers' visit to Australia was followed by a voyage to San Francisco, and, eventually, to a triumphant reception back in Ireland. Michael Davitt traversed the Pacific, observing with interest developments in Polynesia. During the First World War Albert Dryer's Irish National Association maintained clandestine links with American supporters of the Irish Republican Brotherhood (IRB) based on the United States west coast. Later, when Dryer established an Australian League for an Undivided Ireland, he was quick to foster links with like-minded Irish in New Zealand.[27]

Across the Pacific World Irish immigrants also attracted attention – frequently opprobrium – for their dissent towards authority and their participation in and support for radical causes. To this day, Ned Kelly retains iconic status in Australia on this account, but a wider tradition can be identified through the societies of the Pacific World.[28] Though the reputation for dissent homogenises Irish attitudes and experiences, Irish immigrants did figure prominently in campaigns for reform, popular protests, and the emergence of the labour movement on both sides of the Pacific.[29] Another path to be followed is to identify and chart connections (as well as traditions and movements that were not passed) across the Pacific Diaspora and consider the roles of radicalism and dissent in the creation of Irish diasporic identities.

The transmission of culture represents one further avenue of inquiry. Recent scholarship has emphasised the power of music in Irish society to 'form and transform the identity of communities'.[30] But how crucial was it in shaping (and reshaping) the identities of the millions of Irish men and women resident outside Ireland in the period studied here? I will explore the transmission of music and ballads through the Pacific World, questioning their role in the development of diasporic identities. This is very much a new avenue of inquiry, though recent work undertaken on the music of the immigrant Irish in the United States and Australia will underpin the inquiries.[31] An examination of what was (and was not) transmitted should provide critical insights into the process of transfer and exchange through the Irish Pacific, while potentially illuminating significant differences across the societies that constituted it. For example, a striking distinction between Australia and New Zealand appears to be the absence of broadside balladry in New Zealand compared with its presence in colonial Australia – a significant difference given the proximity of the two countries.

In previous work I have utilised comparative history to suggest that similarities exist between the western Americas and eastern Australia, and that these set the Irish experience apart from that of their compatriots within the eastern United States or Atlantic-oriented New World settlements.[32] Paramount among the factors that delineate the experience of the Irish on the edges of the Pacific from the eastern model is the time of their arrival. As Patricia Nelson Limerick wrote of the American west, 'in a society that rested on a foundation of invasion and conquest, the matter of legitimacy was up for grabs, and it remained up for grabs as long as a large sector of the population continued to be migrants from other regions and nations'.[33] Whereas the Irish on North America's Atlantic coast confronted intrinsic hostility and deep sectarian animus, those on the margins of the Pacific World seem to have encountered emerging societies, more fluid and reflexive in their appreciation of newcomers from Ireland. These Pacific-rim societies were marked by identities in a state of constant flux. Indeed, the novelty of the societies was a key ingredient in the way the European populations in both locations defined their identity, marking their communities as different from the Old World. Both societies, through this assertion of difference, paved the way for fuller participation of the Irish than existed elsewhere across the Diaspora, and the immigrants celebrated this difference enthusiastically.

However, the comparative approach is not sufficient to explore fully the interrelationships between the Irish on the edges of the Pacific, nor to accommodate the experience of those who settled on the islands in its midst. In the nineteenth century in particular, the Pacific was a porous site characterised by the frequent movement of peoples, artefacts and ideas. Westward and eastward, the Irish – like other peoples of the Pacific – transgressed boundaries and state authority. The objective now is to move beyond comparison to this widened stage, and to explore with greater determination the relatedness, the interconnectedness, of the Pacific World's entire Irish population.

NOTES

1. George Robertson, *An Account of the Discovery of Tahiti*, Oliver Warner (ed.) (London: Folio Society, 1955), p.19.
2. Ibid., pp.56–7.
3. Ibid., pp.72–3.
4. Ibid., p.5.
5. Richard Davenport-Hines, 'Phipps, Constantine Henry, first marquess of Normanby (1797–1863)', *Oxford Dictionary of National Biography* (Oxford: Oxford University Press, 2004) [http://www.oxforddnb.com.ezproxy.auckland.ac.nz/view/article/22187 [Accessed 19 February 2007].
6. A.H. McLintock, *Crown Colony Government in New Zealand* (Wellington: Government Printer, 1958), pp.98–9.
7. http://www.nzhistory.net.nz/Gallery/brit-nz/where.htm. [Accessed 20 August 2005].
8. http://www.teara.govt.nz/1966/N/NationalGroups/NationalGroups/en. [Accessed 20 August 2005].
9. See James P. Walsh, 'The Irish in Early San Francisco', in James Walsh (ed.), *The San Francisco Irish, 1850–1976* (San Francisco: Irish Literary and Historical Society, 1978), pp.9–25; Roger Lotchin, *San Francisco 1846–1856: From Hamlet to City* (New York: Oxford University Press, 1974), pp.102–3.
10. The Australian colonies accounted for approximately 200,000; New Zealand 30,000; California 55,000; Oregon, Washington Territory and British Columbia 4,000.
11. A. Burchell, 'The Gathering of a Community: The British-born in San Francisco in 1852 and 1872', *Journal of American Studies*, 10, 3 (1976), pp.279–312. This pattern was repeated in neighbouring counties, such as Sonoma, where only 6 per cent of the Irish-born gave their last place of residence as Ireland. See Dennis E. Harris (ed.), *Redwood Empire Social History Project: California State Census, 1852, Sonoma County* (Sonoma: County of Sonoma, 1983), p.37.
12. On the movement of Irish to the West, R.A. Burchell, *The San Francisco Irish 1848–1880* (Berkeley, CA: University of California Press, 1980), pp.34–5; Peter R. Decker, *Fortunes and Failures: White Collar Mobility in Nineteenth Century San Francisco* (Cambridge, MA: Harvard University Press, 1978), pp.13, 19–23. On the operation of the Panama route, as well as alternative routes via Nicaragua and Cape Horn, see H.H. Bancroft, *History of California* (Santa Barbara: Wallace Herberd, 1970, 7 vols.), Vol.vi, p.221; James P. Walsh, 'James Phelan: Creating the Fortune, Creating the Family', *Journal of the West*, 31, 2 (1992), pp.17–23. On the Irish in overland parties, see Gabrielle Sullivan, *Martin Murphy Jr: California Pioneer, 1844–1884* (Stockton: Pacific Center for Western Studies, 1974); Mary McDougall Gordon (ed.), *Overland to California with the Pioneer Line: The Gold Rush Diary of Bernard J. Reid* (Stanford: Stanford University Press, 1983).
13. Burchell, 'Gathering of a Community', pp.282–3; Harris, *Redwood Empire*, pp.36–7.
14. On the Committee and anti-Australian attitudes see Robert M. Senkewicz, *Vigilantes in Gold Rush San Francisco* (Stanford: Stanford University Press, 1985), pp.84–5.
15. Sherman L. Ricards and George M. Blackburn, 'The Sydney Ducks: A Demographic Analysis', *Pacific Historical Review* 42, 1 (1973), p.20; Burchell, 'Gathering of a Community', pp.281–3.
16. I am indebted to a former student, Alfred Soakai, for first drawing my attention to O'Connell.
17. Kevin Kenny, 'Diaspora and Comparison: the Irish as a Case Study', *Journal of American History*, 90, 1 (2003), p.147.
18. Kevin Kenny, 'The Irish in the Empire', in Kevin Kenny (ed.), *Ireland and the British Empire* (Oxford: Oxford University Press, 2004), pp.93, 121.
19. Nicholas Canny, 'Foreword', in Kenny (ed.), *Ireland and the British Empire*, pp.xi–xii.
20. James Belich, *Making Peoples: A History of the New Zealanders from Polynesian Settlement to the End of the Nineteenth Century* (Auckland: Penguin Books, 1996), p.243.
21. Heather McNamara, 'The *New Zealand Tablet* and the Irish Catholic Press World-Wide,

1898–1923', *New Zealand Journal of History*, 37, 2 (2003), p.153. Immigrant letters are the subject of major studies including David Fitzpatrick, *Oceans of Consolation: Personal Accounts of Irish Migration to Australia* (Ithaca, NY: Cornell University Press, 1994); Patrick O'Farrell, *Letters from Irish Australia 1825–1929* (Sydney: University of New South Wales Press, 1984); and Angela McCarthy, *Irish Migrants in New Zealand, 1840–1937: The Desired Haven* (Woodbridge, UK: Boydell Press, 2005).

22. Albert Thomas Dryer, 'The Independence of Ireland: Source Material for the History of the Movement in Australia', National Library of Australia, Dryer papers, MS 6610 Box 1, Folder 11.

23. Hugh Laracy, 'Patrick Hennebery in Australasia, 1877–1882', in Brad Patterson (ed.), *The Irish in New Zealand: Historical Contexts and Perspectives* (Wellington: Stout Research Centre, 2002), pp.103–16; Malcolm Campbell, 'Mannix in America: Archbishop Daniel Mannix's Address at Madison Square Garden New York, 18 July 1920', *Australian Journal of Irish Studies*, 5 (2005), pp.95–107.

24. H.R. Jackson, *Churches and People in Australia and New Zealand, 1860–1930* (Wellington: Allen and Unwin, 1987), pp.48–60.

25. Stuart Piggin, *Evangelical Christianity in Australia: Spirit, Word and World* (Melbourne: Oxford University Press, 1996), pp.57–8.

26. See Malcolm Campbell, 'Irish Nationalism and Immigrant Assimilation', *Australasian Journal of American Studies*, 15, 2 (1996), pp.24–43.

27. Dryer, 'Independence of Ireland'.

28. The literature is extensive, especially for Australia. See Patrick O'Farrell, *The Irish in Australia: 1788 to the Present* (Sydney: University of New South Wales Press, 2000), pp.138–42; Edith Mary Johnston, 'Violence Transported: Aspects of Irish Peasant Society', in Oliver MacDonagh and W.F. Mandle (eds), *Ireland and Irish Australia: Studies in Cultural and Political History* (Sydney: Croom Helm, 1986), pp.137–54; John McQuilton, *The Kelly Outbreak 1878–1880: the Geographical Dimension of Social Banditry* (Melbourne: Melbourne University Press, 1979).

29. See, for example, Colm Kiernan, 'Home Rule for Ireland and the formation of the Australian Labor Party, 1883–1901', *Australian Journal of Politics and History*, 38, 1 (1992), pp.1–11; Catherine Ann Curry, 'Three Irish Women and Social Action in San Francisco: Mother Teresa Comerford, Mother Baptist Russell, and Kate Kennedy', *Journal of the West* 31, 2 (1992), pp.66–72; Frank Roney, *Irish Rebel and Labor Leader: An Autobiography* (ed.), Ira Cross (Berkeley, CA: University of California Press, 1931).

30. Marie McCarthy, *Passing it On: The Transmission of Music in Irish Culture* (Cork: Cork University Press, 1999), p.13.

31. Robert Grimes, *How Shall We Sing in a Foreign Land?: Music of Irish Catholic Immigrants in the Antebellum United States* (University of Notre Dame Press: Notre Dame, Ind., 1996); on the Irish and popular music see William Williams, *'Twas Only an Irishman's Dream: The Image of Ireland and the Irish in American Popular Song Lyrics, 1800–1920* (Urbana: University of Illinois Press, 1996). Newly released in Australia is Graeme Smith, *Singing Australian: A History of Folk and Country Music* (Sydney: Pluto Press, 2005). There is a body of work on Irish balladry in Australia, including Philip Butterss, 'Broadside Ballads', in Gwenda Beed Davey and Graham Seal (eds), *Oxford Companion to Australian Folklore* (Melbourne: Oxford University Press, 1993), pp.48–53; Butterss, '"Convicted by the Laws of England's Hostile Crown": Popular Convict Verse', in Oliver MacDonagh and W. F. Mandle (eds), *Irish Australian Studies: Papers Delivered at the Fifth Irish-Australian Conference* (Canberra: Australian National University, 1989), pp.7–24; and Bob Reece, 'Frank the Poet' in Bob Reece (ed.), *Exiles from Erin: Convict Lives in Ireland and Australia* (Basingstoke: Macmillan, 1991), pp.151–183.

32. Malcolm Campbell, 'Ireland's Furthest Shores: Irish Immigrant Settlement in Nineteenth-Century California and Eastern Australia', *Pacific Historical Review* 71, 1 (2002), pp.59–90.

33. Patricia Nelson Limerick, 'Will the Real California Please Stand Up?' *California History* 73, 4 (1994), p.268.

2

Tracking Irish Migrants in Nineteenth-Century New Zealand: Sources, Methods and Dilemmas

Lyndon Fraser

In the foreword to his magisterial account of New Zealand's west coast gold rushes, Philip Ross May observes that the region 'packed a quarter of century of history under the normal process of colonisation' into three years.[1] Even from our own vantage point, a century and a half after the discovery of payable gold at Greenstone Creek, the events that transformed this distant world seem extraordinary in scale and complexity. We can picture the broad outlines of this vast panorama: the swarming population of miners swagging heavy loads along the sea-beaches and tangled bush trails, clad in their distinctive uniform of moleskin trousers, blue-flannel shirts, tight-fitting boots and 'wide-awake' hats of grey or black, 'dented near the top';[2] the sudden appearance of canvas and calico towns and mining camps near fresh ground, along with the apocalyptic landscapes of re-worked tailings, retreating terraces and extensive tunnelling; the striking architecture of sailing vessels – screw steamers, brigantines, schooners, cutters and ketches – huddled beside crude wharves at the main river ports; and the commemoration of origins or routes in the names of hotels and grog-shanties such as the Edinburgh Castle; the Brian Boru; the Liverpool Arms; the British Lion; the Café de France; Casino de Venice; the All Nations; the European; the Ballarat; the Old Bendigo.

When we view this 'thoroughly colonial' society from a distance we can make out the larger features of migrant lives: directions, numbers and connections.[3] By using a higher degree of resolution, however, we can catch glimpses of the finer details. The extant sources reveal their geographical origins, social backgrounds, mobility paths, ages, gender, occupations, marital status and sometimes their motivations. As our investigation broadens further, we may focus on the activities of migrant networks, the nature of kinship ties, the opportunities for personal and family advancement and the kinds of associations newcomers created, together with topics as diverse as popular culture, religion, marriage and politics. This type of research requires the imaginative exploitation of scattered and fragmented sources, as well as the critical interrogation of oral and material evidence. We must spend time in old graveyards, collect data from cold archival bunkers and survive numerous visits to hotels to meet with informants. But these activities are in vain unless we know what questions to ask and how to develop an appropriate conceptual framework for the historical analysis of migration.

This chapter uses material drawn from a much wider study of Irish ethnicity on the west coast to illustrate the kinds of sources available to historians as they track migrants in nineteenth-century New Zealand. I will focus here on the ways that Irish men sustained themselves in goldfields communities.[4] Historians have shown that the opportunities available to the Irish abroad had a profound influence on the formation of their ethnic identities. Thus, in parts of the United States and Britain, where migrants faced considerable hostility and restricted avenues for social mobility in long established, hierarchical societies, ethnicity assumed far greater historical significance than in the Australian colonies and New Zealand. As William Pember Reeves observed, the Irish here did not 'crowd into the towns, or attempt to capture the municipal machinery, as in America', nor were they 'a source of political unrest or corruption'.[5] Part of the explanation for these differences can be found in the role that newcomers played in the labour markets of host communities, along with other factors like the timing of migration, the size of the migrant group and the extent of anti-Irish prejudice. As we shall see, the west coast Irish males were at the forefront of colonisation and well represented in all sectors of the region's economy. Few accumulated wealth on the same scale as their counterparts in North America and eastern Australia, but the surviving evidence reveals that they matched wider regional patterns of occupational attainment and general prosperity.

I

The movement of Irish migrants to the west coast after the discovery of gold in 1864 formed part of a much larger trans-Tasman flow that 'embraced not one but two generations'.[6] Although some parts of the picture remain hazy, we can see that the migrant stream was highly selective in terms of age, class, county origin, religion, parenthood and marital status. Information contained in the New Zealand census shows that the Irish-born and their descendants constituted about a quarter of the west coast's population between the mid-1860s and the 1920s. The gendered nature of migrant settlement is also clear from the reports, with the urban centres containing a stronger proportional representation of women than the outlying goldfields districts. Turning next to data from the Registrar-General's archives, we find that the regional origins of the inflow were quite distinctive, centring upon a cluster of southern rural districts with strong Australian connections.[7] An important secondary concentration in north and north-east Ulster featured a disproportionate number of Roman Catholics, as well as a chronic excess of migrant males. As we might expect, single men dominated the west coast's intake in absolute numbers, but more than half of all Irish women had married before arriving on the goldfields, three-fifths forming unions in the Australian colonies. In addition, migrants of both sexes were considerably older than their compatriots who ventured elsewhere and the majority had served extensive colonial apprenticeships in Victoria and Otago.[8] Finally, the balance of religious affiliations among the west coast Irish closely matched that of the eastern Australian colonies and included a similar proportion of newcomers from farming backgrounds.[9]

What do we know about the army of itinerant diggers that swarmed through the sodden wilderness? The names of localities like Croninville, Callaghan's, Donnelly's Creek, Capleston and Dunganville show that Irish prospectors were prominent among the toughened colonials keen to relive the excitements 'of Castlemaine and Forest Creek and dear old Bendigo'.[10] But we need to find rich leads if we want to recover detailed impressions of their working lives. A voluminous sequence of correspondence exchanged between the Flanagan brothers, Patrick and Michael, and their associates provides one window into the past. These letters contain revealing commentaries on economic conditions in Australasia and North America, and illuminate the role of social networks in relaying news from one mining camp to another. This personal testimony is rendered all the more important by the fact that the two men made their way to the west coast at the height of the gold rushes. They represent a group that is very difficult to trace in the surviving records: the sizeable, roving population of single males who spent time in the region during the early phases of simple creek and gully work.

The Flanagans came from relatively comfortable backgrounds in the parish of Termonfeckin, County Louth.[11] According to the official surveyors, their paternal grandfather, Patrick, occupied twenty-eight acres in Tobertoby worth £31 annually in 1856 and held additional properties in Balfeddock and Beltichburne valued at £107 and £27 10s respectively.[12] Richard Flanagan, who became a customs clerk in London, was among those who left the parish in that year. It is not clear why his brothers departed in 1857, but a farm account book held by the family shows that their grandfather purchased the tickets: 'Paid Patrick and Michael going to Australia £14'.[13] Both men travelled to Liverpool where they boarded the *Oliver Lang* for a three-month voyage in steerage to Melbourne. Patrick (23) and Michael (17) probably never expected to stay in the southern hemisphere and may have entertained hopes of going home with a tidy pile. In the years that followed, however, only Michael returned to Ireland, an action prompted by a desperate plea from his ailing father in 1890. 'Instead . . . of the lad of seventeen years you last saw', he warned him gloomily, 'you will meet a grey old man of fifty.'[14]

The colonial experiences of these men were marked by extensive mobility in the eastern Australian colonies, New Zealand and California, but the surviving letters affirm the importance of family and neighbourhood networks in structuring the migration process. Michael's enthusiastic account of a reunion with Patrick in Queensland must have provided some consolation to an 'Uncle Priest' in Ireland:

About the end of August last I left Melbourne for this colony to join Pat from whom I had a letter a few days previous to me leaving in which he gave a rather favourable account of the diggings ... The time passed well enough during our journey the nights being pretty cool compensated us a little for the fatigues of the day under the nearly perpendicular sun. On the thirteenth day from our leaving the coast we got a first glimpse of a curiously made up little township composed of bark and slabs and this was the diggings. I was over a week on the diggings before I found Pat. One day I was wending my way amongst the bark and slabs which compose the township and I saw advancing before one curious looking bushman and as I came close and got a nearer view I found I saw the face before not untill he put out his hand and began laughing did I fully recognise the man I was in search of. Pat was a good deal changed since I last saw him before. His appearance would nearly put one in mind of a Maori. The sun of Queensland browned him very much but the climate did not disagree with him. He was in perfect health, but he looked rather thinner than when I last saw him and although New Zealand seems to have agreed well with him during the three years he was there he did not look three years younger after all. There were two Clougher men along with him when I met him who were his mates one of these was the young man who came out along with Dick Sheridan – Pat Kirk.[15]

Significantly, Michael Flanagan emphasised the importance of companionship as a prerequisite for 'getting on' in Australasia:

The friendship of any true friend and especially one who had influence would certainly be a great benefit to any young man in a strange country but to the friendless and the lonely and to those who do not possess the natural gift of being bold and *shameless* and who have not plenty of what in the colony is called 'cheek' it is hard, very hard to obtain a footing amongst a class who make money by means which I would live a poor man all my life rather than descend to.[16]

He struggled to adapt to the harsh nature of goldmining, but his older brother relished the 'bracing freedom' of their nomadic existence.[17] On one occasion, after Patrick visited Charleston from a rush north of the town, Michael told Richard that his 'health is the same as ever. He is one of the very few upon whom the climate or the hardships to be endured in this vagabond life seems to have no effect. The prospects of the rush at which he is looked very well some time ago – indeed I had great expectations of it – but it is very wet ground and expensive to work it so that it is growing lower in peoples [*sic*] estimation.'[18]

As payable ground in the region began to dwindle, Patrick led the way again, this time to Grahamstown on the Thames goldfields in the North Island. His perceptive and finely detailed descriptions of the opportunities available in the area dissuaded Michael and his friends from following: 'There are very few claims getting gold but the extraordinary richness of those few keep the excitment up and the large sums invested by capitalists from other colonies is the stream that keeps the mill going. The amount of gold got in the place would not give tucker to half the population...Most people have a good opinion of it but I think they are dazled.'[19] To make matters worse, Patrick reported that many of their newly arrived associates were struggling to survive as 'wages-men':

The rush of people here has caused the wages to fall again. There are some working for thirty shillings. Hugh Brown and T McKenna went to work for wages next day after land at 2£. It is not so easy to get wages now as all the newcomers look for work as soon as they come. T Keogh is working for wages, Luke Malloy is here and desires to be kindly remembered to the boys. He is not long here. He has been in Melbourn Sydney nearly up to Queensland and over to Hobart Town back to Melbourn and down here. Tom Fox has a claim that stands a good show. He has no gold yet. They have been tunnelling on it more than a year. In fact there is no one that you know has done any good.[20]

By the end of 1869, Patrick was 'working hard' for a subcontractor at a daily rate of 6s 6d, desperate to clear his west coast debts and join his brother, Nicholas, in the United States. 'The worst part of the going to America', he told Michael, 'is the high rate of fare on the overland. I believe the fare over there after getting down would be more than the sea fare but no matter I believe it is the best thing to be done. If you think there is no chance of getting any of the money we cannot do worse than we have been doeing here.'[21] Patrick managed to settle his affairs in the South Island with Michael's assistance and sailed for California in 1870, where he penned glowing reports to his connections around the world. These letters were sufficiently persuasive to lure Nicholas west from Ohio and Michael across the Pacific Ocean inside the next twelve months. It was also news that pleased Richard Flanagan in London: 'If he has gone to California with the intention of settling there and has a little Capital I think he has done wisely as it is most undoubtedly a splendid country – far exceeding in many advantages any of our Australian colonies.'[22]

The nature and availability of employment in different places was a dominant theme of the surviving correspondence. Writing from Ohio, Nicholas Flanagan gave an unembellished account of opportunities in the state, making no attempt to hide the persistent insecurity that characterised his working life:

There is very little doing here in winter. In summer lots of work of all kinds. I am in employ for putry near three years. When I first come here I had to take the about the roughest job in the business but after two years I got something better and better pay. Labouring men as a general thing get $1.40 per day and bord will cost them about $18.00 per month. I am getting 50 dollers per month and bord at present but I do not know whether I can manage to hold my present situation long or not. I have kept it for about 13 months. When I first got it I only got $40.00 per mon. After 10 months they raised it to forty five and last month the raised it to forth 50 which is the highest I can get. My hours are long but I have no hard work. I think there is no better country than this for a man that would have a little capitel. Good land is worth from 40 to one hundred dollars per acre in this state but little west of this a man can get better land and purty convenient from 10 to 20 dollars per acre.[23]

The lure of cheap land in the American west compared favourably with Jeremiah O'Connor's miserable assessment of New York:

Dear Brother you wanted to know if i am contented here after spending eight years here now. I ought to be although i have nothing by my time here only a living as i go along. For i need not tell you that a man never raises out of dally labour but a man is well paid for the time he works.

But it is not steady and then he has to spend a good deal of it to get work for it is nothing but Bribery on every side here and if there is a study [*steady*] job offering there are thousands on top of it.[24]

This kind of information, filtered across the globe, played a crucial role in facilitating or discouraging the mobility of kinsfolk and friends. It ensured that potential migrants were well informed about the economic conditions prevailing in numerous localities and allowed them to measure their progress against their counterparts living elsewhere.

II

How successful were Irish migrants on the west coast? Where can they be found in the region's social structure? The picture of the colonial mining population and its social world that emerges from the Flanagan correspondence suggests that very few succeeded in capturing the elusive pile. Patrick was cash-strapped at the very moment he was planning to purchase a ticket to San Francisco and marry Kate O'Brien, while Michael's estate of £417 3s 1d, which passed to his sister, Judith Garvey, after his death in 1904, was acquired in Tobertoby.[25] There are occasional references to luckier men who made 'homeward-bounders'. Harry McGill, formerly a boatman at the Old Twelve-Mile, sold his farm at Totara Flat for £2,000 with the intention of settling his family back in Ireland; Tom Clinton returned after clearing £800 in 'a mining speculation'.[26] But this was not an experience shared by the other diggers mentioned in the letters. The poorest, however, were those who stayed behind in once-thriving mining townships after the golden years. Writing to Michael in 1884, Philip McCarthy described the declining fortunes of their associates at Charleston: 'The last news I had from the place is that it is very poor & getting worse every day. Bat O Brien, Harry Lavery, Nicholas Sweeny are still on the Township flat getting the Binifit of the Wather! John Woodcock is still on Candlelight flat groundsluicing so is Bill Fox & Jack Gardner.' Brighton was equally miserable, with the local storekeeper, Tom Nevin, supplying only twenty or thirty miners. 'It's surprising how these places holds out and can support a population the length of time it has. No new field has opened since you left except a small flat about half way between Charleston and Addisons Flat which they called Croninville after the prospector Con Cronin.' Their friends with small businesses in prominent west coast towns or in the North Island seem to have been much more successful: 'Hugh & Pat Brennan are at Reifton. Pat is doing very well as legal manager commission agent & for several of the Meefing companys in that locality. Frank McParland has a store & Bakery at Brunnerton 8 or 10 miles from Greymouth. He is doing a very good business is comfortable & happy with his wife & family a large one of Boy & Girls.' Like many of the old hands, William Bohan had gone to Wellington 'and [*was*] doing very well at his trade. He has added the wheelwright buisness to the Blacksmithing'.[27]

Although the Flanagans and their friends were not among those who made substantial fortunes on the west coast goldfields, a small number of Irish men laid the foundations for the accumulation of considerable wealth. Hamilton (d. 1919, £300,000) and Samuel Gilmer (d. 1925, £150,000), for example, constructed a vast commercial empire that consisted of a network of hotels, livery stables, mail services and mining operations stretching from Hokitika to Cobden, east as far as Reefton, and north to Charleston, Westport and Nelson.[28] These business ventures were family affairs that owed some of their success to the participation of various relatives from Mullaghanee, a role that continued after the two men moved to Wellington in the 1880s. The most impressive of their west coast establishments was Gilmer's Hotel on Mawhera Quay in Greymouth, which featured more than fifty rooms, three large billiard tables, a night watchman and a hall with the capacity to hold four hundred people.[29]

Like Hamilton Gilmer, Martin Kennedy of Ballymackey, County Tipperary, gained his initial capital on the Otago goldfields after a brief stint in Victoria. He worked as a merchant at Queenstown in partnership with his brother, Cornelius, before shifting the business to Greymouth at the beginning of 1865. Kennedy was a very prominent figure on the west coast for the next twenty-four years, with financial interests in coastal shipping, coal mining and general merchandise. By the time of his death in Wellington in 1916, he had amassed a six-figure fortune (£150,000), holding directorships in several major companies, including the Bank of New Zealand, as well as sheep runs in the Wairarapa.[30] The estate of Hugh Cassidy (d. 1922, £56,000) was worth much less than Kennedy's, but it still placed him among the very rich in the province of Canterbury. His migration followed the familiar route from Victoria to Otago, where he packed goods to the diggings and from there to Hokitika with the 'noisy, dirty, drinking, smoking, cursing crowd'.[31] Cassidy's success as a storekeeper and wagon-driver was such that he was able to purchase the lucrative coach business known as Cobb & Co in 1873, taking a farm at Springfield some years later. A towering monument in the Hokitika cemetery, still visible from the beachfront, marks Cassidy's grave and contains an inscription consistent with the stipulation in his will 'to the effect that I arrived in Hokitika in December 1864 and is to have a facsimile of a man on a saddle horse driving not less than three pack horses along the beach'.

The careers of men such as the Gilmer brothers, Martin Kennedy and Hugh Cassidy matched the paths travelled by the colonial wealthy in Canterbury and Otago. As Jim McAloon has shown, the rich came from humble origins, arrived early in New Zealand and 'benefited handsomely' from the use of state power to secure land for colonization through the dispossession of Ngai Tahu.[32] At the same time, the labour of family members was crucial in the creation of substantial wealth: indeed 'the family was both the reason for accumulating a fortune and a major aid to doing so'.[33] Not surprisingly, all the men in our case studies were married. Hamilton Gilmer even returned to Monaghan for this purpose, marrying his cousin, Elizabeth, at Broomfield in 1871.[34] The assistance of family networks, the timing of migration, an access to capital and adherence to values such as sobriety, thrift and deferred gratification were clearly critical factors in building wealth.[35] But it is also significant that the Gilmer brothers, Kennedy and Cassidy, worked for very short periods as miners. With a little capital, they became carriers, merchants and hoteliers, services that carried fewer risks than goldmining and quickly 'separated the digger from his profits'.[36]

The success of these men casts doubt on the view that the west coast Irish 'were less evident in business circles, except as small storekeepers and publicans'.[37] It is further undermined when we examine the working lives of other migrants who left large fortunes. Felix Campbell (d. 1922, £300,000) of Maghery, County Armagh, for example, spent time in Melbourne, Invercargill and Dunedin, before moving to the new settlement at Greymouth, where he set up as a general carrier. By 1866, he had sufficient capital to establish himself as an independent wholesale merchant in the river-port town and his business interests gradually expanded to include mining and brewing, as well as the chair of directors at the dispatch foundry. Campbell neatly fitted the profile of the rich in colonial New Zealand, whose commitments were 'concentrated on business and local authority work to the exclusion of most other activities'.[38] He was a member of the Greymouth Chamber of Commerce, served as the Chairman of the Harbour Board and held public office as Mayor in the mid-1890s. Most of Campbell's extensive philanthropic work seems to have been aimed at promoting or sustaining local economic growth, his largesse evident in financial assistance that kept the saw-milling industry afloat before the First World War and in private injections of capital to struggling firms and individuals.[39] In his will, he bequeathed everything to his three children, naming his son, Thomas Henry, and sons-in-law, Patrick McEvedy and Michael Dennehy, as trustees of his estate. They were instructed to pay Thomas an annual income of £2,000 from Campbell's shares in the dispatch foundry and transmit the residuary interest in equal shares to his son and daughters, Catherine and Mary.[40]

The involvement of prosperous businessmen in local government suggests that Irish migrants had considerable influence within their own communities. Patrick Michael Griffen (d. 1913, £14,971), a tenant farmer's son from County Waterford, rose to prominence as a wholesale merchant in Greymouth, eventually forming a successful trading partnership with William Cameron Smith (d. 1895, £3,082).[41] He served on the town's borough council, acted as a Justice of the Peace and achieved renown as a local 'booster'. His brother-in-law, Daniel Sheedy (d. 1909, £5,000), the proprietor of the Brian Boru Hotel on Mawhera Quay, left an estate to his wife, Catherine, that included a large villa on Blake Street with servants' quarters built at the rear.[42] A man of extraordinary energy, he sat on the Greymouth Harbour Board, the Grey River Hospital Board and the Greymouth Borough Council for long periods, as well as continuing a long-standing connection with the Greymouth Jockey Club.[43] There are several similar examples. James Colvin, a Westport merchant with extensive goldmining experience, occupied positions on the Buller County Council, the Westport Harbour Board and the Nelson Education Board, before his election to the House of Representatives in 1899.[44] In Reefton, another veteran digger, Robert Patterson of Killyleagh, County Down (d. 1903, £4,900), ran a store and sat on both the Inangahua County Council and the local school committee.[45] The wealthiest migrants were not the only influential people in the main towns and mining districts, as the careers of local notables like Denis Ryall (d. 1904, £162), James Francis Byrne (d. 1913, £100) and Peter Dungan (d. 1906, £193) make apparent.[46] Yet it is clear that 'local government represented the propertied', even though the rich did not form majorities on borough and county councils.[47] The key point here is that Irish men were prominent among those who amassed fortunes on the west coast and were heavily involved in boosting local development. It is also worth stressing that this success depended on a number of factors, including the role played by wives, children, friends and kinsfolk, and seems to have owed little to the support of ethnic networks.

These claims about the economic position of the west coast Irish are supported by the evidence contained in local death duty registers, which give the value of every estate where probate was granted from 1876 to 1915. Table 1 shows that Irish-born males accounted for one-third of all the estates worth more than £2,000 (33.9 per cent), easily surpassing their share of the region's population. Most striking, however, is the fact that Irish men left six of the twenty probates involving sums over £10,000, the threshold for membership of the colonial wealthy.[48] James William Fair (d. 1913, £20,882) was a prominent Westport draper, who bequeathed a family business at the corner of Palmerston and Brougham Street to his second wife, Teresa, and three of his sons.[49] By contrast, Thomas McKee (d. 1906, £12,000) and Myles McPadden (d. 1913, £10,485) represented family farming wealth in the South Island, a substantial group that held properties 'too small to create vast fortunes'.[50] The three remaining probates belonged to the Hokitika merchant Patrick Michael Griffen (d. 1913, £14,971), the returned migrant William Glenn (d. 1913, £36,000) and Hubert Dolphin (d. 1907, £14,446) of Loughrea, County Galway.[51] In terms of general prosperity, then, the death duty registers indicate, first, that Irish men did as well as other nationalities on the goldfields and often better, and, second, that the best prospects for advancement on the goldfields were to be found in mercantile activities, farming and small urban businesses such as storekeeping.

What were the main occupational characteristics of Irish-born males? The evidence from death certificates shows that these men were found in various kinds of work, even though the dominance of the mining industry limited the range of employment opportunities.[52] A significant minority ended their working lives as professionals or businessmen, among whom publicans like John Shannahan (d. 1905, £1,500) and Richard Cox (d. 1901, £1,043) featured prominently.[53] The Irish-born were well represented in the skilled trades; many were listed as general labourers and farmers constituted the third largest occupation. Predictably, Irish men were concentrated in mining, an activity that accounted for more than half of the entire sample (55.7 per cent). We may surmise that many of those returned as unskilled workers, artisans, shopkeepers and farmers had also spent time as diggers, a career trajectory well illustrated in the case studies cited above. Despite their limitations, then, the Registrar-General's records suggest that Irish-born men matched wider regional patterns of occupational attainment and did not fit the popular image of 'dispossessed proletarians'.

III

The numerical dominance of miners among the migrants is hardly surprising given the narrowness of the west coast's economic base. But we need to move beyond these elementary facts to capture the distinctive flavour of their working lives. It is clear from the surviving inventories of deceased diggers that single men owned few material possessions other than what they carried on their backs. Aside from their tools and clothing, even the most successful died with little more than a handful of shares in a claim, a modest bank account and some petty cash. Whatever their means, diggers endured terrible discomfort in the damp west coast bush.

Persistent rain made prospecting a dreary undertaking as men laboured 'up to the hips in water, picking away at the slatey, gravely bed, moving large boulders, carrying the clayey-looking earth to the "tom" or "cradle" and working all day without seeing the gold', before returning to sodden camps at night.[54] The wretched living conditions and harsh climate contributed to occasional epidemics of typhoid and influenza, as well as the prevalence of debilitating respiratory illnesses. Yet the death toll from disease and ill health appears insignificant when compared with 'the appalling loss of life' from other causes.[55]

Gold-seeking in such rugged terrain was always a dangerous enterprise, especially when it involved tunnelling and shafting. The fate of Michael Caddigan, smothered by tons of stone and debris when he struck 'a jamb-up' with his pick while clearing an old tunnel, typified the most common kind of mining accident.[56] Badly prepared drives collapsed, terrace faces disintegrated and unsuspecting diggers fell to their deaths down mineshafts. Even simple enterprises proved hazardous. John Nolan was about to begin sluicing his claim at Blue Spur when 'a thin layer of dirt' peeled away suddenly, 'knocking him backwards over the tail race' and pinning his right leg. His 'dividing mate', John Keane, watched in horror and could do nothing to save him. A post-mortem examination conducted at Blue Spur township established 'that he had sustained injuries in many places, on top of the head, temple, jaw, chest and other portions of the body, whilst the leg caught in the falling dirt was crushed from the knee down, the bone being in little splinters'.[57]

The most common cause of death from 'misadventure' was drowning. West coast river crossings were notoriously risky and swept many men to watery graves. Robert Moorhead of Smithborough, County Monaghan, lost his life on the Ahaura; John Kane, prospecting at Rutherglen, drowned 'in the Deep Creek between the Lagoon Township and Diamond Gully'; Michael Clune died at the mouth of the Taramakau, his body recovered from the sea breakers the next day.[58] There were occasional cases of suicide. Patrick Martin, a native of Carleston, County Meath, jumped from the SS *Star of the Evening* as it lay in the roadstead outside the Hokitika river, leaving his worldly possessions on deck. Murder and manslaughter claimed few lives.[59] Limerick-born Jeremiah McGrath, who worked with the Hennessy party at Welshman's, near Brighton, was one of the exceptions, 'killed by a stroke of a glass decanter at the House of a woman known as Mary Anderson'.[60]

Although nomadic diggers faced hardship and danger, their daily existence was interesting and exciting. The sudden surge of adrenalin as men left to inspect new fields, the enduring appeal of independence and 'the satisfaction of seeing race and wheel, pump and sluice – all fashioned by "the party" – in full work' were some of the most attractive aspects of life on the goldfields during the 1860s.[61] Above all, diggers seem to have enjoyed the companionship of kinsfolk and old friends, an *esprit de corps* that is plainly evident in the Flanagan correspondence. Their reliance on Old World social connections and notions of 'mateship' are understandable given that mining was a collective endeavour. Men formed small co-operative partnerships of two to six individuals, sometimes amalgamating into larger coalitions or companies to accomplish tasks that required additional capital, technology and labour. As well as retaining their identities for considerable periods, goldmining 'parties' followed the custom of 'dividing mates', whereby any member making a rich strike after they disbanded was obliged to notify the others and re-form the group to work the claim.[62]

How did miners themselves view their chosen vocation? We have seen that Patrick Flanagan was among those who eagerly embraced this distinctive lifestyle and its frenetic pace. David McCullough of County Down, who arrived in the colony much later than Flanagan, seems to have relished his time fossicking at Waimangaroa, Denniston, Charleston and Addison's Flat. He came from a prosperous farming background in Ballycreely, where his father, Samuel, occupied forty-five acres of land with an annual valuation of £52, the sixth highest in the townland.[63] Accompanied by one of his friends, Alexander Young, McCullough travelled first class to Dunedin aboard the *Andrew Reid*, arriving on 19 May 1875 'after a very tedeous and long voyage of 123 days from London'.[64] We know very little about his experiences over the next two decades, but it is clear that he worked initially at the Albion Brewing & Malting Company for £2.10 per week and boarded privately.[65] By the 1890s he had moved to the Buller region and entered the gold-mining industry. In a letter to his parents from Cascade Creek in 1898, McCullough described the nature of his enterprise:

> We are opening up a claim. There are Four of us. We have been over Two years at it now. It will take another six months yet and we may not bottom. The ground is deep and heavy. It is river workings. We hold Four acres. We are going to put on pumping gear. It is rather expensive but we intend to see it out. It is all pay out just now and nothing coming in.[66]

Later in the year the men left their Cascade claim to prospect deep inside 'the Mackley country':

> We took a good supply of rations with us. We carried it in stages. There was not a soul there but ourselves. There is neither roads nor horse tracks

there. We got alluvial Gold would pay about Four pounds per week but that is not good enough in that country. Too much lost time and expense carrying tucker. You have to carry all you eat on our backs and this is a bit hard work. There are plenty of birds pigeons, Kaka and ducks and also the weka or Wood-hen. It cannot fly. The walk or run along the ground. The dogs can easily catch them. Time goes very quick when you are out prospecting shifting camp so often and carrying Tucker. I have had about Eight months of it this time but at any rate we are back again not a bit better off and very little the worse. There is any amount of men in Newzealand and Australia doing the same. The will go into any Country or through any hardship after Gold.[67]

Based at Waimangaroa, several miles north of Westport, where he had bought into another claim, McCullough contemplated returning to Ireland in response to a plea from his parents who were in poor health. 'It would be very awkward at the present time to get away', he told them, 'but I will try and be home in the inside of Twelve months.'[68] It was a journey he never made. Samuel McCullough died two months after the letter was written and stated in his will that the family farm was to pass to his wife for life and then to David, provided that he came home within two years of her death. An inheritance in County Down, however, was insufficient to lure 'Old Davey' from Waimangaroa, where he remained until his own death in 1934.[69]

John O'Regan, a miner from County Cork with experience in the United States, Australia and New Zealand, was the only migrant correspondent to attempt a retrospective assessment of his career. Writing to his grand-niece from Barrytown in 1899, he recalled that 'this day 41 year ago, I was within sight of the Australian coast, and only three months before that time I had bade adieu to all I held dear in the world. Then I was young and full of hope and gave myself two years till I would return again but the unexpected always takes place in this life for an ardent hope is rarely fulfilled and my return now is doubtful as that of the Bark of the Styx whose exile was eternal.' Yet, he confessed, 'my hope never dies, and though old in years my heart is quite young'. O'Regan's eloquent summation of his life on the diggings was tinged with sadness and regret:

You will naturally ask yourself how I fare in this land of gold after my 41 years of work. Well, I got a fair share, that is enough to defray expenses. If I went into a big spec, which I often did, and this failed, it would take a long time to pay back debts. To give you an idea, the last claim I was in before coming to this coast paid the man that worked it $75,000. I sold out for 200 pounds long before the water was on the claim, and being in life's prime I thought I would be able to drop into something good. That was my hope. My father, brother, and sisters being alive, I felt confident that I would see them again but it was not to be. I am alone in the world now. Drunken mates did me no good, but you will ask why not shake them off? This is not easily done, unless you sell out with what result you can judge. I hate drunkards, and the longer I live this aversion will live too. What a curse grog is to a weak mind. What misery to every one about them. I am now making a living but I intend taking some chances in Sweeps and who knows I may be lucky.[70]

We will never know how many of the men who remained on the west coast shared these sentiments in old age. For most, the quest for the elusive pile 'had become the reality' and 'home' was now a small mining locality like Charleston, Waimangaroa or Barrytown.[71]

IV

What impact did these work patterns have on the formation of Irish ethnic identities in the region? The Irish-born were a numerically strong charter group whose members participated actively in the colonisation process and in building local community life. Most had been 'thoroughly colonialised' by the time they arrived on the diggings and many brought with them an extensive array of skills and resources acquired in Victoria and Otago.[72] The surviving evidence shows that Irish men were scattered throughout the region's social structure. Some became very prominent among the wealthy, in local government and within the ranks of local boosters. Others made more modest gains, struggled along in poverty or moved away quickly in search of the elusive pile. Regardless of their motivations, occupations and levels of material prosperity, all migrants encountered an environment where the hardships of daily life were ameliorated by close cooperation between local people, a public spirit that transcended ethnic, religious and linguistic boundaries. The small scale of west coast communities, the relative economic homogeneity of the region's inhabitants and the absence of entrenched anti-Irish élites militated against the rise of sectarian animosities and the development of a strong ethnic consciousness.[73] These conditions were vastly different from those confronting the Irish in parts of the United States, Canada and Britain, where newcomers provided 'a cheap, expendable labour force for the construction of an emerging industrial and urban infrastructure'.[74] The findings presented here remind us that structural factors played a key role in shaping Irish ethnicity abroad and call into question the idea of a single Irish labour diaspora.

Table 1: Number and Value of Men's Estates on the West Coast, 1876–1915

	£0–1,999	£2,000–3,999	£4,000–5,999	£6,000–7,999	£8,000–9,999	£10,000 +	Total
Irish-born Estates							
N	341	18	9	2	2	6	378
%	23.0	33.3	42.8	20.0	50.0	30.0	23.8
Total Estates	1,482	54	21	10	4	20	1,591

Sources: West coast testamentary registers, CH 383, and Probate Files, CH 171, Archives New Zealand (Christchurch); Registry of Births, Deaths and Marriages (Lower Hutt). Additional information on individuals was obtained from family histories, newspaper obituaries and cemetery transcripts held at the West Coast Historical Museum.

NOTES

1. Philip Ross May, *The West Coast Gold Rushes* (Christchurch: Pegasus, 1962), p.13. I would like to express my sincere thanks to the University of Aberdeen for a generous travel grant which made this chapter possible.
2. Ibid., p.314.
3. Ibid., p.310.
4. For Irish women's experiences in the region, see Lyndon Fraser, 'Irish Women's Networks on the West Coast of New Zealand's South Island, 1864–1922', *Women's History Review*, Vol.33, 2006, pp.459–75.
5. William Pember Reeves, *The Long White Cloud: Ao Tea Roa* (London: Horace Marshall, 1899), p.400.
6. Terry Hearn, 'Scots Miners on the Goldfields, 1861–1870', in Tom Brooking and Jennie Coleman (eds), *The Heather and the Fern: Scottish Migration and New Zealand Settlement* (Dunedin: University of Otago Press, 2003), p.77.
7. Death certificates, used in conjunction with literary sources, provide an alternative basis for reconstructing migrant populations, and provide invaluable biographical details about individuals. Moreover, they allow for systematic linkages with other materials such as probates, cemetery transcripts, parish registers and family histories, thereby eliminating some of the ambiguities and omissions found in the extant listings. The analysis presented here is based on a study of 735 Irish-born women and 1,579 men whose deaths were registered on the west coast between 1876 and 1915.
8. The median age of Irish men (29.1) and women in my study (26.6) differed notably from the averages of 22.5 and 21.2 recorded by the *Commission on Emigration and Other Population Problems, 1948–1954* (Dublin: The Stationery Office, 1954) for emigrants leaving the whole of Ireland between 1852 and 1921.
9. The denominational percentages for women were as follows: Roman Catholic (79.6%), Anglican (10.6%), Presbyterian (6.0%) and Wesleyan (0.8%). The percentages for men differed slightly from these figures: Roman Catholic (75.1%), Anglican (12.5%), Presbyterian (7.8%), Wesleyan (1.3%) and Hebrew (0.1%). Data on religious affiliations were unavailable for 3.0 per cent of female and 3.2 per cent of male migrants.
10. May, *The West Coast Gold Rushes*, p.313.
11. See Angela McCarthy, *Irish Migrants in New Zealand, 1840–1937: 'The Desired Haven'* (Woodbridge: Boydell, 2005), pp.20–1.
12. I am indebted to Angela McCarthy for this information.

13. Descendant information, Donald Murphy.
14. Michael Flanagan to John Flanagan, 20 May 1890, courtesy of Donald Murphy.
15. Michael Flanagan to Reverend Richard Flanagan, 18 February 1865.
16. Ibid., 18 February 1865.
17. May, *The West Coast Gold Rushes*, p.286.
18. Michael Flanagan to Richard Flanagan, 10 August 1867.
19. Patrick Flanagan to Michael Flanagan, 8 September 1869.
20. Patrick Flanagan to Michael Flanagan, 18 October 1869.
21. Patrick Flanagan to Michael Flanagan, 6 December 1869.
22. Richard Flanagan to Michael Flanagan, 20 August 1870.
23. Nicholas Flanagan to Richard Flanagan, 5 January 1869.
24. Jeremiah O'Connor to Edward O'Connor, 1 December 1885.
25. Patrick Flanagan to Michael Flanagan, 6 December 1869; Patrick Flanagan to Kate O'Brien, 14 December 1869; descendant information, Donald Murphy. The details of Michael's estate were kindly provided by Angela McCarthy.
26. Andrew Burns to Michael Flanagan, 8 June 1890.
27. Philip McCarthy to Michael Flanagan, 23 May 1884.
28. Will of Hamilton Gilmer, AAOM 27056/1919, Will of Samuel Gilmer, AAOM 36375a/1925, Archives New Zealand, Wellington (henceforth ANZ-W).
29. *Grey River Argus*, 17 March 1881.
30. Will of Martin Kennedy, AAOM 19266/1916, ANZ-W; *New Zealand Times*, 26 August 1916. I am indebted to Brain Wood for additional information on the career of Martin Kennedy.
31. May, *The West Coast Gold Rushes*, p.480.
32. Jim McAloon, *No Idle Rich: The Wealthy in Canterbury and Otago, 1840–1914* (Dunedin: University of Otago Press, 2002), p.174 and *passim*.
33. Ibid., p.75.
34. Descendant information, Ian Cameron.
35. McAloon, *No Idle Rich*, pp.27, 181.
36. May, *The West Coast Gold Rushes*, p.255.
37. Ibid., p.311.
38. McAloon, *No Idle Rich*, p.168.
39. Peter Ewen, 'Wealthy early Coaster was also generous', *The Coaster*, 10 March 1999, p.2.
40. Will of Felix Campbell, GM 365/1922, Archives New Zealand, Christchurch (henceforth ANZ-CH).
41. Will of Patrick Michael Griffen, GM 130/1913, ANZ-CH; Peter Ewen, 'Griffen and Smith survives throughout the year', *The Coaster*, 4 August 1999, p.2.
42. Will of Daniel Sheedy, HK 16/1909, ANZ-CH.
43. *The Cyclopedia of New Zealand, Vol. 5* (Christchurch, 1906), p.549.
44. Ibid.,p.152.
45. Ibid., p.258; Will of Robert Patterson, RN 145/03, ANZ-CH. Patterson died intestate leaving a widow, Catherine, and twelve children, four of whom were minors.
46. *The Cyclopedia of New Zealand, Vol. 5*, pp.580, 491 and 544; GM 298/1904, HK 104/1913 and HK 2101/1907, ANZ-CH.
47. McAloon, *No Idle Rich*, p.147.
48. Ibid., pp.14–16.
49. Will of James William Fair, WP 122/1913, ANZ-CH.
50. McAloon, *No Idle Rich*, pp. 47–9; Will of Myles McPadden, WP 119/1913, Will of Thomas McKee, HK 2088/1906, ANZ-CH.
51. Will of Patrick Michael Griffen, GM 130/1913, Will of William Glenn, HK 674/1897, Will of Hubert Dolphin, WP 46/1910; ANZ-CH.
52. These kind of data have limitations, as I have suggested elsewhere, but they do provide one indication of how well newcomers fared in the local economy. See Lyndon Fraser, *To Tara via Holyhead: Irish Catholic Immigrants in Nineteenth-Century Christchurch* (Auckland: Auckland University Press, 1997), ch. 5.

53. Will of John Shanahan, GM 292/1905, Will of Richard Cox, WP 14/1901, ANZ-CH.
54. May, *The West Coast Gold Rushes*, p.287.
55. Ibid., p.291. Drowning made up 47 per cent of the 239 sudden deaths known to police that occurred on the West Canterbury goldfield between 5 November 1864 and 31 December 1867. Mining accidents accounted for 20 per cent and 'cause uncertain' was returned in 12 per cent of these cases. Only 14 per cent of the deaths were due to natural causes or 'Visitation of God', p.292.
56. *Kumara Times*, 18 and 19 October 1886.
57. Ibid., 21 May 1889.
58. Robert Moorhead, intestate, HK 82/1872, John Kane, intestate, HK 69/1869, Michael Clune, intestate, HK 12/1866, ANZ-CH.
59. Patrick Martin, intestate, CH A52/1866, ANZ-CH.
60. Jeremiah McGrath, intestate, HK D5/1868 and HK 59/1868, ANZ-CH.
61. May, *The West Coast Gold Rushes*, p.286.
62. Ibid., pp.250–1.
63. Descendant information, Angela McCarthy.
64. David McCullough to his parents and sisters, 4 June 1875, courtesy of Angela McCarthy.
65. David McCullough to his parents and sisters, 21 December 1875.
66. David McCullough to his parents, 1 June 1898.
67. David McCullough to his parents, 2 July 1899.
68. Ibid.
69. *Westport News*, 19 December 1934.
70. John O'Regan to his grand-niece, Ellen, 26 January 1899.
71. May, *The West Coast Gold Rushes*, p.287.
72. Ibid., p.310.
73. See Patrick O'Farrell, 'Catholicism on the West Coast: Just How Irish Is It?', *New Zealand Tablet*, 3 May 1973, pp.53–6.
74. Kevin Kenny, 'Diaspora and Comparison: The Global Irish as a Case Study', *Journal of American History*, 90 (2003), p.152.

3

Recruiting Irish Migrants for Life in New Zealand 1870–1875[1]

Ciara Breathnach

In 1870 Julius Vogel (1835–1899), then Treasurer of the Colonial Government, announced an ambitious scheme to develop New Zealand by borrowing capital abroad and spending it on public works and assisted immigration schemes.[2] A recruitment campaign ensued with a view to bringing out good-quality, hard-working migrants. At a time when the multitudes were leaving Ireland for North America, efforts made to encourage Irish migrants to New Zealand were abysmal. Using newspapers that criticised the work of the agent-general in London, Dr Isaac Featherston (1813–1876), this chapter highlights how the colonial media in New Zealand reported on the deliberate exclusion of Ireland in the recruitment efforts.

By 1870 New Zealand consisted of a series of colonies that were governed on a provincial basis but each had representation in a general assembly since 1852. Despite the fact that the provincial councils maintained a great degree of autonomy there was an agreed but basic colonial plan. This was outlined by one of the more notable promoters, Edward Gibbon Wakefield (1796–1862), and other early visionaries, as a plan to reconstruct British society in New Zealand, but without the very rich or the very poor and to trim it of any rough edges.[3] Commenting on the results of his organised colony, Wakefield later wrote:

> Socially, (I can speak from personal observation only of Canterbury and Wellington) there is much to like and much to dislike. The newest comers from England are the best on the whole, more especially the *picked* [emphasis in original] materials with which Canterbury was founded. But I hear that Bellairs is very much pleased with the Otago people and I have myself some gratifying proof of their inflexible worth of the Scotch people there who are the great majority. The Patriarch Cargill is firm as a rock in the principles and ideas with which he emigrated, as he is the trusted leader of that settlement. At

Canterbury I could have fancied myself in England except for the hard-working nature of the upper classes and the luxurious independence of the common people.[4]

The hangover from Wakefield's principles, combined with accounts of the uncouth behaviour of some Irish Catholics in Australia and Britain, created racial and religious prejudices. For example, Akenson notes that the Irish were associated with heavy drinking and this 'scared people. And that was the picture of the Irish that became fixed in the popular mind.'[5] This meant that Irish Catholics were deemed unsuitable candidates for life in the newly organised settlements of New Zealand. While there was no direct mandate to curtail the Irish crossing the Tasman, neither was any concerted effort made to attract Irish people as potential migrants in the 1850s. The provinces employed their own emigration officers, each of whom acted independently in Britain. Little effort was made in Ireland. Richard Davis points to the Otago gold rush of 1861 as a watershed in the pattern of Irish emigration to New Zealand.[6] At that time considerable numbers came from Victoria and California where opportunities for new migrants were exhausted. He describes the arrival of Bishop Patrick Moran in Dunedin in 1871 as another 'landmark in the development of Irish Catholicism politically and ecclesiastically'.[7] When Moran launched the newspaper the *New Zealand Tablet* (hereafter referred to as the *Tablet*) in 1873 it was intended to encourage Catholicism, but it (almost inevitably) became an Irish, political mouthpiece.

By 1869 the flow of migrants to the colony had become a mere trickle, mainly due to economic depression, unemployment and the poor social infrastructure.[8] Census returns highlight that migration patterns were not consistent and numbers were not sustained, and this is why Vogel was driven to public works schemes.[9] Independent travel was prohibitively expensive. Lyndon Fraser estimates that in the 1850s the cost of transport from Britain ranged from £18 to £25.[10] Besides this, with the exception of those with relations in New Zealand, very few in the old world knew about opportunities there. In Ireland, general knowledge was minimal. The *Irish Times* used vague language to describe life in New Zealand, commenting in 1870 that, 'It may surprise those who are interested in watching the course of the waves of emigration from this country to learn that in 1867 there were resident in New Zealand 27,955 Irishmen and Irishwomen, all apparently doing well and pursuing an industrious life.'[11] A week later, the same newspaper noted that the lack of information made migration to New Zealand a very difficult process for the Irish labourer and suggested that part of the funds for assisted emigration be spent on advertising.[12] In the absence of a national recruitment campaign this lack of awareness was inevitable but the Irish tended to rely on personal accounts, which caused a chain migration effect. Slow communications hindered the chain migration process and return migration was rare. Voyages from Ireland to New Zealand could take between three and six months. Irish people who ventured that far independently were seasoned, having usually spent a previous stage of migration in Britain, North America or Australia where they earned the fare. It is also likely, given the time lapse between the first and final stages of migration, that the kinship bonds of such seasoned migrants would have been frayed. Migration to, and life in, New Zealand was something of an enigma in Britain also; in 1869 the Emigration Commissioner confessed to the House of Commons that 'he could not speak with confidence of the colony of New Zealand'.[13] This was not the case in Scotland, where Charlotte MacDonald found that despite economic depression in New Zealand trumped up accounts of wages and conditions appeared in the Dundee newspaper, *People's Journal*, in 1867 in order to increase the response.[14]

The decline in numbers migrating to New Zealand was a source of major concern to colonial authorities. Inconsistent immigration schemes and the heavy reliance on personal connections were simply not enough to meet the economic demands of the fledgling colony.[15] When Vogel introduced his public works schemes, which were to be financed from British funds and built by new migrant labour, he had widespread government support and local newspapers endorsed the scheme. In Nelson, the *Colonist* sold immigration as 'the only power certain to redeem our financial position...Increase in numbers means decrease of average taxation.'[16] Vogel went to London in January 1871 to raise a loan from the British exchequer and a sum of £1.5 million was approved.[17] He also negotiated contracts for the construction of railways.[18] Once Vogel acquired the funding in London, Dr Featherston, previously the superintendent of Wellington, was appointed agent-general to be stationed in London. In March 1871 he set up an office (of reportedly 'palatial prominence') at Westminster Chambers. A correspondent for the *Thames Advertiser* observed that an office in the East End (where there were willing migrants) would have been more appropriate.[19] Featherston's primary duty was to send out numbers from England, Scotland and Ireland in proportion to their respective populations. His remit included the screening of migrants, the organisation of shipping agreements and the employment of agents and sub-agents. He also managed a limited advertising campaign. The *Tablet* seized every opportunity to denounce the new system, stating that between the central agency in London and money paid to local agencies the costs ran as high as £20,000 a year, a figure which did not include the costs of advertising or rents.[20]

In many respects, Featherston had a very difficult job. According to Olssen and Stenson, the subsidised fares were simply not enough to entice emigrants to New Zealand. They cite the great distance, the huge expense involved – at the time the fare to the US was one fifth of the fare to New Zealand – and the bad reputation the New Zealand Land Wars had earned the colony, as the primary prohibitary factors.[21] However, given the dearth of information noted earlier, political unrest in New Zealand cannot explain why the Irish did not avail themselves of the schemes, but the early recruitment policies can. From the outset, Featherston was clearly averse to using Ireland as a potential recruitment area. Although the public works scheme became law in 1870, an agency was not opened in Belfast until June 1872, with a Dublin office set up six months later. Meanwhile, the *Cork Examiner* was reporting large-scale emigration from Queenstown, County Cork, to North America, and the *Tablet* queried 'Why has our New Zealand Rip Van Winkle no active agents there? What a contrast to his habitual lethargy…is presented by the South Australian agent, who in about a month established nearly sixty agencies in the United Kingdom.' The *Tablet* further contrasted the diligence of the Canadian government, which had distributed nearly two million copies of various information leaflets regarding passage to and life in the dominion, with the lethargy of Featherston's office.[22] In short, he made no effort in Ireland and, as was noted by the *Tablet*, he did not attempt to turn the tide of migrants leaving Queenstown towards New Zealand.[23]

The *Tablet* vilified Featherston for an apparent anti-Irish bias but he cannot be blamed exclusively. His policies were sensitive to the general concern in New Zealand about the calibre of migrant being brought into the colony – a concern that was not without reason. Reports in the London *Times* suggested that the current mechanisms of poor law relief be replaced with assisted emigration schemes. One colonial newspaper complained that the London *Times* misunderstood the purpose of assisted emigration as being a 'form of relief afforded to paupers'. However, New Zealanders explained that they did not welcome paupers; the object of assisted passage was 'to assist the friends of persons already in the Colony to join them' and further clarified that 'so far as these Colonies are concerned, that the only form of free immigration shall be limited to the introduction of female servants'.[24] New Zealanders were clear about one thing, they only wanted 'to secure the steady, good workman', not the dregs of British society.[25]

Even though Irish Catholics were relatively poorly represented in the House of Representatives, the uneven nature of Featherston's operations did not go unnoticed. The New Zealand government's response came first in a telegram from Premier, G.M. Waterhouse, directly to Featherston in November 1872, in which he demanded that a central Irish agency be set up in Dublin. Featherston reported that a central office had been open in Belfast since June under the management of H.W. Farnall.[26] Following Waterhouse's telegram a series of letters ensued between the Irish-born George Maurice O'Rorke (1830–1916), who became Minister for Immigration in October 1872, and Featherston. Interestingly this correspondence was published in the *Tablet*. They held opposing views: O'Rorke was more concerned that the low numbers immigrating was not meeting the requirements of the public works schemes. Featherston's policies were clearly more concerned with quality control so that a high calibre of migrant would be guaranteed, but this stemmed numbers. O'Rorke argued that without manpower the public works schemes would inevitably fail, and, furthermore, there was a shortage of ordinary agricultural workers. On being accused of blatant anti-Irish prejudice Featherston replied that he had followed protocol as outlined by the government (to send out proportionate numbers from England, Scotland and Ireland) and that from the north of Ireland '"a proportionate number" [had] been sent out'. The *Lyttleton Times* was one of the few newspapers to defend Featherston, acquitting him 'on what we may call the Irish charge' and agreeing that his numbers were indeed proportionate to population.[27] Featherston also argued that he had fierce competition with the Welsh engineering firm Brogdens, which had won a contract to build railways in New Zealand and was to bring out 6,000 navvies for the task.[28] He felt that the generous conditions under which Brogdens advertised had rendered the government's schemes uncompetitive. Claiming to have eased off his campaign so that the Brogden contract would be filled more quickly, he argued that it was unfair for the government to regard 'Brogden's navvies' as separate from the numbers brought out by him.[29] By the same token, Featherston was careful to add that he took no responsibility for the actions of what he called itinerant agents sent home by the government.[30] O'Rorke was sceptical of the agent-general and dismissed his proportionate representation argument:

> Considering the enormous number that annually leave that country [Ireland] I can hardly be expected to compliment your agents in having induced in a year and a half 900 souls to emigrate to New Zealand ... out of that 900 more than one-third were nominated in the colony and reached this independent of the exertions of your officers.[31]

That Julius Vogel supported Featherston's anti-Irish policies is evident from his silence. Despite the fact that the public work schemes were in danger of failing due to lack of manpower, and that he was aware that the agent-general ignored a populace well accustomed to emigration, shows a degree of support for his friend. Vogel was equally concerned about the implications associated with bringing Irish sectarian affairs to the colony at a crucial time when secularity in all things was the preferred option, such as the proposed secular education system.[32]

O' Rorke criticised the manner in which Featherston liberally doled out hefty pay rises and back pay to his Irish officers, Messrs Birch, Seaton and Farnall.[33] Although they were well paid they were not very productive. The colonial government was instrumental in the appointment of Harry W. Farnall to manage the Belfast agency in 1872 without consulting Featherston. Farnall was not very successful in his attempts – in three months he sent a mere twenty-three migrants. At the time George Vesey Stewart was trying to arrange for a pilot migration project (this later transpired as the Katikati settlement) from Ulster to the Bay of Plenty. Featherston did not like Stewart's approach: he made excessive demands. In addition, his inquiries into the religious and political affiliations of the governor, Sir James Fergusson, and the fact that he prefaced his proposal as land for a '"Special settlement" of Ulstermen' made Featherston dubious about the venture.[34] However, Farnall devoted too much time to negotiating terms with George Vesey Stewart and his general work suffered as a result.[35] On 14 December 1872, Featherston visited Ireland and took great pleasure in dismissing Farnall. On his dismissal as chief Irish agent, Farnall wrote directly to O' Rorke claiming that his efforts to promote emigration among the small farmer class in Ulster were thwarted by Featherston. In this instance Farnall was used as a scapegoat. Featherston believed that he was to blame for the failure to entice Irish people and what emerged as an anti-Catholic bias.[36] When a Mr W. Mason was appointed as chief emigration agent for Ireland after Farnall, little changed; it was noted that by the following August he had yet to submit a report detailing his work.[37]

The *Tablet* continued to accuse Featherston of Irish neglect. It substantiated its claims by highlighting the low numbers of Irish migrants availing of assisted and nominated passage, but it was not the only newspaper to voice discontent. The neglect of potential Irish migrants was also noted by the *Wellington Independent*, which showed that the only efforts made to entice Irish migrants concerned people from Ulster who were destined for Auckland, an enterprise to which Featherston had objected. Furthermore, the newspaper argued, 'the small-cotter class in Ireland are a very desirable field from which to procure immigrants', describing them as 'industrious, sober and thrifty, excellent dairy hands, and good farm labourers'.[38] The article concluded by stating that the dissatisfaction expressed by Irish residents in New Zealand was very well founded, given that conditions on arrival were far better than those at home. For example, of the 161 migrants who arrived in Otago on board the *Celestial Queen* in 1873 nearly all were hired immediately. Married couples were offered wages of between £55 and £65 per annum, single men could earn £40 to £50 per annum while single women were offered between £20 and £25 per annum and most of these arrangements included lodgings. Agricultural labourers were offered a further incentive of £10 if they agreed to stay for one year.[39] Compared to earnings at home –where entire farming families on Ireland's west coast were surviving on between £10 and £50 in 1891 – such wages were very attractive.[40] The *Auckland Star* criticised Featherston's 'irritating conduct' in relation to his shipping agreements. He continued to use the more expensive Shaw, Saville and Co., in spite of the fact that the shipping industry had become competitive and loyalty to this arrangement was an unnecessary drain on the immigration fund. For example, Shaw, Saville and Co. also had hidden extra charges with each adult emigrant having to pay 20s for bedding, blankets and mess utensils before disembarking.[41] Another bone of contention was that London was the main point of departure and New Zealand agents steered clear of Liverpool where poorer migrants – who were generally considered to be of lower calibre – could be found. Irish people favoured Liverpool as a departure point; it was nearer, cheaper to get to and cheaper for migrants to stay there on the night before sailing or if a delay occurred.[42]

The *Tablet* also charged Featherston with doctoring the figures, arguing that of the purported 1,181 Irish migrants sent out by June 1873 between three and four hundred were nominated but that the others had not been seen. It asked, 'Who has seen or spoken to them? Who are they? If he sent them what has become of them?'[43] While Featherston argued that he was following government directives, O' Rorke gleaned proof of his abysmal efforts to recruit Irish migrants from an analysis of newspaper advertisements. For example, when a special advertisement was placed on 29 January 1873 detailing free passages for dairywomen and domestic servants, it appeared in a total of forty-seven newspapers, thirty-seven in England and Wales, ten in Scotland and none in Ireland.[44] By then the agent-general was conducting a general advertising campaign in a total of 154 newspapers, of which only seventeen were Irish and again most were in the north of the country.

The same pattern was evident in the distribution of sub-agents. A disproportionate percentage of local agents worked in Scotland, whose population was approximately two million less than that of Ireland; seventy-eight agents were placed there and a mere forty-six in Ireland (most of whom were sub-agents based in the north).[45] Featherston's own reports show that he failed to advertise in twenty-five Irish counties, that is, the southern counties. This apparent anti-Irish bias or, more specifically, an anti-Catholic bias was exemplified when Featherston went to Scandinavia to recruit 6,000 immigrants in 1872–73 without even trying to fill such quotas in Ireland. According to the *Tablet* this move incensed the majority

British population of New Zealand.[46] At this point it must be noted again that Featherston was acting with Vogel's full consent. Vogel was, according to William P. Morrell, 'the real driving force in the Government'.[47] Ironically, Vogel had personally battled with prejudice because of his Jewish birth. Although he converted to the Anglican faith he wrestled with constant reminders of his past identity. In some respects his personal quest for acceptance as an ambassador of the British empire can partially explain his compliance with Featherston' anti-Irish stance. In response to allegations of neglecting the southern counties of Ireland an isolated advertisement was placed in the *Nation* on 29 March 1873, which read: 'Emigration to NZ; Terms on which assisted passage are granted may be ascertained on application to the agent-general...or, Mr Mason.' That Ireland was neglected in previous years is evidenced by advertisements looking for 'local agents in different counties of Ireland', at a time when a Scottish agent network had been fully operating for a few years. Indeed the informal Scottish links with Otago were established much earlier as the demographic profile of Otago and the letters of Edward G. Wakefield attest.[48] Both of the *Nation* advertisements were clearly just nominal gestures aimed at appeasing the colonial Irish and they did not reappear over the next few months.

Table 2: Advertising, Newspapers and Number of Agents: England and Wales, Scotland, and Ireland

Country	Number of Newspapers	Number of Agents
England and Wales	105	53
Scotland	32	78
Ireland	17	46
Total	154	177

Source: *New Zealand Tablet*, 16 August 1873, p. 8.

In New Zealand it was generally agreed that the best way in which to control the calibre of migrants was through a process of nominated passage, whereby those resident in the colony would nominate relatives and sponsor their passage either financially or as a character reference.[49] For the colonial Irish this was certainly the most important medium for encouraging people from home. In October 1873, Minister for Immigration O' Rorke published new regulations on the nomination of immigrants by those who were resident in the colony. The *Tablet* carried a breakdown of O' Rorke's terms and conditions, aimed at teaching Irish Catholic residents how to nominate their relatives and friends. It explained that copies of the regulations and applications could be found at any post office, but that payment for passages could be made only at bigger centres. It cost £4 to nominate an adult; single females between 12 and 50 years of age travelled free provided they were accompanied by their parents or could obtain proof 'of good character to the satisfaction of the agent-general in London'. Girls who travelled unaccompanied were generally regarded as 'morally suspect',[50] so families bringing out a non-related young girl under their protection received a gratuity of 10 shillings (widows and their families were ineligible). The nomination process was heavily incentivised; colonial residents were given a bonus of 5 shillings for every male nominated and 10 shillings for every female, on their arrival.[51] Nominees were subjected to rigorous scrutiny. Apart from the lengthy process of application the intending migrants had to produce a certificate stating that they could not contribute more than a certain sum and that they intended to 'work for certain wages'.[52]

In spite of the rigid system, the Irish made more use of the nominated scheme than the English, Welsh or Scottish, but it was not as fully exploited as it could have been.[53] The *Tablet* accused Featherston of throwing 'obstacles' in the way of Irish migrants. On 19 September 1873 it was brought to the attention of the House of Representatives that the emigration agent in Galway had refused to issue warrants of passage to eleven migrants because the names of more than one person appeared on the nomination applications. In this instance, the nominator was a Mr Flaherty from Callaghan's Creek, who was, according to the *Tablet*, 'representative of the best class of settler on the coast; and they assure me that thousands of people in the part of Ireland they come from would emigrate to New Zealand'.[54] Subsequently six of Flaherty's nominees left for America and five were still waiting to hear from their relatives. The criteria for nominated passage further stipulated that the agent-general could object to the nominated persons on the grounds of 'unsuitability of occupation . . . *or from any other cause*'. In other words, the office of the agent-general could question the calibre of the nominated migrant. The *Tablet*'s article claimed that the clause 'from any other cause' was being used to exclude potential Catholic migrants on religious grounds. It gave an example of an Irish girl who was refused passage on the grounds that she might 'upset the balance of nationalities'.[55] Charlotte MacDonald cites a few cases where Irish women were even questioned by officials at the London docksides and refused passage. In one instance a woman became ill with dysentery but when it transpired that she was pregnant she was refused passage. Medical officers examined emigrants prior to departure and those deemed unhealthy had their tickets withdrawn.[56] When two Irish women were discovered to be travelling under assumed identities they were also refused passage. It can be argued that these were fair cases for refusal but the pre-embarkation scrutiny was more commonly directed towards Irish migrants. Considering how the tedious application process had previously weeded out undesirables, this persecution at the dockside can be construed as yet another measure to stem the flow of Irish people. The *Tablet* continued to use provocative language in its Irish immigration campaign, citing how 'encouragement would be given to Chinese, Scandinavian and any other system of immigration into this colony; but no encouragement whatever would be given to the immigration of Irish Roman Catholics'.[57]

In 1873 when a special committee was appointed by the House of Representatives to reconsider the emigration question it recommended, amongst other things, that Irish and Scottish migrants should be given the option of leaving from their native ports rather than from London, thus avoiding a considerable expense.[58] The committee deplored the way the agent-general ignored instructions from the New Zealand government and saw his lack of business acumen as a primary factor in the blunders regarding shipping agreements, particularly the old alliance with the more expensive Shaw, Saville and Co. On that note the *Tablet* warned Irishmen to remember how between 1871 and 1873 the colonial exchequer had financed ships from English, Scottish, Prussian and Norwegian ports, but none from Ireland. 'Bear this in mind when asked to applaud the Premier, and his agent-general who is too pious to allow his conscience to be defiled with the aim of permitting Irishmen to come into the country in numbers sufficient to establish Popery here.'[59] The numbers reaching the colony fell far short of the necessary quota. Featherston's action, or inaction, spurred the provincial governments of Otago and Canterbury to appoint their own agents and send them back to the recruiting grounds.[60] Ironically, both provincial governments sent several agents to Scotland but none to Ireland.

The net result of the *Tablet*'s efforts to mount an Irish immigration campaign was that agents employed by, or working in liaison with, New Zealand authorities were sent to Ireland specifically to fill ships that were to leave directly from Irish ports. Throughout the 1870s only ten ships left directly from Ireland and only three were from the south. Indeed the attempts of Dunedin socialite Caroline Howard, who arranged the three ships from Cork, probably did more damage to the Irish immigrant reputation than anything else. She literally filled one ship (the *Asia*) from a Cork poorhouse and the immigrants on arrival in April 1874 were described as 'certificated scum'.[61] Howard was responsible for sending out two other vessels, the *Caroline* and the *Carrick Castle*. Bishop Moran of Dunedin disapproved of the calibre of migrant she brought out and his theory was that it was a conspiracy 'rendering Irish immigration unpopular'.[62] Vogel demanded Howard's dismissal as an Irish agent and following that the Dublin agency was dissolved in 1875.

It became apparent that letters from relatives were of more importance in encouraging southern Irish migration than the work done by government agents and sub-agents. The *Tablet* reiterated that

> the colony...cannot hold itself indebted to any extra activity, or indeed any activity whatever, on the part of the agent-general; the fact of the increase of coming immigrants is due to those who have preceded them, who, writing home to friends and relatives, speaking of the colony and its prospects with high favour, have caused such an impression as to induce a spontaneous desire to the shores of this colony.[63]

Positive letters from the colonial Irish explaining opportunities and prospects attracted more Irish migrants than the advertising conducted by New Zealand officials. By 3 January 1874 the New Zealand *Tablet* was advising Irish residents in the colony to stop requesting permission to nominate their friends because of the 'loss of time' incurred. It stated that direct nomination gave people a choice adding that 'they will not later upbraid you hereafter by saying "You had the opportunity of bringing me out free of cost and you did not".'[64] Nominated passage was definitely a more important component of Irish migration to New Zealand than assisted migration schemes. Numbers of nominated immigrants far exceeded the estimated 'fair proportion' to such an extent that a quota system was later introduced. In 1877 the 'central' Irish agency in Belfast was dissolved; neither it nor the Dublin agency had operated to full capacity, relative to other colonial offices. Southern Irish newspapers were used to great effect in the latter half of the nineteenth century to promote colonial life in Canada, North America and Australia but, apart from general advertisements indicating sailing times, New Zealand was poorly represented. Both Featherston and Vogel adhered to Wakefield's original principles and were more concerned with bringing persons of a high moral character to the colony than bringing in the multitudes. Featherston was very evidently influenced by Vogel's example and the latter treated immigration as a personal crusade, so much so that on Featherston's demise in 1876 he left parliamentary politics to take up the arduous position of agent-general in London.

There can be no doubt that until the late 1870s – a point when chain migration was more firmly established – the personal biases of immigration agents and officers limited the numbers of Irish Catholics reaching New Zealand. Ironically, the *Tablet*'s coverage of Featherston's recruitment policy in Ireland was in itself a very biased affair. He was blamed for a number of issues that were not exclusively his fault. The overall policy was flawed, and the low numbers that emigrated from Ireland to New Zealand in the early 1870s reflected that. Featherston's individual vilification is perhaps unjust but it served to make the colonial Irish more aware of how migration schemes worked. The *Tablet* exposed what was most certainly an anti-Irish Catholic prejudice in the implementation of the colonial immigration policy and if it had not it is likely that it would have been tolerated for longer by the Irish who were resident in New Zealand.

NOTES

1. I would like to thank Lorna Moloney, Dr Lachy Paterson and Dr Rory Sweetman for reading earlier drafts of this chapter. I would also like to thank Dr Laurence M. Geary for his continued support.

2. Erik Olssen and Marcia Stenson, *A Century of Change, New Zealand, 1800–1900* (Auckland: Longman Paul, 1989), p.233.

3. For a further analysis of the early organisation of New Zealand, see William Fox, *The Six Colonies of New Zealand* (Dunedin: John McIndoe Ltd, reprinted 1971). See also W. David McIntyre and W.J. Garner (eds), *Speeches and Documents on New Zealand History* (Oxford: Clarendon Press, 1971).

4. From an early stage Otago was primarily populated by Scottish migrants. British Library, Add. Ms. 35,261, Letters of E.G. Wakefield, 1815–1853, ff.30.

5. Donald Akenson, *Half the World from Home: Perspectives on the Irish in New Zealand, 1840–1950* (Wellington: Victoria University Press, 1990), p.53.

6. For numerous references to the Irish moving between Australia and New Zealand, see David Fitzpatrick, *Oceans of Consolation: Personal Accounts of Irish Migration to Australia* (New York: Cornell University Press, 1994); Angela McCarthy, 'Personal letters and the Organisation of Irish Migration to and from New Zealand, 1848–1925', *Irish Historical Studies*, vol. 33, no. 131 (May 2003), pp.297–319; Angela McCarthy, '"Seas may divide": Irish Migration to New Zealand as Portrayed in Personal Correspondence, 1840–1937' (unpublished PhD Thesis, Trinity College, Dublin, 2000).

7. Richard P. Davis, *Irish Issues in New Zealand Politics, 1868–1922* (Dunedin: University of Otago Press, 1974), pp.3–5.

8. Provisions were not made for the poor until Auckland provincial council passed the Neglected and Criminal Children's Act 1867 and the Sick and Destitute Act 1868. For further information, see W.B. Sutch, *The Quest for Security in New Zealand 1840–1966* (Wellington: Oxford University Press, 1966). For the history of legislation pertaining to children, see O. C. Mazengarb, R. A. Bloodworth, J. Leggat, G. L. McLeod, L. V. O'Brien, J. S. Somerville, F. N. Stace, *Report of the Special Committee on Moral Delinquency in Children and Adolescents: the Mazengarb Report* (Wellington: R.E. Owen, Government Printer, 1954), pp.54–5.

9. Akenson, *Half the World from Home*, p.40, shows a table of census returns.

10. Fraser, Lyndon, 'To Tara via Holyhead: The Emergence of Irish Catholic Ethnicity in Nineteenth-Century Christchurch, New Zealand', *Journal of Social History*, Volume 36, Number 2 (Winter 2002), pp. 431–58.

11. *Irish Times*, 10 January 1870. This is an accurate figure derived from New Zealand census returns.

12. Ibid., 18 January 1870.

13. *The Emigration Commission*, Hansard Parliamentary Debates, 12 April, 1869, vol.195, third series, cols. 579–80; *Colonial Land and Emigration Commissioners, thirtieth general report, 1870* HC, 1870, [C.196], XVII.111.

14. *People's Journal*, 22 June 1867, cited in Charlotte MacDonald, *A Woman of Good Character: Single Women as Immigrant Settlers in Nineteenth-Century New Zealand* (Wellington: Allen and Unwin, 1990), p.46.
15. MacDonald, *A Woman of Good Character,* p.118.
16. *Colonist*, Nelson, 5 July 1870, (also referred to informally as the *Nelson Colonist*)
17. *Correspondence with New Zealand commissioners and authorities on proposed guaranteed loan,* [HC, 1870], C. 298, L.281.
18. Olssen and Stenson, *A Century of Change*, p.233.
19. *Tablet*, 19 July 1873, citing the *Thames Advertiser*.
20. Ibid., 9 August 1873.
21. Olssen and Stenson, *A Century of Change*, p.233.
22. *Tablet*, 20 September 1873.
23. Ibid., 2 August 1873.
24. *Colonist*, 19 April 1870.
25. Ibid., 5 July 1870.
26. Davis, *Irish Issues in New Zealand Politics*, p.29.
27. *Tablet*, 13 September 1873.
28. Olssen and Stenson, *A Century of Change*, p.233.
29. *Tablet*, 23 August 1873; Olssen and Stenson, *A Century of Change*, p.236. Brogdens only managed to bring 1,300 navvies to New Zealand and only 76 of them were still working for the firm in 1874.
30. *Tablet*, 23 August 1873.
31. Ibid., 6 September 1873.
32. Davis, *Irish Issues in New Zealand Politics,* pp.34–5. For further information on the education issue see Rory Sweetman, *A Fair and Just Solution: A History of the Integration of Private Schools in New Zealand* (Palmerston North: Dunmore Press, 2002).
33. *Tablet*, 23 August 1873.
34. Davis, *Irish Issues in New Zealand Politics*, p.32.
35. For further information see Brad Patterson, 'New Zealand's "Ulster Plantation"; Katikati Revisited', in B. Patterson (ed.), *Ulster-New Zealand Migration and Cultural Transfers* (Dublin: Four Courts Press, 2006), pp.85–102.
36. See Davis, *Irish Issues in New Zealand Politics*, pp.35–7.
37. *Tablet*, 6 and 13 September 1873.
38. Ibid., 6 September 1873.
39. Ibid., 18 October 1873, p.10.
40. Ciara Breathnach, *The Congested Districts Board of Ireland: Poverty and Development in the West of Ireland* (Dublin: Four Courts Press, 2005), pp.40–1.
41. *Tablet*, 6 September 1873.
42. MacDonald, *A Woman of Good Character*, p.75
43. *Tablet*, 16 August 1873.
44. Ibid.
45. Ibid.
46. Ibid., 6 September 1873. The *Napier Telegraph* also pointed to Dr Featherston's concentration on other European countries 'when they might have been found in Great Britain and that Ireland has been altogether neglected'.
47. William P. Morrell, *The Provincial System of Government in New Zealand, 1852–76* (London: Longmans Green, 1932), p.191.
48. British Library, Add. Ms. 35,261, Letters of E.G. Wakefield, 1815–1853, ff.30.
49. *Tablet*, 30 August 1873.
50. MacDonald, *A Woman of Good Character*, p.17.
51. *Tablet*, 24 May 1873.
52. Ibid., 7 June 1873, p.8.
53. Ibid., 9 August 1873; Lyndon Fraser, 'To Tara via Holyhead', p.433.
54. Ibid., 18 October, 1873.

55. Ibid., 24 May 1873.
56. MacDonald, *A Woman of Good Character*, p.79.
57. *Tablet*, 20 December 1873.
58. Ibid., 20 September 1873.
59. Ibid., 27 December 1873.
60. Ibid., 20 September 1873; 13 December 1873. See also *Tablet*, 14 October 1873.
61. *Otago Daily Times*, 30 April 1874, cited in Davis, *Irish Issues in New Zealand Politics*, p.38.
62. Davis, *Irish Issues in New Zealand Politics*, p.39.
63. *Tablet*, 9 August 1873. For further studies see Angela McCarthy, '"In prospect of a happier future": Private Letters and Irish Women's Migration to New Zealand, 1840–1925', in Lyndon Fraser (ed.), *A Distant Shore: Irish Migration and New Zealand Settlement* (Dunedin: University of Otago Press, 2000), pp.105–16; A. McCarthy, *Irish Migrants in New Zealand, 1840–1937: 'the desired haven'* (Woodbridge: Boydell Press, 2005); Frances Porter and Charlotte MacDonald (eds), *My Hand Will Write What my Heart Dictates: the Unsettled Lives of Women in Nineteenth-Century New Zealand as Revealed to Sisters, Family and Friends* (Auckland: Auckland University Press, 1996); Miles Fairburn, *The Ideal Society and its Enemies: the Foundations of Modern New Zealand Society* (Auckland: Auckland University Press, 1989).
64. *Tablet*, 3 January 1874.

4

'Be you an Orangeman, you shall meet Orangemen': New Zealand's Ulster Plantation Revisited

Brad Patterson

On 8 June 1875, the 1,400 ton three-masted clipper *Carisbrooke Castle* set sail from Belfast Lough. After putting to briefly off Queenstown, County Cork, the ship headed off into the Atlantic. Aboard was a discrete group of 238 emigrants, including thirty-four families, all recruited in Ulster.[1] Their ultimate destination was Katikati, a scrub and fern covered wilderness on the eastern coast of the North Island in far-off New Zealand. The leader of the party was George Vesey Stewart, a land owner and estate agent from Ballygawley in County Tyrone.[2] Not an especially successful farmer, Stewart started a linen mill in the 1860s, and it was the failure of this speculation, as well as intensification of the Ulster land troubles, which turned his mind to migration. Quite why to New Zealand is still unclear, but it was perhaps related to the New Zealand government's efforts to recruit assisted immigrants from Ulster over the preceding decade, preference for Protestant husbandmen having been invariably expressed.[3] Whatever, Stewart's goal was the establishment of a tight-knit Ulster Protestant settlement, and to this end he had been treating with the New Zealand authorities since 1873. Ultimately he secured favourable terms: free land, and assisted passages for his immigrants.

Arriving in Auckland after a three-month voyage, the party was met with fanfare. They were welcomed by Joseph MacMullen Dargaville, described by the local press as a 'prominent local Irish politician'; perhaps more significantly, also Grand Master of the North Island's Loyal Orange Institution.[4] Bands played, a grand dinner was hosted, and Stewart was hailed as a 'king among his subjects'. Dargaville assured them that they had 'come to a land in which industry, perseverance and frugality were the chief requisites'. He also welcomed them because he and they 'had a deep-seated love for their Queen and mother country', and because he knew they would 'hand down those feelings of loyalty to Britain which would help to maintain that halo which surrounded their native land'.[5]

The would-be settlers then proceeded to the 10,000 acre block that had been set aside, and the practical colonising began. It was as well that many of this first party were practical working farmers, folk used to hard physical labour, for a host of challenges awaited them: clearing, draining, breaking in land, not least the provision of shelter for themselves.[6] In these efforts they were largely successful. Within two years the Crown Lands Ranger responsible for the district was able to report that 'very many of the settlers ... [had] ... done a great deal of work on their lands and as a result now have farms that would be a credit to any district of much longer standing'.[7] He estimated that around 1,900 acres had been cleared, 316 acres were in crops and 1,580 acres were under grass. In the opinion of an Auckland journalist, the planting of the Ulster families 'had been an experiment ... and perhaps at first sight a risky one. But the end crowns the work, and the end has been reached in a manner and with a success and promptitude never before attained in any special settlement ever attempted in New Zealand.'[8]

On the basis of these achievements, Stewart deemed the time ripe to seek a further 10,000 acres from the government, effectively doubling the size of the Ulster settlement. On the eve of his temporary return to the home province to recruit a second party of migrants, those who had accompanied him in 1875 were loud in praise.[9] John Hamilton thanked Stewart for bringing him to a land 'where a man can live under his own vine or fig tree'. At Katikati there need be 'no fear of landlord, agent or bailiff'. The Revd W.E. Mulgan, former Rector of the parish of Donagh, County Antrim, expressed himself as much pleased with the climate, the landscape and the life. His only sorrow was that he had 'not come out when ... a much younger man'. The most interesting encomiums, however, were those placing emphasis on the special character of the settlement. For Robert Stuart, its overwhelming attraction was as a stronghold for Ulster Protestants: 'Be you an Orangeman, you shall meet Orangemen; be you a Blackman, you shall meet Blackmen; be you a Freemason, you shall meet Freemasons; ... you shall always meet a hearty welcome from ... honest and contented countrymen.' Fitz Gibbon Louch, the designer of houses for leading settlers, probably spoke for a majority when he declared it to be 'a matter of thankfulness to the Disposer of all goodness that these fertile lands ... (this Goshen of New Zealand) ... had been reserved by the Almighty to be planted with the sturdy and industrious sons of Protestant Ulster'.

Katikati, then, was an organised Orange settlement, the only such known example in New Zealand. That is not to say that the creation of an Orange settlement was the intention of the New Zealand government – it clearly was not. Indeed, there was considerable nervousness at the prospect.[10] Stewart, however, had made his intentions plain from the outset. In May 1873, long before any arrangement had been concluded with the New Zealand authorities, he had issued a recruitment prospectus.[11] Its circulation had been confined to numbers of the Loyal Orange Order. Though the order had experienced rough times in earlier nineteenth-century decades, Gladstone's programme of Church and land reform, as well as fear of some form of Home Rule for Ireland, had imparted it new vigour. It was becoming a pan-Protestant front, bonding together Presbyterian and Anglican, farm labourer and tenant farmer, the middle class and the aristocracy. The order's full endorsement of his activities, bestowed in December 1873, was thus a great encouragement for Stewart.[12] Over the ensuing eighteen months the Ulster lodges were to be his primary recruitment vehicles.

It is not intended to recapitulate the establishment and maturation of the Katikati settlement in any detail in this chapter, still less to present any radical new findings. As will be demonstrated, Katikati has already been much written about. Equally, new interpretations must await significant new research. Instead, the focus will be on how writers over the past 130 years have portrayed the role of the Loyal Orange Lodge in the settlement. Obviously a whole range of other Ulster cultural traits could be considered, but given the settlement's origins it is surely the most significant. That said, a bald outline of post-1877 events may, nevertheless, be helpful.

Stewart eventually secured agreement for another grant of 10,000 acres, although this time the terms were much stiffer – strictly cash for land. The *Lady Jocelyn* sailed from Belfast in May 1878 with 378 Katikati-bound migrants aboard.[13] A contemporary described this second party as being made up of 'two generals, a major, two or three captains and lieutenants, a canon, a doctor, no end of pretty girls and fine young men'.[14] This was the importation of Ulster gentry, and it was as well that many of them had money. The injection of new capital ensured several more buoyant years, although it seems likely as much was spent on display as on enhancing production. While a few Ulster immigrants subsequently made their ways independently to the settlement, by 1880 the transplantation could be considered complete.[15] Indeed, by this point Stewart was already turning his attention to other promotions, most notably the settlement of Te Puke, further south on the Bay of Plenty coast. The 1880s proved to be difficult years for Katikati. In the course of the decade the initial soil fertility fell away, as in turn did the fortunes of the settlement. Katikati too was soon overtaken by the major depression enveloping the colony in the decade. A peak population of 526 had been recorded in 1881, but ten years later nearly half the original settlers had drifted away, only thirty-nine of the seventy-seven foundation families remaining on their farms.[16] While there was a minor recovery in the 1890s and early 1900s, the population stabilising at around 450 just prior to the First World War, it was on the basis of another form of activity, dairying. In the twentieth century Katikati settled for relatively comfortable obscurity as a small farming district, with a minor rural service centre as its nucleus.

This brief recounting of the foundation and stagnation of Katikati suggests several reasonable questions: how strongly did Orangeism take root in the new soil; were Old World practices and rituals maintained; and just how exclusively Orange was the settlement? In turn, this leads to consideration of what previous writers have said about the Orange Order at Katikati, identification of who those writers were, and assessment of the extent to which their backgrounds may have influenced their expositions.

By far and away the most influential contemporary writer on Katikati was George Vesey Stewart himself. While there is no record of any publication outlining his plans before the despatch of 'the first party', Stewart was to more than make up for this omission once in the colony. Between 1877 and 1887 he produced eleven small books or pamphlets, totalling nearly 700 pages, all promoting his various colonising ventures.[17] Two relate directly to the Katikati settlement. Essentially, they are publicity collages, and they well demonstrate Stewart's capacity to rewrite history to suit his own immediate needs. As a more recent commentator has observed, 'as an historian...Stewart...was essentially a Stalinist'.[18] The settlement leader was a shameless self-promoter, and his constant theme was 'transplanting a little corner of Ulster upon a Garden of Eden in New Zealand'. In these publications the Orange tone tends to be implicit, rather than explicit. It is most marked in settler testimonies, such as those cited earlier, but there is nothing to really frighten the New Zealand government horses! Stewart was too shrewd for that.

Even more circumspect are the memoirs of day-to-day living in early Katikati by Stewart's sister-in-law Adela Stewart, published in 1908 as *My Simple Life in New Zealand*.[19] This slim volume makes no pretence of being a history of Katikati; it is more an elaborated diary, covering thirty years of the development of Athenree, a pioneering farm in the north of the Katikati block. Popular in its time, it still retains a certain charm. There are several layers to the memoir. While major settlement events are mentioned, and the seasonal farm round is faithfully reported, the concentration is on domestic life. The author shows she was an adaptable woman, one prepared to turn her hand to almost anything. The difficulties of making a new life in a scrub-covered wilderness are clearly apparent, though the reminiscences are largely devoid of complaint. What is curious, however, is that only two passing references to lodge activities have been located in the book's 200 pages. On the 'Glorious Twelfth' in 1883, a party of twenty-four sat down to dinner at 'Martray', New Zealand home of Captain Mervyn Stewart, father of George Vesey and the author's husband, Hugh.[20] The meal was followed by loyal speeches and songs. Younger members of the party subsequently proceeded to an 'Orangemen's Ball' in the settlement hall. The only other reference is to a bazaar twelve years later, organised to raise funds for the maintenance of the Orange Hall, which had fallen into disrepair.[21] There are in fact more frequent references to St Patrick's Day picnics! The silence is interesting. It could be assumed that the household was but marginally involved in Orange activities – but for the fact that Captain Hugh Stewart was Worshipful Master of Loyal Orange Lodge No. 30 of Katikati for over a decade.

The only other contemporary reference to the Katikati settlers' lodge activities located is in the subsequently published shipboard diary of Belfast carpenter William John Gray.[22] Unable to curb his impatience, Gray left twelve months in advance of Stewart's first party. Before he left, his lodge – Belfast 492 – presented him with a Bible, and a bottle of brandy to toast the 'Glorious Twelfth' in mid-Atlantic. This he did – but his diary also records a number of displeasing encounters with countrymen of different persuasion throughout the voyage. 'There are that much Popery in them,' he wrote on 20 May 1874, 'that were the hatches down on them in the lower hold, although they number only 8 or 9, it could not be kept from exposing itself.'[23] How different were the seamen, who were of a 'peculiar English and Loyal character'. Gray continued to inveigh against 'that unfortunate class of people known as Irish' throughout the voyage. There are no further records of his views once he arrived in the settlement, but he was to be one of the last surviving of the early settlers. In the decade after Vesey Stewart's death in 1920 'his was the voice that spoke with most authority in Katikati'.[24]

It is a twist of fate that the first systematically researched history of the settlement, *An Ulster Plantation: The Story of the Katikati Settlement*, should be authored by William Gray's grandson, Arthur J. Gray.[25] First published in 1938, and reprinted several times since, it has come to be regarded as a minor New Zealand classic. As late as 1998, sixty years after it first appeared, it was authoritatively described as 'the original and still definitive' history of the settlement and commended for its 'studious attention to detail'.[26] Gray, the grandson, was a scholarly man, and, as far as can be established, did not share his grandfather's trenchant views. A first-class masters graduate of Auckland University, a Rhodes Scholar nominee in 1925, and later a widely respected teacher, he was as thorough in his research as he was able to be.[27] He made good use of the documents available to him, although handicapped by not having access to material available to subsequent researchers. There can be little doubt that Gray intended his book as a memorial. Certainly, the initial sales pitch was overtly celebratory. 'Mr Gray', the publisher enthuses on the dust-jacket, 'is no mere academic outsider selecting a theme for a thesis. He is himself part of Katikati's gift to New Zealand. He is telling the story of his own folk.'[28] He had drawn 'a living picture' of a 'courageous venture'. There were 'statistics of course, the hard facts of history in solid array' but it was 'the warp and woof of history' that gripped the author.

It is perfectly understandable that Gray's emphasis should be on the arrival of the 1875 and 1878 parties and on their pioneering efforts. This is the heroic part of Katikati's story. He does, however, carefully distinguish between the two. If there is a difficulty with the book, it is that by modern standards the study is rather one-dimensional. Gray is more concerned with facts than speculations, with listing first families, establishing a chronology, than inquiring into the durability of Katikati's Ulster heritage. So, what does he say about the Orange Order in the settlement? There are in fact only two short passages in the book directly relating to the lodge. The first bears direct quotation:

> Needless to say there was an Orange Lodge, and a flourishing one, in Kati Kati. The Orangemen's great day was the Boyne anniversary on 12 July, when the brethren donned their regalia and marched in solemn procession to the church headed by the drum and fife band. They then sat down to a heavy and indigestible dinner, winding up with toasts to the glory of Dutch William and Queen Victoria, and confusion to the Pope and Home Rule.
>
> It does not appear that these fervent expressions of sentiment affected the course of events in Ireland, but the Orangemen did confer a lasting benefit on the settlement by undertaking the construction of a public hall. An acre of land was given by James Lockington, and the hall erected in 1883. The extempore celebration that marked its completion was marred by a regrettable incident, when a visiting humorist, begging permission to give an item, favoured the company with 'The Wearing of the Green'.[29]

The only other reference is to the fact that the local public house, run by one Barney McDonnell, described as 'a good Catholic', was the place where Orange gatherings invariably concluded. McDonnell, Gray records, 'stood six foot two and weighed twenty stone...He was at his ease in every class of society...(and)...would have no fights and no blasphemy in his house'.[30] There is also the observation that when one scrupulous local Orangeman objected to liquor for the 'Glorious Twelfth' being procured from a Catholic, mine host resolved the situation by contributing half a dozen free bottles of whiskey to the annual celebrations. There were, Gray notes, 'no further complaints'. There is a simple assumption in Gray's account that a tradition such as the lodge was important, and that it was retained in the settlement. It might also be assumed, given Gray's personal links with several of the settlement's founders, that his interpretation is likely to be accurate.

Perhaps the ultimate compliment to Gray is the extent to which passages from his narrative, both acknowledged and unacknowledged, appear in the pages of his successors. One unabashed borrower was his close acquaintance A.E. (Alan) Mulgan.[31] Another grandson of the first settlers – in fact, the grandson of the Revd W.E. Mulgan – Alan Mulgan, although born in Katikati, had left while still a child. In the twentieth century Mulgan won some transient fame as an Antipodean man of letters but, although he was twenty years older than Gray, it was to be twenty years after the publication of *Ulster Plantation* before his most significant thoughts on Katikati appeared in print. To be fair, however, Mulgan had expressed some doubts about the strength of the settlement's Ulster heritage a decade before Gray took up his pen. In *Home*,[32] an account of a voyage to the United Kingdom (in the course of which, perhaps significantly, Northern Ireland was not visited) he notes that the migrants were constantly exposed to English influences. 'To a boy who had been born in New Zealand, Ulster was a shadowy place. England and English things were always before our eyes.' Perhaps there is the germ of an idea here. Was the Ulster heritage of the settlement worn down by an early form of media pressure? What, for instance, was the impact of the *Illustrated London News*, *Punch* and the *Boys' Own Paper*? In contrast to Gray's certitude about his roots, Mulgan's ambivalence was to be lifelong. In his autobiography, *The Making of a New Zealander*,[33] published in 1958, only four years prior to his death, Mulgan argues that the settlement's social tone, 'was that of a *British* community transplanted into a freer world'.[34] Of course, he goes on, 'there was an Orange Lodge, which had its headquarters in the one hall...On or about the 12th of July, Lodge members would parade in the glory of their sashes for a service in the Anglican Church.'[35] He could 'well remember the impression a small boy got from that processional splash of colour on the tea-tree-lined country road'. The Roman Catholic families in the settlement, Mulgan insists, and it is interesting that there were already some, 'suffered not one whit on account of their religion'. His summation: 'Old passions cooled in the free colonial environment.'

In the three decades after the Second World War there was little scholarly writing on Katikati – apart from the contributions of three historical geographers. While two of the three, Evelyn Stokes of Waikato

University and Noel Mitchel of Queen's University, Belfast, added usefully to the stock of knowledge on the economic and spatial development of Katikati,[36] neither had much to say on the longevity of the settlement's Ulster traditions. The third, a thesis writer at the University of Otago, Thomas L. Stevenson,[37] paid more attention to cultural transfers. In his study of Katikati as a 'special settlement', judged to be possibly the most successful of all the 1870s special settlements, Stevenson seriously questioned the label 'Ulster plantation'. While conceding that Stewart's goal was 'a unified self sufficient community tied by a common bond of "Ulster kinship"', he pointed to a paradox: the settlers had come to Katikati as a united group; yet many had left their homeland to break away from the very way of life that had given them their common bond.[38] For some years the trappings of the Old World were preserved as something of a comfort blanket. This produced a lingering Ulster social atmosphere, despite all the physical signs of settlement development pointing to a way of life totally uncharacteristic of home. 'Orangemen parading in full regalia, retired officers in military uniform, great banquets and dance, were characteristics of Ulster society,' Stevenson notes, but for what strata of Ulster society, and for how long?[39] Katikati proved to be a great leveller of fortunes and social standing. Stevenson suggests that the bond of Ulster kinship, and as a consequence traditional practices, remained relatively strong only so long as Katikati itself was isolated. By the 1890s many of the original settlers had either left the settlement or died, this accelerating the perhaps inevitable erosion of traditional ways.

The most penetrating work on Katikati, to date, has been that of Canadian historian Donald Harman Akenson. While by no means the first professional historian to comment on Katikati, he was certainly the first to study the official records in any depth. The thirty-five-page chapter on Katikati in his 1990 overview of the New Zealand Irish, *Half the World From Home*, is both intellectually rigorous and a model of compression.[40] Akenson brought to his analysis an impressive mix of experience and personal skills. By 1990, the year the book appeared, he was already the author of a dozen volumes on Irish domestic and diasporic history, including two on nineteenth-century Ulster Protestant communities.[41] He thus looked at Katikati through the eyes of an informed outsider. Akenson deliberately set out to investigate the very issues that Gray and those following him had left largely unanswered: just who were the Katikati planters; what was their cultural background; and, arising from these questions, how robust were the distinctively Ulster Protestant aspects of their culture?

Akenson came to the conclusion that, while Katikati may indeed have been 'the purest Irish Protestant community ever to exist in New Zealand',[42] whatever was specifically Ulster about its character diminished quickly. He suggested two new reasons why, both related to the backgrounds of the two settler parties of the 1870s.[43] In his view, the first party, the *Carisbrooke Castle* settlers of 1875, was never the homogenous tight-knit group that has been portrayed. They were not simply a group of tenant farmers from Tyrone. Beneath the surface, Akenson argues, there were long-standing fissures. There were divisions of geography; some were from the insecure border counties (Tyrone, Armagh), others from those deemed fully secure (Antrim, Down). There was a split between those from rural districts and those from the North's growing towns. There was also the religious cleavage between Presbyterians and followers of the Church of Ireland. Exacerbating these differences, the arrival of the second party in 1878 brought another division, that of class. The culture they brought with them was the culture of a gentry plantation rather than an Ulster plantation.[44] It was identical, in Akenson's view, to that anywhere in the British colonies where gentry and would-be gentry settled in any numbers. While these natural divisions may not have mattered much in the north of Ireland, where like could mix with like, they mattered a great deal in a small colonial settlement, and this become obvious in a number of ways.

As an artefact of culture, religion was vitally important to Ulster Protestants. Yet in Katikati, religion was let slide.[45] There was no permanent Presbyterian church in the settlement for over thirty years, and for most of that time no permanent minister. The Anglicans did somewhat better, but not well, their house of worship not being constructed until 1883 and there being no resident vicar until 1886. Until that time, however, Katikati settlers who had taken holy orders filled the gap. Steadily dropping church attendances nevertheless indicate a lesser religious fervour than would have been evident at home; conversely, there is little evidence of strong religious prejudice in the settlement. Small wonder, then, that support for the Loyal Orange Institution also became more half-hearted than in the settlers' by now distant homeland.

Akenson has suggested that the Orange Lodge was the only colonial institution of importance incorporating a specifically Ulster viewpoint.[46] The early signs were that there would be a successful cultural transfer. Not only were the great majority of the settlement's family heads pledged Orangemen; their leaders had also held high office in the order at home. Vesey Stewart himself, for instance, had been Grand Treasurer for Tyrone, while father Mervyn had been County Grand Master.[47] In the colony they were to provide support for Hugh. There was thus every anticipation that traditional Orange celebrations would be replicated at Katikati, one lodge brother writing approvingly of the bands, banners and drums massed in the usual show of territorial intimidation at the Thames in March 1877. Yet, when Katikati's own lodge came into being in the following year, the public triumphalism was subdued. As Akenson notes, 'the brethren did not go on country-wide marches, but held their celebrations at home, and they were not intimidating anyone'.[48] To be sure, in the early 1880s, when Lodge No. 30 was at its strongest, members donned sashes and, with fife and drum band at head, marched the few hundred yards along the main road to the Anglican church. But by the end of the decade even these token marches had been replaced by a more decorous church parade, followed by a dance in the evening. In the colony the lodge steadily assumed a new persona, the nature of its activities changed, and ultimately it declined. Its identity switched from that of an organ of cultural defence to more of a social club, something which may well have better met colonial needs. Akenson is uncertain about just when Orange observances attenuated drastically, but he suggests that after 1900, with the economic base and social mix of Katikati fundamentally altering, the relevance of the lodge came into question.

More recent research, while fully bearing out Akenson's general findings, suggests that the decline of Ulster culture in Katikati may have been even more rapid than he suggested. In a 1998 masters dissertation, Jasmine Rogers[49] subjected three Katikati agencies of socialisation to close scrutiny, foremost among them the Orange Lodge. She found that, after its first decade, the lodge became more egalitarian. Indeed, on occasions, the settlement's Catholics participated in festivities. The second generation, she writes, were 'more given to mix the colours of Orange and Green . . . to produce a unity of colour and feeling'.[50] There was a conscious departure from the sectarian and often bigoted face of Orangeism imported. The lodge instead became a recreational vehicle, fostering neighbourliness and mutual help. Yet in this liberalism lay the seeds of decline. Rogers confirms that by the late 1880s even the short 12 July marches had been abandoned. The lodge's last recorded grand ball was in 1890, and two years later the 'Glorious Twelfth' 'passed over silently'.[51] Orange culture had fallen away in Katikati in less than twenty years. Katikati was 'a settlement of Ulster men and women,' Roger writes, 'but it was not strictly an Ulster settlement. Settlers at Katikati did not establish a mirror community, rather one more suited to their needs in the New World.'[52]

Where, then, does this brief survey of writings on Orangeism in New Zealand's foremost Ulster settlement lead? It surely emphasizes that the occasionally advanced argument that no more research need be done on Katikati, that instead greater consideration should be given to other aspects of the Irish Protestant experience in New Zealand, is premature. Elsewhere, a tentative research agenda has been set out.[53] The most basic challenge is to write a more textured account of the Katikati experiment, if possible using previously unconsulted Ulster sources. To date, all studies have been essentially written from a New Zealand perspective. There are also tangential studies to be considered: of Te Puke, Stewart's third settlement; a biography of Stewart himself. Might not also Katikati be usefully compared with organised Ulster Protestant settlement at other destinations and at other times, for instance Kiama in southern New South Wales, or in the United States and Canada? And, on a broader canvas, why did Irish Protestant culture prove less durable than Irish Catholic culture in New Zealand? The place of Katikati in the history of Irish Protestant migration has yet to be fully established.

By the mid-twentieth century the envisaged Ulster Protestant stronghold in New Zealand was almost forgotten, even by those living in Katikati. And yet, over the past fifteen years, Katikati has begun to rediscover itself and its special character.[54] It would be tempting to attribute this to a questing for roots, and this is probably partially so, but commercial considerations have also been influential. There has been a local realisation that Katikati's Ulster past offers something for heritage tourism. On the ground, Katikati now probably has more murals per head of population than Belfast (there are thirty-six in a small area).[55] While they hark back to those who built the district, there is nothing at all sectarian about any of the art works, no hint of the settlement's Orange origins. There has also been a move to save some of the few remaining historic buildings, the prime example being Hugh and Adela Stewart's 'Athenree' homestead.[56] Though largely ignored for half a century, George Vesey Stewart's monument, erected in the local domain in the 1930s, no longer stands in solitary splendour as an acknowledgement of the small New Zealand rural township's past.

NOTES

1. For an outline of the despatch of the first party see A.J. Gray, *An Ulster Plantation. The Story of the Katikati Settlement* (Dunedin and Wellington: A.H. & A.W. Reed, 1938), pp.17–25.
2. Jinty Rorke, 'Stewart, George Vesey 1832–1920' in *Dictionary of New Zealand Biography* (Wellington: Bridget Williams Books, 1993), p.481.
3. Alasdair Galbraith, '"The invisible Irish". Re-discovering the Irish Protestant tradition in colonial New Zealand', in Lyndon Fraser (ed.), *A Distant Shore: Irish Migration and New Zealand Settlement* (Dunedin: Otago University Press, 2000), pp.43–7.
4. Ibid, p.36.
5. Joseph Carnahan, *A Brief History of the Orange Institution in the North Island of New Zealand from 1842 till the Present Time* (Auckland: Grand Lodge, 1886), p.28.
6. Evelyn Stokes, *A History of Tauranga County* (Palmerston North: Dunmore, 1980), pp.135–65.
7. 'Report and return showing the nature and extent of improvements effected in the Katikati Special Settlement to the end of November 1878', *Appendices to the Journals of the House of Representatives*, H10, 1879.

8. Cited in George Vesey Stewart, *Notes on the Origin and Prospects of the Stewart Special Settlement, Kati-Kati, New Zealand, and on New Zealand as a Field of Emigration* (Omagh: N. Carson, 1877), p.110.

9. Ibid, pp.51, 44, 55, 47.

10. Richard P. Davis, *Irish Issues in New Zealand Politics, 1868–1922* (Dunedin: Otago University Press, 1974), pp 32–7.

11. Gray, *Ulster Plantation*, pp.9–10.

12. *Report of the Proceedings of the Grand Orange Lodge of Ireland ... 3rd and 4th December 1873*, p.25; cited Donald Harman Akenson, 'Katikati: A wee Ulster plantation?' in Donald Harman Akenson, *Half the World from Home: Perspectives on the Irish in New Zealand, 1860–1950* (Wellington: Victoria University Press, 1990), p.128.

13. Gray, *Ulster Plantation*, pp.43–62.

14. Adela B. Stewart, *My Simple Life in New Zealand* (London: Robert Banks and Son, 1908), p.7.

15. Ernest E. Bush (ed.), *The Katikati Story* (Tauranga: Tauranga Historical Society, 1975), pp.42–3.

16. Gray, *Ulster Plantation*, pp.73–4.

17. Details in A.G. Bagnall (ed.), *New Zealand National Bibliography to the year 1960*, Vol. 1 (Wellington: Government Printer, 1980), pp.984–5.

18. Akenson, 'A wee Ulster plantation?', p.125.

19. Stewart, *My Simple Life*.

20. Ibid, p.81.

21. Ibid, p.129.

22. Cited Rory Sweetman, 'Towards a history of Orangeism in New Zealand', in Brad Patterson (ed.), *Ulster-New Zealand Migration and Cultural Transfers* (Dublin: Four Courts Press, 2005), pp.54–5.

23. Ibid, p.54.

24. M. Gray and W.M. Macdonald, 'The journey of William John Gray, 1875', *Auckland-Waikato Historical Journal*, 47 (1985), p.28.

25. Gray, *Ulster Plantation*.

26. Alasdair Galbraith, 'New Zealand's invisible Irish: Irish Protestants in the North Island of New Zealand, 1840–1900' (MA thesis, University of Auckland, 1998), p.12.

27. G.C. Petersen (ed.), *Who's Who in New Zealand*, 7th edn (Wellington: A.H. & A.W. Reed, 1961), p.141.

28. Gray, *Ulster Plantation* (author's copy).

29. Ibid, p.106.

30. Ibid, pp.80–1.

31. Petersen (ed.), *Who's Who*, p.216.

32. Alan Mulgan, *Home: a New Zealander's Adventure* (London: Longmans, Green and Co., 1927).

33. Alan Mulgan, *The Making of a New Zealander* (Wellington: A.H. & A.W. Reed, 1958).

34. Ibid, p.24.

35. Ibid.

36. Stokes, *History of Tauranga County*; Evelyn Stokes, 'The Irish at Katikati', *New Zealand's Heritage* 3:39 (1972), pp.1,083–8; N.C. Mitchel, 'Katikati: an Ulster settlement in New Zealand', *Ulster Folklife*, xiv (1970), pp.203–15.

37. Thomas L. Stevenson, 'The Katikati special settlement, 1875–1900' (MA thesis, University of Otago, 1975).

38. Ibid, p.160.

39. Ibid, p.171.

40. Akenson, 'A wee Ulster plantation?'

41. Donald Harman Akenson, *Between Two Revolutions: Islandmagee, Co. Antrim, 1798–1920* (Hamden, Conn.: Archon, 1979); *Local Poets and Social History: James Orr, Bard of Ballycarry* (Belfast: PRONI, 1977).

42. Akenson, 'A wee Ulster plantation?', p.123.
43. Ibid, pp.133–40.
44. Ibid, p.149.
45. Ibid, pp.149–50.
46. Ibid, p.150.
47. Ibid, p.238 n 14.
48. Ibid, p.151.
49. Jasmine R. Rogers, 'A little corner of Ulster in New Zealand: the Katikati special settlement, 1875–1900' (MA thesis, University of Auckland, 1998).
50. Ibid, p.53.
51. Ibid, p.55.
52. Ibid, abstract.
53. Brad Patterson, 'New Zealand's Ulster plantation: Katikati revisited', in Patterson (ed.), *Ulster–New Zealand Migration,* pp 85–102.
54. 'Welcome to Katikati'. http://www.katikati.co.nz/ [accessed March 2005].
55. 'Katikati Murals'. http://rohrmannspace.net/BRnzl-katikatimurals.htm [accessed May 2005].
56. 'Athenree Homestead'. http://www.katikati.org.nz/athenree.php [accessed May 2005].

PART II
Cultural Transmission

5

William Vincent Wallace and Music in Australia 1835–8

David Grant

Two Irishmen had a major impact on cultural life in Australia in the 1830s, the decade which saw the sowing of its first successful seeds in the colony of New South Wales: the new Liberal (Whig) governor, Richard Bourke (1777–1855), the eighth to hold the post, who was in office from 1831 to 1837, and executant and composer William Vincent Wallace (1812–65), who arrived in late 1835 and left in early 1838, shortly after the governor's own departure. While it was coincidental that the two were thrown together on the opposite side of the world from their birthplace, it was a most fortunate conjunction. Their common Irish Protestant background, coupled with Bourke's love of music, enabled them to empathise, and that empathy led to the first symbiotic relationship in Australian musical history.[1] While highlighting that collaboration is one aspect of this chapter, its main purpose is to furnish as accurate an account as possible of Wallace's time in the colony, and of his considerable impact on musical life there. To that end, all available sources have been utilised, both very recent ones, and also older sources which to date have not received due attention.[2] The whole Wallace family emigrated to Australia in the 1830s, and likewise made a significant musical contribution, and this chapter also provides new information on those family members who stayed on in the colony up to 1850 and beyond. First, however, a brief outline of the origins of Bourke and Wallace, who, coincidentally, both came from a British army background – but there the similarity ends.

GOVERNOR BOURKE

Richard Bourke, born in Dublin in 1777, was a professional soldier whose distinguished family line can be traced back to the first Norman Governor-General of Ireland, William de Burgh (*fl*. 1185).[3]   Bourke, educated at Westminster School and Oxford, was called to the bar in 1798, but never practised. Instead he joined the Grenadier Guards as an ensign, and saw service in Holland and South America. A life-long interest in education began when Bourke, now with the rank of major, was appointed superintendent of the Junior Department of the Royal Military College (the predecessor of Sandhurst).[4] In 1810, Bourke re-established his connection with Ireland by acquiring a 180-acre estate called Shanavoy (which he renamed Thornfields), situated some miles east of Limerick city, and near his family's ancestral lands. Following a further successful campaign in Spain in the Peninsular War, which brought him close to his compatriot, the Duke of Wellington, Bourke continued to be promoted, becoming a major-general in 1821; taking half-pay from the army, however, enabled him to spend time on his Limerick estate with his wife, Betsy, and family. His great-great-grandson, Gerard, who lives on at Thornfields, writes:

> Farming and estate management were high among his extraordinarily wide range of interests...In fact Thornfields quickly became an ideal secluded family residence for my ancestor, a devout, though liberal, Protestant. Right from the beginning, they built up an exemplary rapport with their tenants and neighbours...They knew the duties incumbent on those in a privileged position through good education, especially now owning a property near Castleconnell, so very long associated with the Bourke family.[5]

Characteristically, one of Bourke's first actions on his Limerick estate was to establish a school for the local children at Ahane.[6] This was the calibre of the man who, in his fiftieth year, was called out of semi-retirement by the administration, and served, from 1826 to 1828, as acting governor in the eastern district of the Cape of Good Hope. Then, on 25 June 1831, following the coming to power of the new reforming Whig government of Earl Grey, Bourke was appointed governor of New South Wales, and arrived at Sydney with his wife, family, and entourage on the brig *Margaret* on 2 December 1831.[7]

WILLIAM VINCENT WALLACE

William Wallace, born in Waterford city in 1812, was the first son of Spencer Wallace (1789–1846), of Kilmoremoy, near Ballina, County Mayo. Nothing is known of the composer's mother, Eliza. Originally a rank-and-file musician in the North Mayo Regiment of

Militia, Sergeant Spencer Wallace had, by 1823, graduated to bandmaster of the Twenty-ninth Regiment of Foot; his two sons, William and Wellington (b. 1814) enlisted in the regiment in 1825. When the regiment received a posting to Mauritius in 1826, Spencer bought himself and the boys out of the army. Thereafter, the family moved to Dublin, where the father and sons worked as musicians in the city's theatres.[8] William was an exceptional violinist, and joined the orchestra of the Theatre Royal about 1829, aged 17; by 1834, when he left the post, he had risen to sub-leader. In the meantime, William had fallen in love with one of his violin pupils, Isabella Kelly (c. 1813–1900) of Frascati, Blackrock, County Dublin, and they eloped in 1831.[9] Isabella was Roman Catholic, and Wallace probably converted in order to marry her, his assumption of the name Vincent dating from this time. Two years later their only son, Willy, was born in Dublin. Wallace took part in Paganini's concerts at the Dublin Music Festival in 1831, and was inspired to emulate him.[10] He duly wrote a violin concerto of his own, which he performed in Dublin in 1834.[11] It brought him recognition, but little financial reward. Meanwhile, Wallace's mother had died, his father had remarried, and the extended family was intent on seeking a new life in Australia. William's lack of prospects in Dublin, coupled with his poor health and that of his wife, finally convinced them to emigrate also.[12]

BURGEONING CULTURAL LIFE IN SYDNEY 1832–5

Richard Bourke's period as governor coincided with an upsurge in cultural activity in Sydney and environs, in part a reaction of the city's wealthier class against the harsh regime of the previous governor, Sir Ralph Darling. Both Beedell[13] and Cumes give accounts of this 'quest for culture in the 1830s'.[14] Cumes states that 'the years of Bourke's rule, between 1831 and 1837, were years of substantial progress in cultural activities in the colony'.[15] Within a year of his arrival, Bourke had granted impresario Barnett Levey his first permanent theatre licence, and Levey's Theatre Royal, situated in a warehouse building behind his Royal Hotel, with a seating capacity of 1,000, provided regular if not spectacular theatrical fare up to his death in 1837. Thereafter, the Royal Victoria Theatre was built, which Cumes describes as 'one of the first ... "grand" colonial theatres'.[16] Public performances of music, previously confined to 'at homes', were also in evidence at the Theatre Royal, and were enhanced by the arrival of singers such as Mrs Taylor in 1834, and Mrs Chester, 'a lady from the English Metropolitan Theatres', the following year.[17] April 1834 saw the formation of the Sydney Philharmonic Society, which was patronised by the governor, and which gave a series of rival concerts at the Pulteney Hotel, beginning in July of that year.[18] While these initial concert efforts were only moderately successful, the musical scene was revitalised with the arrival of the Wallace and Deane families in 1836.[19] These families were to play a decisive role in the establishment of music as the jewel in the crown of Governor Sir Richard Bourke's Australian cultural achievements.[20]

THE WALLACE FAMILY EMIGRATES
TO AUSTRALIA, 1835–6

William, Isabella and son, Willy, sailed first, embarking from Liverpool on 9 July 1835 on the ship *Rachel*, captained by R.S. Potter.[21] They went as free emigrants, probably using a bequest which had come to Isabella from her late mother.[22] The scandalous accusation in Flood,[23] of how an alleged shipboard liaison between William and one of Isabella's sisters resulted in the break-up of the Wallaces' marriage, is not true.[24] The Wallaces disembarked at Hobart Town on 31 October 1835.[25] William gave two concerts there, on 4 and 11 December, his first in the Antipodes. It is probably at this time, rather than in 1838 – as given by the Mulligans – that Wallace stayed at New Norfolk, some miles inland from Hobart on the Derwent river. There is a local tradition that Wallace composed some of the tunes that found their way into *Maritana* while staying at the Bush Inn there.[26] If he did, they were 'songs without words', as the play on which the opera is based had yet to be written. In particular, it is said that the melody of 'Scenes that are brightest' was composed at New Norfolk, a tradition which was consolidated in 1924, when Dame Nellie Melba sang the song in public there. This led in turn to the famous broadcast, in 1932, of *Maritana* excerpts from the Bush Inn.[27] The opera's strong connection with Australian culture will be discussed further below.

On 2 January 1836, the Wallaces re-embarked at Hobart Town for Sydney, on the 'Layton', arriving at Circular Quay on 12 January. Following a short stop-over, they moved out to Parramatta, where they stayed at Mrs Nash's Woolpack Inn. Wallace's reputation had preceded him to Sydney from Hobart, and within a month of his arrival, he gave his first 'celebrity' concert, under the patronage of Governor Bourke, at the Royal Hotel on 12 February 1836,[28] a concert that was repeated two weeks later due to demand. These were the first of over twenty concerts given by Wallace and his extended family in the colony over the next two years.

Table 3: Wallace's Concert Appearances in Australia

Date	Place/Details	Reference
1835		
4, 11 December	Argyle Rooms, Hobart Town	29
1836		
12 February	Wallace's debut concert: Royal Hotel, Sydney (RHS)	30
26 February	Repeat concert, RHS	31
16 March	Benefit concert, RHS	32
May	First Wallace family concert	33
1 June, 13 July	Wallace family concerts	34
August	Chamber music series: Wallaces and Deanes	35
14 September	Wallace family concert, RHS	36
21 September	Oratorio Concert, St Mary's, Sydney	37
7 December	Nash's Hotel (Woolpack Inn), Parramatta	38
27 December	Court House, Windsor, Hawkesbury District	39
1837		
1 February–March	Two concerts by Wallace and Deane families, RHS	40
4, 28 May	Wallace family concerts at (1) Catholic Chapel (Sydney) and (2) St Patrick's, Parramatta	41
1 August, 29 September	Joint Wallace/Deane concerts, RHS	42
26 October	Benefit for J.P. Deane, at which Wallace participated	43
1838		
31 January	Second Oratorio Concert, St Mary's, Sydney	44

Meanwhile, on 6 February, the rest of the Wallace family had arrived at Circular Quay, as bounty immigrants on the ship *James Pattison*, which had departed from Cork on 31 October 1835. Spencer Wallace, the composer's father, and his second wife, Matilda (née Kelly), with their two young children, a boy and a girl, were accompanied by his wife's sister, Charlotte; Spencer's daughter, Eliza, aged 16, and his son Spencer Wellington (known as S.W. Wallace) – although he is not listed by name – were also members of the party.[45] This information is confirmed by the *Sydney Gazette* of 1 March 1836: 'Mr. [William] Wallace, Miss [Eliza] Wallace and also his brother [Wellington] and father [Spencer] are all in the Colony; they are excellent musicians.'[46]

MUSIC ACADEMIES AND CONCERT ACTIVITY IN SYDNEY AND SURROUNDINGS IN 1836

By 4 April 1836, Wallace and his family had opened the colony's first ever music academy (nominally but not exclusively for young ladies), at Bridge St., Sydney, under the patronage of Governor Bourke and of his musically minded daughter, Anne Deas Thomson.[47] Although the school did not succeed in the longer term, the present Sydney Conservatoire of Music is, by a remarkable coincidence, situated nearby, in the Botanic Gardens at the end of Bridge St. The Wallaces very soon had competition with their concert and teaching activities. The family of John P. Deane, formerly of London, but since 1822 based in Hobart Town, arrived in Sydney from there about 19 April, and by the end of the month had set up a second music school at Pitt St. in the city.[48] The rivalry was apparently a friendly one: the Deanes and Wallaces collaborated in concert-giving, and the Philharmonic Society, which had gone into decline the previous year, was resurrected with the full participation of the two families.[49] Its first major event was an oratorio concert at St Mary's RC Cathedral on 21 September 1836, which was the highlight of this first year of concert activity. This spectacular concert was timely for Wallace, because by mid-September, the *Sydney Herald* was bemoaning the fact that 'by now his adoring public has grown accustomed to his virtuosic exploits, even to the point of weariness'.[50] The Grand Oratorio Concert changed all that: Holzner describes it as 'the greatest musical triumph of pre-Gold-Rush Australia'. An audience of up to 1,000 people inside, with a similar number standing outside in the moonlight, heard selections from Handel's *Messiah* and Haydn's *The Creation*, with Wallace directing the combined band, choral and orchestral forces.[51]

A FARMING INTERLUDE; MARRIAGE BREAK-UP

Most biographical sources describe Wallace as engaging in farming at some point during his stay in New South Wales. Pougin suggests that this was on the banks of the Darling, on the other side of the Blue Mountains (Great Dividing Range).[52] This is unlikely, however, as the land of Darling Downs was not developed extensively until the 1840s.[53] The Mulligans provide a more plausible account of how Wallace took over the running of a farm near Windsor (Green Hills) in the Hawkesbury district, in partnership with an Englishman who needed time off for medical treatment in Sydney. They describe the holding as follows: 'The farm consisted of sheep...also working horses, and a paddock [i.e. a field] or two ploughed up for cultivation. They should have been very comfortable, for there was a dwelling, stockyard, outhouses etc.'[54] There is a gap of some three months in Wallace's concert schedule from late September until December, which would be an ideal time for such a farming interlude, being of course spring and early summer in these climes. Indirect evidence is provided by the fact that the Wallace family gave two concerts in December–early January in the area. The first was at the Woolpack Inn in Parramatta on 7 December 1836, with the assistance of the twenty-eighth regimental band. A second concert took place at Windsor around Christmas-time, again under the patronage of Governor Bourke, who had a residence there.[55]

The farming enterprise, not surprisingly, failed, as had the music academy presumably, given the Wallaces' absence from Sydney over the previous months. Isabella had never really settled in Australia, and her restlessness was probably increased by concern about their long-term prospects. She persuaded Wallace to return to Sydney in January 1837. There, a letter from home with bad news awaited her: her youngest sister Eliza had died, and her father was also in indifferent health. Isabella immediately seized on this opportunity to leave the colony, and, with their son, Willy, she sailed for home on the next available ship. The Mulligans relate how she arrived home to discover that her father had died just a few days previously.[56] It is generally assumed in the biographies that, when Wallace eventually left Sydney in early 1838, he abandoned his wife and child there. There is no evidence that this occurred, and the Mulligans' account is a plausible alternative.[57]

WALLACE'S ACTIVITIES DURING 1837

In late January, influenced perhaps by Isabella's recent or pending departure, Wallace placed an advertisement in the press announcing his intention of leaving the colony within a few months, and urging all potential pupils to apply immediately for tuition.[58] Whether the announcement was merely a ploy to attract new students, it is difficult to say. Meanwhile, a political scandal involving Governor Bourke had erupted in the colony: his abrupt replacement of the Colonial Secretary, Alexander McLeay, with his son-in-law, Deas Thomson, had opened the governor to charges of opportunism and nepotism. A further disagreement, this time between him and the home government, concerned his suspension of another opponent, the Colonial Treasurer, Campbell Riddell, from the Executive Council. When the government insisted on Riddell's reinstatement, in January 1837, Bourke immediately tendered his resignation, which did not, however, come into effect until December of that year.[59] In the meantime, the Wallace and Deane families continued to enjoy the governor's patronage of their concert activities in Sydney; these received a welcome impetus from the celebrations accompanying the accession of the young Queen Victoria to the throne in June–July 1837. From an announcement in the *Australian* on 31 March 1837, we learn of a new venture by Wallace: his opening of a business in the importation and sale of pianos at Ellard's Music Saloon, George St.[60] In this, however, as in later speculations in America, Wallace showed a complete lack of good business sense: the year 1837 saw a general downturn in the economy, and by April the *Gazette* was commenting that the market in pianos in particular was already oversubscribed.[61] About the same time, William's father, Spencer, followed him into business by establishing a circulating library in Parramatta.[62]

THE DEPARTURE OF GOVERNOR BOURKE, FOLLOWED BY THAT OF WALLACE

Prior to Governor Bourke's departure, his patronage of musical events in Sydney continued. Probably the last such concert he attended was a chamber music recital at the Royal Hotel, on 29 September 1837, in which a string quartet – comprising three of the Deanes and led by Wallace – played one of Beethoven's early op. 18 quartets, another musical first for the colony. Bourke departed in early December 1837, leaving his beloved wife Betsy, who had died in May 1832, buried at Parramatta. Accompanied by his son Dick, he sailed for home across the wide Pacific, calling at Fiji and Valparaiso, and then, following an overland trek across the Andes and the Pampas to Buenos Aires, embarked for England via Rio de Janeiro.[63]

Governor Bourke has a town in the interior of New South Wales, a street in Melbourne, and even a species of Australian parakeet named after him. Undoubtedly, however, his greatest memorials, as inscribed on his statue in Sydney, are his founding of Melbourne, and his enlightened and far-seeing policies which laid the foundation for democracy and civilised living in the colony given to his care.[64]

The departure of Bourke left Wallace without a patron and protector in high places. His business venture had failed, and he was perhaps being pressed by his creditors. Meanwhile, Wallace continued his regular concert routine, the highlight of the second year of which was undoubtedly another (though less successful) oratorio concert at St Mary's Cathedral on 31 January 1838 – postponed from 26 January, the fiftieth anniversary of the foundation of the colony – at which the 18-year-old Eliza Wallace, and her husband-to-be, John Bushelle, assistant choirmaster at St Mary's, sang an affecting duet together.[65] Within a fortnight, and without warning, Wallace had left Sydney: on Sunday, 11 February, the barque *Neptune*, under Captain Nagle, which had arrived in Sydney from Dublin some weeks previously, set sail, with Wallace on board, for Valparaiso via the Bay of Islands, New Zealand. The *Sydney Gazette* of the following week commented: 'Mr. W. Wallace, the Australian Paganini, left the Colony in a clandestine manner...and has sailed for Valparaiso, having contracted debts in Sydney amounting to nearly £2000...'[66] Beedell, however, states that the question of Wallace's debts in Sydney has never been adequately resolved.[67]

WALLACE IN NEW ZEALAND

Berlioz's famous tale of Wallace's adventures among the Maori, recounted to him 'over a bowl of punch' when the two composers met in London during the spring of 1848, could be partly based on fact, or could be totally fictitious.[68] Wallace himself claims to have spent four months in New Zealand prior to his arrival in South America;[69] however, allowing six to eight weeks for a passage across the Pacific, and given that Wallace appeared in Valparaiso in early June,[70] there is no time for such a long sojourn there.[71] New Zealand researcher Inge van Rij confirms the *Neptune*'s arrival at the Bay of Islands (the usual port-of-call there, according to her, being Kororekua – modern-day Russell) on 3 March 1838.[72] Wallace may have spent six to eight weeks in New Zealand, perhaps to put his Sydney creditors off his trail. When Berlioz describes Wallace, in Sydney, taking up the invitation of a whaling captain to participate in a punitive expedition against the Maori, and reports the captain as saying 'the crossing is short', the latter could hardly have been referring to the voyage from Sydney to the Bay of Islands, which took all of two to three weeks. It's much more likely that this episode, if based on fact as vouched by Berlioz, refers to a voyage perhaps from the Bay of Islands to the vicinity of modern-day Wellington, and the Cook Strait, where there was indeed whaling going on in the 1830s. The Mulligans, for their part, place Wallace's sojourn in New Zealand at the remote whaling station of Te Awaiti on Arapawa Island, in the northernmost part of the South Island. There, Wallace supposedly became enamoured of a Maori maid called Waiata (Maori for 'song').[73] She may well have been the model for Berlioz's Maori maid, Tatéa, and the whole rather innocent romantic episode at the whaling station may have become transmuted, by the power of the imagination, into the fantastic adventures found in Berlioz's yarn.[74] On the other hand, Inge van Rij, having carried out a detailed review of possible literary sources – some factual, some fictional, and some a mixture of both – for the story, concludes convincingly that it is largely a literary construct: 'We will probably never know whether it originated in *Wallace's*...or in *Berlioz's* imagination...or, as seems more likely, through some jumbled combination of both, when the two men shared a bowl of punch in London.'[75]

MARITANA

Should the opera *Maritana* be considered an Australian composition, as suggested by the Mulligans?[76] The answer, in typically Irish fashion, is both yes and no! Bearing in mind that, during the period in question, the play on which *Maritana* is based had yet to be written, we are dealing with the composition of melodies, as opposed to completed songs or operatic numbers.[77] Nonetheless, the fact that Australia's foremost contemporary composer, Peter Sculthorpe, included a number from the opera in the original draft of his bicentennial piece, *Child of Australia*, vouches for the iconic status of the opera in the Australian mind. Sculthorpe says about his setting:

> Early in 1987, I completed my bicentennial piece, *Child of Australia*. This is for speaker, soprano, chorus and orchestra, with a text by Thomas Keneally. It was performed on Australia Day in the following year, on the steps of Sydney Opera House . . . I'd originally hoped to begin my bicentennial piece with an arrangement of William Vincent Wallace's 'Scenes that are Brightest', from his opera *Maritana* (1845). It's believed that Wallace wrote it at New Norfolk, in Tasmania. A brass plaque at the Bush Inn, where Wallace stayed while he was there, states this to be so. I completed the arrangement, but it's never been performed. It's scored for soprano, chorus and orchestra, forces that are too impractical for such a short work.[78]

There is no doubt that when *Maritana* was first performed in the Antipodes Australians took the opera to their hearts, and there are many records of performances in Australia and in New Zealand throughout the remainder of the nineteenth century. But how much of the opera was actually composed in Australia? W.H. Deane, a great-grandson of the John Philip Deane who was a contemporary of the Wallaces in Sydney in the 1830s–40s, gives perhaps the most reliable information: in a letter to the Mitchell Library in 1957, in which he corrects a reference to his family in Orchard's then recently published *Music in Australia*, he writes (emphasis added by the present writer):

> There has never . . . been any doubt among any of the Deanes that part of the music of *Maritana* was written in Brougham Place, now Rowe Street, and on the site where the Deane Chambers [the solicitor's office

of William Deane, a son of J.P. Deane] now stands. Brougham Place, adjoining the old Theatre Royal had[,] in earlier times, always been a theatrical street. It is very probable that Wallace, finding there congenial company and atmosphere, here ran off some catching arias which he later incorporated into his Opera...with the eventual production of the Opera here in Sydney[,] these arias[,] *already familiar to the Deanes*[,] were immediately recognised by them ... [79]

Deane's statement does not of course preclude the possibility that some of the melodies in *Maritana* could have been written by Wallace in Tasmania; on the voyage out; or even earlier.[80] However, the heroine of the opera is, of course, a Spanish gypsy, and the opera is now credited with being among the first to have an authentic Spanish flavour. Obviously, Wallace did not assimilate this in Sydney, in New South Wales generally, or in Tasmania; it came from his extensive travels in South America in 1838–40, and his subsequent sojourn in Mexico and in New Orleans in 1840–2.

THE REMAINING WALLACE FAMILY[81]

Spencer Wallace and his wife Matilda continued living at Parramatta. They had two sons in Australia, making a second family of four altogether for Spencer.[82] Spencer's library business apparently did not thrive; Graves' information suggests that he applied for insolvency in the period 1842–4.[83] Spencer died, aged 57, presumably at Parramatta, in 1846; his wife died at Parramatta in 1869, aged 55 years.

Eliza Wallace, aged 19, married bass singer and ex-convict, James ('John') Bushelle, on 30 April 1839, probably at St Mary's in Sydney, where Bushelle was assistant choirmaster. They had three sons.[84] On 28 July 1843, Bushelle died, aged only 37, while the couple were on a concert tour of Tasmania, leaving Eliza a widow at the age of only 23.[85] Known professionally as Mme Bouchelle, Eliza became a well-known singer in her own right. Following a series of farewell concerts in Sydney in the spring of 1847, in which she was accompanied by her brother, Wellington, she left Australia to further her professional career, and had modest success performing both in England and in the USA.[86] The high-point of her career was perhaps her performing the title role in *Maritana* at Covent Garden in 1848, after which she participated with her brother William Vincent in many concerts in the USA. She returned to Sydney eventually, and settled down at Darlinghurst as a noted singing teacher. She died there, aged 58, on 16 August 1878, at her residence in William St.[87]

S. Wellington Wallace, during his more famous brother's stay in

Sydney, seems to have been rather under his shadow, and only after William's departure is he given coverage in the newspapers. He is mentioned as playing flute in the orchestra of the Royal Victoria Theatre, under the direction of John P. Deane, in September 1838.[88] While known mainly as a flautist, he also played violin.[89] Wellington married in Sydney in 1841, his bride being Caroline Green. By 1843, they had a daughter called Elizabeth B. According to information obtained by Graves from the Mitchell Library, either Wellington, or his father – it is not possible to say which because of the similarity between their names – was leader of Sydney's Royal Victoria Theatre orchestra for some years in the 1840s.[90] Following Eliza's departure from Australia, Wellington moved to Adelaide, in South Australia, where according to the newspapers he participated in concerts in 1849–50.[91] There is no information about him after that in the Australian sources consulted.[92]

EPILOGUE

William Wallace's virtuosity and his concert-organising ability had an inspirational and energising effect on the musical life of Sydney in the mid-1830s; in this he was aided by the patronage of Governor Bourke, right up to the latter's departure from Sydney. The wider Wallace family's contribution, though perhaps lacking the finish and flair of its most famous member, was none the less valuable and significant in the longer term. Covell, summing up the Wallace family's contribution to musical life in Australia, writes: 'Wallace became the first creative musician of any renown to take a hand in the musical affairs of the colony... The Wallace family's influence on the improvement of practical music-making was considerable ... '[93] While William Vincent Wallace's impact on cultural life in Australia has now been recognised and recently celebrated, his wider contribution to music in mid-nineteenth century Britain and the USA has yet to be fully acknowledged, and his considerable body of work is only now, as we approach the bicentenary of his birth, being reassessed and made accessible to listeners and performers alike.[94]

I was privileged to be present, in mid-November 2004, at a concert of Wallace's music, 'for Sir Richard Bourke', at Australia House, London, organised by the Tait Memorial Trust, when conductor Richard Bonynge, and many young Australian singers and artists, took part in an impressive musical tribute to the two men who laid the foundations of serious music in Australia. One piece in particular from that concert – Wallace's *Fantasie-Variations de Bravoura* for violin and piano, in the style of Paganini, and based on the melody of Moore's song, 'The Last Rose of

Summer'[95] – was like a long-lost echo of Wallace's opening concert in Sydney in February 1836. The performance, by Naoko Miyamoto (violin) and Rosemary Tuck (piano), conjured up a vivid aural impression of how 'the Australian Paganini' must have sounded all those years ago in Sydney's Royal Hotel, in the presence of his patron, Governor Bourke, and the other colonial dignitaries, 'the room...crowded by much of the rank, beauty, talent and fashion in the colony'.[96]

NOTES

1. Maximilian Holzner, 'Wallace and Music in Australia during the Governorship of Sir Richard Bourke, 1831–1838' (B.Mus. Honours sub-thesis, Australian National University, Canberra, 2003). Maximilian Holzner, 'Music under the Governorship of Sir Richard Bourke 1831–1838: The Humanisation of the Colony' (a paper read at the New Zealand Musicological Society and the Musicological Society of Australia Combined Conference, Victoria University of Wellington, 27 November 2003). I am indebted to Mr Holzner for providing copies of both these papers. Governor Bourke's love of music is alluded to by his descendant, Anthony Richard Ulick Burke, in his preface to Max Waugh, *Forgotten Hero: Richard Bourke, Irish-born Governor of NSW 1831–1837* (Melbourne: Australian Scholarly Publishing, 2005), p.xiv.

2. Annie de Meurant Mulligan and Louise Kelly Mulligan, 'In Happy Moments: The Romance of William Vincent Wallace', *Munster Express* (Waterford), thirteen weekly instalments from 9 September 1931. The original typescript (with accompanying correspondence) is in the National Archives of Australia, Canberra (Series Accession No. A1336/1; Item 19660). Page references are to the typescript. (I am grateful to local historian, Mr Dermot Power, formerly of the Waterford City Library, for drawing this important newspaper source to my attention.) Perceval Graves, 'The "Maritana" Wallace: His Life and Times', (unpublished typescript, n.d. [*c*. 1940s], in private hands). Kathleen Hellyar Myers, 'William Vincent Wallace: Life and Works', (doctoral dissertation, Bryn Mawr College, PA, USA, 1980; UMI Ref. 8103604).

3. William de Burgh (called 'William the Conqueror' by Irish annalists) was the progenitor of the Burkes in Ireland. He came to Ireland about 1185, and was made Governor of Limerick; he later succeeded Strongbow as Chief Governor. See www.araltas.com/features/burke/ [accessed 15 January 2007].

4. A seminar, 'Major-General Sir Richard Bourke, Educationalist', took place at Thornfields, Lisnagry, in October 1999.

5. Gerard Bourke, *Out On A Limb* (Victoria BC: Trafford Publishing, 2003), pp.7–8.

6. The school was built in 1823; in due course it came into the Irish national school system. See Mary Moloney, 'Memories of Ahane National School', *An Chaisleán* (parish magazine of Castleconnell, County Limerick), Autumn 2000.

7. For a general biography of Bourke, see Hazel King, *Richard Bourke* (Melbourne, New York: Oxford University Press, 1971). For a recent account of his period as governor, see Waugh, *Forgotten Hero*, passim.

8. Mulligan and Mulligan, 'In Happy Moments', p.3.

9. Ibid., pp.20–1.

10. In a letter to the *Sydney Gazette and New South Wales Advertiser*, 28 April 1836, Wallace wrote: 'I have had the honour to lead four of Paganini's concerts in Ireland ...'; quoted in Holzner [2].

11. William Henry Grattan Flood, *William-Vincent Wallace: A Memoir* (Waterford: Waterford News, 1912), p.13.

12. Mulligan and Mulligan, 'In Happy Moments', pp.24–5.   For an up-to-date biographical

article on Wallace, see the entry by the present writer in the new six-volume *Dictionary of Irish Biography* (Cambridge: Cambridge University Press, forthcoming).

13. A.V. Beedell, *The Decline of the English Musician 1788–1888: A Family of English Musicians in Ireland, England, Mauritius, and Australia* (Oxford: Oxford University Press, 1992), pp.257–91.

14. James William C. Cumes, *Their Chastity Was Not Too Rigid: Leisure Times in Early Australia* (Melbourne, Longman Cheshire/Reid, 1979), pp.174–96.

15. Ibid., p.174.

16. Ibid., p.184.

17. Mrs Chester disembarked first at Hobart Town (*Colonial Times*, 28 July 1835); she moved on to Sydney some months later (Holzner [1], p.16). She took part in Wallace's concerts in Hobart Town in early December 1835, and in Sydney up to late September 1836 (ibid., p.25).

18. Cumes, *Chastity*, pp.189–90.

19. Beedell, *Decline*, p.257.

20. Bourke's efforts as governor of NSW were rewarded in 1835 with the bestowal of a knighthood (KCB). Waugh, *Forgotten Hero*, p.154.

21. Graves, 'The "Maritana" Wallace', Ch. 2, p.4.

22. Mulligan and Mulligan, 'In Happy Moments', pp.24–5.

23. Flood, *Memoir*, p.14.

24. The sister is not named, but is generally assumed to be Anna Kelly; in fact she never went to Australia, and at this time was happily married to James Jones, a solicitor in Mallow, County Cork. Cumes cites the journal, *Imperial Review*, as the origin of this apocryphal story, and it is the likely source of Flood's account also.

25. 'Trade and Shipping', *Hobart Town Courier*, 6 November 1835, quoted in Myers, 'Life and Works', p.11.

26. Mulligan and Mulligan, 'In Happy Moments', pp.30–1.

27. See www.australianbeers.com/pubs/bushin/bush.htm

28. Beedell, *Decline*, pp.263–6.

29. *Hobart Town Courier*, 4, 11 December 1835, p.3; *Colonial Times*, 8 December 1835.

30. *Australian*, 29 January 1836, p.3; *Sydney Gazette*, 11 February 1836; ibid., 16 February 1836, p.2.

31. *Sydney Gazette*, 25 February 1836; William Arundel Orchard, *Music in Australia* (Melbourne: Georgian House, 1952), p.10.

32. *Sydney Gazette*, 19 March 1836; J.P. McGuanne, *Music and Song of Old Sydney* (Sydney: Mitchell Library, Press Contributions 1886–1916), p.24.

33. *Sydney Gazette*, 3 May 1836; Orchard, *Music in Australia*, p.13.

34. Orchard, *Music in Australia*, pp.14–15; quoted in Myers, 'Life and Works', pp.26–7.

35. *Australian*, 19 August 1836; *Sydney Gazette*, 27 August 1836.

36. Orchard, *Music in Australia*, p.15.

37. Full details of the concert are in Beedell, *Decline*, pp.276–9. See also the *Sydney Gazette* and *Australian*, 23–4 September 1836.

38. McGuanne, *Music and Song*, p.24; *Sydney Gazette*, 1 December 1836.

39. *Sydney Gazette*, 24 December 1836.

40. McGuanne, *Music and Song*, p.24; *Sydney Gazette*, 2 February 1837.

41. *Sydney Gazette*, 4 May 1837.

42. Ibid., 3 August 1837; Orchard, *Music in Australia*, p.18; *Sydney Herald*, 2 October 1837.

43. McGuanne, *Music and Song*, p.24.

44. Orchard, *Music in Australia*, pp.19–20; *Sydney Herald*, 5 February 1838.

45. Graves, 'The "Maritana" Wallace', Ch. 2, pp.5–6.

46. Quoted in Holzner, 'Wallace and Music in Australia during the Governorship of Sir Richard Bourke, 1831–1838', p.21.

47. *Sydney Gazette*, 30 March 1836; also Orchard, *Music in Australia*, pp.11–12, quoted in Myers, p.22. Following the death of the governor's wife in 1832, shortly after their arrival in Sydney, his daughter Anne, who had married the future Colonial Secretary, Edward (later Sir

Edward) Deas Thomson, took over her late mother's official duties.

48. Beedell, *Decline*, pp.286–7, provides details of both schools.

49. Holzner, 'Wallace and Music in Australia during the Governorship of Sir Richard Bourke, 1831–1838', p.25.

50. *Sydney Herald*, 19 September 1836.

51. Holzner, 'Wallace and Music in Australia during the Governorship of Sir Richard Bourke, 1831–1838', pp.26–7; Beedell, *Decline*, pp.276–9; Myers, 'Life and Works', p.28.

52. Arthur Pougin, *William-Vincent Wallace: Etude Biographique et Critique* (Paris: Ikelmer & Cie., 1866), p.6.

53. Beedell, *Decline*, p.257n. See also Ernest Favenc, *Explorers of Australia* (Christchurch, Melbourne and London: Whitcombe and Tombs, 1908; repr. Tiger Books, 1998), p.95.

54. Mulligan and Mulligan, 'In Happy Moments', p.27.

55. Ibid.

56. Ibid., pp.28–9.

57. The *Sydney Gazette*, in relating Wallace's departure, states: 'in one or two cases we could mention, his conduct has been heartless in the extreme'; had Wallace in fact abandoned his wife and son in Sydney, would the *Gazette* have neglected to make the most of such a damning fact?

58. *Sydney Gazette*, 31 January 1837.

59. Waugh, *Forgotten Hero*, pp.141–51.

60. Myers, 'Life and Works', p.31.

61. Beedell, *Decline*, p.288; *Sydney Gazette*, 22 April 1837.

62. Holzner, 'Wallace and Music in Australia during the Governorship of Sir Richard Bourke, 1831–1838', p.21.

63. Waugh, *Forgotten Hero*, pp.173–4. This route, although arduous, was seen as an alternative to the even more hazardous sea-passage of Cape Horn. In his book, *Extracts from a Journal Written on the Coasts of Chili, Peru, and Mexico in the Years 1820, 1821, 1822* (London: Moxton, 1840), Captain Basil Hall RN, FRS, an English traveller in South America, states that there was a well-established overland route from Santiago to Buenos Aires. Gentlemen would travel most of the 1,200-mile route, across the flat lands of the Pampas, by carriage; only the crossing of the Andes necessitated the use of a horse or mule. I am indebted to Wallace researcher, Mr Peter Jaggard of Bristol, for this latter travel information. Its significance is that Wallace probably attempted the same route home later in 1838, but was unable to embark at Buenos Aires because of a blockade.

64. Bourke's name survives in the town of Bourke (originally Fort Bourke), on the Darling river; in Bourke St., one of the principal thoroughfares of Melbourne, and in Bourke's parakeet. Bourke's statue, raised by public subscription in 1842, is now situated appropriately outside the Mitchell (State) Library of New South Wales in Sydney.

65. *Australian*, 6 February 1838; quoted in Beedell, *Decline*, p.288.

66. *Sydney Gazette*, 14 February 1838. There is considerable confusion in the newspapers as to the exact date of Wallace's departure from Sydney. However, *Lloyd's List and Shipping Gazette* is authoritative in this matter, and gives 11 February as the date in question.

67. Beedell, *Decline*, p.290.

68. Hector Berlioz, *Evenings in the Orchestra*, trans. by C.R. Fortescue (London: Penguin/Peregrine Books, 1963) pp.310–20.

69. Memoir by Wallace in the *Daily Picayune*, New Orleans, 22 June 1842. I am again indebted to Mr Peter Jaggard for this reference.

70. Graves, 'The "Maritana" Wallace', Ch. 4, pp.1–2.

71. *Lloyd's List* of 1838 gives the following information for the voyage of the *Neptune*: 'Prev. to 12 Mar 1838 "Neptune", [Master] Nagle, arrived in New Zealand from Sydney and sailed for Valparaiso; prev. to 20 May 1838 "Neptune", Nagle, arrived in Valparaiso from New Zealand.' I am grateful to Ms Lorna Hyland, Assistant Librarian, Maritime Archives and Library, Merseyside Maritime Museum, Liverpool, and to Mr Anthony Brophy of Waterford, for this shipping information.

72. From Rhys Richards and Jocelyn Chisolm, *Bay of Islands Shipping Arrivals and Departures 1803–1840* (Wellington: Paremata Press, 1992). My thanks are due to Dr Inge van Rij, Victoria University of Wellington, New Zealand, for the reference.
73. Mulligan and Mulligan, 'In Happy Moments', pp.31–6.
74. Berlioz, *Evenings*, p.310, gives the location the whaler sailed to as 'Tavai-Pounamu Bay'; this appears to be merely a corruption of 'Te Wai Pounamou', the Maori name for the whole South Island of Aotearoa/New Zealand. Wallace's story could also be based on the real-life adventures of English seamen and adventurers, John Guard and Richard (Dicky) Barrett, (also known by his Pakeha Maori name, 'Tiki Parete'), in early colonial New Zealand. Guard set up the whaling station of Te Awaiti, and his hair-raising early adventures among the Maori were well-known in Sydney in the mid-1830s. Barrett took over Te Awaiti from Guard, and was whaling there during the period that Wallace's visit may have taken place. See www.teara.govt.nz/1966/G/GuardJohn /GuardJohn/en and http://www.pukeariki.com/en/stories/immigration/default.asp [both accessed 15 January 2007].
75. Inge van Rij, '"Take them for true": Berlioz, Vincent Wallace and New Zealand exoticism'. (A paper read at the Music Colloquia, University of Cambridge, on 21 April 2004.) I am grateful to Dr van Rij, both for providing a copy of her paper and for clarifying numerous incidental details in subsequent correspondence.
76. Mulligan and Mulligan, 'In Happy Moments', Title page and p.30.
77. In support of this, Wallace's friend, Heyward St Leger, who, according to his own account, introduced Wallace to Edward Fitzball, the librettist of *Maritana*, in London, mentions 'an old oblong notebook' in which Wallace had noted down many melodies, some of which he played for Fitzball at their first meeting in summer 1845. Heyward J. St Leger, 'Reminiscences of Wallace', The *Orchestra*, 16 and 23 December, 1865.
78. Peter Sculthorpe, *Sun Music: Journeys and Reflections From a Composer's Life* (Sydney: ABC Books, 1999), p.253.
79. William Harrison Deane, 'Errata to Dr Orchard's Music in Australia', letter to the Mitchell Library, 30 October 1957, quoted in Myers, 'Life and Works', p.33.
80. The Mulligans, for their part, claim that the tune of 'Scenes that are brightest' was inspired by Wallace's first view of Sydney harbour, while that of 'In Happy Moments' they associate with the birth of the Wallaces' first son in Dublin in 1833: Mulligan and Mulligan, 'In Happy Moments', pp.24–5.
81. Apart from specific references given, the Wallace family information in this section is from internet searches on the NSW Registry of Births, Deaths, and Marriages website: http://www.bdm.nsw.gov.au/ [accessed 15 January 2007].
82. Arthur F. was born in 1836, and Alfred in 1840. The latter died in 1850.
83. Graves, 'The "Maritana" Wallace', Ch. 2, p.5.
84. Twins John B. and Theobald T. ('Toby') in 1840, and William B. in 1843.
85. Beedell, *Decline*, p.289, 289n.
86. Orchard, *Music in Australia*, p.28; Myers, 'Life and Works', p.24.
87. Joseph Michael Forde, *Some Fragments of Old Sydney* (Sydney: McCarron Stewart, 1898), p.15, quoted in Myers, 'Life and Works', p.25.
88. Beedell, *Decline*, p.291.
89. Quoting an un-named newspaper critic of February 1839, Orchard, *Music in Australia*, p.22, states: 'The violin playing of S.W. Wallace served as a reminder of the ability of his more gifted brother.' Also, Eliza's farewell recitals in Sydney in 1847, in which she was accompanied by Wellington, are described as 'song and violin recitals', ibid., p.28; quoted in Myers, 'Life and Works', pp.24–5.
90. Graves, 'The "Maritana" Wallace', Ch. 2, p.5.
91. Cumes, *Chastity*, pp.338, 340.
92. The next mention in the sources of a descendant of Wellington is of his grandson, George Liddell Wallace, who lived at Walsall, near Birmingham, England, in the 1940s (Graves, 'The "Maritana" Wallace', Introduction, p.1); his daughter in turn, Hazel Vincent Wallace, of London, a noted actress and theatre manager, now an octogenarian, is the last known living

descendant of the Wallace family.

93. Roger Covell, *Australia's Music* (Melbourne: Sun Books, 1967), pp.10–11, quoted in Cumes, *Chastity*, p.195.

94. Myers, 'Life and Works', Part 2, contains an extensive catalogue (c. 400 pp.) with incipits of Wallace's published music; George Biddlecombe, *English Opera 1835–1864: with particular reference to the works of Michael William Balfe* (New York and London: Garland, 1994); David Grant, 'A Reappraisal of W. Vincent Wallace 1812–1865, with new documentary information on his death', *British Music*, 25 (2003), pp.60–79; Margaret McCann, 'The Piano Music of William Vincent Wallace (1812–1865)' (MA thesis, NUI Maynooth, 2003); Rosemary Tuck, CD recordings of Wallace's piano music: 'The Meeting of the Waters': Celtic Fantasies, Cala United CACD 88042 (2001); 'To My Star', Cala United CACD 88044 (2005).

95. The piece, dedicated to Henri Vieuxtemps, and very likely revised, was eventually published by Schuberth & Co., of Hamburg, Leipzig and New York, in 1856, and is in the Music Collections of the Library of Congress, Washington DC.

96. 'Mr. Wallace's Concert', *Sydney Gazette*, 16 February 1836, p.2.

6

Eva of the *Nation* and the Young Ireland Press

Brega Webb

The major thrust of the Young Ireland movement was a marshalling of the media to generate an intellectual pressure on the status quo establishment of the Dublin Castle regime. It took every opportunity to put before the readership what the editors perceived to be the *sine qua non* of the current polity – initially parliamentary reform by peaceful methods and the achievement of civil rights for Catholics, although, ultimately, some of the protagonists resorted to physical force. It was against this background of cultural nationalism that the poets of the Young Ireland period began to write their passionate verses and within this environment that Mary Ann Kelly, later to be known as 'Eva' of the *Nation*, was to develop her own ideological brand of literature. Verse was an effective way of educating the people because it appealed to the intellect as well as to the emotions.

Although the Young Ireland writers were concerned with the political context of Daniel O'Connell's Repeal movement they continued in the vein of the literary nationalism of the United Irishmen's political songs. Much of the verse took the form of ballads using traditional tunes that were easy to learn so the message had a more dramatic impact and could be spread very rapidly. Recurring themes in the verse of these poets were concerned with the acceptance of nationalism and national claims as fundamental realities which could not be compromised, and which were superior to religious differences and group prejudices. Such themes were expressed with eloquence and used as a very powerful tool, although some of the poetry was somewhat immature. Though often hackneyed, with inflexible metre and rhyme, it was easy to memorise and became a good vehicle for propaganda.

Poems and articles were mostly published anonymously, under the contributor's initials or under a pseudonym, the pseudonyms varying according to the personality of the individual. Thomas D'Arcy McGee is known to have used eight different names, John D. Frazer called himself

'Maria', whilst James Clarence Mangan used 'Terrae Filius' as well as his initials and at least seven other different names. Mary Ann Kelly wrote under the names 'Sumalla', demonstrating her familiarity with the Ossianic poems of James MacPherson, 'Aoife', 'Ella', 'Anne', 'Fionnuala' and 'E' before settling on 'Eva'. Her choice of 'Eva' probably originated from the legend of Strongbow, and such was her eventual popularity she became known as Eva of the *Nation*.

Whilst 'Eva' was not the only female poet whose work was being printed in the *Nation* and other newspapers, none of her female contemporaries achieved the same level of fame as she. 'Speranza', later Lady Wilde, mother of playwright Oscar, came close when, as the first female editor of a newspaper in Ireland, she took over that role, together with a Mrs Callan, following the arrest of Charles Gavan Duffy, editor of the *Nation*. Sadly the presses of the *Nation* were seized before they could publish and an article prepared by 'Speranza', entitled 'Jacta Alea Est', was used in evidence against Duffy at his trial.

Most of the early poetry written by 'Eva' followed a romantic vein, the first poem published, in 1844, being 'The Minstrel's Invocation'.[1] Frequent references to the River Shannon, Tipperary and nature appeared in her verse but by1847 she had abandoned this genre as she moved into the political arena, probably influenced by her mother's brother, Martin O'Flaherty, who was a prominent solicitor and supporter of the Young Irelanders. She began to take a militant stance, becoming more patriotic as well as intensely inflammatory. An example of this militancy is 'The Awakening of the Sleepers', a poem very much in the Ossianic, bardic style:

> Yes! The *time* is come! – it is the hour,
> Warrior chiefs of Eire, now for your pow'r!
> Lift those mail'd hands from your brow – ...Now! – now![2]

Her language became increasingly warlike with her metaphors evoking 'gallant knights' and 'flashing steel' while she called on the people of Ireland to rise up united against sectarian and political divisions as she looked to Heaven for help in achieving this aim:

> 'Gainst England all', gainst England all,
> Up! up! all you Irish races –
> Shall the English hoof trample down your roof,
> And tread in your ancient places?
> For Ireland All.[3]

'Eva' also wrote poetry with a metre suitable for transferring to a broadside – verses that could be out on the street within hours and easily memorised. 'The Irish Mother, A Ballad of '98', a poem that recalled the events of the rebellion of the United Irishmen in 1798, was a good example of this type of work. The opening lines of 'The Irish Mother' are:

> Come tell us the name of the rebelly crew,
> Who lifted the pike on the Curragh with you;
> Come, tell us the treason, and then you'll be free,
> Or right quickly you'll swing from the high gallows tree.[4]

She also wrote seven stanzas of rousing verse for a new national anthem at the request of the editor of the *Nation*, which were published on 18 March 1848, the first of which reads:

> God Save the People all –
> Tho' Thrones and Sceptres round them fall,
> Shout aloud the sacred call –
> God save the People![5]

Eva began a campaign to involve the citizens of Ireland in the politics of the Young Ireland movement through the medium of letters to the editor of the *Nation*. Calling upon the dissenting political parties to put aside their differences and work together towards the cause of Repeal, she emphasized that their warring attitudes were unacceptable and overtly threatened them: 'let them beware how they attempt to impose any opinions on us'.[6] She promised that the voice of the people would not be silent and in a letter published in the *Nation*, 25 March 1848, she specifically addressed 'The Women of Ireland': 'What is virtue in man is virtue also in woman. Virtue is of no sex. A coward woman is as base as a coward man...It is not unfeminine to take sword, or gun, if sword or gun are required...Plead not in this hour the miserable excuse – I am a woman.'[7]

She was clearly influenced by the leaders of the Young Ireland movement at the time through knowing Charles Gavan Duffy and John Mitchel, editors of the *Nation*. She wrote three poems to Thomas Francis Meagher, the first of which was published shortly after he made the famous speech in which he dissented from the 'Peace Resolutions' proposed by Daniel O'Connell because he felt there were times when only arms could be the means to the end. This speech earned him the sobriquet 'Meagher of the Sword' and inspired her second poem to him, 'Hymn of the Sword':

Where is our sword, O God?
Where is our flaming steel,
To make the desecrating foe
Before thy footstool reel?
Where is our guardian sword,
Before the gate to stand,
A free and holy land.[8]

John Mitchel, author of *Jail Journal*[9] in which he recounts his trial, transportation and eventual escape from Van Dieman's Land, deeply affected Eva when he was convicted, as is seen in her poem 'The Felon'. She uses his words as he is led away from the dock – 'the victory should be with me and it is with me'[10] – to give her the last line of the verses written to 'The Felon':

Oh! Surely shall we show
To that base, defeated foe
That, e'en in every wrong or woe,
'The Victory' was thine.[11]

Eva was a great admirer of William Smith O'Brien, the leader of the 1848 uprising. Arraigned and convicted of high treason, he was sentenced to be hanged, drawn and quartered, a sentence which, despite his protests that he wanted to die, was commuted to transportation across the seas for life, the Castle authorities not wanting martyrdom to inflame popular opinion. She presented him with a small book of her poems inscribed with the dedication: 'To William Smith O'Brien in the truest spirit of Reverence and Love. These twelve poems published in the *Nation* newspaper are dedicated by Eva. May 16 1849.'[12]

Eva not only wrote patriotic verse: she had the courage of her convictions to become actively involved in the movement. John Blake Dillon's flight to America disguised as a Catholic priest following the 1848 uprising has been well documented, but the mechanics of the escape remained unknown until Eva's conversation with P.J. Dillon was published in 1933.[13] One evening a sister of Eva's answered a knock at the door of Killeen House, the family home near Portumna, Co. Galway. A gentleman asked for Miss Eva Kelly but she was not able to recognise him. He identified himself thus: 'John Dillon and there is £300 on my head. I have come to see if you will hide me.' The request put Eva in a very awkward position. Her acquaintance with Dillon was slight; her father was away but his antipathy to the nationalist movement was legendary and he certainly would not countenance any law breaking. However, after momentary consultation with her sister they both agreed that they would help. They secreted Dillon in a back room. All but one of their servants was considered trustworthy so Eva decoyed him and locked him in a stable. She sent a letter, by hand, to a priest in Ballyvaughan, Co. Clare, appealing for help in securing Dillon's escape but the reply came back that he could only help if Dillon could be brought to his house – a seemingly insurmountable problem as in order to reach the priest's house Dillon would have to pass the Constabulary barracks situated about 200 metres from Killeen House. Dillon shaved off his whiskers, donned a clerical type of broad-leafed hat and cloak and, accompanied by her sister, the three strolled out of the front door – only to meet the police sergeant 'taking the air in front of the barracks'. Since Eva and her sister were known to him he accepted the identity of 'His Reverence' and allowed the three to pass. Dillon was then taken to safety in 'the family out-side car' which had been waiting for him on the far side of the barracks. He eventually escaped to America via Tuam, Galway and the Aran Islands.

Once he had effected his escape, Eva released the servant, who immediately went to the barracks and reported the incident. The sergeant returned with a search party, much to the indignation of Eva's father, who had returned home. Eva did not relate her father's reaction to the part she and her sister had played in this episode!

No reliable documentary evidence exists of Eva's meeting with Kevin Izod O'Doherty, the man who was later to become her husband. There is some evidence that their acquaintance came about through her Uncle Martin with whom she frequently stayed in Dublin. Martin O'Flaherty, her mother's brother, was a solicitor, in partnership with Valentine Dillon, brother of John Blake Dillon, and a silent but trusted Young Irelander. He gave Eva encouragement, as she was later to write that she had 'received stimulus for the Young Ireland notions from Uncle Martin'.[14] A reference in the unsigned and undated memoirs of P.J. Smyth, another nationalist, who later went to rescue John Mitchel from Van Diemen's Land, noted that he and Kevin O'Doherty were visited in prison by Smyth's Aunt Mary, Miss Bruton, who was accompanied by 'a young girl, Miss Kelly, who at that time was charming everybody by the sweetness of her poems'.[15] One visit to O'Doherty followed another until the meetings became a weekly occurrence.

O'Doherty and Richard Dalton Williams had started a newspaper, the *Irish Tribune*, which was only published for six weeks before both were arrested for treason-felony. They gave up their careers as medical students to join the cause, though it remains a mystery to this day why they decided to use the medium of a newspaper to convey their support for the Young Ireland movement. Eva was in court the day O'Doherty was sentenced, at the third trial, to transportation. She went to see him in prison on the following day where, according to P.J. Smyth, she promised to remain faithful, with a hope that he might one day come back to claim the promise she now gave him to be his wife. Richard Dalton Williams was acquitted.

O'Doherty had been tried, but not convicted, on two previous occasions, despite carefully selected juries. In a biographical note prefacing her book *Poems by Eva of the Nation*,[16] published in 1909, Justin Mc Carthy who prefaced the volume, stated that prior to O'Doherty's third trial, it was suggested to him that, if he would publicly plead guilty, the proceedings would be abandoned and he would be discharged. After consultation with Eva, who promised to wait for him rather than agree to anything so dishonourable, he rejected this offer. The third trial went ahead; he was found guilty and sentenced to transportation for seven years to Van Diemen's Land. Eva kept her promise – and wait for him she did.

Eva's poetry during O'Doherty's period of incarceration in Richmond Penitentiary could only be printed in the *Irishman*, all other newspapers which supported the Young Irelanders having been closed down. In the first three months of 1849 she had eleven poems published, all of which reflected her melancholy, but with the coming of the new *Nation* (1 September 1849), following Duffy's release from jail, she recovered her spirits and renewed her campaign against what was perceived to be the English tyrant. Duffy, however, had changed. The series of trials and incarcerations had taken their toll and most of his brilliant writers had been transported or were in exile. Eva implored him not to give up the fight in a long poem entitled 'The New Time'[17] but his thoughts had turned to the Tenant Right League which was then in an embryonic stage.

Released from jail Duffy returned as editor of the *Nation* and chose verses by four poets, one of whom was Eva, to be the motto for the eighth volume. Though published in the 'Answers to Correspondents' column, none of the verses actually appeared in the new editions. Eva's contribution, which she later expanded, is the fifth verse of her poem 'The Oath of Allegiance':

> Like a rainbow in the night,
> Hope still anchors o'er the right;
> From the land the fount shall burst
> Good men, true men, stand ye forth.
> East and west, and south and north;
> Raise the chorus deep and loud,
> 'Life and limb to thee are vowed. – Ireland!'[18]

She started to write about the Tenant Right League, apparently accepting that the answer to the political problems in Ireland did not lie with violence. A new pacifism appeared in her poetry as seen in 'The War of the League'.

> No glowing dreams are yours,
> With rainbow colours fraught,
> But stern and high resolves,
> With cool and bronzed thought.
> For you no sabres flash –
> For you no rifles ring;
> But true man's voice and true man's hand
> Are 'stronger than a king!'[19]

The year 1851 saw new subjects – eviction and death from hunger – a surprising departure, for Eva particularly, as she had not written any poems with a famine theme despite living in areas that were particularly badly affected. Headford, where her grandparents lived, for example, was devastated and had 80–100 per cent of the population on Poor Law Union food rations in July 1847. She did, however, write three poems for the *Nation* on the theme of the conditions being created by what she called The Gentry: 'The Ruined House',[20] 'Mysteries',[21] and 'A Scene for Ireland':

> Sad was the wretched mother's brow,
> Her baby's wailings hushing:
> She has no food to give it now,
> Save those hot tears outgushing ...
> Far, far away, with pearls and gold,
> My lady's hair is gleaming:
> For every gem our eyes behold,
> A crimson drop is streaming –
> For all the grace of silks and lace,
> Some wretches naked shiver;
> For every smile upon her face,
> Some death-blue lip will quiver.[22]

The last poem to appear in the *Nation* for this period of her life, waiting to be reunited with O'Doherty, was 'The Dream of Eden'. She is in a deeply melancholic mood, comparing her own lost love with the plight of Ireland, chastising herself for believing in impossible dreams:

> Never again to mortal eyes
> Can be unclosed earth's paradise.[23]

Eva apparently took herself into mental exile as no poetry can be found published between 1852 and 1856. She said she 'had lost heart',[24] and when Duffy was elected Member of Parliament for New Ross in 1852 and Bernard Fulham, whom she did not like, took over the editorship of the *Nation* her poetry ceased to appear. Duffy sold the *Nation* in 1855 and emigrated to Victoria, Australia, where he embarked on a political career in a colonial administration that he had previously despised, and one that eventually brought him a knighthood. A rebel no longer, Eva went home to Killeen.

Released in 1856, after seven years' incarceration, on the proviso that he did not set foot in Ireland or England, O'Doherty clandestinely came to Eva in Ireland and proposed marriage. They travelled to London with her father and a priest, and there they were secretly married. This marriage, which has been widely reported by the biographers of O'Doherty, was said to have been conducted by either Cardinal Wiseman or the Rector, James Patterson. Eva, herself, records in the *Family Register* that she was married in 'Moorfields Chapel in the presence of her father and her parish priest, the Rev. J Whelan'.[25] Moorfields Chapel was, at that time, the pro-cathedral in London, but no physical evidence exists in the archives of Westminster Cathedral, which replaced it. O'Doherty, as a convicted felon who had no right in England because he was only partially pardoned, could not fulfil the legal requirement to register the marriage, without identifying himself. It is to be presumed that neither he nor Eva would countenance either elopement or cohabiting without benefit of matrimony and so a secret marriage in London was a necessity. They then went on to Paris, where O'Doherty returned to his medical studies. They were married officially in Paris on 30 November 1856 at the office of the British Consul, six months before the birth of their first child, a marriage presumably performed to 'legalise' the Catholic ceremony that had taken place in London earlier in the year.

In Paris they lived a quiet and frugal life as O'Doherty continued with his studies. Eva wrote some articles for the newspapers and one can presume that there was some interaction with the former Young Irelanders who had settled there, such as John Martin, who had been transported with O'Doherty and James Stephens, who had been involved with the uprising and who was later to become involved with another revolutionary movement, the Irish Republican Brotherhood (the Fenians). She did publish some translations of poems by Béranger, Hugo and de Lamartine in the *Nation*, so obviously she was able to keep occupied until the imminent birth of their first child. She returned to Ireland for her confinement whilst O'Doherty stayed in Paris to continue his studies. This pattern was subsequently repeated on several occasions.

O'Doherty was granted a full pardon on 19 May 1856. He returned to Ireland a year later where the experience gained in St Mary's Hospital, Hobart, and in Paris, coupled with his pre-1848 work, qualified him to apply for admission to the Royal College of Surgeons as a Fellow. He graduated from there on 11 June 1857 and worked as a surgeon at St Vincent's Hospital, Dublin. He was also employed as a Dissector at the 'Original Theatre of Anatomy and School of Medicine and Surgery'[26] and the Ledwich Medical School.[27]

O'Doherty was examined and admitted as Licentiate of the King and Queen's College of Physicians of Ireland on 28 December 1859 and also passed the higher diploma awarded by that college in 'midwifery and diseases peculiar to women'. By 1862 he was assistant to the Master at the Coombe Lying-In Hospital,[28] a prestigious position, and both he and Eva were living in comfortable surroundings near St Stephen's Green, Dublin.

O'Doherty found it hard to settle in Dublin despite having built a lucrative medical practice. Although he disagreed with the politics of the time he chose not to get involved with the emergent revival of nationalism, and so it was with some surprise that he decided to emigrate. After discussions with former Young Irelanders in France and America he decided, having met with Bishop James Quinn in Dublin, to settle in Australia. Eva, now pregnant with her fourth child, sailed with O'Doherty and their three children for Liverpool on 4 July 1860, and thence to Sydney, on the *Ocean Chief*.

They arrived in Melbourne some eighty-five days later after what must have been a very difficult voyage for a pregnant woman with three small children. When her son Kevin Izod Louis was born, just over a month later, on 8 November 1860, in Geelong, Victoria, she was alone, as O'Doherty had already set sail for Sydney, where the press greeted him enthusiastically: 'We are rejoiced to find that Mr K. J. [*sic*] O'Doherty, with his family has resolved to settle down among us in Sydney to practise his profession.'[29]

The article went on to describe his previous sojourn in Australia, to praise his 'high accomplishments' and to hope for success for 'our fellow-countryman'. He must have felt greatly reassured by these attentions. Days later he inserted an announcement in the Sydney *Freeman's Journal*, stating that 'Dr K. I. O'Doherty, late Surgeon to St Vincent's and Assistant Physician to the Coombe Lying-in Hospitals, Dublin, may be consulted at his residence, 27 Botany-street, Sydney'.[30]

In December Eva sailed with her four young sons to join him and by January 1861 she had begun contributing to the Poet's Corner in the *Freeman's Journal* (Sydney), receiving a salary for her work. Between 30 January and 11 December 1861, fifty-one poems were published, including the translations of Béranger, de Lamartine and Hugo, as well as some of her own translations of poems from 'Old Irish'. It is interesting to speculate why she chose to publish translations, as this was a comparatively new departure from her usual practice. Of these fifty-one poems, thirteen were from Béranger, two from de Lamartine and two from Hugo, in other words, 33 per cent of her published output in ten months constituted translation work.

It is possible that she needed to produce some work in a hurry because, as Kevin was in the process of setting up a new practice, money would have been in short supply, and she had a young family making demands on her time so may not have had the opportunity to prepare original verse. Some of these had already been prepared in a portfolio, since four of the translations and several of the other poems had already appeared in previous editions of the *Nation* during her sojourn in France. One could also hypothesise that she was trying out a genre that had been popularised by James Clarence Mangan and Speranza who had had this type of work published.

At first, her poetry suggests that she was happy and enjoying life in Australia:

> Long years ago in grief and toil,
> Our infant nation first was planted,
> Upon this fair and fertile soil;
> And sad the exile's hymn was chanted.
> But now we sing a purer day,
> A glorious future's rosy dawning
> By the bright waters of our bay,
> Beneath the clear skies' peaceful awning.[31]

However, the mood did not last, and she began to yearn for Ireland. Her poetry became melancholy, filled with sadness and despair, as shown in 'Dead Leaves':

> Dead leaves are sadly falling
> Down from the tree of life;
> With every blast, they drop so fast,
> And lie all rank and rife.
> Upon the ground I see them –
> Yellow, and pale, and cold;
> In every one, some hope is gone,
> Dead in the wintry mould![32]

The family soon came to the notice of James Quinn, Bishop of Brisbane, whom they had previously met in Dublin. At his insistence they were, by the end of 1861, preparing to move yet again, to Ipswich in Queensland. Quinn, a forceful man determined to build up the Irish population of his Queensland Catholic empire (dubbed 'Quinnsland' by critics)[33] with persons from the professional classes, found the O'Doherty family were ideal to promote his policies! By 7 March 1862 O'Doherty had a new practice in his residence at Thorn Street, Ipswich, and on 17 March, at the St Patrick's Day banquet, he was given the honour of replying to the toast of 'Fatherland'.[34] Following their move to Queensland, two further children were born in rapid succession, neither surviving beyond infancy.

In 1865, the family moved to Brisbane. O'Doherty was by now getting a reputation as a fine surgeon and in January 1866 he joined the staff of the Brisbane Hospital and the Queensland Lying-In Hospital as a visiting consultant. In 1882 he built a splendid house, Frascati, in Ann Street and had a very comfortable standard of living.[35] But as his private practice went from strength to strength, he became more politically motivated.

Little is known of Eva's life during this period. Her daughter Gertrude was born in 1869, the only child not to predecease her parents. The argument that she may have been too busy with her family does not bear scrutiny when one knows that she had managed to write for the *Freeman's Journal* (Sydney) for almost a year, turning out an average of one poem a week. The majority of poems included in *Poems by Eva of The Nation*,[36] published in 1877, probably written about this time, are introspective and melancholic, perhaps indicating a form of depression.

O'Doherty was elected to the Queensland Legislative Assembly in 1877 but the mention of Eva's name comes only rarely, appearing only in the social advertisements of the *Brisbane Courier*, as a member of a committee organising a ball and in a notice advertising the 'Building Fund of St Stephens Cathedral a Bazaar under the patronage of His Excellency Sir Maurice O'Connell and Lady O'Connell: Mrs O'Doherty was one of eight ladies who have kindly consented to hold Stalls'.[37]

In 1877, she travelled to San Francisco with her two elder sons to try to get her first book *Poems by Eva of The Nation* published. It was not a commercial success. The dedication read: 'To the memory of John Mitchel and John Martin, "Felons" of '48. These Poems (Associated with the cause for which they suffered), are dedicated by their friend and compatriot, Eva.'[38] She then continued her journey, taking William to study dentistry in Philadelphia and Edward to Dublin to study medicine at the Royal College of Surgeons. Both eventually returned home qualified and put up their plates at Frascati. With the sons well established, O'Doherty began to have thoughts of home – and in particular of Home Rule.

In 1881, he became involved with the Brisbane branch of the Irish Land

League, and in 1883 resigned from the Ipswich and Brisbane Hospitals in order to focus on his private practice and political career.[39] Hints dropped in the *Australian*, a Catholic weekly newspaper, appear to suggest that he could possibly expect to win a seat in the House of Commons in London (should a vacancy present itself). So, with this in mind, early in 1885, following a progression of banquets and meetings, culminating in a farewell dinner at which he was presented with a purse of sovereigns (£250 at least is known to have been subscribed) he sailed for Ireland.[40]

O'Doherty had a great reception and was presented with the Honorary Freedom of the City of Dublin. When Gladstone's Liberal government resigned in June he accepted the nomination to represent County Meath in the forthcoming election and was elected unopposed. He returned to Brisbane to sort out his business affairs only to be met with an unfriendly reception from the *Brisbane Courier*. At that time, the Australian newspapers received their information from agencies in England, and so printed the English version of any events, together with editorial opinion that reflected these views. The *Brisbane Courier*, which had in the past supported him as a doctor, now castigated him for belonging to a political party, 'whose chief characteristic is almost insane hatred of Britain and of the British' and '...who have again and again shown their indifference – except as a source of money contributions – for the colonial Empire of our Sovereign'.[41]

O'Doherty returned to London in the spring of 1886 to take up his seat. However, with the fall of the government, following the defeat of the Home Rule Bill, he decided not to stand again and returned once more to Australia. There is some evidence from his daughter that he may have been experiencing financial difficulties.[42]

This was the start of the road to ruin. By the time O'Doherty returned, his medical practice, affected by his political views, had fallen off considerably. He moved in October 1886 to Sydney for a fifteen-month locum but did not complete the contract, moving in August 1887 to be the government medical officer at Croydon in the north of Queensland, a very inhospitable location. During his spell in Croydon, 'Frascati', the family home, had to be vacated and his son, who had taken over the medical practice, was declared bankrupt.[43]

The downturn in their fortunes was followed by sorrow and anguish for Eva and O'Doherty as within a space of ten years their four sons died: Vincent was knocked down by a horse-drawn cab on 3 November 1890, and fractured his skull; William died of an unspecified illness on 9 October 1893; Kevin Junior died of pneumonia in Kalgoorlie on 15 February 1900, and Edward died from a brain haemorrhage on 5 July 1900, having slipped and hit his head on a kerbstone.

Kevin and Eva O'Doherty slid into poverty, supported only by a meagre pension and their daughter Gertrude, who had a small salary. By the late 1890s official records give their address at a boarding house in Wickham Terrace, Brisbane. After forty years of marriage the couple were back in lodgings similar to those they had at the beginning of their marriage in Paris. Early in 1900 they were able to move to a small cottage which they rented in Rosalie, a suburb of Brisbane, where O'Doherty, who had lost his eyesight in his declining years, died on 15 July 1905. After his death, without his small pension, Eva and Gertrude had to move out of Brisbane to an even smaller house in Toowong.

Moved by Eva's plight, the Revd William Hickey, a clergyman in Yorkshire, England, and an admirer and collector of memorabilia pertaining to the Young Irelanders, managed to raise a small fund and arranged for the publication of her collected works. Gill & Co. of Dublin agreed to print and publish at their own expense and pay the author £20 sterling on the day of publication plus a royalty of 10 per cent on each copy sold on the first edition, as well as 20 per cent on subsequent editions. *Poems by Eva of The Nation*, edited by Seamus MacManus, was published in Dublin in 1909. Dedicated 'To the Memory of the Dead: A Hortus Siccus', the last poem in this book, 'Tenebrae', finds her looking back over her shoulder at the ghosts of the past:

> Thus one by one in gathering fear and gloom
> The plaintive voices murmuring low between,
> Each light goes out with cruel stroke of doom,
> Until upon the scene
> The dreadful darkness falls,
> A silence that appals,
> The darkness and the silence of the tomb![44]

The publication of this book generated a small profit which helped to improve Eva's circumstances as her health deteriorated. She died of bronchitis and exhaustion a year later, on 22 May 1910, over 80 years of age.

Eva is buried alongside her husband in the Catholic portion of the Toowong Cemetery. Her daughter Gertrude married but had no children. She died in 1949. Eva's only surviving grandson, Louis, died in 1918, wiping out the O'Doherty male line, but her surviving granddaughter, Mignon, married and had children. Eva has two living great-great granddaughters – Caroline Nesbit, a novelist, and Vivian Nesbitt, an actress and musician.

On 25 February 1912 a ceremony was organised by the Queensland Irish Association, to raise a memorial Celtic Cross in honour of Eva and her husband. The Hon. F.M. O'Donnell, MLC, who had been a family friend and had visited Eva just a few days before her death, said in his oration that he had found her

> frail and weak physically, but mentally as clear and as bright as in the days when she wrote 'The Banshee' [*sic*].[45]... the rebel of sixty years before expressing the same grand sentiments ... the same fire, the same fervour, the same undying love for poor old Ireland, the same hope, aye, the same wish, the same indomitable unflinching spirit ... She spoke of the present fight in Ireland, and in all, showed that though in her eightieth year, practically on the brink of the Great Unknown, her love was as warm, her spirit unbroken.[46]

Eva did not exist as a passive icon. She was part of a movement that fought for Irish nationality and Irish identity – regardless of race and creed – and she paved the way for other women to be accepted as activists. John O'Leary, who suffered imprisonment, extreme hardship and exile for his nationalist views, said in later years that 'she is more intimately associated in my memory, probably, than any one now living, with all I have felt and thought and done for Ireland since "boyhood's fire was in my blood", down to that sad present when my blood is growing cold, and all the fire has long gone out of me'.[47]

Through her poetry she participated in the struggle for Irish nationality and identity and deserves to be remembered. Her 'oath of allegiance' to Ireland was paramount as she said in the poem of the same name:

> Good men, true men, stand ye forth,
> East and West, and south and north;
> Raise the chorus deep and loud,
> 'Life and limb to thee are vowed.'
> Ireland![48]

NOTES

1. *Nation*, 7 December 1844, p.139.
2. Ibid., 23 February 1845, p.314.
3. Ibid., 17 July 1847, p.649.
4. Ibid., 12 April 1845, p.440.
5. Ibid., 18 March 1848, p.184.
6. Ibid., 11 March 1848, p.168.
7. Ibid., 25 March 1848, p.200.
8. Ibid., 24 December 1848, p.1018.
9. John Mitchel, *Jail Journal; or, Five Years in British Prisons* (Dublin: Gill, 1921).

10. T.D. Sullivan, A.M. Sullivan and D.B. Sullivan, *Speeches from the Dock or Protests of Irish Patriots* (Dublin: Gill & Son, 1945), p.96.
11. *Nation*, 3 June 1848, p.360.
12. National Library of Ireland (NLI), Ms. 465.
13. P.J. Dillon, 'Eva of The Nation', *Leabhar Bliadhna na gCapuisineach* (Dublin: The Father Mathew Record Office, 1933), pp.261–6.
14. NLI, Ms. 10521.
15. NLI, Ms. 4758, pp.12–13.
16. Eva, *Poems by Eva of The Nation*, intro. William Hickey, ed. Seumas MacManus, pref. Justin McCarthy (Dublin: Gill, 1909).
17. *Nation*, 15 December 1849, p.251.
18. Ibid., 27 July 1850, p.760.
19. Ibid., 24 August 1850, p.827.
20. Ibid., 15 March 1851, p.475.
21. Ibid., 29 March 1851, p.523.
22i. Ibid., 29 March 1851, p.491.
23. Ibid., 28 February 1852, p.410.
24. NLI, Ms. 10521.
25. John Oxley Library, Brisbane, OM 6/7.
26. *Thoms Almanac and Official Directory of the United Kingdom and Ireland* (Dublin, 1858), p.631.
27. Ibid. (1859), p.994.
28. Ibid. (1862), p.808.
29. *Freemans Journal* (Sydney), 20 October 1860, p.2.
30. Ibid., 27 October 1861, p.1.
31. Ibid., 30 January 1861, p.6.
32. Ibid., 26 June 1861, p.6.
33. Patrick O'Farrell, *The Irish in Australia* (Sydney: New South Wales University Press, 1993), p.107.
34. *Freemans Journal* (Sydney), 20 March 1861, pp.9–10.
35. R. Patrick and H. Patrick, *Exiles Undaunted: The Irish Rebels Kevin and Eva O'Doherty* (Brisbane: Queensland University Press, 1989), p.9.
36. Eva, *Poems by Eva of the Nation* (San Francisco: P.J. Thomas, 1877).
37. *Brisbane Courier*, 17 May and 23 May 1871, p.1.
38. Eva, *Poems* (1877).
39. Patrick and Patrick, *Exiles Undaunted*, pp.239–43.
40. *Brisbane Courier*, 25 April 1885, p.4.
41. Patrick and Patrick, *Exiles Undaunted*, p.251.
42. John Oxley Library, Brisbane, OM71-6/3.
43. Patrick and Patrick, *Exiles Undaunted*, pp.258–64.
44. Eva, *Poems* (1909), p.115.
45. *Nation*, 3 May 1845, p.13, entitled 'The Benshi'.
46. John Oxley Library, Brisbane, OM 71-6/3.
47. John O'Leary, *Recollections of Fenians and Fenianism* (London: Downfy, 1896, rpt. Shannon: Irish University Press, 1969), p.108.
48. *Nation*, 27 July 1850, p.760.

7

'We got on splendidly!' – The Irish Players in Queensland in 1922

Peter Kuch

Leafing through their copy of the *Queensland Times* for 3 October 1922 after breakfast the Ipswich reader would have come across the following advertisement on page 7:

Table 4: Advertisement from the *Queensland Times*

SYDNEY, MELBOURNE, ADELAIDE AND BRISBANE HAVE PAID HOMAGE TO

THE WHITE-HEADED BOY

AND ACCLAIMED IT AS A TRIUMPH

THE MOST WONDERFUL CHARACTER ACTING EVER SEEN ON THE AUSTRALIAN STAGE

The MELBOURNE ARGUS said: 'Those who miss this play will miss the treat of a lifetime'

MARTOO'S OLYMPIA

TO-NIGHT (TUESDAY) TO-NIGHT

(ONE NIGHT ONLY)

J.C. WILLIAMSON LTD

Present 'A PLAY OF ALL PERIODS AND ALL LANDS'

THE WHITE-HEADED BOY

A COMEDY IN THREE ACTS BY LENNOX ROBINSON, DROLL AND WHIMSICAL THROUGHOUT, YET FILLED WITH HAUNTING WISTFULNESS

WITH

MAIRE O'NEILL

And the Original Abbey Theatre Company of 12 Irish Players, from the Ambassadors' Theatre, London,

INCLUDING

ARTHUR SINCLAIR

JOAN SULLIVAN	MAUREEN DELANEY	MARGARET DUNNE
J.A. O'ROURKE	GERTRUDE MURPHY	MAY FITZGERALD
NORAH DESMOND	SYDNEY MORGAN	ARTHUR SHIELDS
	HARRY HUTCHINSON	

BOX PLANS open at Wertheim Piano Co. Book early to avoid disappointment
POPULAR PRICES: Reserved seats 5/-, unreserved 3/- and 2/-; Plus Tax
CHILDREN, HALF-PRICE TO ALL PARTS, PLUS TAX

Arrangements have been made with the railway department to attach a carriage to 11pm goods train; stopping at Booval, Bundanba, Dinmore and Redbank, thus enabling patrons coming by train to see the performance to its conclusion.[1]

Elsewhere, in the same paper, the Ipswich reader would have encountered, in the 'Entertainment' section under the subheading, Martoo's Olympia, the following, as it turns out, syndicated paragraph, most likely drafted by the publicity department of J.C. Williamson:

The visit of the Abbey Theatre Players to Ipswich is a dramatic event to be made much of. These famous players have a reputation of world-wide renown, and it was not lightly acquired, it was won by sterling acting, and local playgoers, who visit Martoo's Olympia tonight will learn how good that is. According to southern critics they give the most wonderful display of character acting ever seen on the Australian stage. The debut in Ipswich of the Abbey Theatre Company, headed by Miss Máire O'Neill, the renowned star, and incidentally a sister of Miss Sara Algood [sic], of Peg O' My Heart fame, constitutes a landmark in our theatrical history, for the organisation comprises the original artists in the original and complete production. The combination of 12 Irish players has appeared together in this comedy for over six years, and Australia is the sixth country visited in the course of a triumphal world tour.[2] It is said that the charm of The White-Headed Boy will instantly captivate the theatre-goers of this city. The brilliance of the comedy is due to the triumph of individuality. Each member of the company is an artist. The White-headed Boy is a crisp comedy, full of wit and satire, and possesses a powerful dramatic touch. Miss O'Neill will be seen in the part of Aunt Ellen, Arthur Shields is the white-headed boy who disappoints his family, and Arthur Sinclair gives a wonderful characterisation as John Duffy. The minor roles are all said to be capitally played. To sum up, local playgoers may look forward to a night of hearty laughter and delightful acting. The box plan is at Wertheim's Music Warehouse. The prices are on a popular scale and children half price, plus tax.[3]

But what were a troupe of Irish actors with a 'world-wide reputation' doing in Ipswich, Queensland, in the late autumn of 1922 with a 'one night only performance' of The White-Headed Boy? Founded in 1826–7 on the banks of the Bremer river, and lying some 40 km west of Brisbane, this coal-mining and meat-producing centre was enjoying a period of prosperity as it approached its centenary. Even so, despite the implication of the first line of the newspaper advertisement announcing the play, Ipswich could hardly be said to rank alongside Sydney, Melbourne, Adelaide and Brisbane, nor could it be said to be one of the most sought-after places to tour after having played London, regardless of whatever arrangements could be made with the railways. Yet Ipswich was where they were. But who were they?

The actors who arrived in Ipswich on 3 October were not, as claimed in the advertisement, the 'original Abbey Theatre Company of 12 Irish Players, from the Ambassadors' Theatre, London'. They did not belong to the Abbey Theatre; they were not from the Ambassadors' Theatre, London; and of the twelve on the Ipswich cast list only seven had taken part in the London production.[4] These seven belonged to a group of disgruntled actors who had broken away from the Abbey Theatre six years before, in 1916, shortly after the Easter Rising. Deeply concerned about the financial viability of the Abbey, which had been teetering on the edge of bankruptcy for several years, and in revolt against Yeats's autocratic rule and St John Ervine's, the current manager's, dictatorial methods, they had decided some time in May 1916 to take the name the Irish Players and form their own touring company. After appointing Arthur Shields as their leader, they played two weeks in Belfast in July 1916 and then toured England and the Irish provinces, before appearing in Dublin in October.[5] Though their first tour was a success, it nevertheless disclosed both the strengths and weaknesses of the new company. The Irish Players' great strength was their ensemble acting for which, over time, they were to establish an international reputation – and in this respect both the advertisement and the paragraph in the *Queensland Times* is correct. The Irish Players' great weakness was that they were essentially an actors' company, with the result that they themselves never initiated any new scripts of merit.[6] For the ten years or more the company was active they had to rely on securing permission from playwrights whose work was not already under contract. At first this was made all the more difficult by Yeats and Lady Gregory taking out an injunction against The Irish Players to prevent them from using any of the plays from the Abbey's repertoire.

Consequently, when Lennox Robinson, a former Abbey director, who in 1916 was working for the Carnegie Trust, wrote *The White-Headed Boy*, a shrewdly crafted, whimsical three-act comedy that unmasked the intrigues of provincial Irish society, and which was first staged at the Abbey with moderate success on 13 December 1916, the Irish Players could only eye the script from a distance while, for his part, Lennox Robinson could only wish that such talented performers were interpreting his work.[7]

Yet time did bring the two together. After 1916 the Irish Players continued to grow as a company. Touring, particularly in England, saved them from risking their fortunes in an Ireland that had become increasingly unpredictable and violent in the years following the 1916 Easter Rising. Bombings, shootings and curfews made going to the theatre at best dangerous and at worst impossible. At the same time Yeats's opposition to the Irish Players subsided. Though the Abbey pressed on doggedly, opening for short seasons when it could, the aging poet, who married in

1917 and who subsequently spent more and more time at Ballylee and abroad, intervened much less frequently in its affairs. During the same period, Lennox Robinson returned to the theatre, enhancing his reputation as a playwright with the success of *The Lost Leader* and achieving a level of rapprochement with and a degree of independence from Yeats and the Dublin theatrical establishment by combining work with the Abbey with fostering a new venture, the Dublin Drama League.[8]

Lennox Robinson's success with *The Lost Leader* also restored his relationship with the London-based actor-manager and playwright, James Bernard Fagan,[9] who approached him late in 1919 or early in 1920 for permission to produce *The White-Headed Boy* in England and cast it with the Irish Players. After trialling the production in Manchester for a run of twelve nights from 13 September 1920, Fagan took it to the Ambassadors' Theatre in London, where the Irish Players' interpretation of *The White-Headed Boy* drew laudatory reviews and enjoyed such popularity at the box office that it ran for some 300 performances. In this respect the advertisement in the *Queensland Times* is misleading rather than inaccurate – the Ambassadors' Theatre in London being the venue for the Irish Players' greatest success rather than a place they would have called 'home'.

The early months of 1921 proved to be a particularly difficult period for the London theatres. On 23 May 1921 *The Times* quoted one 'leading manager' to the effect that everybody 'connected with the theatrical business had joined the "Clan Micawber" and were waiting patiently for something to turn up'. 'At present there are few signs of a break in the "slump"...and there is little prospect of a general revival of business before the opening of the autumn season,' the writer noted. In the same column it was announced that *The White-Headed Boy* had been withdrawn from the Ambassadors' that weekend,[10] advance notice having been given in *The Times* almost a month previously, on 21 April 1921, that the play, which was nearing its three hundredth performance, was in its last weeks.[11]

Not that the withdrawal of the play from the Ambassadors' marked the end of the relationship between the Irish Players and *The White-Headed Boy*. In the summer of 1921 most of the members of the original company left for a tour of America and Canada while those who remained formed themselves into a second group. Produced by Charles Dillingham, the original Irish Players' *Whiteheaded Boy* [sic] opened at Henry Miller's Theatre, New York, on 17 October 1921. From there they went to Chicago, Pittsburgh, Toledo, South Bend, Indianapolis, Louisville, St Louis, Detroit, Toronto, Buffalo, Philadelphia, Washington, and Baltimore, with a final season in Boston.[12] By May 1922 the original group was opening in Sydney, in advance of a tour that took in Goulburn, Albury, Melbourne and Adelaide with a return to Sydney. Back in London the second group, also known as the Irish Players, opened with a revival of *The White-Headed Boy* at the Aldwych on 10 April 1922.[13]

Here again the advertisement in the *Queensland Times* is misleading when it claimed that

SYDNEY, MELBOURNE, ADELAIDE AND BRISBANE HAVE PAID HOMAGE TO
THE WHITE-HEADED BOY
AND ACCLAIMED IT AS A TRIUMPH

In fact, the Irish Players met with only moderate success in Sydney and Melbourne, while they were pulled in Adelaide after a run of only four nights to free up the Theatre Royal for a production of *The Peep Show*. It seems that the advertising copywriter for the *Queensland Times* was either hoping that his Ipswich readers had short memories, did not subscribe to the southern papers, or did not recall the sarcastic comments in the *Bulletin* on 20 July 1922 on the debacle in Adelaide,[14] barely three months before the Ipswich opening.

Yet, despite the misleading information and the puffery, the actors seem to have enjoyed their time in Ipswich. There was also a very good response from audiences; the Ipswich issue of the *Queensland Times* reporting the following day that the audience had been 'enthusiastic' and that 'the brilliant individual acting of the twelve players [had been] greatly appreciated'.[15] Ipswich was the Irish Players' first venue after their one-week engagement in Brisbane had been extended by a further week, with the result that they were in Brisbane from 13 September to 2 October 1922. The competing attractions when they opened were *The Tivoli Frolics* at the Cremorne; *Turn to the Right* at the Theatre Royal; *One Clear Call* at the Majestic; *Hail the Woman* at the Strand de Luxe; *Waiting for the Dawn* at the Tivoli Theatre; with *The White-Headed Boy* opening at His Majesty's.[16] Reviews of the opening night were enthusiastic, the Brisbane *Daily Mail* reporting:

The debut in Brisbane of the Abbey Theatre Company, headed by Miss Máire O'Neill, the renowned star, constitutes a landmark in our theatrical history, for the organisation comprises the original artists in the original and complete production. The charm of the production instantly captivated the theatre-goers of Brisbane, and the efforts of the artists heightened the piece immensely.[17]

In addition to playing *The White-Headed Boy*, the Irish Players also performed William Boyle's *The Building Fund*, James Bernard Fagan's *Dr*

O'Toole, St John Ervine's *The Mixed Marriage*, and a light-hearted curtain-raiser entitled *Tactics*. St John Ervine's *The Mixed Marriage* in particular made a significant impression on the audience, the *Brisbane Courier* of 21 September noting that

> If the Abbey Theatre Players were happy in *The White-Headed Boy*, they were much more at home in the dual attraction, *Mixed Marriage* and *Tactics*, which was presented to a delighted house at His Majesty's Theatre last evening. The former is the principal play, and it must rank as one of the most engrossing subjects exploited for some time. Written by St John Ervine ... it deals with the religious bigotry and intolerance in Ireland which existed to such a large extent prior to the present tumult in that troubled country. But there is nothing in the story which is likely to hurt the susceptibilities of the most rabid northern or southern Protestant or Roman Catholic. Many deep and sensible thoughts on the Irish political and religious controversies were expounded in a way which compelled the rapt attention of the listeners. Although the theme embraced such a serious subject, there was a vast amount of wholesome good humour in[f]used into it, and on numerous occasions the theatre rang with laughter at the merry Irish quips and jests. Humour, pathos and drama were intermingled with masterly ability, and the closing scenes were exceptionally telling.[18]

In fact the entire fortnight was something of a minor triumph, the Governor of Queensland, Sir Matthew Nathan, and his entourage attending performances of *The Building Fund* and *Doctor O'Toole* in the second week.[19] Reviews were uniformly flattering, particularly of the acting, the *Brisbane Courier* observing of the closing performance:

> The artistic merit of The Abbey Theatre Company and their naturalness have appealed to the mind of the Theatre lover who demands a high standard. In *The White-Headed Boy* the acting is of a high standard, and the entire play is borne on the shoulders of a cast which is so skilled in its work that the onlooker can with ease forget that he is an onlooker, and imagine that he is observing some human drama in a real home instead of a stage home.[20]

From Brisbane the tour proceeded at a frantic pace, taking in Ipswich on 3 October; Toowoomba on the fifth; Warwick on the sixth; and Gympie on the seventh. Most of the regional papers simply adapted the press releases supplied by J.C. Williamson, though the 'drama critic' of the *Gympie Times*, 7 October 1922, was sufficiently emboldened to venture the following:

This is what a leading Sydney critic wrote of *The White-Headed Boy*,
J.C. Williamson's big comedy attraction, which will be produced in the
Olympia tonight: "Bernard Shaw discovered that the Irishman was not
sentimental. England has, of late, discovered it, too. And now Lennox
Robinson, the author of *The White-Headed Boy*, admits, in three
delightful acts, the terrible fact. The comedy is another *Bunty Pulls the
Strings*, but in the Irish and not in the Scotch language. It is also
another *On Our Selection*, in its clever presentation of characteristic
national types; and, like the other national plays, it does not flatter the
nation that produced it. But as comedy it is delightfully packed with
humour, Irish, no doubt, but universal in its appeal, and very human."
Greater praise could not be given, and the cast is a strong one. The
leading comedienne, Máire O'Neill, is described as another Marie
Tempest in another metier.[21]

After Gympie, the Irish Players performed *The White-Headed Boy* in
Maryborough on 9 October, Bundaberg on the tenth; and finally, for three
nights, at Rockhampton, from 11–14 October.

In many respects the reviews of the Rockhampton performances sum
up the Queensland tour, a tour that is not mentioned in any of the histories
of the theatre, either Irish, British or Australian. On the one hand, the Irish
Players, regardless of whether it was Brisbane, Gympie or Rockhampton,
were obliged to negotiate a stereotype of Irish identity that they must have
found created problems for their interpretations of character. The advance
notices, in particular, over which they probably had little or no control,
contained lines like: 'Wit and humour will flow voluminously...
tomorrow night when The Irish Players, from the Abbey Theatre, Dublin,
...make their first appearance...' As for the play – *The White-Headed
Boy* was said to be composed of 'threads of life's story fashioned into a bit
of exquisite Irish lace', and to be 'droll and whimsical throughout, yet
filled with haunting wistfulness'. 'It is a realistic presentation of a certain
phase of Irish life and character. Intensely human and bubbling over with
subtle humour, which is closely allied to tears, it is a masterpiece of
character drawing and character acting.' 'Droll and whimsical', laughter
and tears – all the clichés of Irish identity that Shaw had pilloried in *John
Bull's Other Island* merely a decade before.

On the other hand, the Queensland tour, as with the tour of Sydney,
Melbourne and Adelaide, gave the Irish Players an opportunity to confront
and confound these stereotypes, particularly at a time when Ireland was
much in the Australian news as newspapers daily reported a bewildering
array of atrocities – killings, bombings, massacres, murders, executions,
shootings, ambushes and assassinations. What audiences were presented

with was a different Ireland; an Ireland that was prepared to laugh at itself, an Ireland that Australian audiences enjoyed encountering. For example, the *Bundaberg Mail* spoke for many Queenslanders when it reported the Irish Players' one-night performance in their town:

> This unique company appeared in the Queen's Theatre last evening, when they staged that brilliant three-act comedy *The White-Headed Boy* to a very large and most enthusiastic audience. Each...of the 12 artists gave of their best, and throughout the entertainment kept the audience bubbling over with laughter. The various artists...were vociferously applauded time and again by the delighted audience who were unanimous in declaring the company to be one of the best and the most popular to visit Bundaberg and a return visit from them will be anxiously awaited.[22]

And as for the actors themselves; when Arthur Shields eventually returned to Dublin he was interviewed by the *Evening Telegraph*.

'Did you have a good time in Australia?' asked [their] representative.

> – 'On the whole we had. After our arrival we played for some weeks *The White Headed Boy*...Our performance got very good notices – in fact there was only one unfriendly paper. From Sydney we went to Melbourne, playing at three small towns on the way. Then we did Adelaide, and later Newcastle, and then Brisbane. We played more in Queensland than in any of the other states, visiting many towns such as Ipswich, Warwick and Gympie – the latter being one of the oldest towns and the spot where gold was first discovered in the Southern Continent. We moved north until we got to Rockhampton. This was the farthest north the company went.'

'How were you received in these places?'

> – 'We got on splendidly. Everywhere we went, in all the cities and towns, we found Irish people with their clubs and social circles, and they all treated us splendidly.'[23]

In terms of the 1922 tour of Australia, getting on 'splendidly' was doubtless more true of the treatment the Irish Players received in the cities and mining and agricultural towns of Queensland than of the treatment they received in South Australia, New South Wales and Victoria. As the most recently settled of these states, Queensland was more open, more rural, and more ethnically diverse – and consequently more accepting of the Irish. This was particularly true of the north of the state, which in many respects was still a 'frontier'.[24] Patterns of migration and assimilation were also different. Queensland had found favour with the Irish from as far back as 1865 when Bishop Quinn had inaugurated a well-organised and highly successful campaign of chain migration that encouraged young emigrants to sponsor not only siblings but also parents and close relatives with the consequence that the Queensland Irish were at once more recent and more 'familial' than their southern counterparts.[25]

Finally, in Queensland, Irish identity was not being as vigorously contested in 1922 as it had recently been in South Australia and New South Wales and was still being in Victoria, where, between 1913 and 1923, the rise and rout of the highly controversial Archbishop Mannix, the chief architect of an Irish Catholic triumphalism unparalleled in Australian history, intermittently irritated, flummoxed or outraged the Anglo-Protestant establishment and the new federal government. It was Melbourne rather than Brisbane that experienced the monster Saint Patrick's Day parades of 1918 and 1920, the latter led by the Archbishop, who was escorted by twelve Victoria Crosses and 10,000 First World War veterans marshalled to rebut accusations of cowardice and disloyalty.[26] And it was Melbourne that hosted the 1919 Irish Race Convention.[27] Furthermore, it was Sydney rather than Brisbane where four of the seven members of the Irish Nationalist Association were arrested and imprisoned late in 1918.[28] And it was from Sydney that Mannix departed for his triumphal 1920 tour of America, though when he attempted to proceed to Ireland, the passenger ship on which he was travelling was intercepted by two British destroyers and the archbishop was unceremoniously landed at Penzance with the warning that he was forbidden to visit Ireland or any city in the British Isles with a large Irish population.[29] Sensing that he was now a spent force, the Australian government did not deem it necessary to support a resolution to require Mannix to take the oath of loyalty to re-enter the country in July 1921.[30] After all, Irish-Australians had failed to rally around the Labor member for Kalgoorlie, Hugh Mahon, when he was expelled from federal parliament in November 1920 for holding a protest rally in Melbourne organised by the Irish Ireland League in support of Terence MacSwiney, the Lord Mayor of Cork, who had died the previous month after a seventy-four day hunger strike in protest at the Black and Tans' burning of his city.[31] Not surprisingly, given the mood, the 1922 Melbourne St Patrick's Day parade, held in spite of a Melbourne City Council ruling, was a low-key affair.[32] Similarly, only muted protests attended the deportation of Fr Michael O'Flanagan and Mr J.J. O'Kelly, envoys from the *de facto* Irish Republic, in June 1923.[33]

By the time the Irish Players reached Queensland the dominant mood in the 'clubs and social circles' that Arthur Sinclair spoke about to the *Evening Telegraph* (Dublin) was of an idealized rural community celebrated by Fr P.J. Hartigan's (John O'Brien's) verse collection *Around the Boree Log*, first published in 1921 and achieving immediate and lasting popularity.[34] This was a world ordered by kind but firm priests that revolved around the 'little Irish mother' as the embodiment of piety and the hearth – an intensely tribal, closed community insulated by language and custom from the baleful effects of politics, modernism and secularism. That the bill of fare the Irish Players offered their Queensland audiences gently but incisively questioned rather than challenged this world might seem a modest accomplishment, but given the heightened sectarianism being experienced in Australia, and, in Yeats's phrase, the 'blood-dimmed tide' of violence unleased in Ireland, such questioning, made all the more searching by brilliant ensemble acting and a mastery of comedy, was no mean accomplishment.

NOTES

1. *Queensland Times* (Ipswich), 3 October 1922, p.7.
2. In fact *The Times* (London), 28 September 1920, p.8 lists the London cast as:
    Cast of *The White Headed Boy*

Mrs Geoghegan	SARA ALLGOOD
George	SYDNEY MORGAN
Peter	HARRY HUTCHINSON
Kate	NORAH DESMOND
Jane	URSULA TREMAYNE
Baby	MIGNON O'DOHERTY
Denis	ARTHUR SHIELDS
Donough Brosnan	J.A. O'ROURKE
John Duffy	ARTHUR SINCLAIR
Delia	NAN FITZGERALD
Hannah	KITTY MACVEAGH
Aunt Ellen	MAIRE O'NEILL

3. *Queensland Times* (Ipswich), 3 October 1922, p.4.
4. The London cast list included Sara Allgood, Ursula Tremayne, Mignon O'Doherty, Nan Fitzgerald, and Kitty MacVeagh.
5. Robert Hogan and Richard Burnham (eds), *The Modern Irish Drama: A Documentary History, V: The Art of the Amateur, 1916–1920* (Dublin: Dolmen, 1984), p.47.
6. Ibid.
7. Note Christopher Murray, 'Lennox Robinson: The Abbey's Anti-Hero' in Masaru Sekine (ed.), *Irish Writers and the Theatre* (Gerrards Cross: Colin Smythe, 1986), p.125: 'Robinson's comedies ... represent his best work. [A] feature necessary to emphasise is their strong theatricality. The characterisation is so varied and the scenes in the comedies so tellingly arranged that they offered from the start excellent playing roles to the Abbey company, a matter of considerable importance where a repertory theatre is concerned.'
8. R.F. Foster, *W.B. Yeats: A Life II: The Arch Poet 1915–1939* (Oxford: Oxford University

Press, 2003), pp.153–4. Murray, 'Lennox Robinson', p.133, notes a letter from Robinson to James Stephens, dated 27 September 1918 cited in Michael J. O'Neill, *Lennox Robinson* (New York: Twayne Publishers, 1964), p.113, to support the contention that The Dublin Drama League was Robinson's brain-child; whereas Hogan and Burnham, *The Art of the Amateur*, pp.152–3 claim that Yeats was the prime mover. Finally, Ann Saddlemyer, *Becoming George: The Life of Mrs W.B. Yeats* (Oxford: Oxford University Press, 2002), p.194, points out that Yeats chaired the inaugural meeting.

9. Anon, 'London Theatres: The Ambassadors: *The White-Headed Boy*', *The Stage*, 30 September 1920, p.16, reports that J.B. Fagan was 'responsible for the scene design and the production'.

10. Anon., 'The Theatres: Waiting for Something to Turn Up', *The Times*, 23 May 1921, p.8.

11. Anon., 'The Theatres', *The Times*, 21 April 1921, p.8. (Note: 27 September 1920 to 23 May 1921 equals approximately 238 nights, though it is not possible to know whether or not there were matinee performances.)

12. Interview with Arthur Shields in *Evening Telegraph*, 15 January 1923.

13. Anon, 'The Theatres', *The Times*, 10 April 1922, p.12.

14. *Bulletin*, 20 July 1922, p.34: '*The White-Headed Boy* has found heavy support in cultured Adelaide before being literally pushed out of the Royal by preparations for a first-in-Australia revue. Máire O'Neill is the popular success of the Irish comedy, and her frequent appeals to the Deity are always (for some obscure reason) received by the house with delighted laughter. Equally acceptable in a different way are the quiet women who fit into their dull-grey characters as if they were not acting at all, notably Maureen Delany and Nora Desmond. The men are Irish types finely differentiated.'

15. *Queensland Times* (Ipswich), 4 October 1922, p.9.

16. *Brisbane Courier*, 14 September 1922, p.11.

17. Quoted in *Maryborough Chronicle*, 9 October 1922, p.4.

18. *Brisbane Courier*, 21 September 1922, p.7.

19. Ibid., 28 September 1922, p.11.

20. Ibid., 30 September 1922, p.8.

21. *Gympie Times*, 7 October 1922, p.5.

22. *Bundaberg Mail*, 11 October 1922, p.4.

23. *Evening Telegraph*, 15 January 1923, p.10.

24. M.E.R MacGinley, 'The Irish in Queensland: an Overview', in John O'Brien and Pauric Travers (eds), *The Irish Emigrant Experience in Australia* (Dublin: Poolbeg Press, 1991), pp.103–19. For the experience of Biddy Burke, who emigrated to Queensland, see David Fitzpatrick, *Oceans of Consolation: Personal Accounts of Irish Migration to Australia* (Melbourne: Melbourne University Press, 1995), pp.139–58.

25. Patrick O'Farrell, *The Irish in Australia* (1986; Kensington: The University of New South Wales Press, 1993), p.107.

26. Ibid., pp.273–4; James Griffin, 'Daniel Mannix and the Cult of Personality', in Oliver MacDonagh and W.F. Mandle (eds), *Ireland and Irish-Australia* (London: Croom Helm, 1986), p.99; Caroline Williams, 'Moran, Mannix and St Patrick's Day', in Philip Bull, Frances Devlin-Glass, and Helen Doyle (eds), *Ireland and Australia, 1798–1998: Studies in Culture, Identity and Migration* (Sydney: Crossing Press, 2000), pp.143–51.

27. O'Farrell, *The Irish in Australia*, pp.279–81.

28. Ibid., pp.273–9.

29. Ibid., pp.282–4; Dermot Keogh, 'Mannix, de Valera and Irish Nationalism', in O'Brien and Travers (eds), *The Irish Emigrant Experience*, pp.196–225; Michael Gilchrist, *Daniel Mannix: Priest and Patriot* (Melbourne: Dove Communications, 1982), pp.90–4.

30. O'Farrell, *The Irish in Australia*, p.284.

31. Ibid., pp.284, 286.

32. Ibid., p.291.

33. Ibid., pp.291, 293.

34. Ibid., pp.191–2.

8

The Irish in Grass Castles:
Re-reading Victim Tropes in an
Iconic Pioneering Text

Frances Devlin-Glass

The bush nationalist tradition in Australia is replete with hero myths relating to explorers and pioneers/settlers and with pastoral histories which paint the settler/pastoralist as benign. His (rarely her) conquest of the land is legitimized in narratives of suffering and endurance. Despite the decline of the cattle industry in the late twentieth century, romanticisation of pastoralism remains one of the bulwarks of Australian nationalism, symbol-formation and identity partly because of the nation-building fictional enterprises of the 1890s (like the poems and fiction of Paterson, Lawson and Furphy), which were re-read and revalued and made canonical in the 1940s and 1950s.[1] Bush nationalism and the pioneer mythos and their icons, and their ways of institutionalising the narrative of settlement, are, however, increasingly contested territory, as Aboriginal perspectives are more often registering as active agents in the national conversation and their influence on white settlers more likely to be noted, a phenomenon even registering in popular culture mobilisations of bush nationalism, for example *Crocodile Dundee*. Indeed, in the north-west of Western Australia, the Bunuba warrior Jandamarra, sometimes dubbed 'the Black Ned Kelly', who offered serious resistance to the premier iconic settler family of Australia in the 1890s is celebrated in schools, by a tourist trail which documents his daring exploits, and by an annual celebration.

INTERDEPENDENCE OF PASTORALISTS
AND ABORIGINES

Since the early 1970s, revisionist historians and anthropologists have problematised colonialist pioneer/settler narratives, Australia's sanctifying myth of origin.[2] They have documented the pastoral industry from both sides of the frontier, often using Aboriginal oral testimony as part of their methodology.[3] What is interesting about the histories that were subsequent to those of Reynolds and Rowley is their strongly regional nature, which points to a sea-change in understanding among mainly white historians of the independent nature, indeed sovereignty, of Aboriginal 'nations', and a backing away from pan-Aboriginalist assumptions.[4] Most of them are, significantly, highly collaborative in nature. They also concur in foregrounding the extent to which Aborigines in a number of different communities not only offered resistance to white settlers, but also cooperated with them in order to be able to continue to safeguard and properly tend their own country, and at the same time minimised the costs of an economically questionable industry. In the era before welfare services took over with rations in the 1950s and pensions in the 1960s, and full wages had to be paid to station-workers after the Wave Hill strikes in the 1970s, white pastoralists were undoubtedly guilty of benign paternalism (at best), exploitation (at least), massacres at worst (Roberts). Massacres on the frontier have rarely been successfully prosecuted in Australia as Roberts convincingly demonstrates in the first volume of his history of the Gulf of Carpentaria, and perpetrators have employed a lexicon rich in euphemism: 'dispersals' and in the Duracks' case, 'inevitable punitive expeditions'. This chapter does not seek to minimise the gross, often criminal, abuses of physical and economic power which marked the frontier.

However, the evidence is strongly available in these works and in a body of Aboriginal life-writing and *testimonii* that Aboriginal stockmen (and women) often avoided the victim/resistance stereotypes, leading truncated ceremonial lives on their own land, and deriving a measure of satisfaction from their roles as skilled bushmen/stockmen.[5] The absolute debt which explorers owed to their guides, and pastoralists to their workers' intimate knowledge of land that was otherwise lethal for Europeans, and police to their trackers (who often engaged in unsavoury expeditions and massacres European police themselves did not dare to undertake) has been richly and continually documented, by historians rather than by the hagiographical dynasty memoirists.[6] Foster makes it very clear that there were significant advantages to pastoralists in having Aboriginal people live on their own country and exercise their traditional rights on pastoral leases as a form of subsidised access to a cheap and flexible workforce. Rations could be provided, with government subsidy, when the workforce was needed in the dry, and bush tucker (cost-free to the pastoralist) resorted to in the wet.[7] Pastoralists and their Aboriginal workforce constituted a highly complex interdependent system, which allowed indigenous people a measure of cultural continuity:

Fishing and visiting waterholes, hunting and collecting bush foods and medicines, travelling across country on musters, sharing information with younger workers, checking on sites of significance, speaking language with contemporaries, sitting at camp fires retelling stories or listening to grandparents, sharing rations and learning to ride were all activities which allowed for the transmission and integration of existing secular knowledge.[8]

Certainly, secular European knowledge was garnered by Aboriginal people working as station hands, but the distinction between secular and sacred knowledge in relation to Aboriginal knowledge is not apposite in relation to Aboriginal culture, and Jebb's comment makes little sense. On the indigenous side of the frontier, to engage in the maintenance of country, to eat its symbolically invested produce and to enact Aboriginal forms of sociality is to be engaged in what Bradley, avoiding the European sacred/secular distinction, would call *super-vital* activities,[9] on the boss's time but also securely within Aboriginal time, in which dreamtime and historical time are coterminous. It was also, before the end of the pastoral era, in important ways, to be at home.

In the light of post-colonial histories and *testimonii*, it is instructive to re-read one of the iconic texts of the pastoral era, *Kings in Grass Castles* by Mary Durack,[10] a popular often-reprinted best-seller.[11] In this context, I wish to draw attention to its ideology drawn often quite explicitly from Irish nationalist land policy, and to point out the extent to which it is riven with instabilities. In particular, I intend to demonstrate the ways in which at crucial points in the narrative tropes of Irishness, usually associated with victimhood, are mobilised to rationalize the land-grab and to deflect attention from Durack complicity in massacres.

Kings in Grass Castles reveals the extent to which Irish-identified land-hunger and pragmatism drove the enterprise of pioneering within the extensive Durack pastoral dynasty, which settled vast tracts of remote south-west Queensland and the Kimberleys. Consciously in the writing, Aboriginal resistance is a mere footnote to the swelling theme of pioneer heroism in the face of murdering natives. But the repressed text demonstrates that their success intimately depended on their ability to co-opt Aboriginal stockmen, in particular Pumpkin, Ulysses and Boxer. These real-life characters are sentimentalised: for example, Pumpkin, a general factotum and 'mainstay of the station' (stockman, horse tailer, blacksmith, butcher, gardener and general handyman), is referred to as a 'guardian angel'. Pumpkin's authority was such that he was deemed by Patsy to have run the Cooper's Creek property (p.274). He was a rare Aboriginal stockman, confident enough to argue with his employers, and to resist their authority if the situation warranted it (pp.273–4). Such a degree of give and take across what was not just a racial divide but also a class one was uncommon.[12] Pumpkin is not, however, listed in the index;[13] indeed, no Aborigine is. The familiar humanity of known and trusted Aborigines (often given demeaning European names; for example, Melonhead, Kangaroo, Pintpot and Pannikin) is not extended to other more hostile defenders of territory in the Kimberleys. And, although Patsy understood that his retainers would suffer 'broken hearts' and illness away from their own country and kin (pp.179, 276), he nevertheless committed his most loyal retainers to permanent exile, and undoubtedly mortal danger, in the Kimberleys.

The Duracks' very survival they unwittingly owed to Boxer, a skilled indigenous diplomat, linguist and law-man who, described as 'unreliable' by his European bosses because of his frequent absences on Aboriginal business (pp.330–1), was both serving his own ends by keeping up his traditional knowledge base, and presumably gathering/distributing intelligence friendly to the Duracks to whom he remained loyal. The point of his absences is clearly not understood by the writer, who uses the phenomenon of Boxer's two-way life as a grandstand for enunciating the family's defence against charges of slavery. For Durack, to be an Aborigine living outside the pastoral domain was to be 'skulking in the hills' (p.332). Mary Durack in 1959 was talking of events that happened half a century and more before. She was certainly not self-conscious of the extent to which her language 'others' and dehumanises Aborigines: 'boys' change hands in return for a jar of jam (pp.306–7); they are 'strange, wild people whose ways they [Europeans] would never understand', and in discussing the 'yella-fella' issue, 'genetically remarkably good specimens, better adapted to the environment than the whiteman and better to the new way of life and philosophy than their full black brothers' (p.372), a language no doubt identical with that used of stock.

Unlike many settlers,[14] or even their near-neighbours in the Channel Country, Alice Duncan-Kemp and her father, the Scottish amateur ethnologist, William Duncan,[15] the Duracks demonstrated very little curiosity about Aboriginal culture, language or law. In pursuit of his own 'civilising' agendas, Costello (a Durack associate) unwittingly exposed a young couple on Thylungra intent on making a 'wrong-way' marriage to death, without questioning the ethnocentrism of his mission (p.129). Their mission was to make money and homes for their own tribes in the wilderness, and particular Aborigines were viewed as potential friends only if they were instrumental in achieving those objectives. Despite the strength of their own clannish mores,[16] their awareness of Aboriginal kinship loyalties and ties to land was non-existent. The Irish Bishop

Gibney, an outspoken critic of settlers of the north-west of Western Australia, was perhaps harsh in his assessment of pastoralists of the period when he described their lack of fellow-feeling in these terms:

> In the main, the civilizing influence of the employing white settler over his 'niggers' has been that of the shepherd to a good dog – he is treated well if he works well. They are made useful animals – white labour-saving machines and nothing more ... [17]

The family saga makes clear too that it is not the country itself which the Duracks find homely: 'they found it no land for loving at first sight' (p.39). Indeed, Giblett's case that they experienced it as cruel and sadistic is compelling.[18] Rather, the motive force for the Duracks was to people the Cooper Creek region, and later the Kimberley with their own numerous tribe of interdependent Irish families:

> ...what sort of a father is it would hear of country like this [the Kimberleys] for the taking and not be securing it for his boys? How could I expect them to settle down here knowing of this pastoral paradise out west? (p.207).

Although the writer makes some gestures of common cause between the tribalism of the colonialised Irish and the Aborigines (p.150) and some solidarity as 'underdogs' (p.341), both being understood to be outsiders (Richardson), and Patsy Durack can intellectually endorse the view that the Aborigines were 'the original owners of the soil' (p.340), this amounts to little more than class-based rhetoric in the first case, and intellectual liberalism which did not give any cause for pause or interfere with in any way the wholesale appropriation of that land. He assumes it is 'for the taking'. Patsy, from 1869:

> rode about throwing open thousands of square miles of country between Kyabra Creek and the Diamentina [sic]. Sometimes this 'throwing open' meant no more than riding through, making contact with the local tribespeople, observing the waters and general topography for future reference, but often it entailed the careful selection and pegging of properties for relatives, friends or possible purchasers (p.125).

It was the better-Australian-educated nephew of Patsy, Michael, who was more aware than Patsy of the systemic injustice done to the Aborigines, though his daughter Mary Durack quite self-consciously draws veils over the 'inevitable unauthorized punitive expedition' (pp.329–30), often writing as if these were unavoidable, despite her father's insistence that they were.

THE MATTER OF IRELAND AND TROPES
OF VICTIMHOOD

The matter of Ireland looms large in Durack's family saga and is deployed strategically at crucial points in the narrative. Chapter 1, entitled 'Roots', is a highly conventional framing narrative of 'ancient wrongs and of glories still more remote' (p.27), laden with Irish historical tropes drawn from nineteenth-century nationalist primers (she tracks a well-worn path from Brian Boru, via the Book of Ballymote, confiscation of the monasteries during the Reformation, Wild Geese and the Famine, and brewing poteen as a consolation for tenancy). Two essentialising details serve the pioneer mythologizing and chime with wider already well-institutionalised discourses of Australian identity: she melds the Irish stereotype, of a '[stubborn] refusal to bend the knee' (p.28) with the Australian stereotype of the laconic bushman. Irish nobility/kingship is the subtext which explains this identity formation of rebelliousness (p.28). Their Irish past may be 'a blank to [the] Australian-born' Duracks (p.29), and she may be aware of the dangers of victim narratives, but this cultural amnesia does not stop Mary Durack, two generations later, from invoking its tropes, in the spirit of 'join-the-dots', at the start of her narrative and at *cruces* in the narrative. Her first paragraph, inscribing the family's Irish experience, becomes in fact a leitmotif for experience in a different kind of land and very different colonial conditions half a world away:

> Generations of Duracks were born around Magerareagh, which belonged to Galway until 1899, when it was moved within the boundary of Clare, and the farm on which they paid rent to some 'upstart landlord' lay close by on the slopes of Sleive [sic] Aughty Mountain. The land was poor and subject to the whims of shifting bog, serving as a constant reminder to my people of the chip they had carried on their shoulders since the year 1542 when their ancient heritage of Ogoneloe [sic] had been granted, in fee simple, to their traditional enemies. (p.27)

This passage articulates a sense of being embattled, both by the nature of the land itself (too wet in the northern hemisphere; too dry in the southern) and also by their own sense of entitlement/loss. The sense of victimhood is simply transposed and inverted in Australia, the lessons of colonialism well learnt, and compassion for the disinherited Aborigines was not part of the learning.

Australian settlement is imaged in *Kings in Grass Castles* as an unstoppable tidal movement, and later (citing John Dunmore Lang, whom she regards as a race-enemy), as a 'flood of Irish popery' (p.35), beyond the constraints of the law. She cites Governor Bourke (is his Irishness significant to her?) approvingly: 'Not all the armies in England . . . , not a hundred thousand soldiers scattered through the bush could drive back these herds within the limits of the Nineteen Counties' (of New South Wales) (p.34). She strategically mobilises another trope of the rebel Irishman to obscure a silence in the narrative, that of the literal decimation of the Karuwali within a ten-year period in the Channel country of south-west Queensland.[19x] In the account of the pacification of the Channel Country Aborigines, Grandfather Patsy is represented as having a 'thoroughly Irish antipathy' and 'half-humorous contempt of the police' (p.155). The context is an account of the savagery of the native police:

> When news [of the murder of several Aborigines in retaliation for the murder of Maloney] reached Thylungra Grandfather rode after the police party in a towering rage, demanding an explanation of their policy.
>
> 'What kind of a law is it that will train blacks to murder their own countrymen?'
>
> 'Nothing of the sort,' he was informed. 'We never recruit blacks for service in their own district. A Kalkadoon will shoot a Boontamurra at the drop of a hat and vice versa. They've been at each other's throats for generations.'
>
> Whether or not they ever made an honest attempt to reason with the now totally unpredictable tribespeople it was soon clear to all that the black troopers rode to kill – to shatter the old tribes, the Boontamurra, the Pita-Pita, the Murragon, the Waker-di, the Ngoa, the Murrawarri and the Kalkadoon, to leave men, women and children dead and dying on the plains, in the gullies and river beds. (p.154)

Although Durack's memoir must be given credit for naming these realities and for its moral sensibility (the pioneering sagas of de Satgé, Collins and Costello, by contrast, fudge such realities),[20] nevertheless the displacement of responsibility for massacres from pastoralists onto indigenous people for their own demise and the fissures in her own narrative are breathtaking when, barely a page later, she reports:

For years the black police would ride, until the country could at last be declared safe from menace – safe and quiet and the songs of dreaming stilled for all time. The police would earn the praise and thanks of the settlers for their work and a few die in the cause of duty (p.155).

In the sequel, *Sons in the Saddle*, Durack makes clear that Boxer, one of the Aboriginal retainers, was used to lead police parties to cattle spearers and rewarded for his work.[21] Although Watson admires the transparency of Durack's memoirs (pp.26–9),[22] there is much in Durack's chronicle to disturb a contemporary reader, and 'Irishness' is the discursive formation designed to generate affect and disarm the reader at critical points like the one above. The tropes she mobilises are a curious amalgam: the wild west is invoked, with the Aboriginal police, dutifully and heroically, acting as the bringers of peace in the 'unsettled districts', and this inapposite referent is yoked, contradictorily and sentimentally, with social Darwinist melancholia for the demise of whole nations. What these tropes obscure is the role of the native police as murderous agents of even more murderous settlers. Mary Durack's jocular reminder of her grandfather's Irish foible of police resistance, 'I'd sooner have an outlaw put his feet under my table … than any of that murthering gang' (p.155) (that is, the police, or native police), is a strategic attempt to rebuild semantic coherence, to paper the fissure in her own narrative, by returning to the subject of injustice towards indigenous peoples. It is, however, inapposite and inadequate to the gravity of the situation, and serves to rationalize in retrospect 'land hunger' (p.177), a land-grab, or wealth-creation enterprise (complete with account books, p.185). Patsy Durack may not have been a killer, may have had distaste for it, but the grand-daughter's writing reveals that she was obscurely aware that the family profited from it, and was complicit in silencing it, and that she must continually displace and repress the guilt in constructing the family-focused pioneer mythology by taking refuge in tropes of Irish victimhood.

The text offers further Irish-inflected rationalisations for the pioneering enterprise. When Patsy is criticised by his sons as excessively reliant on Church advice, wearing his religion on his sleeve in a specifically Irish form, his defence of the pioneer enterprise is couched in biblical (and tribal) terms:

And who could say that he had not been blessed when he rode into the lonely land with his hand in the hand of God? He had loved the country and its wild people and both had served him well. His family had grown up about him with strong bodies and good minds, his flocks and herds had increased and multiplied. He had brought people and life to the wilderness. There were homes now on the inland rivers and roads criss-crossed the vast, grass plains. He had been self-reliant, hard-working, purposeful, but every day he had acknowledged the help of God and his need of it. Some of the young people, like his own son Michael, could run rings around him in a theological argument, but their religion had become a formal thing and the saints who were so close and real to an Irish generation were far away from them – high and strange upon their heavenly thrones.

Would these young fellows, riding a new wilderness, be equally blessed? Had he done right to set them upon this adventure without wives and families to soften the harshness and loneliness of their pioneering work? Many may have considered John Costello and himself imprudent in bringing women and children to Cooper's Creek and yet it would never have occurred to them to have left their families behind. Nor would they have considered postponing their marriages until life seemed plain sailing. It had seemed to them that little worthwhile could be achieved alone. How could the country have come to life without the families – the women he had sometimes wished to the bottom of the sea, the children who had not all been spared to them? (p.280)

The rhetoric is familiar in colonialist writing,[23] but it begs a raft of questions, especially in relation to questions of land and ownership. Curiously, Patsy's repressed guilt is ameliorated by his relationship with Pumpkin: 'Somehow talking to Pumpkin helped him to cast aside his doubts. He saw it as a sign of age to lose faith in youth.' (p.281). His consolation and purpose in living was his dynasty, and biblical tropes served to give these desires shape. Curiously, too, he bound his retainers into his religion by conferring on them medals of St Patrick and St Christopher and, with their freedom, gave them horses (p.280). There is no mention of money changing hands at the point of the retainers' release.

The pastoral lands they finally acquired as a result of their epic two-year, 5,000 kilometre overland journey from Coopers Creek via the Gulf to the Ord river are also designated the 'Promised Land' (p.221), despite having to share them with hostile indigenous defenders of the territory, and crocodiles. Even termite mounds are accorded the language of sublimity and bring biblical images to mind (p.222). Mary Durack represents her family's first view of the promised land (curiously from a hill abutting a river they named after themselves, the Durack river) in a register not previously heard in the memoir, that of gothic and emphatically anti-romantic sublimity: the alien and intimidating nature of the country is acknowledged and immediately assimilated in a metaphor drawn from liturgical or regal splendour:

> Now plains and parklands faded into rugged country where they rode in weird cities of termite strongholds. Scarcely a shape that human sculptors might devise had not been wrought by these myriad white ant builders, working in the dark, conjuring fantastic biblical images, hooded and cloaked, squat Buddhas, gorillas, and madman's castles with domes, turrets and minarets. Each took its colour from the surrounding earth – red, ochre, dun-grey – some so small and fine as to crumbles under the horses' hoofs, others looming fifteen feet above the spinifex ... Far and away to the north and west ranges fell from flat tops or rugged pinnacles in folds like sculptured drapes of pallid gold studded with emeralds of spinifex (p.222).

> ...Meanwhile Stumpy Michael and Emanuel rode on through speargrass foothills and climbed ridge upon ridge to a range summit broken like the battlements of an ancient castle. Far below stretched the golden Kimberley savannah lands, cut through by green ribbons of timbered gullies and creeks (p.225).

Dominion rather than homeliness is the note struck here,[24] though the sense of being potentially mastered by the earth itself is also strong. What makes the landscape homely are the tenuous waterways, their chief reason for abandoning the Cooper Creek area where water was far less reliable or provided in oversupply in the wet.[25] Gothic sublimity and utopic rhetoric are in the above quotation strangely dialogical: they serve both to legitimate appropriation but also to defend it as much is made of the much more aggressive resistance they experienced in the East Kimberley compared with the Channel country. The landscape description also displaces the nature of the threat. Stumpy Michael and his party only narrowly escaped attack by a ceremonially decked attack-force of Kimberley defendants, courtesy of the vigilance of Pintpot and Pannikin, the Channel country retainers (p.224). Durack both criticises her ancestors and simultaneously disarms criticism by talking of the pastoral invaders as 'bound to the context of their times' in regarding indigenous people as 'another hazard to be overcome with the rest' (p.256). However, there is a defensiveness in the strategy on a range of issues: the dangers to stock and pastoralists, and the lethal stealth of Aborigines are continually insisted upon (pp.307); she is fatalistic about antagonism being reduced to an 'us or them' fight for survival (p.320); there is an avoidance of the ethical implications of the manoeuvre whereby they acquired new biddable station workers:

overlanders had somehow acquired a few native boys between eight and fourteen years old. How they got hold of them was nobody's business, but whether by fair means or foul they were to stand a better chance of survival in the years to come than their bush tribespeople (p.291).

The narrative makes clear that Ulysses and Maggie were survivors of a massacre in retaliation for a spearing (p.330). Most tellingly, and the language reveals a repressed knowledge of complicity, she lays at the feet of police 'the *inevitable* unauthorized punitive expedition' (present writer's emphasis, pp.329–30) in retaliation for individual European deaths. The subtext of massacres is strong and frequently the narrative hints that it knows more than it will divulge, even naming '[t]he conspiracy of silence that sealed the lips of the pioneers' (p.301); nevertheless, every time she approaches the subject of massacres, there is a deflection of the narrative with Irish tropes. For example, 1892–3 was a very turbulent period in the East Kimberley with twenty-three Miriwoong people killed in retaliation for the death of trooper Collins near Durack's and Kilfoyle's Rosewood Station.[26] Durack reports it in these terms:

> At Argyle the old year '92 ushered out to the tune of 'Auld Lang Syne' lustily rendered by the family and a large police party under Sergeant Lavery then organising a 'surprise drive' on the persistent cattle spearers. (p.340)

Durack complicity in the raid would seem almost certain, if only to the extent of providing a base for the troopers' 'military campaign'.[27] However, the narrative minimises the settlers' campaign, and again at a strategic point deflects the argument into Irish victim tropes that are only tangentially relevant but designed to represent Patsy in the best possible light and draw attention away from the perpetrators. Patsy is represented as siding with Irish-born Bishop Matthew Gibney, widely regarded as one of the most outspoken critics of 'punitive expeditions' against Aborigines.[28] In October 1892, Gibney had been critical of the north-west settlers for engaging in indiscriminate killings of Aboriginal people in response to sheep killings. The report of his speech (originally published in the *West Australian Catholic Record* on 13 October) ignited a correspondence in the *West Australian* between 1 and 27 October 1892. Attacked by the (Protestant) squatter, Charles Harper of De Grey Station (Port Hedland), Gibney had risen to the sectarian bait and defended the 'few real atrocities committed by the Irish...against the strong' and Durack cites Gibney's article, with strategic omissions.[29] Mary Durack registers that Irish atrocities constitute a red herring in the massacre debate, but this insight does not prevent her from elaborating at length, again making reference to a suite of narratives of Irish victimisation:

A keen admirer of the forthright Bishop and a loyal supporter of Parnell and the Nationalist movement, much of his old fire returned as he now denounced the increased powers of the police and the flogging of cattle spearers. His brother Galway Jerry disagreed with him, insisting that nothing short of flogging was merited by blacks who would cut the tongues and tails from living animals.

'And how are we to teach them that such things are cruel and that the branding, ear-marking and castrating that we do to the living beasts are not?' Grandfather demanded. 'Just read here now what the Bishop has to say of it all.'

Galway Jerry glanced cursorily through the letters.[30]

'What! Not the Irish question again!'

'The Irish question!' Grandfather exclaimed indignantly.

And you but for the Grace of God born to starve in the poor famine stricken country! Ye are like the rest of them, Jerry, born with a silver spoon in your mouth and little thought in your head for the under-dog.'

'It's precious little silver we can lay our hands on these days,' Jerry laughed, 'and there'd be none at all soon if we left the running of the country to you and the Bishop.'

Grandfather had no higher opinion of the police in Kimberley than he had had for the same body in Queensland.

'Ye're all useless anyway without the blacks to help you with the dirty work,' he remarked in reply to the sergeant's complaint that they had found the patrolling of the countryside a thankless task. (pp.340–1)

What the Bishop Gibney-initiated newspaper slanging match was about was not punishments for mistreating animals but the much more sinister enterprise of payback for the death of trooper Collins and eliminating a guerrilla force led by Jandamarra.[31] Stock-spearing was just the visible manifestation of this warfare, and to render it the central issue was to trivialise the power and tenacity with which the Bunuba attempted to hold onto their lands, and the effects of the answering massacres conducted by the settlers. The *Catholic Record* of 10 August 1893 talked of a 'pile of dead victims' and a 'massacre'.[32] The story of Bunuba resistance, mutinies by armed native police, and the (overly romanticised?) Jandamarra whose daring exploits, designed to humiliate the police, made Ned Kelly look like an amateur must have been known to the Duracks because their associate, Isadore Emanuel J.P., was closely involved with prosecuting the Bunuba resisters.[33] What interests me here, though, are the ways in which tropes of Irish victimisation (in this case the fall and death of Parnell which had occurred only two years previously) are mobilised to render the squatters the victim class. Patsy, Irishman and 'underdog' (p.341), is constructed as standing out against his own more complicit sons in an attempt to distance the family from the Protestant squatters more active in warfare against the hostile defenders of territory.

There is, of course, a palpable irony in the use of such terms as 'Irish' and 'underdog' on the frontier. While the Duracks may have a much more distinguished record in relation to Aborigines than many of their squat-tocratic peers, sentimental mobilisation of the tropes of Irishness is clearly a diversionary tactic and a means to cheap affect in *Kings in Grass Castles*, used in tricksy and slippery rhetorical ways as counters in the construction of a pioneer hero mythos. Durack's identification with her own pastoral class may not be transparent in this text, but it is implied despite the smokescreen of class-based difference identified as Irish in this text. Further, what it demonstrates is the way in which institutionalising pioneer discourses which underline suffering, victimhood and fellow-feeling, enable the too-easy transformation of the 'wild' and 'savage' into the 'tame', and in turn paradoxically legitimate the theatre of cruelty on the frontier. Just who deals out terror is the barely repressed sub-text.

NOTES

1. David Walker, *Dream and Disillusion: A Search for Australian Cultural Identity* (Canberra: Australian National University Press, 1976).
2. Pamela Watson, *Frontier Lands and Pioneer Legends: How Pastoralists Gained Karuwali Land* (St Leonards, NSW: Allen & Unwin, 1998).
3. Henry Reynolds, *Aborigines and Settlers: The Australian Experience, 1788–1939* (North Melbourne, Vic.: Cassell Australia, 1972); Henry Reynolds, *Dispossession: Black Australians and White Invaders* (Sydney: Allen & Unwin, 1989); Henry Reynolds, *Frontier: Aborigines, Settlers and Land* (Sydney: Allen & Unwin, 1987); Henry Reynolds, *Race Relations in North Queensland* (Townsville, Queensland: History Dept. James Cook University of North Queensland, 1978); Henry Reynolds and James Cook University of North Queensland. History Dept., *The Other Side of the Frontier: An Interpretation of the Aboriginal Response to the Invasion and Settlement of Australia* (Townsville, Qld.: History Dept., James Cook University, 1981); C.D. Rowley, *Outcasts in White Australia*, Vol.2 (Canberra: Australian National University Press, 1971); C.D. Rowley, *The Destruction of Aboriginal Society* (Ringwood, Vic.: Penguin Books Australia, 1972).
4. More localised histories include those of F.S. Stevens, Bruce Petty and Academy of the Social Sciences in Australia., *Aborigines in the Northern Territory Cattle Industry* (Canberra: Australian National University Press, 1974); L.A. Riddett, *Kine, Kin and Country: The Victoria River District of the Northern Territory 1911–1966* (Darwin: Australian National University, North Australia Research Unit, 1990); Deborah Bird Rose, *Hidden Histories: Black Stories from Victoria River Downs, Humbert River and Wave Hill Stations* (Canberra: Aboriginal Studies Press, 1991); Watson, *Frontier Lands and Pioneer Legends*; Noel Loos,

Invasion and Resistance: Aboriginal–European Relations on the North Queensland Frontier, 1861–1897 (Canberra: Australian National University Press, 1982); Ann McGrath, *Born in the Cattle: Aborigines in Cattle Country* (Sydney: Allen & Unwin, 1987); Dawn May, *Aboriginal Labour and the Cattle Industry: Queensland from White Settlement to the Present* (Cambridge and Melbourne: Cambridge University Press, 1994); Heather Goodall, *Invasion to Embassy: Land in Aboriginal Politics in New South Wales, 1770–1972* (St Leonards, NSW: Allen & Unwin in association with Black Books, 1996); Watson, *Frontier Lands and Pioneer Legends*; Richard Munro Baker, *Land Is Life: From Bush to Town: The Story of the Yanyuwa People* (St Leonards, NSW: Allen & Unwin, 1999); Mary Anne Jebb, *Blood, Sweat and Welfare: A History of White Bosses and Aboriginal Pastoral Workers* (Nedlands, WA: University of Western Australia Press, 2002); Tony Roberts, *Frontier Justice: A History of the Gulf Country to 1900* (St Lucia: University of Queensland Press, 2005).

5. Bill Rosser, *Dreamtime Nightmares* (Ringwood (Victoria): Penguin Books, 1987); Jolly Read and Peter Coppin, *Kangkusho: The Life of Nyamal Lawman Peter Coppin* (Canberra: Aboriginal Studies Press, 1999); May, *Aboriginal Labour and the Cattle Industry: Queensland from White Settlement to the Present*; McGrath, *Born in the Cattle: Aborigines in Cattle Country*; Peter Read, Jay Read and Institute for Aboriginal Development (Alice Springs, NT), *Long Time, Olden Time: Aboriginal Accounts of Northern Territory History* (Institute for Aboriginal Development Publications, Alice Springs, NT, 1991); Paul Marshall and Eric Lawford, *Raparapa Kularr Martuwarra: All Right, Now We Go 'Side the River, Along That Sundown Way, Stories* (Broome, WA: Magabala Books, 1988).

6. Watson, *Frontier Lands and Pioneer Legends*.

7. Robert Foster, 'Rations, Coexistence, and the Colonisation of Aboriginal Labour in the South Australian Pastoral Industry, 1860–1911', *Aboriginal History*, xxiv (2004), pp.2–26.

8. Jebb, *Blood, Sweat and Welfare*, p.168.

9. Franca Tamisari and John Bradley, 'To Have and to Give the Law: 'Animal Names, Place and Event', Unpublished paper, 2003, http://www.istitutoveneto.it/iv/attivita/convegniescuole/animali/IV_Tamisari.DOC [accessed 28 July 2005].

10. Mary Durack, *Kings in Grass Castles* (London: Corgi Books, 1959). References hereafter are to this edition.

11. Rod Giblett, 'Kings in Kimberley Watercourses: Sadism and Pastoralism', *SPAN Journal of the South Pacific Association for Commonwealth Literature and Language Studies*, 36 (1993), p.541.

12. Riddett, *Kine, Kin and Country*, p.xi.

13. Omissions of this kind are remedied in *Sons in the Saddle* (London: Constable, 1983), with many Aboriginal retainers being listed and more frequent deployment of the names of Aboriginal nations, and occasional references of an ethnographic nature, pp.74, 77, 138.

14. Tom Griffiths, *Hunters and Collectors: The Antiquarian Imagination in Australia* (Cambridge and Melbourne: Cambridge University Press, 1996).

15. Watson, *Frontier Lands and Pioneer Legends*.

16. Ibid., p.27.

17. Matthew Gibney, 'Bishop Gibney and the nor'-West Settlers. To the Editor,' *West Australian*, 25 October 1892.

18. Giblett, 'Kings in Kimberley Watercourses', pp.448–9.

19. Watson, *Frontier Lands and Pioneer Legends*, *passim*.

20. Ibid., pp.11–25.

21. Durack, *Sons in the Saddle* (London: Constable, 1983).

22. Watson, *Frontier Lands and Pioneer Legends*, pp.26–9.

23. Giblett, 'Kings in Kimberley Watercourses', p.541.

24. See also Giblett, 'Kings in Kimberley Watercourses'.

25. Ibid., p.542.

26. Howard Pedersen and Banjo Woorunmurra, *Jandamarra and the Bunuba Resistance* (Broome, WA: Magabala Books, 1995), p.92.

27. Ibid.

28. John W. Harris, *One Blood: 200 Years of Aboriginal Encounter with Christianity: A Story of Hope* (Sutherland, NSW: Albatross Books, 1990), pp.431–49; D.F. Bourke and Catholic Church, Archdiocese of Perth (WA), *The History of the Catholic Church in Western Australia* (Perth: Archdiocese of Perth, 1979), pp.100, 143–56.

29. Durack cites Bishop Gibney's response to Charles Harper of De Gray Station very selectively on p.340 of *Kings in Grass Castles*. She omits the reference to murders by settlers, and Gibney's claims that attacks on sheep were occasioned by drought-induced famine, and overlooks his claim that the north had been depopulated by 50 per cent. The original text reads, with Durack's omissions or changes in italics:

> ... the few real atrocities in Ireland were those of the weak against the strong, and founded on centuries of misrule. *Not so with the white settlers whose deliberate murders in no single instance met with the punishment that invariably overtook the blackfellow convicted of a similar crime against the invaders of his country. I can point to manifesto after manifesto* issued by Nationalist leaders against genuine atrocities in Ireland, but I have never yet seen the squatters of this Colony, as a body, or their representatives, do anything but take part against the efforts of the Government to stamp out the willful and deliberate murders by the alleged 'few', *of the original owners of the soil*. (*West Australian*, 19 October 1892, p.3).

Nor does she pick up the point made by Quabba, one of the defenders of Gibney, that Maoris had been recompensed for their land (Letter to the editor, *West Australian*, 15 October 1892, p.6).

30. Galway Jerry was subsequently murdered in 1901 by Aborigines. Although Durack denies that he had been involved with an Aboriginal woman and that payback for stealing women was unusual motivation for Aboriginal-initiated murder on the frontier, subsequent histories of black/white relations on the frontier would suggest that the intention to steal flour and stores was unlikely to have been the motive and that murders over women were common both among Aboriginal men themselves and also against white men who did not honour their reciprocal obligations (Roberts, *Frontier Justice*, p.107). Durack demonstrates her awareness of the breach of 'tribal marriage laws' white liaisons with indigenous women entailed, and declares such liaisons to have been 'purely physical ... devoid of any emotional involvement' (Durack, *Sons in the Saddle*, p.197).

31. Pedersen and Woorunmurra, *Jandamarra and the Bunuba Resistance*.

32. Ibid., p.92.

33. Ibid., p.97.

9

A Sense of Place: Monastic Scenes in Irish-Australian Funerary Monuments

Pamela O'Neill

James Stapleton, only son of Stephen and Bridget Stapleton of the Harp of Erin Hotel, Queen Street, Melbourne, died on 17 April 1881, shortly before his thirteenth birthday.[1] His parents sought out the prominent firm of monumental masons, Jageurs and Son, to erect a memorial over his grave in the Melbourne General Cemetery (see Figure 1).

The monument is now in a sad state of disrepair, but we can obtain a very clear idea of its original grandeur by reference to a monument created some ten years later by the same Jageurs and Son, and erected in the Kilmore Catholic Cemetery in memory of Bridget Rush (see Figure 2).

These two monuments are part of a very small group of Irish-Australian funerary monuments which allow us to trace an interesting development in the expression of a sense of place, seen very clearly amongst many Irish migrants to Australia. This same phenomenon that I call sense of place[2] can also be seen in the high proportion of Irish-Australian funerary monuments, including several of those that I consider here, which proclaim the Irish county or parish of origin of the decedent.

On their deaths, Stephen and Bridget Stapleton were interred with James in the family burial plot and added to the inscription on the monument. We thus learn that Stephen Stapleton was a native of Roscrea, County Tipperary. Bridget was also born in Tipperary.[3] They married in Australia,[4] and opened the Harp of Erin Hotel in 1868,[5] the same year that James was born. Presumably the hotel was successful and Stephen and Bridget good at business, for when tragedy struck twelve years later they commissioned an impressive and expensive monument from a leading monumental mason, who had previously practised in Tullamore and Dublin.[6]

Unfortunately, the damage to the Stapleton monument means that we cannot retrieve its full iconographic programme. However, of the significant inserts on the upper tier which probably all bore visual, rather than textual, embellishment, one can be almost fully reconstructed (see Figure 3).

Figure 1: Memorial to James Stapleton

Figure 2: Memorial to Bridget Rush

Figure 3: Close-up of Memorial to James Stapleton

This depicts a landscape scene, which can readily be associated with Ireland. Against a background of gentle hills, a round tower with a conical roof rises in high relief. Reclining at the foot of the tower is what is undoubtedly an Irish wolfhound. The scene is quite pastoral, and although the tower is almost certainly monastic in origin, that aspect of it is not given particular prominence in this depiction.

What, then, can we say about this scene? I suggest that it refers to a remembered Ireland of Stephen Stapleton's past. The sweeping hills, round tower and wolfhound are archetypal images of rural Ireland. Roscrea is in a typically agricultural district of rolling hills, and is home to an early monastic site with a round tower. These symbols compare to the Irish harp, and indeed the female personification of Ireland playing a harp, which became a prominent motif in Celtic revival iconography.[7] Those motifs and this scene all represent Irishness. However, unlike the woman or the harp, I would argue that there is a stronger sense in which the tower scene represents specifically the Irish landscape as a place, whether of geography or of the imagination. The simple lines of this sculpture are remarkably evocative for such an economical arrangement and testify to the skill of the masons.

This, however, is a relatively early work for the Jageurs firm in Australia. Although there is not currently evidence to date it precisely, it seems likely to have been erected in the 1880s, within a few years of James Stapleton's death. Peter Jageurs had been working in Melbourne since

Figure 4: Memorial to Patrick Moloney

1870,[8] but had not previously included specifically Irish iconography of this order in his monuments, and it seems that his son Morgan had not yet joined him in the business. Morgan is reported as having joined the firm in 1892, after travelling and studying abroad.[9]

A slightly later memorial was made by Jageurs and Son and erected, also in the Melbourne General Cemetery, to Patrick Moloney after Moloney's death in 1888 (see Figure 4).

It is likely that by the time this monument was made Peter Jageurs' son Morgan had begun to have some involvement in the business.[10] Two of the panels on the front of the cross feature quintessentially Irish landscape scenes. The upper, in low relief, has the female personification of Ireland, seated in the countryside playing an Irish harp with an Irish wolfhound at her feet (see Figure 5).

In the other landscape, in very high relief, a round tower on a small hill is flanked on the right by a tall church with a gothic window and on the left by a high cross in its stone base (see Figure 6).

Figure 5: Close-up 1 of Memorial to Patrick Moloney

Figure 6: Close-up 2 of Memorial to Patrick Moloney

The tower in this particular depiction is broken off at the top, as are many of the surviving examples at monastic sites. This scene differs from that on the Stapleton monument in that, although the round tower is still central to the scene, the composition is now clearly monastic, attested by the presence of the cross and the church. I would suggest that this scene may be intended to represent an actual physical place in Ireland, since it seems to be a one-off design. It is conceivable that it represents Clonmacnois, County Offaly, where there is a similar high cross, a broken round tower on a small hill, and a ruined cathedral with a window of roughly the same shape as that in the church on the monument. The disposition of the three elements in the scene is not as it is at Clonmacnois, which is not unexpected. Rather than a realistic rendition, it is more likely to be a representational depiction, tailored to fit the space on the monument.

Patrick Moloney, to whom this monument was initially erected, was born in Ireland in 1817. He married in Ireland, and had a son called Patrick, born in 1843, whom I shall call Patrick Junior for the sake of clarity. When Patrick Junior was still a child, the family migrated to Victoria. Patrick Junior attended St Patrick's College and, subsequently, was one of the three students to enrol in the first intake for the medical degree at the University of Melbourne in 1862. He became a successful medical practitioner, active in the Medical Society of Victoria, a university lecturer at Melbourne Hospital, and doctor to the St Vincent de Paul orphanage for boys. He edited the *Australian Medical Journal*, contributed to *Punch*, wrote and published poetry, and associated with Australian writers like Marcus Clarke and Henry Kendall.[11] He was clearly a professional, social and financial success.

Patrick Senior, by contrast, was not a particularly prominent citizen, and there is no reference in the inscription to his place of birth or any other accomplishments. Why, then, did his son commission this distinctive memorial with its overt references to Ireland and the Irish landscape? Although involved, at least in a professional capacity, with organisations such as St Vincent de Paul, Patrick Junior showed no strong attachment to Irish institutions in Australia or Ireland and no particular affection for a real or imagined Ireland. His poetry is replete with classical references, and those of his poetic compositions which refer to place are preoccupied with his adopted home, rather than the land of his birth.[12] He died in Lancashire, England, in 1904,[13] apparently not returning to Ireland, despite his proximity to it for the last six years of his life.

Patrick Moloney Senior probably retained an emotional attachment to the land and landscape of his birth, and at the time of his death either his son Patrick or his widow Ellen deemed it appropriate to signify this on his grave marker. The monastic scene, possibly Clonmacnois, occupies the most prominent position on the monument and is in the most distinctive sculptural style (the tower, in particular, is more than half-round, while all the remaining sculptural panels are in low relief). This prominence argues a particular attachment to this specific aspect of the Irish landscape, that is the legacy of the early monastic movement, and possibly to the actual site at Clonmacnois, if indeed it is that which is depicted.

The memorial to Bridget Rush in the Kilmore Catholic Cemetery is a complex and highly symbolic monument (see fig. 2), as indeed the Stapleton monument may once have been. The symbolism on the Rush monument primarily reflects Catholic beliefs and the memory of the departed. There is a range of sentimental poetry, symbolic floral emblems, sacred monograms and sacred heart emblems. The Celtic cross atop the monument features a harp surrounded by shamrocks, declaring the Irish associations implicit in the decedent's Christian name.

There is a monastic landscape scene on one side of the monument, in a similar inset panel to that on the Stapleton monument. Like the Stapleton scene, the landscape on the Rush monument is dominated by the central round tower in high relief (see Figure 7).

Figure 7: Close-up of Memorial to Bridget Rush

This round tower is surmounted by a conical roof like the Stapleton one. There is a high cross to the right of the tower, and a large church to its left. In the background, the setting sun's rays can be seen between the mountains. I believe that the scene represents the early monastic site at Glendalough, County Wicklow. The round tower at Glendalough has remained intact except for a short period in the nineteenth century, when the roof was struck by lightning and then reconstructed.[14] There are several high crosses and churches in the vicinity of the round tower. A view towards the Upper Lake at Glendalough would place the cathedral, the largest church building, to the left of the tower, as in the depiction on the Rush monument.

Bridget Rush was apparently much loved and greatly mourned, having apparently died in the course of giving birth to an only son.[15] The words 'beloved' and 'deeply regretted' feature heavily in the newspaper notices, which is somewhat unusual. Bridget's death and funeral notices appeared in the *Argus* on two consecutive days, and a full requiem mass was celebrated for her at St Patrick's church, Kilmore, an expensive undertaking and not at all commonplace.[16] The evidence of the monument suggests that it was erected within two years of the funeral,[17] again, not at all commonplace. The significant expense of this grand memorial was apparently overshadowed by the mourners' urge to commemorate Bridget publicly.[18]

Both Thomas's and Bridget's parents were probably migrants from Ireland, although Thomas and Bridget may have been born in Australia. I suggest that the use of this scene deliberately looks back to a remembered landscape. It is interesting that the idea of a remembered landscape seems in this case to have been transmitted to the next generation, a generation which had perhaps never seen Ireland.

The Jageurs' masons – and I would suggest that responsibility for the design of this monument rests firmly with Morgan Jageurs[19] – clearly rose to the challenge of portraying the early Irish monastic scene with considerable competence, if not outright relish. If the resemblance of the scene to Glendalough is not mere coincidence, it could be that Morgan Jageurs, too, was referring to a remembered Ireland. This memory could have been quite a recent one. He had last left Ireland in 1890, and although we have no clear idea of his activities whilst in Ireland it is not unlikely that he travelled there. I contend that the Rush monument was completed less than three years after Jageurs' return to Melbourne.

An informed, politically active and well-travelled expatriate, it would have been natural for Morgan Jageurs to have taken an interest in the antiquities of his homeland. They were a source of considerable pride, and also something of a rallying point, for nationalists with an antiquarian or scholarly bent. They demonstrably pre-dated English or Norman interference in Ireland and were thus a just source of pride in the Gaelic past (although not without complications).[20] Several leading scholars of early Ireland were also political activists, such as Eoin MacNeill, Professor of Early and Medieval Irish History at University College Dublin, who was imprisoned for some years for his political activities. Information about Ireland's monastic sites would have been readily available to Jageurs through his extensive network of political contacts on both sides of the world. Some indication of this network is given, for instance, by the fact that Michael Davitt was godfather to Jageurs' son, John.[21]

Books about Ireland's antiquities were published throughout the nineteenth century, many lavishly illustrated with drawings of monastic ruins and high crosses. Some were printed or reprinted in Sydney by McNeil and Coffee.[22] Others were undoubtedly included in the regular shipments received by such establishments as Melbourne's Catholic Book Depot, and some were acquired by the Melbourne Public Library.[23] Patrick O'Farrell suggests that Jageurs based many of his designs on 'models' in Henry O'Neill's *Illustrations of the Most Interesting of the Sculptured Crosses of Ireland*.[24] This seems unlikely, since the book's illustrations do not include many of the features found on Jageurs' monuments. Specifically, the only monastic scene illustrated in O'Neill's book is Monasterboice, which is distinctly unlike any of the monastic scenes sculpted by Jageurs and described here. O'Farrell's suggestion is also taken up more generally by Jonathan Wooding,[25] but I think that both overlook the proliferation of such books at the time, and their ready availability in Australia. This proliferation implies that the Melbourne Irish community was well-informed and highly interested in the early medieval monastic antiquities of Ireland, which probably generated the conditions necessary for Jageurs to create his designs, without necessarily implying his direct reliance on any such models. Jageurs had spent the first four years of his life in the immediate vicinity of the high cross at Durrow, and on his return trips to Ireland almost undoubtedly visited family members in the Tullamore–Durrow region. It is inconceivable that Jageurs, who was passionately interested in Irish history and spent time in Ireland, would have been entirely reliant on illustrations printed in a book for models for his designs.

The monument to Henry O'Brien in the Melbourne General Cemetery contains mixed symbolism (see Figure 8).

It was made by J. Robinson of Carlton. The monument is primarily classical in design, featuring draped urns and classical decorative motifs, but it is surmounted by a Celtic cross. On the front and back faces of the cross are a harp with shamrocks, a wolfhound in front of a setting sun, and a landscape scene. This landscape is, on first impressions, very similar to the Jageurs' monastic landscapes, but it is not identifiably monastic (see Figure 9).

It has no high cross, and the building is not necessarily a church. The round tower is very like a monastic round tower, but its top is neither conical nor broken, but crenellated, so it is not an accurate depiction of a monastic round tower.[26] The Jageurs' masons were able to represent such details correctly, doubtless through a combination of personal familiarity, access to illustrations and sheer skill. It seems likely, though, that the mason Robinson, whose mark is clear on the monument, but of whom I can find no record, had considerably less familiarity with Ireland and its antiquities.

The monument reveals that Henry O'Brien was a 'native of Co. Louth' but 'late of Victoria Hotel Port Melbourne'. He died in 1898 at the age of either 70 or 71 years,[27] and his monument uses the formula 'in loving memory of', suggesting that there was someone left behind to remember him lovingly. He seems not to have had children, though, and his property, including the Victoria Hotel, was inherited by a Mary Josephine O'Brien,[28] later MacGregor, who appears to have been his niece, and who, after her death in 1932, was added to the inscriptions on the monument. O'Brien's death and funeral notices appeared in both the *Argus* and the *Age*. Interestingly, there is an explicit request in the death notice for 'Home papers' to 'please copy'. The notice indicates that he was the 'son of Andrew O'Brien of Black Rock, county Lough [*sic*], Ireland'.

Figure 8: Memorial to Henry O'Brien

Figure 9: Close-up of Memorial to Henry O'Brien

Henry O'Brien was clearly Irish, and presumably Catholic. The Catholic Irish mason of choice, Jageurs, may not have been available to make his monument. O'Brien died in 1898, and we know that Jageurs was in Ireland in 1901.[29] Given that monuments were usually constructed some years after interment, it seems likely that O'Brien's monument may have been commissioned while Jageurs was in Ireland. The monument nonetheless makes an overt visual association with an Irish place, in its landscape scene and associated symbols. It may have been commissioned by Henry's niece, Mary, or by one of Henry's brothers.[30] Combined with the evidence of the death notices, it suggests that Henry retained very strong ties with Ireland, to the extent that news of his death was expected to be of interest to the 'home' newspapers and their readers. The quasi-monastic scene is very interesting, in that it presents yet another version of this motif, and if indeed it is intended as a monastic scene, it shows yet again this attachment to a remembered Ireland represented by the remains of the early Christian monastic past.

Henry O'Brien was from County Louth, home of Monasterboice, one of the most significant early monastic sites. Not only is Monasterboice significant, it was also the recipient of considerable antiquarian attention in the eighteenth and nineteenth centuries, and therefore well publicised and presumably well known. It was the only monastic scene illustrated in Henry O'Neill's 1857 book of drawings.[31] If Henry O'Brien had retained his ties with Ireland, as is suggested by his death notices, it is quite likely that his brothers had done so too, and he may even have regaled his niece

Mary with stories of the venerable antiquities of his home. It is not unexpected to find that the commissioner of Henry's grave marker sought to immortalise his connection with that place. Interestingly, because they commissioned Robinson, and not Jageurs, to construct the monument, the representation is not quite as one might expect. One can only speculate as to the likelihood of Robinson having based his depiction on an imperfectly understood observation of the Jageurs' monuments, although with published drawings of the scenes so readily available this should not have been necessary. One can, however, say with reasonable certainty that his depiction was not informed by the same familiarity and skill as those by Jageurs and Son.

Here, then, over something like seventeen years, is a sequence of funerary monuments which tell an interesting story. An enduring sense of place and attachment to a remembered Ireland are expressed through the medium of depictions of early Irish monastic remains. The brilliant monumental mason Morgan Jageurs, whose family had migrated from Tullamore to Melbourne, was at the heart of this expression. The appropriation of Ireland's venerable monastic past by antiquarians devoted to the nationalist cause must surely underlie this fascinating regional development, which seems to have been unique to Melbourne in the late nineteenth century, where Irish nationalist politics also found fierce expression.

NOTES

1. *Argus*, 18 April 1881, 'Deaths': 'STAPLETON – On the 17th inst., at the residence of his parents, Harp of Erin Hotel, Queen-street, Melbourne, James, the beloved and only son of Mr Stephen Stapleton, aged 12 years and 10 months.'
2. The term has frequently been used when discussing the Irish: see, for example, Patrick O'Farrell, 'Defining place and home: are the Irish prisoners of place?', in David Fitzpatrick (ed.), *Home or Away? Immigrants in Colonial Australia* (Canberra: Australian National University, 1992).
3. 'Marriages', *The Victorian Pioneers Index 1837–1888* (Melbourne: Royal Melbourne Institute of Technology and Registry of Births, Deaths and Marriages Victoria, 1994) CD-ROM.
4. 'Marriages', *Victorian Pioneers Index*.
5. Clare Wright, *Beyond the Ladies Lounge: Australia's Female Publicans* (Melbourne: University of Melbourne, 2003), p.4.
6. *Advocate*, 1 January 1881, p.2: 'Monumental masons'.
7. The motif of the woman playing the harp, often accompanied by other 'Irish' symbols such as the shamrock or wolfhound, is to be seen on many funerary monuments, as well as other Celtic Revival objects.
8. Geoffrey Serle, 'Jageurs, Morgan Peter', in *Australian Dictionary of Biography* (Melbourne: Melbourne University Press, 1983), Vol 9, p.462.
9. Serle, 'Jageurs', p.462. However, shipping records show that Morgan Jageurs returned to Melbourne on the SS Orient, arriving in October 1890: 'Voyages to Victoria', http://shippinglists.museum.vic.gov.au/voyage.asp?ID=1002 [accessed 28 September 2005]. It

seems unlikely that he would have left Melbourne again for any protracted period between this arrival and his marriage on 17 February 1892. I suggest that Morgan may have taken on an 'official' role in the business, such as partnership, in 1892, but that he participated in the design and execution of monuments from his arrival in 1890.

10. Particularly since he was apparently present in Melbourne from 1890; see note 9 above.

11. 'Moloney, Patrick', *Australian Dictionary of Biography*, Vol 5, p.266.

12. For example, 'O sweet Queen-city of the golden South', from 'Sonnets – Ad Innuptam', in W. Murdoch (ed.), *A Book of Australasian Verse* (London: Oxford University Press, 1924), p.42.

13. 'Moloney, Patrick', *Australian Dictionary of Biography*, Vol. 5, p.266.

14. P.J. Noonan, *Glendalough and the Seven Churches of St Kevin* (Kilmantin Hill: P.J. Noonan, 1959: 7th ed), p.37. The reconstruction was carried out in 1876 by the Board of Works.

15. *Argus*, 4 September 1893, 'Deaths': 'Rush – on the 1st inst., at Kilmore, Ormond Thomas Murray, only son of T.J. and the late Bridget Francis Rush, aged 2 years and 3 months. R.I.P.' Ormond's death at the age of two years and three months occurred two years and three months after Bridget's. The births of four daughters were recorded before Ormond's birth: 'Births', *Victorian pioneers index*.

16. *Argus* 15 and 16 June 1891, 'Funerals' and 'Deaths'.

17. The layout of the inscription strongly suggests that the portion referring to Ormond is a later addition, a suggestion strongly supported by the differing scripts of the two portions. Surely, if the completion of the monument post-dated Ormond's death two years after his mother's, the entire inscription would have been made at one time and in a single script.

18. Dianne Hall and Lindsay Proudfoot, 'Memory and identity among Irish and Scots migrants in nineteenth-century Stawell', in Elizabeth Malcolm and Brad Paterson (eds), *Celtic Connections: Irish and Scottish Studies Down Under* (forthcoming), demonstrate that a 'polished marble monument' would cost the price of a small house in a town in Victoria: Bridget Rush's monument probably cost considerably more.

19. If, as I argue (see note 17), the monument was designed and created between Bridget's death in June 1891 and Ormond's in September 1893, Morgan Jageurs was certainly present in Melbourne, and probably involved in monument design for the family business.

20. See, for example, Clare O'Halloran, *Golden Ages and Barbarous Nations* (Cork: Cork University Press, 2004), passim.

21. Jageurs to Henry Bournes Higgins, 19 February 1917: National Library of Australia MS 1057: 273.

22. For example John Savage (ed.), *Picturesque Ireland: A Literary and Artistic Delineation of its Scenery, Antiquities, Buildings, Abbeys, etc* (New York: Thomas Kelly, ND [c1880]; repr Sydney: McNeil and Coffee, ND [c1880]); Martin Haverty, *The History of Ireland from the Earliest Period to the Present Time* (Sydney: McNeil and Coffee, 1882). I am very grateful to Tony Earls for his assistance in identifying these works and those listed in note 23.

23. For example S.C. Hall, *Ireland: Its Scenery, Character &c* (London: How and Parsons, 1842); George Petrie, *The Ecclesiastical Architecture of Ireland, anterior to the Anglo-Norman Invasion* (Dublin: Hodges and Smith, 1845); Henry O'Neill, *Illustrations of the Most Interesting of the Sculptured Crosses of Ancient Ireland* (London: Henry O'Neill, 1857).

24. Patrick O'Farrell, *The Irish in Australia* (Sydney: University of New South Wales Press, 1986), pp.178–9.

25. Jonathan Wooding, 'Irish-Australian monuments and the discourse of the Celtic Revival', in Rebecca Pelan, Noel Quirke and Mark Finnane (eds), *Irish-Australian Studies: Papers Delivered at the Seventh Irish-Australian Conference* (Sydney: Crossing Press, 1994), p.4.

26. Except that the round towers at Cloyne, County Cork, and Kildare, County Kildare, were rebuilt with crenellated parapets: Kathleen Hughes and Ann Hamlin, *The Modern Traveller to the Early Irish Church* (New York: Seabury, 1977), p.70.

27. *Argus*, 15 August 1898, 'Deaths': 'O'Brien: On the 13th August, at his residence, Victoria Hotel, Bay-street, Port Melbourne, Henry O'Brien, son of Andrew O'Brien, of Black Rock, county Lough, Ireland, in his 71st year. R.I.P. Home papers please copy.'

28. David Thompson, Port Melbourne Historical & Preservation Society, personal communication, 10 January 2005.
29. Jageurs to Higgins, 19 February 1917.
30. Mary's father James seems likely to have been Henry's brother, as also does Edward O'Brien, who was occupier of the Victoria Hotel during Henry's ownership: Thompson, personal communication.
31. O'Neill, *Illustrations*, p.36.

PART III
Citizenship

10

Irish Influence on Van Diemen's Land/Tasmania from Bushrangers to the Celtic Tiger[1]

Richard P. Davis

In his influential book *The Irish in Australia*, the late Patrick O'Farrell claimed that the Irish provided the true dynamic of Australian history. He argued that the Australian Irish, unlike their counterparts in North America, were more concerned to assimilate with the local majority than to establish an Irish-oriented enclave.[2] Surveying the impact of the Irish on the small island state of Tasmania, O'Farrell's striking generalisations can be tested in the Australian island state, whose area is close to that of the Republic of Ireland.[3]

Established in 1803 as a convict colony, Van Diemen's Land, formally renamed Tasmania, in 1856 became a self-governing colony. In 1900 it joined the Australian Federation as a state. Irish influence can be summarised under seven categories: the convict period, the establishment of infrastructure, Orange and Green rivalry, education (primary and university), support for Irish independence, democratisation through the Labor party, and the attempted emulation of Ireland's recent economic success.

1. THE CONVICT PERIOD, 1803–53

The convict period from the first settlement at Risdon Cove in 1803 to the arrival of the last convict transport in 1853 fully engaged Irish people at all levels. The initial settlement included Irish convicts, male and female, ordinary criminals and political prisoners from the 1798 Rebellion, Irish soldiers and an Anglo-Irish officer. The first white child to be born in Van Diemen's Land was the daughter of an Irish woman convict.[4] Altogether, Ireland sent 14,000 convicts to Tasmania, one-fifth of the total.[5] The number would have been larger, but, until transportation to New South Wales was virtually ended in 1840, the authorities were reluctant to send convict ships direct to Van Diemen's Land. Thus earlier Irish convicts arrived via New South Wales.

This reluctance to populate Van Diemen's Land with Irish people did not prevent Ireland from producing several of the colony's most celebrated bushrangers. In the 1820s Matthew Brady's gang roamed freely throughout the island before defeat by a posse led by an Irish officer. Brady was originally transported for stealing food in Lancashire in 1820. Three years later, he escaped by boat from Macquarie Harbour, Van Diemen's Land's penal settlement for repeat offenders on the west coast. Two years of dramatic bushranging ensued. Brady and his gang moved north and south. In one famous episode they captured the southern town of Sorell, releasing prisoners in the gaol. They also held up former United Irishman Richard Dry's fine Quamby residence at the opposite end of the island. Pitched battles were fought with their pursuers. When the government raised the reward for their capture, Brady coolly offered twenty gallons of rum for the apprehension of Lt. Governor Sir George Arthur. Brady was invariably courteous towards defenceless or female victims. When possible he avoided cruelty and murder. Commandeering a settler's house, Brady played courteous host to the guests who turned up for dinner. Brady's chivalry made him a popular hero when he finally confronted the Hobart gallows. The novelist Richard Flanagan, himself descended from Irish convicts, has made Brady the hero of his best-selling *Gould's Book of Fish*,[6] a scorching satirical denunciation of the convict system.

Another highly publicised Irish bushranger was Martin Cash. Born in 1808 at Enniscorthy, County Wexford, Cash was transported to Sydney in 1827 for housebreaking, not, as he claimed in his ghosted memoirs, for shooting his mistress's lover. Though he gained his ticket-of-leave in New South Wales, he fled to Van Diemen's Land with his current mistress to evade prosecution for cattle duffing. Soon in trouble again, Cash was sentenced in Van Diemen's Land to seven years for housebreaking, but continued to abscond. Returned to the dread penal station of Port Arthur, which had replaced Macquarie Harbour, Brady's place of misery, Cash made his most daring escape with two other convicts. To avoid the savage dogs placed across the narrow spit of Eaglehawk Neck, Cash and his mates braved sharks to swim naked across the bay. From a log fortress at the top of Mt Dromedary, north of Hobart Town, Cash and his allies became successful bushrangers, robbing inns, stage coaches and settlers' houses with apparent impunity. Like Brady, Cash adopted the gentlemanly style, treating the poor and unfortunate with consideration, but humbling domineering or haughty free settlers who were made to wait on their own servants, carry bags of stolen possessions and beg for mercy on their knees. On the arrest of his mistress, Cash, as contemptuous of the establishment as Brady, promised Governor Sir John Franklin a flogging were she not released.

Hearing his mistress had a new lover, Cash rashly entered Hobart Town, only to be captured after a gun battle in which Cash killed one of his assailants. Although defended by the eminent Irish barrister, Edward MacDowell, Cash was found guilty and condemned to death. As in Brady's case, popular support was forthcoming, and the governor commuted Cash's sentence to transportation for life on Norfolk Island.

Cash now collaborated with the authorities. He married a convict transported from Clare for stealing potatoes. Returned to Tasmania, he obtained a ticket-of-leave and appointment as a constable. He worked as an overseer at the Hobart Botanical Gardens before spending four years in New Zealand as a constable in the Canterbury Province armed police force, and also running brothels. Addicted to drink, Cash died on a small farm in Glenorchy, near Hobart Town. James Lester Burke, a soldier from Westmeath transported for striking his sergeant in India, wrote up his story in a colourful, if inaccurate, account. Richard Flanagan read Cash's memoirs over and over again as a child.[7]

Less attractive was Alexander Pearce, who twice escaped from Macquarie Harbour. The terrain was so difficult that in the first party of eight the stronger men killed and ate the weaker. With only two convicts remaining, Pearce axed his sleeping companion. A second escape with one ally ended the same way. Before facing the executioner, Pearce provided some useful geographical information of a hitherto uncharted area. A painting of his death mask reveals not an inhuman monster, but a handsome young man.

A later Irish convict of the 1840s, Michael Rogers, a literate shoemaker from Meath, had been a Ribbonman, whose Catholic objectives might be deemed partly political. Escaping with two hard-bitten Irish companions, Dublin burglars Patrick Lynch and John Reilly, the trio terrorised northern Tasmania from late January to late May 1848, showing some courtesy to captured ladies. In a violent encounter these bushrangers shot dead Joseph Howard, a convict policeman. Taking a boat to South Australia the bush-rangers were finally captured and brought back to Tasmania. Rogers was hanged, but his companions were reprieved. After many vicissitudes Lynch escaped from the colony. Reilly, having done his time on Norfolk Island, surprisingly became a convict constable. The bushranger turned policeman was not a success. Irresponsible firing at a suspect earned Reilly further serious punishment. In 1863 he was set free on condition he left Tasmania.[8]

Later in the year of Rogers' execution, the highly publicised Young Ireland rebels, whose rebellion had failed in 1848, appeared in the colony. Smith O'Brien and John Mitchel wrote journals covering their exile, while

Patrick O'Donohoe edited a paper, the *Irish Exile*, of considerable interest to historians. Others, John Martin, Thomas Meagher, Terence McManus and Kevin O'Doherty, left letters or fragmentary accounts of their experiences. Most assisted the anti-transportationist and self-governing cause against the hated Governor, Sir William Denison, but O'Donohoe in his newspaper backed former convicts against exclusivist upper class free settlers. He also regarded the Aborigines as the true owners of Tasmania and even defended the much-maligned women convicts, a considerable number of whom were Irish. O'Brien was similarly sympathetic towards the dispossessed Aborigines and, unlike Mitchel, towards male convicts in general. Though both O'Brien and Mitchel rejected women convicts as a bad lot, many Irishwomen, especially from country areas, did make good in the colony, leaving numerous descendants.

After the escapes of Mitchel, Meagher, McManus and O'Donohoe to the United States, Smith O'Brien, O'Doherty and Martin were pardoned in 1854.[9] Only William Paul Dowling, a Young Irelander liaising with the Chartists in London, elected to remain in Tasmania, where he married and achieved success as a photographer and portrait painter. Seven working-class insurgents from the 1849 attack on Cappoquin barracks worked their way through the system to conditional pardons. The publicity accorded to the Young Ireland rebels has skewed thought on Irish convicts in general, only eight per cent of whom can be categorised as political.[10] The Famine nevertheless played a distinct role in the conviction of a considerable number of Irish people transported in the 1840s. Although some sank further into recidivism and punishment, others took advantage of their opportunity to build more comfortable lives than were possible in mid-nineteenth-century Ireland. Some ended as lunatics, like the unfortunate 'Paddy', a cattle stealer who hoped, when interviewed by the Irish journalist James Grattan Grey, to return to Ireland overland in a day and a half.[11] The detailed Tasmanian convict records, which provide occupations, personal statements of offences and sometimes of motivation, are an important source for Irish Famine analysis. In general, the labour of Irish convicts, like that of their fellows, played an important part in establishing the state of Tasmania.[12]

If Ireland sent many criminals to Tasmania, the Irish also played a role in the maintenance of law and order, originally dependent to a considerable extent on convict police. Irish bushrangers like Martin Cash and John Reilly, who had escaped with Rogers, were later appointed constables. Surprisingly, the system was seen by some contemporaries, including O'Donohoe, as providing security for law-abiding settlers. At a higher level, Chief Justice Valentine Fleming and Attorney-General Edward Macdowell were Irishmen educated at Trinity College, Dublin.

Superintendent James Coulter transferred to Tasmania after service in the Royal Irish Constabulary. Thomas Patrick Reidy from Tralee became governor of the Hobart Gaol, while John Donnellan Balfe was rewarded with the post of Assistant-Comptroller General of Convicts for informing on the Young Ireland insurgents in Ireland in 1848.

2. EMINENT CITIZENS AND BUILDERS OF INFRASTRUCTURE

Emphasis on Irish convicts should not distract from the Irishmen who established large Tasmanian estates, giving them political clout, before and after the establishment of responsible government in 1856. Most of these were Protestants. In 1821, for example, a younger son of the Talbot family of Malahide Castle was granted 3,000 acres in Fingal, establishing the Tasmanian estate of Malahide. This sheep station remains in the Talbot family, while the Irish Malahide estate was sold in 1973 on the death of Milo, Lord Talbot de Malahide.[13] An exception to Protestant success was Roderic O'Connor, half-brother of the Chartist leader Feargus, who built up the huge Benham station to become one of the largest landowners in the colony. O'Connor, however, was a convert to Catholicism in Tasmania.

Two Irish Anglicans, Richard Dry and Michael Fenton, were leading examples of powerful landowners significant in politics. The father of Dry was transported as a United Irishman, but built the large Quamby estate in northern Tasmania after securing his freedom. Dry and Fenton, a former army officer, became leaders of the anti-transportation movement and framers of the Tasmanian Constitution of 1856. Fenton, with a holding, Fenton Forest, at New Norfolk, served as speaker of the Tasmanian parliament, while Dry, knighted, died in office as premier of Tasmania in 1869. Both men, especially Fenton, supported Smith O'Brien in Tasmania, Fenton by entertaining him frequently at his house, and Dry by attending a banquet in O'Brien's honour.

In preparing the colonial infrastructure, James Meehan, transported for his part in the 1798 Rising, proved a surveyor of genius. Mapping the Derwent river region after the initial landing in 1803, he nominated the site of the colony's capital, Hobart Town. John Lee Archer, son of an engineer in Dublin and County Tipperary, designed a number of stately Tasmanian buildings, including Tasmania's Parliament House in 'Georgian Renaissance' style. A more recent Irish architect in Tasmania was Esmond Dorney, influenced by Frank Lloyd Wright in his public and private buildings characterised by sweeping curvatures.

Although Tasmania lacked the gold discoveries which so greatly enriched mainland Australia, there was a boom in copper and zinc on the west coast late in the nineteenth century. Irish convicts absconding from the Macquarie Harbour penal settlement, including the cannibal Pearce, provided early geographical information. This was finally exploited by James Crotty, a Catholic from Clare, and Anthony Bowes Kelly, a Protestant from Galway. Prospecting for gold, Crotty cheaply bought a share in what became the rich Mt Lyell copper mine. After a contest, beginning in 1891, with Bowes Kelly, originally a drover now wealthy through the Broken Hill Mining Company, Crotty sold out his interest, using some of his fortune to build St Patrick's Catholic Cathedral, Melbourne. Bowes Kelly went from strength to strength in Tasmania. Humbler Irish workers obtained jobs in the mines which, as will be shown below, became the cradle of an Irish-led Labour party.

3. ORANGE AND GREEN RIVALRY

While the majority of Irish, bond or free, were Catholic, probably only about one-fifth of Tasmanian Irish had Protestant backgrounds. Irish Catholics joined a colonial Church where most of their co-religionists and clergy were fellow countrymen. Irish Protestants, on the other hand, more easily merged into the general community. Church of Ireland members formed a minority amongst Tasmanian Anglicans; Scots dominated the local Presbyterian Church. Nevertheless, two early Anglican archdeacons were Irish, and likewise two Presbyterian ministers. While the first Catholic bishop of Hobart, Englishman Robert Willson, found himself in conflict with an Irish missionary priest, Fr John Joseph Therry, the first Anglican bishop, Englishman Francis Nixon, faced an evangelical opposition led by the Rev. Henry Phibbs Fry, graduate of Trinity College, Dublin. At the end of the nineteenth century, Henry Montgomery, better known as the father of the field marshal, was appointed Anglican bishop of Tasmania. The Montgomery family were Ulster planters of the seventeenth century.

Some Irish Protestants maintained their culture by membership of Tasmanian Orange lodges. These began fitfully in the 1830s and 1840s. Encouragement came from Victoria and the advent in 1879 of a French-Canadian anti-Catholic revivalist and former priest, Pastor Chiniquy, who specialised in public celebration of a mock mass. When the local council granted Chiniquy use of the Hobart Town Hall, local Catholics were reinforced in protest by coreligionists from other areas. The governor, himself a Catholic, somewhat prematurely, called out the Volunteer Corps. The fracas inspired the establishment of a number of Orange lodges, especially in Hobart and Launceston. The Royal Black Preceptory was introduced in 1888 and a Grand Orange Lodge for Tasmania set up in 1890. The mining areas of the west coast also acquired lodges in the period after 1870 when Irish Home Rule became a serious issue in Britain and Ireland. As Orangemen were strongly opposed to state aid for Catholic schools, those with Ulster backgrounds may have been outnumbered in the movement by opponents of state aid without Irish links.

Between 1882 and 1894 Orangemen paraded publicly in the city of Launceston on every twelfth of July. For a time there was an Orange newspaper, the *Protestant Standard*. Relatively little disorder occurred. The Catholic community, fearing bias against them, was outraged by the appointment as governor in 1913 of Sir William Elliston-Macartney, a prominent Orange leader in Britain. Even though his tenure extended into 1917, when war, conscription and Irish insurgency had fuelled sectarian tension, Elliston-Macartney appears to have been relatively circumspect in his public activities. On the other side were two Irish-Catholic governors, Lord Gormanstown (1893–1900), a senior Irish peer, and Sir James O'Grady (1924–30), a British trade unionist of Irish antecedents. More recently, Lt.-General Sir Charles Gairdner, from Tyrrellspass, County Westmeath, was governor from 1963 to 1968.[14]

4. EDUCATION (1) THE HUNDRED YEARS' WAR OVER STATE AID FOR CATHOLIC SCHOOLS

After 1868 an educational compromise involving Catholic and Protestant churches was replaced by a system of state education without aid to private institutions. The Catholic Church, as in other colonies, endeavoured to establish their own network of primary schools, at the same time campaigning vigorously for government assistance.[15] Non-Catholic opinion, however, remained adamant that the claims should not be met. Protestant churches organised some private secondary schools, but initially managed to operate satisfactorily on fees from middle-class parents. Teaching orders of nuns and brothers, mainly from Ireland, helped to provide low-cost education for the poorer Catholics. These instructors, aided by clergy of Irish background, perpetuated a modicum of Irish spirit in second or third generation Irish. The refusal of successive governments to grant aid encouraged a sense of injustice akin to that originally experienced in Ireland. O'Farrell argued that the politicising of Australian Irish through the state aid struggle helped to integrate them into the community. More likely, it encouraged alienation and a greater concentration on their traditional Irish resources. Irishmen in the Tasmanian parliament, such as J.D. Balfe,

Christopher O'Reilly, a papal knight and minister for lands with comprehensive plans, James Dooley and Daniel Burke, who had helped John Mitchel to escape, battled for state aid with little success. Later Irish Labour leaders were constrained to find a middle way between denunciation by their church for state aid apathy and the loss of Protestant votes by its promotion.

In the 1920s the last Irish-born Catholic Archbishop of Hobart was succeeded by Australian-born prelates of Irish descent. The struggle continued until the 1960s. Protestant opinion, finding their secondary schools unviable without state aid, completed a U-turn and accepted Catholic leadership in securing government assistance. While concession of the principle of state aid in Tasmania and Australia as a whole did not end all conflict, the 1960s appear to have marked the beginning of an Anglo-Celtic establishment confronting post-Second World War immigrants from continental Europe and Asia. Reviled in the nineteenth century as unwelcome convicts and pauper newcomers, Tasmanian and Australian Irish now represented a conservative middle class. By 2000 the Tasmanian Catholic historian Fr Terry Southerwood estimated that Catholics of Irish background constituted only 60 per cent of the Church in Tasmania.

4. EDUCATION (2) THE IDEA OF HIGHER EDUCATION

Deeply involved in the primary education debate, Irish people also played a significant, if ambiguous, role in Tasmanian higher education. Fr Thomas Kelsh, locally born of Irish descent, was a member of the group pressing for the establishment of the University of Tasmania in 1890. Bishop Montgomery sat on its early council. An early graduate, later Chief Justice Sir Herbert Nicholls, ably defended the infant university in parliament when its funds were about to be slashed. The son of H.R. Nicholls, an economically dry Ulster editor of the local *Mercury*, Herbert exhibited liberalism in law and politics.[16]

While the University of Melbourne was originally staffed extensively by Irish Protestants, the first senior academic of Irish descent in Tasmania was Professor T.T. Flynn in biology. Better known as the father of the swashbuckling actor Errol, Professor Flynn became an expert on Tasmanian marsupials. A supreme individualist, frequently at loggerheads with the university council, Flynn evaded drastic salary cuts in the Great Depression by transferring to Queen's University, Belfast, where he eventually ended his distinguished academic career.

In the 1950s a philosophy graduate of the same Belfast institution caused a major upset in Tasmanian higher education. After the Second World War the university was grossly overcrowded at its original location, staff salaries were low, adequate housing was almost unobtainable, lay members of the council interfered in academic matters, and the Tasmanian government refused to release finance earmarked for a new campus. Ignoring existing negotiation procedures, Professor Sydney Sparkes Orr published a passionate open letter to the Premier detailing grievances and asserting a high notion of academic freedom and the value of unrestricted scholarship in the maintenance of democracy. A royal commission on the university, to the annoyance of the government and university council, endorsed many of the complaints and insisted on the rapid construction of the new campus, more academic control of professional issues and a re-jigged council.

Some months later, after irregular *ad hoc* hearings of several accusations against Orr, including the seduction of a student, he was summarily sacked in early 1956. Persistently denying intercourse with the student, Orr took legal action against the University of Tasmania, but failed in the courts. The struggle, however, continued. Orr was supported by the Australian philosophers who black-banned his chair, the Federal Council of University Staff Associations, the Tasmanian Presbyterian Church, Guilford Young, the Catholic Archbishop of Hobart, and several of his colleagues. Finally, in 1966 the University of Tasmania awarded Orr compensation without reappointment. Orr died suddenly in the same year. The University of Tasmania accepted new regulations giving it the strongest tenure rules in the country. By this time it had moved to a bright new campus at Sandy Bay outside Hobart.

Since Orr, there have been several other Tasmanian academics of Irish background, but none has achieved the same notoriety. Orr supporters of Irish background, George Wilson and Tony Kearney, were respectively appointed warden of Hytten Hall of residence and registrar of the university. Many of the changes resulting from the conflict have been swept away in the late twentieth century by Australian governments reorganising universities to accord with market forces. The Orr episode remains a precedent for academic assertion in a more favourable period.

5. SUPPORT FOR IRISH INDEPENDENCE

While Ireland struggled for self-government in the nineteenth century, Irish-Tasmanians could not ignore its problems. Many Tasmanians had supported Smith O'Brien and his colleagues, while the anti-transportation movement linked its demands with those of Ireland. Poorer Irish workers were glad to join local branches of the Hibernian Australasian Catholic Benefit Society, important in the days before a welfare state. With the development of C.S. Parnell's Home Rule movement in the 1880s, financial needs necessitated an appeal to the Irish abroad. Between 1881 and 1912, Tasmania accordingly received seven visits from Home Rule delegates. These included some of the best-known nationalist leaders: William Redmond, John Dillon, Michael Davitt and Joseph Devlin. When Redmond visited in 1883, the Phoenix Park murders of the previous year deterred some potential supporters, but by the outbreak of the First World War general Tasmanian public opinion saw Irish Home Rule as equivalent to Tasmanian self-government. Meanwhile hardline Orangemen, who feared for Ulster under a Home Rule parliament, busily extended their lodges. Nevertheless they no longer represented mainstream opinion. The last Home Rule delegates received support across the political spectrum. The local branch of the United Irish League, an organisation paralleling the movement in Ireland to provide funding and support for the Irish Parliamentary Party, maintained liaison with leaders at home.

On the outbreak of war in 1914, most Irish leaders and clergy were strongly supportive of Irish Nationalist leader, John Redmond, who called on the nationalist Irish Volunteers to enlist in the British army. Edmund Dwyer Gray, formerly proprietor of the Dublin *Freeman's Journal* and now editor of the Tasmanian Labor *Daily Post*, encouraged recruitment. At the 1916 St Patrick's Day celebration, immediately before the Easter Week Rising in Dublin, there appeared amongst Tasmanians a comfortable consensus in favour of moderate Irish Home Rule. Hard words were levelled at the extremist minority in Ireland who undermined John Redmond, the chosen leader.

Soon the consensus was broken by the Dublin Rising and the Australian conscription referenda of 1916 and 1917 in which Tasmania voted 'yes' on both occasions, against the national decision. Catholic Archbishop Delany came out strongly against the insurgents, as did many of his clergy and Dwyer Gray in the *Daily Post*. The issue was, however, subsumed in the conscription contest. Archbishop Mannix's stand in Melbourne against conscription was interpreted as support for the Sinn Féin Rising. Irish people, especially those opposed to conscription, were almost forced by angry opponents into the Sinn Féin camp. The end of the war in November 1918 failed to lessen the frenzy. Loyalty leagues, popular extensions of the Orange lodges, sprang up to denounce Archbishop Mannix and an alleged conspiracy against the British empire, organised by an unlikely alliance of Sinn Féin, the papacy, and the Bolsheviks. Several members of parliament were involved in the leagues.

On the Irish side, Katherine Hughes, a Canadian supporter of de Valera, toured a range of countries to establish self-determination for Ireland leagues. In May 1921 a meeting in Hobart, chaired by Dwyer Gray, established the league in Tasmania. Gray became its local president. One hundred members joined immediately and paid their 2s fee. The league was relatively successful in Tasmania. It hired an organiser to tour the state enrolling members and sent four representatives to a national self-determination league convention at Melbourne in July 1921.

The Anglo-Irish Treaty of December 1921 came as a great relief to Tasmanians. Dwyer Gray and his allies had no sympathy for opponents of the treaty. Gray considered the difference between de Valera's Document No. Two and the treaty not worth fighting over. Nor were the insurgents in the resultant civil war popular in Tasmania. Archbishop Barry of Hobart, though supportive of Irish self-determination, on hearing of the murder of Kevin O'Higgins in 1927, declared that Ireland was no longer the country of his dreams. Local Irish descendants now focused on their own affairs. Orange lodges, mollified by the separation of the six counties of Northern Ireland from the Irish Free State, declined in the 1930s, finally petering out in the 1960s, the decade when state aid triumphed.

Dwyer Gray was dead when de Valera visited Tasmania after losing office in the Irish election of 1948. De Valera himself was pleased with the visit, during which he was entertained by the Irish-led Labor government, Catholic Archbishop E.V. Tweedy and the vicar-general, Monsignor John Cullen. But the local Catholic *Standard* was uncharacteristically reticent, probably because de Valera's Second World War neutralism was unpopular with a number of Tasmanians, including Athol Townley, later Australian minister for defence, himself a Protestant of southern Irish descent.[17] Catholic authorities appeared to fear that association with such neutralism would damage their campaign to obtain state aid for their schools. Here local issues clearly took precedence over vestigial Irish patriotism.[18]

6. DEMOCRATISATION THROUGH IRISH-LED LABOR

On his visit to Tasmania in 1895, Michael Davitt had criticised the local Irish for tardiness in establishing a Labor Party.[19] After several false starts a parliamentary Labor Party of four was inaugurated in 1903. Though one, James Long, was a west coast miner of Irish descent, the ultimate Labor leader was John Earle, who had also worked on the coast. Earle's mother was Irish and he was brought up as a Catholic but ceased to practise his religion. Helped by the Hare Clark proportional voting system, Labor under Earle was enabled to take office for a few days in 1909 and for two years, 1914–16. Short of a majority, Earle was kept in power by an eccentric Irish conservative, Joshua Whitsitt, upset that a previous government had not enabled him to sell his infected potatoes on the mainland. Earle could to do little more than administer. He annoyed the local unions by refusing them preference.

During the conscription crisis of 1916 and 1917, Earle broke with his party and joined the conscriptionists. The new leader, Joseph Lyons, a former teacher, had strong Irish credentials on both sides of the family and supported Irish self-determination. Though Labor did badly in the 1921 election, a split in the opposition enabled Lyons to take office in a minority Labor government in 1923. Premier until 1928, Lyons adopted consensus politics, disliked by radicals in the Labor movement, some of whom were also of Irish descent. Losing office in 1928, Lyons moved to federal politics. During the depression he formed a new United Australia Party to maintain orthodox finance. In 1932 Lyons became Prime Minister of Australia, holding the position until his death in 1939.

While the first two Tasmanian Labor leaders were now denounced by current members as traitors for leaving the Labor Party, the third, Albert Ogilvie, a Catholic lawyer with an Irish mother, took a more radical line, flirting with social credit as an answer to the depression. He scored a narrow victory in the state election of 1934. With Irish-born Edmund Dwyer Gray as his treasurer, Ogilvie restored confidence in the state with a programme of more generous finance, hydro-electric development and public works. Historians see him as the architect of modern Tasmania. Nevertheless he met considerable union opposition like his predecessors, his chief opponent being Bill Morrow, the Ulster-descended local president of the Amalgamated Railways' Union.

The momentum of Ogilvie helped the Tasmanian branch of the Australian Labor Party to a record thirty-five years of unbroken government. After Ogilvie's sudden death in 1939, Dwyer Gray held the premiership for six months before reverting to treasurer until his death in 1945. The next leader, Robert Cosgrove, a grocer of impeccable Irish-Catholic descent, was premier for an unprecedented seventeen years before relinquishing it in 1958 to the Methodist, Eric Reece. Reece, married to an Irish Catholic, completed the thirty-five years of unbroken power, before experiencing temporary defeat in 1969. These premiers were backed by a caucus and ministers, many of whom were of clear Irish descent. One, Jack Dwyer, had won the Victoria Cross for capturing a German machine gun at Ypres.

Since 1969 Tasmanian Labor has held office for the majority of the period but the Irish-Catholic dominance has been broken. In the current Labor government both the Premier, Paul Lennon, and his former deputy, David Llewellyn, are of Irish descent, but citizens of Irish ancestry are so integrated into the country's mainstream that they arouse little interest. During its Irish-Catholic heyday, the Tasmanian Labor Party, despite some radicals of Irish descent on the left, was an extremely moderate party of development, which eschewed socialism, impossible under federal law. The continuing problem was the state aid issue. Irish leaders endeavoured, uncomfortably, to grant minor assistance short of direct capitation. Cosgrove as premier removed the party's bar against state aid but was blocked by the Legislative Council from passing the necessary legislation. His non-Catholic successor, Eric Reece, achieved this in 1967.

7. FROM THE IRISH JOKE TO THE CELTIC TIGER

Despite the very considerable contribution of the Irish to Tasmanian development, the 'Irish joke', resembling some nineteenth-century attitudes to poor Irish migration, was still prevalent in the 1980s. The Irish economy was seen as a 'basket case' and the country itself appeared a byword for ignorance. Irish Catholics on the other hand looked to Ireland as a place of religious inspiration compared with the secular materialism of Australia. By the 1990s attitudes were reversed. The growth of the 'Celtic Tiger' economy in Ireland, with a soaring GDP, a reversal of emigration and a reputation as the computer software centre of Europe, made Tasmanians highly envious. Could not Tasmania, the economic basket case of the southern hemisphere, derided by mainlanders, develop her resources in the Irish manner? Contempt and ridicule for Ireland gave way to obsequious emulation. Irish visitors pontificated on how it could be done, failing to realise that Tasmania lacked economic sovereignty and the strategic advantages of Ireland.

Meanwhile, Tasmanians of Irish Catholic descent, visiting Ireland, no longer found a religious utopia, but a materialistic secularised society racked by religious scandals identical to those appearing throughout the world.

The retention of Irish characteristics in Tasmania became problematic. As Irish journalist Fintan O'Toole has demonstrated, the compromises necessitated by the Ulster Troubles render Irish identity less clear. The demand by both national and unionist traditions for 'parity of esteem' makes the precise nature of Irish culture difficult to define. Unlike the Irish War of Independence, the Ulster Troubles made scarcely a ripple on Tasmanian life. Irish associations in Tasmania now emphasise music and dancing. With little local celebration of St Patrick's Day, readings on 16 June of James Joyce's *Ulysses*, for many years discouraged, if not formally banned in the Irish Republic, have become the most characteristic celebration of Irishness.

Since the foundation of the colony in 1803, the Irish and their descendants in Tasmania have played a role in education, politics, religion, economics, more significant than their numbers, never much greater than 20 per cent of the population, would indicate. The Irish, moreover, have appeared on both sides of every important question. Catholic and Protestant assimilation into the mainstream, after a more combative nineteenth-century role, has been complete, suggesting that the model has been a melting pot, rather than the multiculturalism so emphasised for migrant groups today.

NOTES

1. Where not otherwise stated, material for this chapter will be found in Richard P. Davis, *Irish Traces on Tasmanian History, 1803–2004* (Hobart: Sassafras Books, 2005).
2. Patrick O'Farrell, *The Irish in Australia* (Kensington: New South Wales University Press, 1988), pp.8, 10.
3. The Republic of Ireland, 70,282 square kilometres, Tasmania 68,358 square kilometres.
4. Phillip Tardiff, *John Bowen's Hobart: the Beginnings of European Settlement in Tasmania* (Hobart: Tasmanian Historical Research Association, 2003), pp.37, 116–17.
5. John Williams, *Ordered to the Island: Irish Convicts and Van Diemen's Land* (Sydney: Crossing Press, 1994), pp.9 and 168–9: 10,988 tried in Ireland; 3,504 Irish-born tried elsewhere; 4,637 were women.
6. Richard Flanagan, *Gould's Book of Fish* (Sydney: Picador, 2001).
7. See Maree Ring, 'Martin Cash: His Life in the Colonies', in R. Davis, et al. (eds), *Irish-Australian Studies: Papers Delivered at the Eighth Irish-Australian Conference, Hobart July 1995* (Sydney: Crossing Press, 1996), p.501; Maree Ring, *Martin Cash: Life after Bushranging* (Hobart: M. Ring, 1993); Frank Clune, *Martin Cash: The Lucky Bushranger* (Sydney: Angus and Robertson, 1968), p.154; *Australian Dictionary of Biography (ADB)*, Vol.1, pp.214–15 (L.L. Robson & Russel Ward).
8. Richard and Marianne Davis, *The Whistling Irish Bushrangers: Tasmania and South Australia, 1848–63* (Hobart: Sassafras Books, 2002).
9. For Young Ireland writings, see Davis, *Irish Traces*, p.38; *Revolutionary Imperialist: William Smith O'Brien, 1803–1864* (Sydney and Dublin: Crossing Press and The Lilliput Press, 1998); R.P. Davis (chief ed.), *'To Solitude Consigned': The Tasmanian Journal of William Smith O'Brien, 1849–1854* (Sydney: Crossing Press, 1995); R.P. Davis, 'Patrick O'Donohoe: Outcast of the Exiles', in Bob Reece (ed.), *'Exiles from Erin': Convict Lives in Ireland and Australia* (London: Macmillan, 1991), pp.246–83.
10. Williams, *Ordered to the Island*, p.44.
11. 'The New Zealander in Tasmania', *Evening Post*, Wellington, New Zealand, 30 April 1883.
12. See Williams for more details and R.P. Davis, '"Not so bad as a bad marriage": Irish Transportation Policies in the 1840s', *Tasmanian Historical Research Association Papers & Proceedings*, Vol. 47, No.1, March 2000, pp.9–64.
13. Alison Alexander (ed.), *The Companion to Tasmanian History* (Hobart: Centre for Tasmanian Historical Studies, University of Tasmania, 2005), p.351.
14. See *Irish Times*, 17 May 1951 for background.
15. R.P. Davis, *A Guide to the State Aid Tangle in Tasmania* (Hobart, Cat & Fiddle Press, 1975); *State Aid and Tasmanian Politics, 1868–1920*, 2nd edition (Hobart: University of Tasmania, 1980).
16. For a general coverage of this topic, R.P. Davis, *Open to Talent: The Centenary History of the University of Tasmania, 1890–1990* (Hobart: University of Tasmania, 1990); R.P. Davis, *100 Years: A Centenary History of the Faculty of Law, University of Tasmania, 1893–1993* (Hobart, University of Tasmania, 1993).

17. *Mercury*, Hobart, 19 May 1948. De Valera was also attacked by the Tasmanian Protestant Federation, *Examiner*, Launceston, 31 May 1948. See also in this volume the chapter by Rory O'Dwyer, '"A roof-raising affair"? Éamon de Valera's tour of Australia and New Zealand'.

18. *Standard*, 25 May 1948. The emphasis was entirely de Valera's Catholicism: 'quite apart from and above any questions of politics'. No mention was made of any churchman who supported de Valera.

19. For a general coverage of the Tasmanian Labor Party, R.P. Davis, *Eighty Years' Labor: The ALP in Tasmania* (Hobart: Sassafras Books, 1983).

11

From Connerville, County Cork, to Connorville, Van Diemen's Land. The Irish Family Background and Colonial Career of Roderic O'Connor (1786/1787? – 1860)

Laurence M. Geary

'...Let the world be your republic, Ireland your country, to do good your religion, be humane, but above all, be united.'[1]
'...Countrymen awake...unite your hands – unite your hearts – remember that you are men – that you are Irish men – embrace.'[2]

In a swingeing attack, the American scholar and literary critic Robert Tracy depicted the author of these sentiments, County Cork-born Roger O'Connor, as 'a bad son, a bad brother, a bad husband, a bad tenant, and a bad neighbour'; damned him as 'a liar, a swindler, a thief, and a plagiarist'; and likened his extra-literary activities to those of a character who had sprung from the pages of *Castle Rackrent*, or Sir Jonah Barrington's memoirs.[3] This intemperate, unleavened assessment ignored O'Connor's positive attributes, among them a capacity for friendship and loyalty, his charm, political courage, spirited patriotism, and a commitment to United Irish ideals that exposed him to the odium of his caste and jeopardised his life and liberty. Roger O'Connor was bombastic, eccentric, imaginative, turbulent and unconventional, with an exaggerated self-esteem and an inflated sense of his own family's origins and importance, and these attributes, I suggest, defined the man more accurately than the deliberate or evil intent implicit in Tracy's portrayal.

The recipient of Tracy's invective was born at Connerville, County Cork, in 1762.[4] In the 1780s, he and his brother, Arthur (b. Connerville, 4 July 1763), rejected their patronymic, Conner, in favour of the surname O'Connor, after the ancient line of Irish high kings. Specifically, they claimed lineal descent from the O'Connor Kerry branch of the O'Connor royal family. By 1828, six years before his death, Roger O'Connor was brazenly describing himself as 'a man of the blood-royal of Ireland'.[5] There is no direct evidence to support such an exalted lineage. A more likely ancestry is a London merchant family,[6] one of whom prospered in trade in Bandon, County Cork, in the late seventeenth century and, in the custom of the upwardly mobile of the time, began to acquire land. He bequeathed his business acumen and his property interests to the next generation of Conners, who consolidated and built on them. The family's success was given concrete expression in the erection of Connerville, a substantial Georgian mansion, near Ballineen, some twenty miles west of Cork city, by Roger O'Connor's grandfather, William Conner.[7]

Whatever the family's questionable origins, there can be little doubt about the sincerity of the political beliefs of Roger and Arthur O'Connor, or of Roger's integrity and courage, and his commitment to Ireland. 'For that country I have lived', he wrote in middle-age, 'and for that country I am always prepared to shed the last drop of my blood, thinking no sacrifice too great to promote her happiness and welfare.'[8] The brothers exchanged their youthful tory leanings for radical politics and rose to prominence in the United Irish movement in the closing decade of the eighteenth century. Roger became a leading figure in the organisation in Cork, and for a time was its chief director. Arthur, a member of the executive of the United Irishmen, was, according to a recent assessment, a man of domineering personality and ironic disposition.[9] Marianne Elliott describes him as irresponsible, ambitious and egotistical and believes that his megalomania wreaked havoc within the United Irish movement.[10] Having served a period of imprisonment for his political activism, Arthur spent half a century in exile in France, where he became a Napoleonic general, married seventeen-year-old Eliza, Condorcet's only child, and acquired Mirabeau's estate at Le Bignon.

Roger and Arthur's commitment to United Irish ideals in the 1790s was matched by the fervour with which their older brothers William and Robert rejected them. William, a Lieutenant-Colonel in the Cork Militia, and Robert, who lived at Fortrobert, a neighbouring property to Connerville, remained staunchly loyal to Protestant ascendancy and the political establishment, and their attempts to secure the execution of their treasonable siblings shocked even the Irish authorities. According to W.J. O'Neill Daunt, a neighbour and cousin of the family, Robert Longfield Conner 'did all he could to get his brother Roger hanged'.[11] On 27 September 1797, Roger was arrested and lodged in Cork gaol on Robert's trumped-up charge. In the following March, while still in prison and awaiting trial, Roger launched a radical, stridently anti-government paper, *Harp of Erin*, under the motto: 'It is newly strung and will be heard'. He was largely responsible for the content of the four issues that appeared before the militia suppressed the paper on 17 March 1798.[12] Two weeks later, Robert informed the army commander at Bandon, General John Moore, that pikes, firearms and ammunition were concealed in the gardens at Connerville. 'It was unpleasant for him to declare against his brother,' he said, but 'he was determined to do his duty to his country.' Moore organised a military search of the grounds but no arms were found.[13]

On 12 April 1798 Roger was tried at the Cork spring assizes on three indictments for high treason, and was acquitted and discharged. He went to London immediately afterwards, for the dual purpose, he explained, of educating his eight young children and of 'avoiding any interference in politics'. However, when his brother Arthur was arrested at Margate, while trying to flee to France, Roger was taken into custody in London and, on 2 June 1798, after undergoing what he described as 'a variety of toils and hardships', he was transferred to Newgate gaol in Dublin. While there, his home, Connerville, was taken over by the military for six weeks, an occupancy marked by 'every excess which barbarity could devise, and cruelty execute', an incensed Roger recorded.[14] On a broader level, he was exercised by the proposed union between Great Britain and Ireland, which he denounced in a pamphlet written in prison as a 'ruinous and wicked project', claiming that it was nothing less than 'a farrago of nonsense'.[15]

In April 1799, Roger, his brother Arthur, Thomas Addis Emmet, and other state prisoners were transferred to Fort George in the north of Scotland. Roger was released two years later and spent some time on the Continent before he was allowed to return to Ireland, on condition that he resided within thirty miles of Dublin. On 1 October 1803, he took out a perpetual lease on Dangan Castle and demesne, the ancestral home of the Wellesley family, earls of Mornington, at Trim, County Meath, which was then owned by Colonel Thomas Burrowes. The annual rental was £2,000, reducible to £1,000 by payment of £20,000, in two sums of £10,000. The first payment was due on or before 29 September 1806 but O'Connor was unable to fulfil the agreement and on 6 March 1807 he mortgaged his entire holdings, including Connerville, the family home in County Cork, to John Claudius Beresford of Dublin to secure the sum of £10,000.[16] In the following year, 1808, part of Dangan Castle burned down, and Roger was suspected of deliberately setting the fire for the insurance money.[17] Many years later, Roger's second son, Frank, exonerated his father and accepted responsibility for the blaze; he recorded in his memoirs that he had accidentally spilled molten lead on the floorboards when casting bullets for the pistols he used for target practice.[18]

Roger, with a large family and a considerable establishment to support, appears to have been a hopeless spendthrift. He squandered his patrimony, mismanaged or misappropriated his exiled brother Arthur's property, over which he had been given power of attorney, and was indebted to friends like Sir Francis Burdett, the English radical MP.[19] On 2 October 1812, four years after the partial burning of Dangan Castle, over which a cloud of suspicion still hung, a gang of highwaymen robbed the Dublin–Galway mail coach at the Hill of Cappagh, about six miles from Dangan, in the course of which the guard was shot and killed. As with the fire at his home, Roger was suspected of master-minding the hold-up, in which a large amount of cash, in the form of bank notes and remittances, destined for the annual fair at Ballinasloe, was taken, along with letters and securities of various kinds, lottery tickets and post-bills. It was almost five years before O'Connor was formally charged with the crime, following a plea-bargain struck by one of the gang.

On 5 August 1817, the case was heard before Mr Justice Daly at Trim Assizes, in a courthouse 'crowded to suffocation', and with large numbers awaiting the verdict in the street outside. According to one report, the defendant was 'dressed in blue, and looked extremely well; his deportment was dignified; he had a smile on his countenance during the entire time, and from the bar saluted some gentlemen in court'.[20] The charge against O'Connor was that, through his steward, Martin McKeon, he had organised and armed an eight-man gang, including four of his own labourers at Dangan, to rob the mail coach. The prosecution argued that the party returned, by previous agreement, to the Dangan demesne, where the proceeds of the robbery were equally divided among O'Connor and the gang members. Over the following years, six of the gang were apprehended, convicted and hanged. One of the two remaining members, Michael Owens, was acquitted on three separate occasions of passing stolen bank notes, but in February 1817 he was convicted of robbery in County Dublin, and sentenced to death. Some three weeks later, Owens turned king's evidence in return for a free pardon, and implicated O'Connor in the mail coach robbery. His evidence was subsequently corroborated by the other surviving gang member, Daniel Waring. According to the prosecution, Owens's confession formed 'a body of irrefragable testimony, from which the prosecutors could not recede, or under any pretext of humanity, deference to rank, or compliment to birth or talent, avoid taking notice of, or pursuing that line of conduct which became imperative on them'.[21]

In his evidence against O'Connor, Owens stated that he was sworn in as a Carder, a member of an oath-bound rural secret society, by O'Connor on 1 January 1812:

Mr O'Connor swore him to secrecy; and to aid and assist in taking arms; he had a conversation with him about religion; the contents of the oath were "That they shall not pity the moans or groans of Orangemen, but should wade knee deep in their blood". Mr O'Connor said that when the Carders would supply themselves with arms, he would make them surprise the "plans of government".

Daniel Waring was also sworn in as a Carder by O'Connor, and pledged 'to aid anarchy, and overturn monarchy'.[22]

Owens testified that on the evening of the robbery, O'Connor gave him two blunderbusses, two cases of pistols and eighteen rounds of ammunition. Part of Owens's information against O'Connor was that the blunderbusses used in the robbery would be found either at Dangan Castle, or in the cottage that Roger's son Roderic occupied at Saints' Island on the estate. The local magistracy instituted a search, and the weapons were discovered in Roderic's bedroom.[23] The latter's younger brother Frank testified in court that after the burning of Dangan Castle, Roderic built the house at Saints' Island, and that Roderic, Frank, and their two sisters lived there. Their father resided in another house on the estate, and did not visit Roderic's cottage. According to Frank, 'there was a family reason for it', which suggests a degree of estrangement between father and son. Frank stated that he found the blunderbusses, without locks and full of sand, in a rabbit hole a month after the robbery. He kept them and brought them to Roderic's house when it was built.[24]

For the defence, O'Connor's land agent, Michael Barry, gave evidence of his employer's finances and rental income, observing: 'If Mr O'Connor wanted money to buy sheep at the fair of Ballinasloe, he could have got it easier than by robbing the mail.' Barry added that he had never met 'a more honourable, a more just, or a more generous man'. Jeremiah Keller, 'father of the Munster Bar', who had known O'Connor for some thirty-five years, testified to his character, as did O'Connor's friend of many years, Sir Francis Burdett, who had travelled from London specifically for that purpose. Keller characterised O'Connor as 'honest, honourable, frank and generous', and regarded him as unimpeached and unimpeachable.[25]

The case for the prosecution rested on the evidence of a convicted robber, one who was under sentence of death, and who was given a free pardon in return for informing on O'Connor. The jury acquitted the defendant, having been strongly recommended to do so by the presiding magistrate. O'Connor then thanked the judge and jury, observing that though he had suffered a great deal, 'what would not a man suffer for such a day as this'. He and Burdett were cheered in court and when they emerged onto the street. According to one account, 'the shouting and huzzaing continued in the town for near an hour after Mr O'Connor got into the street; and the cheering of Sir Francis Burdett, by name, was loud and general. At night there were bonfires in the town.'[26]

Despite O'Connor's acquittal, rumours persisted about his involvement in the robbery and, in an attempt to clear his name, he charged Daniel Waring with perjury. At the latter's trial in Dublin on 31 October 1817, the jury took a mere ten minutes to return a verdict of not guilty,[27] after which Roger O'Connor stood condemned in the eyes of the public of robbing the Galway mail.[28] It was subsequently rumoured that the mail coach was targeted to secure compromising letters between Sir Francis Burdett and Lady Oxford, rather than for the money on board. However, Burdett's biographer, M.W. Patterson, dismissed the rumour as baseless; he blamed it on O'Connor and claimed that there was not 'a scrap of contemporary evidence to support the tale'. Patterson believed that O'Connor was an 'utter impostor', and was, in addition, certifiably insane and should have been in an alienist's or psychiatrist's care.[29]

It may have been the notoriety that attached to the Trim and Dublin trials, coupled, perhaps, with on-going financial difficulties, that led to O'Connor's departure from Dangan some time after December 1817. He settled in Paris, where he embarked on what was probably the most extraordinary undertaking of his career, the composition of a two-volume history of Ireland, entitled *Chronicles of Eri*, the name he applied to the country before the arrival of the Anglo-Normans in 1169.[30]

The frontispiece depicts O'Connor in a Gaelic chieftain's cloak, with a scroll in one hand, and the other hand resting on a crown.[31] Underneath are the words: 'O'Connor cier-rige head of his race, and O'Connor chief of the pro-strated people of his nation. *Soumis pas vaincus*' (beaten but not conquered).

The title page shows a device, 'The Ring of Baal', with thirteen radiated points, marked clockwise, 1–13: Tionnscnad, Blat, Bael tetgne, Sgit, Tarsgit, Meas, Cruinning, Tirim, Fluicim, Geimia, Sneacda, Siocan, Deirionnae, with Baelainn in large type in the centre of the circle or ring.

In the second volume the frontispiece represents 'the interior of the high chamber of Teacmor on Tobrad during the convention of the national assembly of Eri'. The Ard Rí, or High King, with his mitred crown of gold, sits in the chair of state, and along the walls hang the shields of the chieftains and warriors.

The author of the two volumes is listed simply as O'Connor. The work, which was completed in Paris in 1821 and published in London in the following year, is grandiloquently dedicated to O'Connor's 'faithful friend', Sir Francis Burdett, who probably financed the undertaking.

In his prefatory remarks, O'Connor described his work as 'a faithful history' of his country, his 'beloved Eri'. He began the study when he was in prison in Dublin in 1798–9, 'charged by the oligarchy of England with the foul crime of treason'. His first attempt to complete the project was

Figure 10: Frontispiece, Volume I, *Chronicles of Eri*

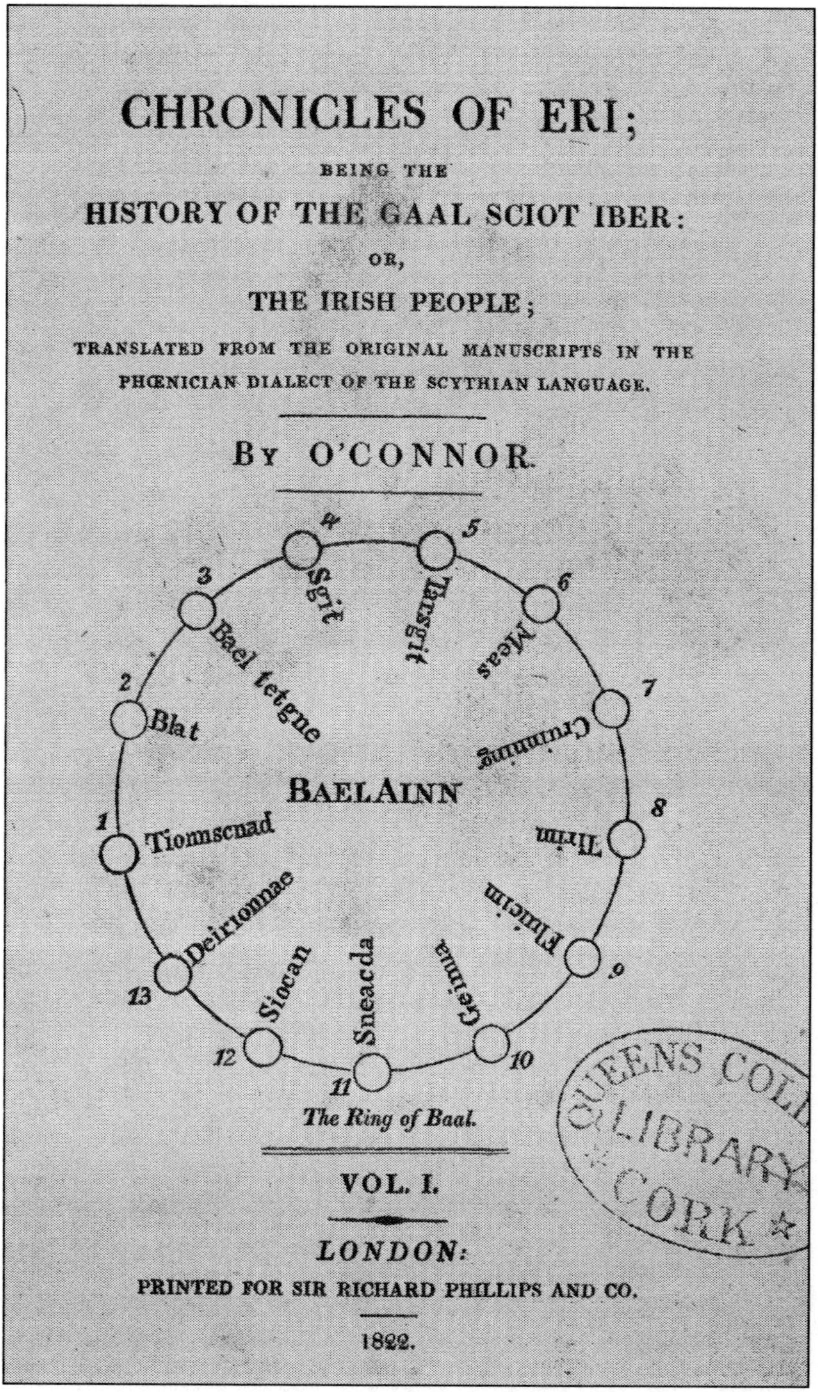

CHRONICLES OF ERI;

BEING THE

HISTORY OF THE GAAL SCIOT IBER:

OR,

THE IRISH PEOPLE;

TRANSLATED FROM THE ORIGINAL MANUSCRIPTS IN THE
PHŒNICIAN DIALECT OF THE SCYTHIAN LANGUAGE.

BY O'CONNOR.

The Ring of Baal.

VOL. I.

LONDON:

PRINTED FOR SIR RICHARD PHILLIPS AND CO.

1822.

Figure 11: Title page, Volume I, *Chronicles of Eri*

Figure 12: Frontispiece, Volume II, *Chronicles of Eri*

thwarted when an armed force of militia entered his cell and 'outrageously' stripped him of the manuscript, which has 'never since been recovered'. He returned to the task after he was transferred to Fort George in Scotland in 1799 but burned the manuscript on his release two years later, his wife fearing that his liberty would be compromised by its discovery. He resumed the project when he returned to Ireland in 1803, having reclaimed 'from the bowels of the earth the most ancient manuscripts of the history of Eri', and had brought the story down to the year 1315, the date of Edward Bruce's arrival in Ireland, when the manuscript and most of his possessions were destroyed in the fire at his home, Dangan Castle. After his trial at Trim in 1817, O'Connor promised Sir Francis Burdett that he would present him with an authentic history of Ireland, a pledge that spurred him to complete the project. O'Connor described the work as 'a literal translation into the English tongue (from the Phoenican [*sic*] dialect of the Scythian language) of the ancient manuscripts which have, fortunately for the world, been preserved through so many ages, chances and vicissitudes'. In an anticipatory move, O'Connor stated that the parchments on which he based his history might not be as old as the events they recorded, but they were 'faithful transcripts from the most ancient records', adding that it was not possible, 'either from their style, language, or contents, that they could have been forged'.[32]

CHRONICLES OF ERI;

BEING THE

HISTORY OF THE GAAL SCIOT IBER:

OR,

THE IRISH PEOPLE;

TRANSLATED FROM THE ORIGINAL MANUSCRIPTS IN THE
PHŒNICIAN DIALECT OF THE SCYTHIAN LANGUAGE.

By O'CONNOR.

VOL. II.

LONDON:

PRINTED FOR SIR RICHARD PHILLIPS AND CO.

1822.

Figure 13: Title page, Volume II, *Chronicles of Eri*

The two volumes published in 1822 were part of a projected five-volume work, whose entirety would constitute 'a complete continued history of this noble island', under the name of Eri, to the year 1169, and of Ireland from that time onwards. O'Connor intended that the third volume would bring the story of Ireland down to the Anglo-Norman invasion in 1169, the penultimate one would cover the period from 1169 to the date of the author's birth, and the final volume would record the history of his own times.[33] He concluded the second volume by 'wishing health and happiness to all the good people of the earth, and speedy amendment to the vicious', and hoped, health permitting, to publish early in the following year the third segment of the history of his 'adored Eri'.[34] Roger O'Connor lived for another twelve years but no further volumes appeared.

Robert Tracy, in a characteristically robust analysis, characterised *Chronicles of Eri* as a concoction, 'a literary fraud', in which the author, 'heavily disguised, figured as Ireland's king, law-giver, and historian'. Tracy added that the history of Ireland, as O'Connor narrates it, 'turns into a disguised and fantastic autobiography, a compensation for the shady and rather futile activities that figure in his biography'.[35] Other commentators described the work variously as the product of O'Connor's imagination;[36] a 'gigantic' lie;[37] 'a bare-faced fabrication';[38] and 'one of the most extra-ordinary and impudent literary forgeries ever palmed off as history upon the public'.[39] These dismissive and rather po-faced assessments overlooked the magnitude of the undertaking, which was obviously laborious and costly, and which underlined O'Connor's romanticism and the great fertility of his imagination.

In 1783, Roger O'Connor married Louisa Ann Strachan, who bore him two children, Louisa Anne and Roderic. After his wife's untimely death, he married, in 1788, Wilhelmina, daughter of Nicholas Bowen of Bowenscourt, Farrahy, County Cork,[40] a marriage that produced at least four sons: Francis Burdett (b. 12 June 1791), who appears to have been named William originally,[41] and who was known to his family and friends as Frank; Arthur; Feargus Edward; and George Roger; and two daughters: Wilhelmina and Harriet. Three of Roger O'Connor's sons – Roderic, Frank and Feargus – carved out careers and reputations for themselves in Australia, South America and England respectively in the first half of the nineteenth century.

Roger bequeathed several of his traits, not least his bombast, pomposity, impulsiveness and turbulence, to his second youngest son, Feargus. In the general election of December 1832, Feargus, standing as a repealer, headed the poll for County Cork, and in the general election of July 1847 he was returned as an MP for Nottingham. As leader of the Chartists in the 1830s and 1840s, Feargus was simultaneously the movement's most revered and most reviled figure. Daniel O'Connell bestowed the sobriquet 'Poor Balderdash' upon him, and described Feargus's newspaper, the *Northern Star*, as 'a literary curiosity. The first page is filled with praise of Feargus; second page, praise of Feargus; third page, ditto; fourth page, ditto; and so on all through till we come to the printer's name.'[42] Feargus's increasingly eccentric behaviour in the late 1840s and early 1850s toppled over into certifiable insanity in June 1852. He was committed to a private lunatic asylum after striking a fellow MP in the House of Commons, and died agonisingly, on 30 August 1855, of general paralysis of the insane, a physical and mental disease due to syphilis of the nervous system.[43] Feargus never married but had a succession of lovers and fathered several illegitimate children.[44]

Long before his younger brother's arrival on the political stage, Frank, who had received a military training, had become involved in the Spanish-American wars of independence. He left Dublin in July 1819 as part of the Irish Legion that had been raised and equipped to help liberate South America from the Spanish. According to his grandson's pietistic – and highly colourful – account, Frank, now Francisco Burdett O'Connor, abandoned 'his land, his possessions, his fortune and his health to come in search of a new fatherland in those parts of a new world where the great Bolivar had just proclaimed the liberty and emancipation of the Spanish colonies'; his grandson claimed that his motivation was 'his ardent love of liberty and of the republic, his aspirations and democratic ideals'.[45] Frank became successively a general in the Bolivian army, minister of war, and chief of the general staff, and his South American adventures, in his father's estimation, 'shed additional lustre even on our name'.[46] He remained in South America after the final surrender of the Spanish in 1826, married, bought a farm and settled in southern Bolivia, where he died in 1871.[47]

Frank's original intention was to accompany his older half-brother Roderic to the Australian penal colony of Van Diemen's Land, where the latter arrived in May 1824, accompanied by his sons, William and Arthur, and in possession of letters from the under-secretary of state, permitting Frank and himself to proceed to the colony as free settlers and to receive a grant of land in proportion to their means of cultivating it.

It is difficult to sketch anything other than a hazy account of Roderic's life in Ireland before his departure for Australia. What is not in doubt is his closeness to his full sister, Louisa, who may have been the older sibling, and with whom he corresponded affectionately for many years. He wrote to her from London in November 1797, where he appears to have been living with his grandmother and attending school.[48] In June 1810, he complained of a difficult relationship with his younger brother Frank, who, like himself, was then living on the Dangan estate. Roderic was severely critical of Frank's cavalier existence, opining, *inter alia*, that he was 'a selfish brat'.[49] Roderic was in his cottage on the property when the police authorities, acting on information provided by Michael Owens, the approver, searched the premises, sometime between February and mid-April 1817, and found the blunderbusses used in the mail coach robbery in 1812.[50] Roderic was in west Cork with his father and Sir Francis Burdett on 22 September 1817,[51] thereby discounting any possibility that he was in Van Diemen's Land on 9 August 1817, as has been tentatively suggested.[52] The three were at Dangan early in the following December, from where, on the eve of Burdett's departure for his home in England, Roderic informed his sister that their 'invaluable friend Sir Francis' had come there 'for no other purpose than to settle our affairs', adding enigmatically, '*he has done everything*' (Roderic's emphasis).[53]

James Dunkerly suggests, convincingly, that Roger O'Connor's eccentricity and nonconformism destabilised his family, created social difficulties and tensions for his children and constituted one of the factors that precipitated Frank's involvement in the military affairs of Latin America.[54] The same push factor applied to Frank's siblings, not least to his older brother Roderic, Roger O'Connor's heir-apparent, whose economic and social prospects must have been dented by his father's court appearances in the summer and autumn of 1817, and which were rendered even more problematic by the severe economic depression, famine and fever epidemics that crippled the country in the wake of the Napoleonic wars and that carried over into the 1820s.

Frustrated economic and social expectations, and, possibly, family tensions may explain Roderic's departure for Van Diemen's Land on 13 November 1823. He did so on board his own ship, *Ardent*, which called at Madeira, and Rio de Janeiro, landing there some nine weeks after its departure from Dublin,[55] before finally docking at Hobart on 7 May 1824.[56] On arrival, Roderic listed his assets as one ship, which was subsequently sold in Sydney for £1,500, 'one large Waggon; two carts; farming implements; and one large Town Clock and Bell: value, £600'.[57]

He received a free 1,000-acre grant on the Lake river and within four years had trebled his acreage. In 1826, Lieutenant-Governor Arthur appointed him to the Commission of Survey and Valuation, which had been established following the British government's orders to have the colony divided into counties, hundreds and parishes, and to have the waste lands of the crown valued so that quitrent could be levied. For two years, O'Connor and fellow commissioner Peter Murdoch examined all of the island's settled districts. Their reports were largely O'Connor's handiwork and were recorded, according to his biographer, P.R. Eldershaw, in 'vivid and uncomplicated language' that went far beyond the usual limits of official returns.[58]

There is only one reference to Ireland that I could detect in the land commissioners' published journals, but it is one that encapsulated O'Connor's style and temperament. The subject of the journal entry was an Irishman named Gilligan, who farmed a hundred-acre holding on the South Esk river, not far from the junction with St Paul's river:

> He has become a rich Man in the course of seven years, having now about thirteen hundred Sheep and two hundred and fifty Head of Cattle, which he is about to sell and intends returning to Ireland and misery. He is now old, and he fears to die in this unchristian place, as he calls it, where he cannot conveniently confess his Sins before he departs or have the rights of his Church, nor can he have in this wilderness the same numerous attendance at his Wake or Funeral, reflections nearest and dearest to an Irishman's heart, here he dies unpitied and unknown, there he is attended by a host of friends and relations, paying the last sad offices to his remains with tears and loud lamentations, which luckily are all forgotten in the nearest Public House, when all their grief is drowned in a glass of good Potteen.[59]

According to Eldershaw, the land commissioners' journals 'reflect a hot-tempered, outspoken, worldly-wise, contentious and egotistical Irish personality, but one possessed of wit and common sense',[60] a characteristic he shared with his brother Feargus, according to Karl Marx's assessment of the latter.[61] The journals provide a detailed picture of the practices and mores of the island's landed community in the years 1826–8, as perceived by a sharp and often cynical observer. In Eldershaw's opinion, the journals illustrate, 'better than many volumes of report and despatch, one of the main reasons why the British government decided to discontinue the free grant of land in the Australian colonies. Nowhere else are the abuses attendant on the free grant system more clearly set forth; the journals could be called a handbook on the art of defrauding the Crown in land.'[62]

After the completion of his survey work, O'Connor was appointed inspector of roads and bridges in April 1829, a position he held until December 1835, and one that put him in charge of hundreds of convicts engaged in public works. He was a committed transportationist and a large private employer of convict labour. O'Connor served two terms as a member of the Legislative Council, 1844–8 and 1852–3, and served also as a magistrate for many years. He was notoriously litigious and quarrelsome, much given to airing his grievances in public. According to Lady Franklin, wife of the Lieutenant-Governor, he was a man of 'viperous tongue and pen', which he dismissed as simply a facet of his 'red hot' Irish temperament.[63]

Throughout the period of his public life, O'Connor consolidated and expanded his private concerns, ending up as one of the colony's largest land-holders, owner of eleven properties, totalling 65,000 acres, and lessee of another 10,000 acres. He installed his son Arthur at 'Connorville' in or about 1829, and gave another property, 'Brook Lodge', to his younger son William.[64]

Roderic O'Connor contracted influenza, and died at his home, 'Benham', Avoca, in July 1860, and was buried in the Catholic cemetery at Avoca, having converted to that religion late in life. According to his headstone, he was seventy-two years of age when he died.[65] An obituary in the local press lauded his commitment to Tasmania, comparing him favourably to most of the early colonists who fled the place as soon as they acquired wealth. O'Connor, on the other hand, 'made Tasmania his home, retaining for her use all his means'. The newspaper account was less sure footed in its depiction of his Irish background, describing him as 'a zealous Irish patriot' who had been actively involved in the 1798 Rebellion and had fought in the defining battle of Vinegar Hill.[66] Perhaps he was a boy soldier; he was certainly his father's son!

Roderic was predeceased by his father, Roger, who died of a stroke in 1834. According to an account of his death written by Feargus to his brother Frank in Bolivia almost a decade after the event, Roger got up one morning 'in perfect health and being dressed, he stooped to put on his boot, seized the bed post and never spoke more, although he lingered some days in perfect consciousness. He also died a Catholic and was buried according to the ceremonies of that religion.'[67]

Roderic's son William died childless in 1855 and he was succeeded by his other son, Arthur, who inherited the bulk of the Tasmanian estate. Roderic was also survived by his brother, Frank, who lived a soldier's life and emerged unscathed from wars and revolutions to die of old age at his home in Tarija, Bolivia, on 5 October 1871. Like his father and older brother, he, too, was buried according to the rites of the Catholic Church.

The various O'Connor lines that sprang from Roger and his brother Arthur continue, in Europe, Australia and South America. In Tasmania, the current representative of the family, Roderic, lives in a house that bears the name of the one it replaced in 1922, 'Connorville'. The original family residence in County Cork, 'Connerville', has long since fallen into ruin.

NOTES

1. Roger O'Connor, *Letters to Earl Camden* (Cork, 1798), pp. 21–2.
2. Roger O'Connor, *An address to the people of Ireland; shewing them why they ought to submit to an union* (Dublin, 1799), p.16.
3. Robert Tracy, 'Self-fashioning as pseudo-history. Roger O'Connor's *Chronicles of Eri*', in

Robert Tracy, *The unappeasable host. Studies in Irish identities* (Dublin: UCD Press, 1998), pp. 47–56, at p.48.

4. His date of birth is incorrectly given as 8 March 1763 in *Burke's Irish Family Records* (London: Burke's Peerage Ltd., 1976), p.266, and in the chapter on the O'Connors of Connorville (sic), Co. Cork, in Bernard Burke, *Vicissitudes of families* (London, 1861, second series), pp.28–54, at p.33.

5. [Roger O'Connor], *Letters to his majesty, King George the Fourth, by Captain Rock* (London: B. Steill, 1828), p.202. The use of the pseudonym Captain Rock may indicate sympathy with the Rockite movement, an agrarian agitation that was widespread in Cork and other Munster counties in the 1820s, or ROCK may be an acronym for Roger O'Connor, King.

6. 'The Connor or, more correctly, Conner family was descended from a rich London merchant, and its claims to ancient Irish descent were totally spurious', W.J. Fitzpatrick, 'O'Connor, Roger (1762–1834)', rev. Thomas Bartlett, *Oxford Dictionary of National Biography* (Oxford: Oxford University Press, 2004), online edition, accessed 3 April 2007 [hereafter *ODNB*].

7. Jane Hayter Hames, *Arthur O'Connor: United Irishman* (Cork: Collins Press, 2001), pp.7–13.

8. Roger O'Connor, *View of the system of Anglo-Irish jurisprudence, and of the effects of trial by jury, when individuals consider themselves belonging to a faction, rather than to the community* (London, 1811), p.72.

9. James Livesey, 'O'Connor, Arthur (1763–1852)', *ODNB*, online edition, accessed 4 April 2007.

10. Marianne Elliott, *Partners in Revolution: The United Irishmen and France* (New Haven and London: Yale University Press, 1982), pp.99–100. See also Frank MacDermot, 'Arthur O'Connor', *Irish Historical Studies*, 15 (March 1966), pp.48–69; for a less critical assessment, see Hames, *Arthur O'Connor*.

11. William J. Fitzpatrick, *Ireland Before the Union; with Extracts from the Unpublished Diary of John Scott, LL.D, Earl of Clonmell, Chief Justice of the King's Bench, 1774–1798. A Sequel to the Sham Squire and the Informers of 1798* (Dublin: W.B. Kelly, 1867), p.225. See also Hames, *Arthur O'Connor*, pp.166–7.

12. The publication dates were 7, 10, 14 and 17 March 1798. Seán Ó Coindealbháin, 'The United Irishmen in Cork County', *Journal of the Cork Historical and Archaeological Society*, liii (July–December 1948), pp.126–7. See also, R.R. Madden, *The United Irishmen: their lives and times* (London: J. Madden, 1843, 2nd series, 2 vols), 2, p.294; David Dickson, *Old world colony. Cork and south Munster* (Cork: Cork University Press, 2005), p.467.

13. Diary of General John Moore, quoted in Ó Coindealbháin, 'United Irishmen in Cork County', p.124.

14. Roger O'Connor, *To the People of Great Britain and Ireland* (Dublin, 1799), pp.72–4.

15. Ibid., pp.86, 88.

16. Registry of Deeds, Dublin: 554.556.371048 (reg. 1803); 558.227.371049 (reg. 1803); 583.482.399006 (reg. 1807). At the time of these transactions, Connerville house and demesne were leased to Edward and Herbert Gillman at £557 per annum. See also John P. Prendergast, 'Dangan and Roger O'Connor', *Irish Monthly*, 12 (January 1884), pp.35–47, at pp.35–7. By June 1812, O'Connor had fully discharged the principal, interest, and costs associated with the mortgage, Registry of Deeds, 694.378.476663.

17. Burke, *Vicissitudes of Families*, p.38; Fitzpatrick, 'O'Connor, Roger', *ODNB*; W.J. O'Neill Daunt, *A Life Spent for Ireland* (London: T. Fisher Unwin, 1896, repr. with an introduction by David Thornley, Shannon: Irish University Press, 1972), pp 249–51. The suspicion of Roger's involvement persisted. Almost a century and a half later, an essayist observed: '… the house passed to a Mr Roger O'Connor, who cut down all the trees that he could sell and skinned the rooms of every saleable fitting. Finally, after it had been well insured, the house burst into flames. No great effort was made to quench them.' Hubert Butler, 'Dangan revisited', in Hubert Butler, *Grandmother and Wolfe Tone* (Dublin: Lilliput Press, 1990), pp.105–7, at p.105.

18. James Dunkerley, 'The third man: Francisco Burdett O'Connor and the emancipation of the Americas', in idem., *Warriors and Scribes. Essays on the History and Politics of Latin America* (London and New York: Verso, 2000), pp.145–67, at p.153.

19. Fitzpatrick, 'O'Connor, Roger'; Livesey, 'O'Connor, Arthur', *ODNB*; Burke, *Vicissitudes of Families*, pp.38, 46; *A full and accurate report of the arraignment and subsequent*

extraordinary and highly interesting trial of Roger O'Connor, Esq. of Dangan Castle, County Meath, and Martin McKeon, his gate-keeper, on a charge for feloniously conspiring, aiding, and abetting in the robbery of his majesty's mail from Dublin to Galway, at Cappagh Hill in the county of Kildare; on the second day of October, 1812; and for the robbery of Bartholemew St. Leger, at the same time and place. Tried before the Right Hon. St. George Daly, one of his majesty's justices of the Court of King's Bench, and a most respectable jury, at summer assizes held in Trim, in the county of Meath, on Monday the 4th, and Tuesday the 5th days of August, 1817 (Dublin, 1817), p.46.

20. *A full and accurate report of the arraignment and subsequent extraordinary and highly interesting trial of Roger O'Connor*, pp.2, 8.

21. Ibid., pp.12–20.

22. Ibid., pp.21–5, 34–5.

23. Ibid., pp.30–3.

24. Ibid., p.42.

25. Ibid., pp.44–6.

26. Ibid., pp.45–7.

27. Richard Wilson Greene, *A report of the trial of Daniel Waring upon the prosecution of Roger O'Connor, Esq. At an adjournment of the Commission for the County of the City of Dublin, before the Hon. St. Geo. Daly and the Hon. Edward Mayne, for perjury* (Dublin, 1817), p.85; *A full report of the trial of Daniel Waring, at the prosecution of Roger O'Connor, Esq. for perjury. Tried at the Commission Court, Friday, October, 31, 1817* (Dublin, 1817), p.19.

28. Prendergast, 'Dangan and Roger O'Connor', pp.41–2.

29. M.W. Patterson, *Sir Francis Burdett and his Times (1770–1844)* (London: Macmillan, 2 vols, 1931), 2, pp.429, 434, 446.

30. [Roger] O'Connor, *Chronicles of Eri; being the history of the Gaal Sciot Iber: or, the Irish people; translated from the original manuscripts in the Phoenician dialect of the Scythian language* (London: Sir Richard Phillips and Co., 2 vols, 1822).

31. The representation is derived from Roger O'Connor, by Thomas Goff Lupton (1791–1873), after Abraham Wivell (1786–1849), mezzotint, 1822, National Portrait Gallery, London, D3715.

32. O'Connor, *Chronicles of Eri*, 1, pp.vii–ix.

33. Ibid., p.xi.

34. Ibid., 2, p.509.

35. Tracy, 'Self-fashioning as pseudo-history', p.48.

36. Fitzpatrick, 'O'Connor, Roger', *ODNB*.

37. *Ulster Journal of Archaeology*, 7 (1859), p.177.

38. Ibid., p.264.

39. Prendergast, 'Dangan and Roger O'Connor', pp.43–7.

40. For this family, see Elizabeth Bowen, *Bowenscourt* (London: Longman's, Green and Co., 1942).

41. W.J. Williams, 'Bolivar and his Irish legionaires', *Studies*, 18 (December 1929), pp.619–32, at pp.630–1.

42. O'Neill Daunt, *A life spent for Ireland*, p.25.

43. Laurence M. Geary, 'O'Connorite bedlam: Feargus and his grand-nephew, Arthur', *Medical History*, 34 (1990), pp.125–43.

44. Donald Read and Eric Glasgow, *Feargus O'Connor: Irishman and Chartist* (London: Edward Arnold, 1961), p.142; James Epstein, 'O'Connor, Feargus Edward (1796?–1855)', *ODNB*, online edition, accessed 23 April 2007.

45. Francisco Burdett O'Connor, *Independéncia Americana: recuerdos de Francisco Burdett O'Connor, coronel del ejercito libertador de Colombia y general de división de los del Perú y Bolivia* (Madrid, ND), quoted in Alfred Hasbrouck, *Foreign legionaries in the liberation of Spanish South America* (New York: Columbia, 1928), p.60.

46. O'Connor, *Chronicles of Eri*, 1, p.iv.

47. Laurence M. Geary, 'Fraternally Yours: Roderic and Francis Burdett O'Connor', *Journal of*

the Cork Historical and Archaeological Society, xcv (1990), pp.120–3.

48. Roderic to Louisa, 11 November 1797, Conner Papers, Manch House, Ballineen, County Cork. I am grateful to Oriana Conner, Manch House, for permission to cite the Conner Papers in her possession. I would also like to acknowledge the assistance of Julian Walton, who is currently cataloguing these manuscripts.

49. Ibid., 26 June 1810.

50. *A full and accurate report of the arraignment and subsequent extraordinary and highly interesting trial of Roger O'Connor*, pp.25, 30–2, 41.

51. Patterson, *Sir Francis Burdett*, 2, pp.448–9.

52. P.R. Eldershaw, introduction to Anne McKay, ed., *Journal of the Land Commissioners for Van Diemen's Land, 1826–28* (Hobart: University of Tasmania in conjunction with the Tasmanian Historical Research Association, 1962), p.xix; Roderic O'Connor MSS, copies of letters, mostly addressed to Roderic O'Connor, National Library of Ireland, P 5074 [Hereafter NLI].

53. Roderic to Louisa, 3 December 1817, Conner Papers. Some six years later, Burdett reassured Roderic, who was en route to Australia, of his friendship for his father. Despite the latter's 'misfortunes', he was, according to Burdett, 'comfortable and happy'. Roderic O'Connor MSS, NLI, P 5074], Sir Francis Burdett to Roderic O'Connor, 28 December 1823.

54. Dunkerley, 'The third man', pp.154–5.

55. Roderic to Louisa, 23 January 1824, Conner Papers.

56. Roderic O'Connor MSS, NLI, P 5074.

57. Eldershaw, introduction to Anne McKay, ed., *Journal of the Land Commissioners for Van Diemen's Land*, p.xix.

58. P.R. Eldershaw, 'Roderic O'Connor', *Australian Dictionary of Biography* (Melbourne: Melbourne University Press, 1966–), Vol. 2, pp.296–7 (Hereafter *ADB*); idem, introduction to Anne McKay (ed.), *Journal of the Land Commissioners for Van Diemen's Land*, pp.xiii–xvii.

59. McKay (ed.), *Journal of the Land Commissioners for Van Diemen's Land*, p.68.

60. Eldershaw, 'Roderic O'Connor' in *ADB*, 2, pp.296–7.

61. Review of May–October 1850, *Neue Rheinische Zeitung Revue*, in D. Fernbach (ed.), *Marx: the revolutions of 1848* (Harmondsworth, 1973), pp.308–9, cited in Dunkerley, 'The third man', p.163.

62. Eldershaw, introduction to Anne McKay (ed.), *Journal of the Land Commissioners for Van Diemen's Land*, p.xxi.

63. Eldershaw, 'Roderic O'Connor' in *ADB*, 2, pp.296–7; Eldershaw, introduction to Anne McKay (ed.), *Journal of the Land Commissioners for Van Diemen's Land*, pp.xxii–xxv.

64. Roderic O'Connor MSS, NLI, P 5074.

65. http://eheritage.statelibrary.tas.gov.au/ [This State Library of Tasmania site was accessed on 16 March 2007]. O'Connor's headstone suggests that he was born in 1788. This is unlikely, given that his father remarried in that year, following the death of his first wife, Roderic's mother, Louisa Ann. Eldershaw gives 1784 as the year of Roderic's birth. A more likely date is 1786 or 1787. In a deed of 1803 it is stated that Roderic, oldest son of Roger O'Connor, was then aged seventeen years and that Francis Burdett O'Connor, his second son, was then aged thirteen years. Registry of Deeds, Dublin: 554.556.371048.

66. Roderic O'Connor MSS, NLI, P 5074, obituary in unnamed, undated Tasmanian newspaper.

67. Feargus O'Connor to Frank O'Connor, 28 September 1843, quoted in Dunkerley, 'The third man', p.162.

12

'The opportunity of being useful': Daniel O'Connell's Influence on John Hubert Plunkett

Tony Earls

In the introduction to *The Irish in Australia*, Patrick O'Farrell made an important assertion:

> The direct Irish contribution to Australian liberties is very great, in terms of effective protest against religious and political monopolies, refusal to accept discriminatory laws, and demands for social equality. Perhaps even more vital is the impact of their energetic activities and independent opinions in liberalizing and humanizing the climate of Australian life, on freeing the atmosphere of authoritarianism, pretence and cultural tyranny. The Irish had no philosophic notion of an open pluralistic society. It might be argued their pretences were ideally the opposite. Yet an open society in Australia was the effect of their determination to prise apart a society which threatened to become closed.[1]

The extent to which O'Farrell pressed this social dynamic as formative of an Australian ethos was bold and controversial. Although O'Farrell's proposition is obviously to be understood in a much wider context, the career of the New South Wales Attorney General, John Hubert Plunkett, provides a supportive and informative case study. It may also suggest that although the Irish did not come from an 'open pluralistic society' they were, perhaps, not without philosophical notions favourable to such a society.

The years 1824[2] to 1856[3] in New South Wales mark a period of transition from a penal colony to a civil government, the foundation of the modern democratic culture. The dominant political model that Irish immigrants of that period brought with them was that engendered by Daniel O'Connell. At its most fundamental level, it was a model that believed civil rights and justice could be obtained by vigorously working within the framework of English constitutional forms. The successes of the Catholic Association in Ireland in the 1820s can be seen as a factor which encouraged the Irish to actively participate in the developing legal and political institutions through the 1830s, 1840s and 1850s in New South Wales. The context of that political engagement is apparent when one compares the New South Wales and Irish newspapers of the period. The similarity in sectarian rhetoric points strongly to a conclusion that the gradual extension of the franchise and civil rights in Australia involved not only a contest between emancipists and exclusives, but religious and ethnic debates that had been well rehearsed in the homelands. John Hubert Plunkett was at the centre of events during this period. For over twenty years, at a crucial stage of the colony's development, he was the most influential legal officer in New South Wales. The ideals behind the exercise of that influence were informed not just by his legal training, but by his involvement with Daniel O'Connell and the Catholic Association.

The Plunkett family had a long involvement in Catholic politics, particularly through the conservative aristocrat, Arthur Plunkett, the Earl of Fingall. John Hubert Plunkett attended Trinity College Dublin with Daniel O'Connell's eldest son Maurice; they also read for the bar together in London and Dublin, and were to remain close friends. It is likely that Plunkett was an intimate at the home the O'Connell family kept at Southampton while Maurice was reading for the bar at Gray's Inn. Plunkett had been studying in Dublin during the debates that led to the formation of the Catholic Association, and, at age 22, he was one of the association's early members, (according to a membership card from 1824 which he kept with him all his life).[4] Lawyers were the most significant group involved in the formation of the Catholic Association. Of its sixty-two founding members, thirty-one were lawyers.[5] Young barristers of Plunkett's ilk were relied upon to spread the word and promote the business of the association as they travelled from town to town on circuit. In addition, they were sometimes deployed to legally assist members of the association, such as tenants in land disputes. Plunkett was admitted to the Irish bar in 1826,[6] established himself on the Connaught Circuit and involved himself in the business of the Catholic Association.

Oliver MacDonagh has drawn attention to the influence of Godwin's *Political Justice* on O'Connell, and in particular three principles that O'Connell took from that work.[7] First, that violence in pursuit of political objectives was counter-productive. Second, that any political objective could eventually be achieved by marshalling public opinion, and, third, that civil liberties were universal, irrespective of class, colour or creed. MacDonagh was of the view that, notwithstanding the many vacillations of O'Connell's pragmatic political career, these were three principles from which O'Connell never wavered. These values were central to the aims and methods of the Catholic Association. Plunkett's correspondence with O'Connell[8] suggests that he was close enough to O'Connell at a personal level, not least through his friendship with Maurice O'Connell, to have been exposed to such thought at first hand,[9] They are principles that are wholly consistent with the manner in which Plunkett conducted his own legal and political career.

Another intellectual tenet to the cause of Catholic emancipation was the separation of Church and state. This was a necessary counter to the view that because Protestantism was integral to the British constitution only Protestants could be trusted to uphold that constitution. Catholics were seen as a particular threat in this regard because of their supposed allegiances to a foreign power. O'Connell met this by proclaiming a respect for, and loyalty to, the crown and the British constitution uncompromised by his, or any other Catholic's, faith, because so far as the business of the state was concerned that faith involved no contradictions. The spiritual did not interfere with the secular. This message was somewhat obscured by the fact that the Catholic Association relied on the resources of the Catholic Church to mobilise popular support and collect the Catholic Rent.

The general election of 1830 was the first opportunity after Catholic Emancipation for a Catholic to win a parliamentary seat, and Plunkett successfully managed the campaign for the head of an ancient Catholic family in County Roscommon, The O'Conor Don. O'Connell was delighted at the victory for a seat which had been seen as something of an Orange stronghold, and called for a dinner to be held in Plunkett's honour. In response to the dinner, Plunkett said:

> Enlarging our exultation at the independence of a district, into a fervent wish for the prosperity of our beloved country, let us hope the example will not be forgotten. To the people, let it be a suggestion of the existence of resources...To the individual let it be a lesson, that to none is denied the opportunity of being useful, however limited his capacity, or humble his condition.[10]

Plunkett himself was a man of considerable capacity, his condition was by no means humble, and he was to be given a unique opportunity to be useful far from his native land.

The number of seats won by O'Connell's supporters in 1830 had given O'Connell substantial bargaining power with the new Whig government. In 1831 O'Connell, together with the Earl of Fingall, lobbied to have Plunkett appointed as Solicitor General to the Colony of New South

Wales. Keen to see the principle of Catholic Emancipation converted to actual appointments, O'Connell was alert to suitable vacancies. The New South Wales post was a particularly quick piece of opportunism on O'Connell's part. He somehow became aware that there was discontent in the Colonial Secretary's office with a newly appointed Solicitor General who was taking too long to leave England to assume his duties, and, in what appears to have been a hastily arranged affair in back corridors, that appointee was replaced by Plunkett.

No doubt Plunkett had sought, in general terms, whatever preferment his influential mentor could obtain for him, but a position in far away Australia must have given him pause for thought. Indeed he walked around with the application for appointment in his pocket for two weeks before he could bring himself to tell his father.[11] Plunkett's biographer, John Molony, recounts family legend that Plunkett was motivated to leave Ireland because he was heartsore over a broken engagement.[12] However, Plunkett married another before he set out for New South Wales (although after his appointment), and it would seem valid to give at least equal weight to professional ambition. A solicitor-generalship was unlikely to come his way in Ireland, where opportunities at the bar were few. His family circumstances were not such that he could lightly dismiss a government salary of £800 per annum, and there was good reason to believe that a young man of his talents would have prospects to advance further in the growing colony of New South Wales. As someone who had dedicated himself to the cause of Catholic emancipation, he cannot have been unaware of the fact that, by virtue of the appointment, he would become the first Catholic appointed to high office in Australia.[13] Even if he was, then O'Connell would surely have pointed it out. There was a sense of duty involved.

Plunkett took up the position in Sydney in 1832, where he effectively became de facto Attorney General. The then Attorney General, John Kinchela, a Kilkenny man, was hard of hearing and essentially unfit for court work. This impediment did not inhibit Kinchela's later elevation to the bench in 1836, allowing Plunkett to be formally confirmed as Attorney General for New South Wales, a post he was to hold until 1856.

For over twenty years Plunkett was the most influential legal officer in the colony. He decided which cases would be prosecuted, and prosecuted most of them personally. He ensured the proper administration of the legal system, with respect to matters such as the compilation of jury lists, and supervised the conduct of legal practitioners and magistrates. He was at the forefront of measures taken to restrain the excesses of the New South Wales magistracy, particularly with regard to the punishment of assigned convicts.[14] In 1835 he wrote Australia's first published legal text, An

Australian Magistrate, which remained the country's most influential legal practice book for the remainder of the nineteenth century.[15] He was the primary legal advisor to the governor, and to all legal departments. As a member of the Executive Council no major legislative reform escaped his attention, indeed he drafted many of the bills personally. He was a prominent figure in council debates, and a key member of many of the council's committees. Through all of this, his enduring reputation, even amongst his critics, was one of diligence and impartiality. He consistently promoted a 'one law for all' principle. He promoted the right for emancipated convicts to sit on juries. He argued against assigning convicts as labour to private individuals. In 1847 he stood alone in the council chamber in opposition to the resumption of transportation. He was a key figure in each of the steps towards the establishment of representative and responsible government, from the Market Commissioners Act of 1837 through to the New South Wales constitution of 1856.[16]

In popular Australian histories, he is most frequently remembered as the prosecutor in the Myall Creek massacre case. During the expansion of the colony westwards, there were many clashes between white settlers and indigenous Australians, and many appalling atrocities. Much of this occurred beyond the frontiers of the territory the government was able to administer. It rarely found its way into the courts. However, in 1836 an overseer reported to the authorities a massacre of approximately twenty-two Aboriginals, mostly women and children, near Myall Creek cattle station, about 350 miles north-west of Sydney. (The overseer was subsequently dismissed by his employers.) Remarkably, a police magistrate, a Kerryman named Edward Denny Day, was able to track down and arrest twelve of the white men responsible. Plunkett had long proclaimed that he would prosecute whites and blacks equally, without fear or favour. He did not shirk the opportunity to prove it. It was a case attended with significant difficulty because the bodies had been burnt beyond recognition. The defendants received solid support from the economically powerful grazing lobby, and a significant body of public opinion held that regardless of the crime, it would be wrong to hang a white man for killing a black. At least one juror in the first trial, where the men were aquitted, admitted as much. Undeterred, Plunkett prosecuted a second trial, claiming, controversially, that he could run a separate case for each of the slain. This time he prosecuted only seven of the twelve men, hoping to break their solidarity. During the course of the second trial he exposed the tactics of the powerful land owners who sanctioned the extermination of the native peoples, and secured a guilty verdict. On the scaffold each of the condemned men confessed, and said that such events were so commonplace they did not think they would ever be prosecuted.

The case caused a public furore. It was the first and last such case ever brought, even though the massacres continued, albeit covertly. Even to the end of his career, Plunkett suffered the open enmity of those who disagreed with his prosecution of the cases, to which his standard reply was that he would have been ashamed had he acted otherwise.

One of the reasons Plunkett had been confident from the outset that the men were guilty was because he had access to an eye-witness of the events. However, that witness was an Aboriginal, and under the law an Aboriginal could not give evidence. Plunkett saw this as the greatest handicap to securing the protection of the law for Aboriginals. For over twelve years Plunkett made strenuous efforts to secure this right for them, pleading that he was powerless to bring prosecutions for the mass poisonings and slaughter which was continuing, without their evidence. That he failed is one of the saddest stains on the history of New South Wales.

Plunkett considered his greatest achievement to be his part in the introduction of the Church Act in 1836. The early founders of New South Wales intended the development of a society built on the values of the established Church. Accordingly, the Anglican Church was entitled to one seventh of all crown land and its proceeds. For a large part of the colony's early history Catholicism and other faiths were actively discouraged. During Plunkett's early years in the colony, the governor was Richard Bourke, an Irishman, whose career and management of his Limerick estates vouched for his liberal principles. Although a sincere Anglican himself, Bourke shared the tolerance of his relative and mentor, Edmund Burke,[17] and had long held the view that, for the purposes of civic life, the various Christian faiths had more in common than they had apart, such as an adherence to the ten commandments. He was concerned that if a substantial part of the population could not have the guidance of their own faith, they would have none at all, and lawlessness and moral degradation would ensue.

Plunkett and Bourke had become friends during Plunkett's time as Solicitor General, and Plunkett spent many pleasant weekends at the governor's Parramatta residence. During that time they hatched a plan, which was to create an opportunity for all Christian faiths to be placed on an equal footing. According to Plunkett's account of events, they privately drafted a bill over several months to provide for all the major Christian denominations to receive equal government funding, relative to the size of their congregations. The reason for the secrecy was that the governor alone could not force the measure through. It had to be passed by a local Legislative Council of seven. Bourke and Plunkett were well aware that conservative members of the council, including the local colonial secretary, would oppose the measure. So they lobbied in secret and successfully introduced the already-drafted bill at the most opportune moment. [18]

The Church Act was of enormous importance to Australia's social development. In its time it was seen as a Magna Carta of religious freedom, in advance of anything at that time possible in either England or Ireland. It effectively disestablished the Anglican Church in New South Wales thirty years before such a measure could be achieved in Ireland. Plunkett made it clear that had he had his way the provisions would also have been extended to those of the Jewish faith, and indeed before the end of his career he had them included by an amendment to the Act in 1856, providing a sinecure for rabbis. The importance of the Act is sometimes overlooked because it was repealed as early as 1862. But by then it had already done its work. The major Christian Churches had built up enough of a critical mass to be self-sufficient, and their equal status as part of a multi-faith society had been put beyond doubt.

The major credit for the Church Act belongs to Sir Richard Bourke. It was his vision, backed by the application of his authority to his convictions. But, equally, Plunkett's role in carefully drafting and negotiating the terms of the Act, and as an active advocate for it in the Legislative Council, was crucial. Perhaps due to the unexpected introduction of the Church Act, the conservative forces were better prepared to offer resistance when Richard Bourke attempted to introduce a parallel liberal measure which was close to his heart – government-funded public education. Education at that time was held to be the preserve of religious bodies, but they were poorly placed to meet the needs of the growing colony, and many thousands of children, dispersed over a wide territory, went uneducated. Bourke had worked with Thomas Spring Rice on the formulation of the non-denominational Irish National School system, and had fostered a Kildare Place Society school on his own estate in Limerick (a precursor to the Irish National School system). However, his attempts to introduce the system in New South Wales floundered as the various Churches bickered over issues of curriculum and control. Stung by the Church Act, the Anglicans were not prepared to make any concessions, and the Catholic Church insisted that it alone was fit to meet the needs of young Catholics. Plunkett was familiar with the Irish National School system, due to the success of Kildare Place Society schools amongst the poor of his native county, Roscommon. Intriguingly, there are the ruins of an old National School on the estate of Mount Plunkett were Plunkett was born and grew up. It appears the structure was built after Plunkett had left for Australia, but may well have had antecedence reflecting family support for such ventures. At any event Plunkett was a staunch supporter of 'national', non-denominational public schooling and where Bourke failed Plunkett eventually succeeded. Plunkett continued to press for non-denominational public education long after Bourke had departed the colony, and in 1848 was part of a group, led by Robert Lowe, which achieved the introduction of such a system, and Plunkett acted as the unpaid chairman of the relevant board overseeing the system's first twelve years.

The leading Catholic layman of his day, on no point did Plunkett come into greater conflict with his Church than on the issue of education. That he was prepared to stand his ground on such matters was of the utmost importance to the public perception of Catholics in Australia. The greatest fear of the Protestant establishment was that empowered 'Papists' would follow the dictates of their Church rather than the intelligence of their conscience. This had always been a fundamental objection to the full citizenship of Catholics. In New South Wales, Plunkett was the example par excellence that Catholics were capable of drawing a line between secular duties and spiritual life. His career was prominent enough and long enough for his conduct in that regard to be recognised as a matter of public record. In this sense, Plunkett was truer to the intellectual underpinnings of Daniel O'Connell's various causes than many others who used O'Connell's name as a rallying cry in the colony. For many Irish in Australia, O'Connellism meant the alignment of political objectives with the organisational power of the Church. Plunkett, who was a leading light in both spheres, never sought this.

The correspondence between O'Connell and Plunkett is revealing as a demonstration of the confidence and familiarity between the two men. There appears to be no record of Plunkett's letters to O'Connell, but extracts from some of O'Connell's letters suffice:

From Derrynane, on 19 September 1832

My dear Plunkett,
This letter will be handed to you by a young gentleman, an ally of mine, Mr Murphy. You will not like him the less for being a near relation of your friend Maurice.
This young gentleman has got some situation in New South Wales which as he is one of a large family he accepts of but I believe he will require some friendly aid to advance him into a situation of more competency. I have no hesitation in assuring his relations that your friendship for me would instigate you to do anything in your power to serve him, and I am quite sure it will ... If he were my son I could not feel more grateful for any attention shewn him.
This is not an opportunity to canvass politics but I may tell you though you are on the high road to the Bench that I am *repealing the Union*. When you come to see your friends having sat some years with credit

to yourself and benefit to the Colony as Chief Justice[19] you will I trust find Ireland as she ought to be. You know the rest.[20]

From Tralee, on 1 January 1835

My dear Plunkett,

I have often and often proposed to write to you and postponed doing so at the pressure of my various occupations so long that I am also ashamed to do so now but there is a case of justice and suffering humanity which will not permit me to defer it any longer.

Before I go into the case which demands my writing at present allow me to tell you that I saw your letter to Maurice and had the pleasure of receiving one from you dated in May last and handed to me by your friend Surgeon O'Donoghue who has impressed me with very favourable sentiments on his behalf. I am delighted to find that you are in such good spirits as to your future prospects ...I am glad you think so favorably of Chief Justice Forbes. I shall take my next opportunity to speak of him in the house as I perceive he deserves, and I entirely agree with you that your colony should have a representative body of legislators as speedily as possible. The success of the trial by jury affords an omen of and an argument for the second great experiment. I think I remember reading in some old law book that jury trial arose from the principle of representation.

We are in an unpleasant state now in the Country with our Orange Rulers but it is only a passing cloud which will give a brighter glow to the light of liberty when it shines out again. You see I am getting poetic, but not less of the spirit of prophesy on that account. The Tory dominion believe me *will* not and cannot last.

[O'Connell then, at some length, outlines the case of one of his clients, a Kerryman named James Daly, who O'Connell thought had been wrongly convicted of rape and asks Plunkett to secure whatever freedom he can for Daly in the colony.]

Many many thanks for your kind attentions to my young friend Mr Murphy. It was truly gratifying to me to have you respond so completely to my wishes for his interests ...[21]

The last letter Plunkett received from O'Connell came from O'Connell's Dublin residence in Merrion Square. It is dated 10 April 1845, and follows from O'Connell's period of incarceration in Richmond Prison.

My dear Plunkett,

I beg leave to introduce to you the bearer of this letter Mr Thomas R

Purdon – a young gentleman in whose fortune I take a deep interest, for this reason that he is the son of Mr Purdon the Governor for many years of Richmond Penitentiary in which capacity I received from him the kindest and most constant attention during our unjust imprisonment ... If you can in any manner promote his interests you will confer a great personal favour on your very faithful and affectionate friend, Daniel O'Connell.[22]

These examples are representative of the whole correspondence. O'Connell could assure relatives, friends and clients destined for New South Wales that his influence extended to the other side of the world, and that his man there would do what he could for them. O'Connell's trust that the influential Plunkett would do so is apparent from the letters: a trust borne not just from a personal connection, but the recognition of like-minded convictions.

Between March 1841 and August 1843, Plunkett took leave to return to Ireland, ostensibly to attend to affairs on the death of his father. Whilst there he entertained the possibility of making it a permanent return, but he appears not to have been offered a position. He visited his former governor, at Richard Bourke's Thornfield estate in Limerick, and no doubt met with O'Connell also. It is interesting to reflect that whilst in Ireland Plunkett would have seen the first editions of Gavan Duffy's newspaper the *Nation*. He was of the same generation as the Young Irelanders, but by the time of their break with O'Connell in 1845, Plunkett was back in New South Wales. Perhaps he might have felt differently had he been closer to the scene, and experienced the Great Famine at first hand. As it was, he remained steadfast to the O'Connell line. He thought the Young Irelanders ruined Ireland, and broke O'Connell's heart.[23] However, when Gavan Duffy came to Sydney in 1856 he seems to have enjoyed good relations with Plunkett, and recognised Plunkett's contribution fulsomely:

I am proud to see a man of my own creed and nation, who for five-and-twenty years had a power almost uncontrolled over the course of legislation, secure for himself the adherence of the most adverse classes by his systematic liberality and justice. Every clergyman of the Church of England voted for this Irish Catholic; the Wesleyans supported him; the Jews supported him. And why? Because when power was centred in his hands, he protected and secured their religious liberty. [24]

Plunkett stood down as Attorney General in 1856, and in recognition of his service he was appointed Australia's first Queen's Counsel.[25] He sought an elected position in the newly constituted legislature. What was significant about his first election campaign was that he did not seek to appeal to the Irish Catholic constituency alone, but sought and obtained support across all classes and sects of society – this was at the expense of losing many Irish voters who sought a more partisan approach. He had the worst of both worlds during the election, as his opponents ran a smear campaign based on his Irish Catholicism. He lost by a mere 101 votes, out of 15,061 cast. O'Connell was a controversial figure in New South Wales and Plunkett rarely referred to his connection with him. Perhaps thinking his public career was over, he spoke unguardedly at the poll about many matters, including his achievements and principles, in the course of which he noted that 'it had been said by the celebrated O'Connell that the man who infringed the law was an enemy to freedom'. Plunkett said that he adopted that sentiment and believed that the man who did not rely on law to obtain justice did not deserve the name of a freeman.[26]

He was soon returned as the representative of another constituency, and went on to serve as President of the Legislative Council. He continued to make a useful contribution to the government of New South Wales, as a respected and impartial elder statesman until his retirement to Melbourne, where he died in 1869. On his death his body was returned to Sydney, where he was accorded a public funeral, attended by representatives of all political factions and the leaders of all the major faiths. The funeral procession down George Street to Sydney Cemetery was reported to tail for three-quarters of a mile.[27] The esteem of his contemporaries is well recorded. The Chief Justice, Sir Alfred Stephen, said of him, '...there will be no name recorded by the pen of history, in Australian annals, with juster or more enduring praise than that which belongs to Mr Attorney-General Plunkett'.[28] In an editorial the *Sydney Morning Herald* stated that 'future times will not furnish a sphere of trial, and therefore of virtue, such as Mr Plunkett occupied for so long'.[29] In 1998, at a joint sitting of the houses of the New South Wales parliament, Premier Carr acknowledged that, save for W.C. Wentworth, no one was more important than Plunkett to the constitutional development of the parliament they now sat in.[30] Today, Plunkett lies in an unmarked grave.

On his deathbed it was Plunkett's wish to be buried as close as possible to a priest he had brought out to Australia with him, his friend Fr McEncroe. Attempts were made to comply with that wish at Sydney Cemetery. But in 1901 that cemetery was closed to make way for what is now Central Railway Station. Fr McEncroe was re-interred in the crypt of St Mary's Cathedral, and a cousin paid to have Plunkett re-interred in a family grave at Waverley Cemetery, on Sydney's coast. The grave has a fine Celtic cross, but only names of immediate family members are named; John Hubert is unacknowledged.

There are no public monuments to Plunkett in Sydney. His name is painted above the inside of the doorway to the NSW parliament, and there is a plaque in memory of him at the home of the Sisters of Mercy, at Potts Point. (Plunkett and McEncroe were instrumental in bringing the sisters out as the first nuns in Australia, and were their greatest supporters.) However, by a quirk of serendipity there is an apt metaphorical tribute in Melbourne. In 1863 Plunkett had led the drive for Australian subscriptions towards the O'Connell monument in Dublin. By 1891 Australia had its own statue of O'Connell, erected in the grounds of St Patrick's Cathedral, Melbourne. For over a hundred years that statue stood at the door of the cathedral. In recent years the statue has been moved around the corner and into the gardens of the cathedral to make room for the statue of another famous Irishman in Australia, Archbishop Daniel Mannix. From its current position O'Connell's statue now looks out over the road towards the very house that Plunkett died in, which was then 5 Burlington Terrace (now in Albert Street).[31]

Daniel O'Connell held hopes that, unburdened by centuries of an entrenched hierarchy, Irishmen in Australia would find it easier to achieve the liberties that he sought for Ireland itself. He is reputed to have said that 'it is in New South Wales that Irishmen would first come to love the British Constitution', because there they would have 'English law fairly administered'.[32] For over twenty years, O'Connell's protégé and Australia's longest-serving Attorney General[33] did much to make that so.

NOTES

1. Patrick O'Farrell, *The Irish in Australia* (Sydney: New South Wales University Press, 1987 Reprint), p.11.
2. 1824 – The founding of Australia's first independent court, The Supreme Court of New South Wales.
3. The New South Wales Constitution of 1856, establishing Australia's first form of responsible government.
4. Plunkett ended his days in Melbourne, and some of his papers were given to the Church there. They include letters from Daniel O'Connell and his Catholic Association membership card. The papers are now with the Melbourne Catholic Archdiocesan Historical Commission.
5. James A. Reynolds, *The Catholic Emancipation Crisis in Ireland* (New Haven, CT: Yale University Press, 1954), p.31.
6. Edward Keane, Beryl P. Phair and Thomas U. Sadlier (eds), *King's Inn Admission Papers 1607–1867* (Dublin: Irish Manuscripts Commission, 1982).
7. Oliver MacDonagh, 'O'Connell and Parnell', in Richard Davis, Jennifer Livett, Anne-Marie Whitaker and Peter Moore (eds), *Irish Australian Studies: Papers Delivered at the Eighth Irish-Australian Conference Hobart July 1995* (Sydney: Crossing Press, 1996), p 6. See also Oliver MacDonagh, *The Hereditary Bondsman* (London: Weidenfeld and Nicolson, 1988), p.41.

8. Maurice R. O'Connell (ed.), *The Correspondence of Daniel O'Connell* (Dublin: Irish University Press for the Irish Manuscripts Commisssion, Vol. 8, 1980), letters 3138a, 3343, 3430, 3432, 3433, and 3439.

9. Towards the end of his career, Plunkett donated his books to the library of the NSW parliament. The library holds a copy of Godwin's *Political Justice* from that time. Unfortunately it is not possible to ascertain whether it belonged to Plunkett. The book has limited markings pencilled in the margins that are not dissimilar to those contained in other books identifiable as Plunkett's, but this is not conclusive.

10. *Sydney Morning Herald*, 17 May 1869.

11. John M. Bennett (ed.), *Callaghan's Diary* (Sydney: Francis Forbes Society, 2005), p.25.

12. John N. Molony, *An Architect of Freedom* (Canberra: Australian National University Press, 1973), pp. 5–6.

13. A claim for this title could be argued on behalf of Roger Therry. Prior to Plunkett's appointment as Solicitor General, Therry, in 1829, within weeks of the Catholic Relief Act, was appointed Commissioner for the Court of Common Requests in New South Wales. However, Catholics, theoretically, had not been excluded from this post prior to the Catholic Relief Act. It was not a judicial position or a high government office.

14. Molony, *An Architect of Freedom*, p.162.

15. Ibid., p. 164.

16. T.L. Suttor, in *Australian Dictionary of Biography* (Melbourne University Press, Volume 2, 1967) pp. 337–40.

17. Max Waugh, *Forgotten Hero* (Melbourne, Australian Scholarly Press, 2005), p.76.

18. *Sydney Morning Herald*, 21 March 1856.

19. Plunkett almost became Chief Justice. He applied for the post when C.J. Dowling died in 1844. His only rival was Alfred Stephen who received the appointment. Governor Gipps felt that Plunkett was most hard done by in this instance.

20. O'Connell (ed.), *The Correspondence of Daniel O'Connell*, Vol. 8, letter 3430; see also O'Farrell, *The Irish in Australia*, p.11.

21. Ibid., letter 3343.

22. Ibid., letter 3138a.

23. Molony, *An Architect of Freedom*, p.227.

24. Cited in James F. Hogan, *The Irish in Australia* (Melbourne: G. Robertson, 1888), p.314.

25. John M. Bennett, 'Of Silks and Serjeants', *The Australian Law Journal*, 52 (1978), p.271.

26. *Sydney Morning Herald*, 21 March 1856.

27. Ibid., 17 May 1869.

28. Ibid., 26 June 1856.

29. Ibid.

30. NSW Parliamentary Debates (Hansard), 8 September 1998.

31. I am grateful to Dr Pamela O'Neill of the University of Melbourne for helping me to discover this.

32. Patrick O'Farrell, 'The Image of O'Connell in Australia', in Donal McCartney (ed.), *The World of Daniel O'Connell* (Dublin and Cork: Mercier Press, 1980), p.112.

33. Twenty years, one month and eighteen days (April 1836 to 5 June 1856) and a further period of four months and twenty-eight days (25 August 1865 to 21 January 1866). See website of the New South Wales Parliament:
http://www.parliament.nsw.gov.au/prod/parlment/members.nsf/0/b19e88d7a0727cc2ca 256cbb00837d9b?OpenDocument [accessed 20 December 2006].

PART IV
Politics, War and Remembrance

13

'A New World full of Youthful Hopes and Promise': Michael Davitt in Australia, 1895[1]

Carla King

Although best known in Ireland as 'The Father of the Land League', by the mid-1890s Michael Davitt's name was also familiar in Britain and further afield as a labour leader. He was a regular speaker on radical and labour platforms, in support of issues ranging from land nationalisation to Scottish crofters and trade union rights. In 1885 workers in Sheffield had invited him to stand as their candidate for parliament, while in the 1890s he mediated in several labour disputes, most notably the large dockers' strike in Liverpool in 1890. In 1890–1 he published a newspaper called *Labour World*, and in 1891 he helped to found a trade union for agricultural labourers in Cork, the Irish Democratic Trade and Labour Federation.[2]

However, in December 1890 the Parnell split had dragged Davitt back into the centre of Irish politics, when he led the attack on the Irish Party leader. In December 1891, he was defeated by John Redmond in a by-election in Waterford, while in July of the following year he was elected for North Meath, only to be disqualified on grounds of clerical interference.[3] Standing once more, this time for North-East Cork, Davitt was elected to Westminster in February 1893, during the debates on the second Home Rule Bill, to which he contributed in his maiden speech. He had long been opposed to standing for parliament, but felt constrained to do so in the crisis caused by the weakness and dissention in the aftermath of the Parnell split. Nevertheless, shortly after taking his seat, he was declared bankrupt and had to resign his seat as a consequence, only to be re-elected in 1895, this time to seats in South Mayo and East Kerry. By the mid-1890s Parnell was dead, the Irish Parliamentary Party sundered into three warring factions, and public opinion in Ireland and abroad deeply alienated. The defeat of the Home Rule Bill in September 1893, followed by Gladstone's resignation six months later, signalling the postponement of hopes for Home Rule, only added further to the party's difficulties.

It was against this background that Davitt decided, in 1895, to undertake a seven-month tour of Australia and New Zealand. He had been interested in the region since his youth, when he read John Mitchel's *Jail Journal*, and he was acquainted with several Fenians who had served time there. He was also well known among the Irish in Australia, having contributed regular articles as Irish correspondent of the Melbourne *Advocate*. He had planned a visit on several occasions since 1885, when he set off on what he had intended as a long tour of Europe, the Middle East, India, Australia and the United States, but was drawn back by events in Britain and Ireland before he got further than Jerusalem. Other projected trips were also abandoned, so as not to conflict with lecture tours by other Irish nationalist leaders,[4] or in 1893 because he devoted his efforts to supporting the second Home Rule Bill.[5]

At last, he sailed from London on 5 April 1895 on the *Octavia*, of the Orient Line, travelling through the Suez Canal and Indian Ocean. On reaching Columbo he received the tragic news that his 7-year-old daughter, Kathleen, had died after a short illness. His first impulse was to return to Ireland but his wife persuaded him to carry on with the trip as planned, partly because the family needed the income his lectures were expected to earn. When in Australia he toured extensively, combining lectures with close observation of the society he encountered. With their large Irish populations the Australasian colonies had provided considerable funds to support the Irish land and Home Rule campaigns and Davitt addressed some seventy-two meetings during his visit. He received a warm welcome from the Irish settlers, despite the disgust felt by many Irish-Australians for the factionalism besetting the nationalist movement in Ireland in the years following the Parnellite split and notwithstanding Cardinal Moran's initial coolness towards him.[6] However, Moran's attitude seems to have softened, as he received Davitt warmly in Melbourne in July, contributing twenty-five guineas to the Irish Parliamentary Party's election fund a few days later.[7] (The cardinal's support was important as he was rapidly establishing himself as the leader of the Irish community in Australia.) Considerable assistance in planning and organising the trip was provided by Joseph Winter, proprietor and editor of the *Advocate*.[8] Joseph and his brother Samuel owned a printing business in Melbourne, and were prominent in the Irish-Australian community there from the 1870s on. Joseph Winter became honorary treasurer of the Australian League, on its establishment on 7 November 1883. In *The Fall of Feudalism in Ireland,* Davitt described him as 'the most earnest and active worker for Ireland among all the stanch [*sic*] volunteers in Australia who have rendered valued aid to the Irish movement continuously from 1880 to the present day'.[9]

Davitt filled six journals with details of experiences and impressions garnered on his visit, and made a collection of press cuttings, on which he subsequently based his book, *Life and Progress in Australasia*, written on his return and published in 1898.[10] This was aimed to introduce what were then seven separate colonies to a British and Irish public and in what is more thoughtful than most travelogues, he engaged with the society he found, focusing on the issues that interested him most – from mines and the lives of the miners, to the political systems of the colonies. He criticised the mistreatment of the Aboriginal people by white settlers and investigated the conditions of the Kanakas, South Sea islanders imported to work on the sugar plantations. He visited farming communes on the Murray river in South Australia and wrote approvingly of the contribution of the Catholic religious orders to the development of Australian education. Something of a specialist on prisons (having been in jail on four occasions), he remained concerned with prison reform throughout his life. So he included, in Part IX of his book, a survey of 'Australasian Prisons'. He not only examined and described them, he also assessed them, making recommendations in some places and criticising in others. Davitt was fascinated by the emerging medium of photography. He had an extensive collection of photographs and from the 1880s he took a camera with him when he travelled.[11] There are 109 photographs of this journey in the Davitt papers, together with thirty-three more of Samoa and eight of Honolulu, taken on stops on the return from Australia.[12]

It would be impossible within the scope of a single chapter to do justice to the range of Davitt's experiences and thoughts concerning his encounter with Australia. Instead, the reader might be directed to his book, *Life and Progress in Australasia*. In this chapter, it is proposed to focus on just two subjects of Davitt's interest during his visit, the mining settlements in various colonies and the Murray river colonies of Western Australia.

A likely, although unstated, purpose of the visit was the reinforcement of ties with the Irish-Australian community, alienated by the infighting of previous years. Irish-Australians had provided valuable support in the past: in their response to the economic crisis of 1879–80 they had donated some £95,000 for Irish famine relief,[13] while Dillon's lecture tour in 1889–90 had netted £33,000 without which the plan of campaign could not have continued.[14] Moreover, Davitt had always been keenly aware of the political and strategic, as well as economic, importance of the Irish diaspora. He was well suited for the purpose of re-engaging with Irish-Australians, partly because much of that community shared his sense of betrayal by Parnell over the divorce crisis.[15] In addition, by the closing years of the nineteenth century many activists among the Irish in Australia were in a process of replacing their preoccupation with Irish issues by a more local focus on labour questions facing them in their working lives. With his involvement in both Irish and labour movements, Davitt was able to span both spheres. He was very interested to observe the growth of Labour parties in Australia and their policies, whilst he could inform Australian audiences of developments in the British labour movement.

It would have been difficult to visit Australia in the late nineteenth century and not have been aware of the effects of the gold rush. The Australian gold rush had been in spate since the discovery of gold deposits near Bathurst in New South Wales in 1851,[16] but the territory was so large that new fields were continually being discovered. The latest, prior to Davitt's visit, had been opened in Western Australia, and he reports that more than half his fellow passengers on the ship to Australia were on their way to the west Australia goldfields.[17] In the course of his travels he visited seven gold-mining areas in Australia: Coolgardie and Hannans (later renamed Kalgoorlie) in Western Australia; Ballarat and Bendigo in Victoria; Gympie, Mount Morgan and Charters Towers in Queensland; a silver mining area at Broken Hill in New South Wales; and three goldmines in New Zealand: Kumara, Hokitika and Auckland. The phenomenon of the gold rush clearly interested him sufficiently to travel very long distances in difficult conditions. In the case of Coolgardie, for example, it took him three days to reach the mine. At the time of his visit the railway ran only as far as Barrabin, so the train journey was followed by a fifteen hours' drive by coach. By the time he wrote *Life and Progress* the rail line had been extended as far as the Hannans field and, as he put it, 'coaching experience, with its bush "hotels" and gunyah "taverns" and alfresco "restaurants" are now things of the past.' He continued:

> The traveller need not mourn at this. What he may have lost in the element of novelty he gains in the matter of solid comfort, with freedom from dust, flies, stenches, thirst, and many other afflictions not nameable even in touring sketches.[18]

However, if the route by coach was difficult, he speculated in his diary: 'What must this journey have been for those who had to tramp the whole distance of 360 miles from Perth?'[19] Travelling in the same coach was Major Alexander Forrest, whom, Davitt claimed, resembled Cecil Rhodes.[20] Forrest's brother, John (later Sir John) Forrest, was Premier of Western Australia.

Working conditions at most of the mines were harsh, the heat and dust almost unendurable and the housing rudimentary. Coolgardie was built of timber and corrugated iron, the buildings were vulnerable to fires and the insanitary conditions of the town left it prone to outbreaks of typhoid. The worst problem was the lack of water, particularly at Hannans. Davitt notes that at one of the mines on the Hannans field (perhaps ironically named

'Lake View'), while there were heaps of ore lying around in huge quantities without protection, a notice was posted up in large letters, warning the employees against taking water without leave, and he commented: 'Here at least, water required more watching than gold.'[21] The price of water in the area had reached 6d per gallon and there was a serious outbreak of typhoid the year before Davitt's visit with predictions of an even worse one to come.[22] He lost no time in voicing the discontent of the communities of Coolgardie and Hannans about the water situation both in speeches during his visits and in a press interview in Perth on his return. He charged the Forrest administration with apathy and neglect, urging it to carry out a scheme of its own or to permit private enterprise to undertake one.[23] The problem was the scale and cost of any such project and the government had been overwhelmed by the rapidity of the developing goldfields. The most promising scheme would involve piping water some 300 miles from the Swan river near Perth, a project so costly it was likely to make any government quail. In fact, in the year after Davitt's visit, Sir John Forrest commenced the scheme, requesting the Western Australian parliament to authorize £2.5 million and sparking off a protracted political battle. Eventually, after taking five years to complete, the Goldfields Water Supply Scheme was opened by Forrest in 1903, and was considered one of the engineering feats of its day.[24]

Another grievance of the communities on the goldfields to which Davitt drew attention was the conditions endured by the telegraph operators, which he compared to 'white slavery'. He deplored the inadequate and insanitary working conditions, inadequate attention to safety measures, long hours and low rates of pay. With only one telegraph line between Coolgardie and Perth, messages were often delayed for days. There was, in fact, a great deal of dissatisfaction with the government in the communities; Davitt noted in his diary that: 'The miners charge the government with neglecting the field – shirking obvious duty – looking after Perth interests – making these paramount to the duties they owe to the richest part of W[estern] A[ustralia] ...Men of all nationalities and all shades of opinion join "agin" this government.'[25] When fire had broken out in Kalgoorlie a few days before he arrived, destroying much of the leading thoroughfare, some people were engaged in another part of the street burning an effigy of the town's mayor.[26]

Some of the goldfields were enormous; for example, the Coolgardie and Hannans fields extended over 10,000 square miles and Davitt noted that the Murchison goldfields, at 32,000 square miles, was the same size as Ireland.[27] In many cases towns had developed and after an initial settling-down period, some, such as Ballarat, in Victoria, had become large and prosperous. Davitt observed that a stranger unaware of Ballarat's history would find it hard to believe (if he had any experience of other mining centres) 'that the handsome city of today, with its stately streets and splendid public buildings, could ever have been a diggers' camp'.[28] Huge fortunes were still being made and lost in speculation on the goldfields. He was keen to visit the Londonderry mine, on which the Earl of Fingall had lost a substantial sum, and which he described as 'very disappointing', with few men apparently at work.[29] At the 'Bayley's Reward' nearby he was taken 500 feet down a mineshaft and he describes the society beginning to take shape in Coolgardie. Everybody, he noted, seemed to have plenty of money:

> Somers' hotel was crowded with agents of London, Adelaide and Melbourne syndicates, experts, mine managers and fortunate and other prospectors...Typhoid was prevalent, it is true but that...was only a matter of trivial concern to men who had come thousands of miles in search of a mine or a fortune...No miner was idle unless he wished it. Work was plentiful, at a pound a day, and a significant aspect of this absence of poverty and idleness was seen in a crimeless town, numbering five or six thousand men, engaged in gold hunting.[30]

As a journalist, Davitt was well aware of the interest in the Australian mines among the British public and as a result of his decision to send £900 of the money he had raised in lecturing to the Irish Parliamentary Party's fund, when an election was called in July, he realised he would have to find further sources of income to fulfil the original purpose of the trip, to support his family. Thus his decision to prolong his stay in Australia and visit Western Australia was partly determined by a commercial consideration to pen material that editors would find attractive, and he spent nine days at the Coolgardie and Hannans fields.

The lives of the miners interested Davitt and everywhere he went he noted their daily or weekly wages and working and living conditions. He had visited mines and mining areas in the United States, during lecture tours in 1880 and 1886. As was the case in the US, many of the miners in Australia were Irish or of Irish parentage. In Hannans, Davitt noted that around one-third of the mining population was Irish.[31] In Gympie, which boasted the first Australian branch of the Land League, Davitt met some old friends from his Fenian days and relates that he had, 'in the American sense of the saying, "a very good time"'.[32] Indeed, in 1881, when Davitt was imprisoned in Portland Jail, the Gympie branch of the Land League had sent a letter of protest to the Home Secretary in London.[33] Shortly after Davitt's visit, a Goldfields National League held its inaugural meeting, its name, no doubt, based on the Irish National League. Its demands included political rights for the miners, an extension of the railway line into the goldfield and reductions in railway and customs charges, improvements in the postal and telegraphic services and an expansion of public works, especially regarding water.[34]

Two main themes emerge from Davitt's accounts of the mining settlements he encountered. One was the great difference between mines supported by local capital and those owned by absentee individuals or companies. In the former case, he argued, the settlements and towns that emerged were much better supported, as was the situation in Gympie and Bendigo. By contrast in the cases of Coolgardie, Mount Morgan and Charters Towers, where nearly all the capital came from external sources, working and living conditions tended to be poor and the towns badly maintained. In Charters Towers he noted in his diary the contrast between the wealth yielded by the mines, averaging over the previous three years some £835,000 per annum, and the dilapidated streets, the houses built of corrugated iron and timber and the primitive sanitary arrangements. He was told that three-quarters of the annual dividends of the mine went directly to England, which meant that very little was reinvested in the town. In Mount Morgan, when the township was marked out the company drew the boundary so that the mount where the mine lay was outside the precincts of the town, in order that it would be exempt from paying any rates. As Davitt put it: 'They carefully excluded the mine from the town boundary, so as to free themselves from the legal obligation of helping to render it a healthy and decent place of abode for their workmen and others who make the fortunes of the proprietors.'[35] He doesn't make the point explicitly but the parallel with Irish absentee landlords is clear.

The other theme that emerges in Davitt's treatment of mines and agricultural settlements is the superiority of agrarian life to that of the miners. In line with contemporary attitudes and in particular, with a radical tradition on which he drew, from William Cobbett to John Ruskin to William Morris, agrarian community life was seen as the more natural, more fulfilling. When he visited Toowomba in south Queensland in August 1895, he contrasted the comfort of its agrarian settlements with the misery of the mining towns: 'Talk about Charters Towers and its wages; Mount Morgan & its mountain of gold! The view of Toowomba (10,000 pop) from the hill overlooking the [Darling] Downs is one of almost ideal social comfort and independence.'[36] In his description in *Life and Progress in Australasia*, he quoted the poem by Robert Buchanan, 'The Perfect State', where to the question 'Where is the perfect State?' the answer is given:

> 'Tis where the soil is free,
> Where, far as the eye can see,
> Scattered o'er hill and lee,
> Homesteads abound . . . [37]

Davitt's account depicted broad streets, ornamented with trees, an absence of poverty and a prison containing only eight inmates for a population of 40,000 people.[38]

The mining settlements also contrasted sharply with an attempt at socialist community building that Davitt was keen to observe: the labour colonies on the Murray river. These nine settlements originated as a response to unemployment in Adelaide in the winter of 1893, resulting from a severe economic crisis in 1892–3, during the worst of which perhaps 20 to 30 per cent of Australian skilled tradesmen were unemployed, with a higher figure for the unskilled.[39] Some of the unemployed had turned to gold prospecting in New South Wales and Victoria, while the discovery of rich goldfields in Western Australia came just at the right time to offer opportunities to others. Another alternative was settlement on the land. The coexistence of unemployment and vast acres of unworked land in the surrounding area led the Trades Council of Adelaide and some members of the government to undertake the initiative of setting up villages along the Murray river. They were able to take advantage of legislation passed in 1893, which allowed the government to make grants of land and loans available to groups of settlers. On 22 February 1893 the first 100 families had left Adelaide on a special train to commence the first of the settlements. Davitt visited them twenty-eight months later in June 1895.

These colonies were of particular interest to him because Davitt, who on occasion described himself as a 'state socialist', saw these communal experiments as potentially offering a solution to problems of unemployment in providing labour of a non-exploitative character. There was a long tradition of socialist communities in the nineteenth century, influenced by theorists such as Charles Fourier and Robert Owen; relatively few of them survived for any considerable length of time, but reformers continued to look to agricultural settlement as a solution to urban unemployment and poverty. The Murray river labour villages were not the only such experiment undertaken in Australia – there were settlements in Queensland,[40] New South Wales,[41] Victoria and Tasmania – but these were the most successful. Their likely success was due, according to Davitt, to the fact that Murray river settlers had been provided with good-quality land, which was not the case elsewhere. Davitt devoted five chapters of the book (of eighty-four) to the Murray river settlements.

He set off to visit the Murray river communities on 14 June, travelling the first hundred miles from Adelaide by train to Morgan, followed by an all-night mail coach journey of seventy miles through the bush. The party: the coach driver, the Inspector-General of Schools in Southern Australia, J.A. Hartley,[42] and Davitt, arrived at the first of the settlements, Lyrup, late on 15 June.

The settlements, situated along the Murray river between Renmark and

Morgan, varied in size from Murtho, the smallest, with thirty-six people, to Lyrup, the largest, with 186. In all, there were 775 settlers listed in 1897 in government statistics quoted by Davitt. The soil was good but the land was very dry, so the villages were dotted along the river, to allow water to be pumped into irrigation channels. Large grants of land having been obtained from the government, the settlers grew a combination of wheat, some barley, some lucerne (alfalfa), vegetables, vines and fruit trees. The settlements kept cattle, horses, pigs and sheep, and there were plentiful supplies of rabbits for hunting and fish in the river to supplement the diet. Clearing and sowing the land had taken priority over housing, so the settlers were still living in 'humpies', of frame and canvas with corrugated iron roofs, when Davitt visited them. He pronounced them 'warm and comfortable', although he experienced them in winter and they may have been less pleasant in the heat of the summer. Each community had its own school for the children of the community. The men worked an eight-hour day, while the women were employed primarily in the home. No money was used in the settlements but in some a coupon system served to pay for provisions from a common store. No drink was kept in the camps.

A crucial role in the initial formation and subsequent support of the settlements was played by the government of South Australia. Improvements carried out by the settlers were periodically valued by a government commissioner, and loans of 50 per cent of the value of the improvements were advanced for ten years at 5 per cent, the first three years' loan being interest free and with this the settlers could purchase necessary supplies from the merchants in the nearby towns of Morgan and Renmark. The communities governed themselves through regular meetings and committees and Davitt was invited to attend some of these. The settlers expressed pride in what had been accomplished and appeared content with their new way of life, one mother commenting that she found it a safer and happier environment for her children than life in Adelaide.[43] Some of the colonists called themselves communists, some co-operators, but there was a general leftward orientation, and the communities had received assistance from two Labor MPs (E.L. Batchelor and T. McPhearson). Murtho, one of the colonies, was founded by supporters of Henry George. This association, according to Davitt, originated not in unemployment, but in 'a desire on the part of a body of intelligent and industrious men for a newer and healthier life, away from wage servitude and landlordism'.[44] In another of the settlements, Kingston, Davitt encountered a Cork woman, nicknamed 'the communist midwife', who claimed she had never had a busier time than when she moved to the Murray river. Yes, she told him, she was a firm believer in communism. There was little of it in her native city by the Lee, it is true. But Cork, she said, had many things to learn yet, though no other city could turn out better doctors or more efficient midwives. The settlers were of various backgrounds, Australians, English, Scottish and Irish, with one or two Germans, Swedes, Italians, and others. They were also of mixed religions, but, according to Davitt, when ministers came from Morgan or Adelaide, all the members of the community took part in the ceremony, whether Catholic or Protestant.[45]

After thirteen years and the repayment of state loans, the members were to be free to decide whether to continue on their co-operative plan or to distribute the land among themselves. Davitt hoped to see the experiment succeed, remarking:

> Everything I saw contrasted most favourably with the ordinary conditions of wage-earning life, in even the highest-paid labour centres of Australia. There was no poverty or want felt by anybody. The work, though necessarily rough in the main, was not exhausting, while it was robbed of that which links the task of ordinary daily toil to servitude – the feeling that you were at the disposal of somebody for so much.[46]

Davitt expressed optimism about their future in an interview in the *South Australian Register* shortly after his return to Adelaide.[47] However, even there he recognised that there had been some difficulties, and by the time he went to write his book one of the communities he had visited, the very small New Residence village, had ceased to function as a labour settlement. While hailing the courage of the South Australian government for its support and encouragement of the Murray river colonies, Davitt made several recommendations to increase their chances of success. In the first place, he suggested that the larger settlements appeared to suffer the most from disagreements, so he recommended an optimum size of twenty-five settlers, which with their families would give a population of around one hundred. Secondly, the establishment of a consultative council of all the settlements would allow the exchange of information, the conciliation of disputes, and so on. Finally, recognising the difficulties involved in transferring a group of artisans into an agricultural environment, where they had to learn to be farmers, he advocated the government making available an adviser to teach them the necessary skills.[48]

There had been moves to foster land settlement in other parts of Australia. Charles Gavan Duffy, when Minister of Lands in Victoria, had passed 'Duffy's Land Act', which provided cheap land and land at low rent to settlers, while the Settlement of Lands Act, passed in Victoria in 1893, had been intended to promote village settlements, labour colonies and homestead associations. However, Davitt was told that the government of Victoria had little interest in applying them and there had been little response among the public since the passage of the law.[49] None of the agricultural communities discussed by Davitt survived in co-operative form for more than a few years. The settlers, drawn from the cities, lacked experience of agriculture and knowledge of co-operative principles. Most of the settlements were under-capitalised and those that survived invariably switched to individual ownership, frequently following internecine strife.[50]

Patrick O'Farrell has written of Davitt's visit to Australia that he was interested less in expounding the Irish cause than in observing the new society of the colonies, in other words, that 'He came to learn, not to teach.'[51] So what effect did Australia have on him? It may be argued that it was not so much that Davitt brought home new ideas but that what he encountered there renewed his hopes for reform. In this new society he saw in practice things he had long advocated but which in the Old World existed only as aspirations. One example was Home Rule, which seemed further away than ever for Ireland following the election of 1895, bringing a Conservative government to power. Yet in Australia, not only had the individual colonies enjoyed a form of Home Rule since the 1850s, but six years after Davitt's visit they came together to form a federal commonwealth.

The years since 1890 had seen the emergence in several Australian colonies of a vigorous labour movement, a feature that impressed Davitt. He repeatedly contrasted the unity he observed among Australian labour to the divisions within the movement in Britain, censuring Keir Hardie's Independent Labor Party for dividing the working class vote between itself and the Radical Liberals. Nevertheless, in the years that followed, he drew closer to the political organisation of labour and in 1906 campaigned in its support in the general election. He was present at the formation of the British Labour Party in 1906, only months before his death.

A strong supporter of women's rights, Davitt welcomed the granting of women's suffrage, introduced in New Zealand in 1893 and South Australia in 1896. However, he criticized the measure in New Zealand, which while granting women the vote debarred them from sitting in parliament. He commented: 'This lack of courage of doing the right in whole and not in halves, will some day be as apparent as was the injustice of depriving one half of the population of the right of citizenship before women suffrage became law.'[52]

This had been at times a gruelling visit, with constant travelling and public speaking, coupled with the pain of the loss of his daughter, evident in his sombre expression in several photographs taken at this time. Nor was it very rewarding in financial terms, as Davitt donated a large portion of his earnings from the trip to the Irish Parliamentary Party toward its expenses in the general election. However, in terms of renewing his spirit, strengthening him for the frustrating life of a Home Rule MP at Westminster that faced him on his return, and providing him with models of a more democratic society, the journey was important to his intellectual development. He had noted both strengths and weaknesses in Australian politics and society. But as he told his readers:

> Australia is...an industrial empire of unfederated Labour nations, where neither wars nor foreign policies intrude their demoralising influences upon the peaceful programmes and progress of domestic government. The people have the fullest and most effective control of their own affairs. There are no ruling classes.[53]

It was in this state of affairs, where the people were 'well and wisely trusted with the full responsibility of organizing the constitutional guardianship of their own concerns in their own way',[54] that Davitt found an inspiration and vindication of his own democratic ideals.

Table 5: Mining Settlements Visited by Davitt in 1895

Western Australia:	Coolgardie
	Hannans (Kalgoorlie)
New South Wales:	Broken Hill Silver Mines
Victoria:	Ballarat
	Bendigo
Queensland:	Gympie
	Mount Morgan
	Charters Towers
New Zealand:	Kumara
	Hokitika
	Auckland

TABLE 6: Murray River Settlements, 1897

	Acres	Acres cultivated	Pop. of village
Murtho	2,000	548	36
Lyrup	14,060	550	186
Pyap	9,145	531	105
Moorook	3,200	341	78
Kingston	3,925	375	93
Holder	7,560	1,159	141
Waikerie	3,330	838	86
Ramco	3,680	487	50
TOTALS	46,900	4,829	775

By 1897, one of the communities, New Residence, had ceased to function as a labour settlement. (From Michael Davitt, *Land and Progress in Australasia*, p.104; based on *Report of the Surveyor-General of Lands, June, 1897*)

NOTES

1. I should like to gratefully acknowledge the award of a Government of Ireland Research Fellowship from the Irish Research Council for the Humanities and Social Sciences, during which research for this chapter was carried out. I should also like to thank the Board of Trinity College, Dublin for permission to quote from MSS 9565 and 9622 in the Davitt papers.

2. T.W. Moody, 'Michael Davitt and the British Labour Movement, 1882–1906', *Transactions of the Royal Historical Society*, 5th ser., iii (1953), pp.53–76.

3. Davitt's disqualification was brought about by the interference of Bishop Thomas Nulty of Meath in the campaign. In its aftermath he was forced to declare bankruptcy.

4. John and William Redmond travelled to Australia on a fund-raising tour in 1883; in the following year Davitt postponed plans to visit Australia on learning that Thomas Sexton and John Redmond were planning a visit, while a later trip was postponed in 1889, the year that John Dillon made the journey.

5. He had planned a visit in July 1893 but Davitt's involvement in campaigning in support of the second Home Rule Bill brought a further postponement. See Trinity College Dublin (TCD) MS. 9324/73, Winter to Davitt, 28 March 1893.

6. In 1885, following the death of Archbishop Edward McCabe, Davitt, who was in Rome during part of that year, was known to have advocated the appointment of William Walsh as his successor, rather than Moran, who was also considered for the position. However, it is highly unlikely that Davitt would have had any influence on the appointment.

7. TCD MS. 9562/59, diary 10 July 1895 and 9562/64, diary 16 July 1895. Davitt immediately telegraphed news of the donation to Ireland, which was published in the *Freeman's Journal*, 17 July.

8. His assistance was acknowledged in letters from Davitt. See TCD MS. 9324/76, 31 October 1895 and MS. 9324/77, 19 February 1897.

9. Michael Davitt, *The Fall of Feudalism in Ireland; or the Story of the Land League Revolution* (London & New York: Harper, 1904), p.384.

10. Michael Davitt, *Life and Progress in Australasia* (London: Methuen, 1898); reprinted in Carla King (ed.), *Michael Davitt: Collected Writings*, vol. 5 (Bristol: Thoemmes Press, 2001).

11. On Davitt's photographs, see Carla King, 'Photographs in the Davitt Papers,' in *Irish Archives, Journal of the Irish Society for Archives*, 9 (Winter 2003–4), pp.58–66.

12. Davitt's Australian photographs are among the 515 photographs in MS. 6949 in the Davitt papers in Trinity College Manuscript Library. Davitt appears to have taken more photographs in Australia than are now in the Davitt papers, but some of these may not have been developed successfully.

13. This figure is from the final report of the Mansion House Committee, *The Irish crisis of 1879–80: proceedings of the Dublin Mansion House relief committee, 1880* (Dublin, 1881), p.83, quoted in Laurence M. Geary, 'The Australasian Response to the Irish Crisis, 1879–80', in Oliver MacDonagh and W.F. Mandle (eds), *Irish-Australasian Studies: Papers Delivered at the Fifth Irish-Australian Conference* (Canberra: Australian National University, 1989), p.115.

14. F.S.L. Lyons, *John Dillon, a Biography* (London: Routledge & Kegan Paul, 1968), p.106.

15. Patrick O'Farrell, *The Irish in Australia: 1788 to the Present* (Sydney: New South Wales University Press, 1986; 2nd edn., Cork University Press, 2001), p.233.

16. The first man to discover gold in Australia was Edward Hargraves. See Manning Clark, *Manning Clark's History of Australia* (Melbourne: Melbourne University Press, 1993), pp.219, 224–5.

17. Davitt, *Life and Progress*, p.4.

18. Ibid., p.7.

19. TCD MS. 9565/31, Journal, 10 October 1895.

20. TCD MS. 9565/27, Journal, 10 October 1895.

21. Davitt, *Life and Progress*, p.17.

22. For example, *Western Mail*, Perth, 25 October 1895: 'Now that summer has begun it becomes increasingly evident that the typhoid epidemic on the goldfields will be considerably worse this season than it was the last.' TCD 9622/24. Press cutting collection.

23. *Western Mail*, Perth, 25 October 1895, TCD MS. 9622/23, press cutting collection.
24. Gavin Casey and Ted Mayman, *The Mile that Midas Touched* (London: Angus and Robertson, 1964), pp.118–19.
25. TCD MS. 9565/128, Journal, 12 October 1895.
26. Ibid.
27. TCD MS. 9565/31, Journal, 10 October 1895.
28. Davitt, *Life and Progress*, p.157.
29. Arthur James Francis Plunkett, 11th Earl of Fingall (1859–1929). Fingall was a Catholic Unionist peer, cousin of Horace Plunkett, founder of the Irish co-operative movement.
30. Davitt, *Life and Progress*, p.19.
31. TCD MS. 9565/110, Journal, 15 October 1895.
32. The Gympie society was formed by Revd Matthew Horan in 1880. In 1882 it criticised the Vatican condemnation of Land War tactics, an unusual step for Australia, according to Patrick O'Farrell, *The Irish in Australia*, pp.222–3.
33. PRO HO 144/5/17869/75, letter of protest to the Home Secretary at Davitt's imprisonment, signed by Marcus Collisson and James G. Pollard, Gympie Branch of the Irish National League, Queensland, 7 September 1881.
34. A handbill setting out the programme of the Goldfields National League was sent to Davitt on 17 October by Henry A. Ellis, a few days prior to its publication. The inaugural meeting was due to be held on 2 November. TCD MS. 9622/7a.
35. Davitt, *Life and Progress*, p.267.
36. TCD MS. 9564/18.
37. Robert Williams Buchanan (1841–1901) was a British poet, novelist and dramatist. The son of Robert Buchanan, Owenite lecturer and journalist, he was born in Staffordshire but studied in Glasgow before moving to London in 1860. His poems display a sympathetic insight into the lives of the poor.
38. Davitt, *Life and Progress*, p.308.
39. P.G. Macarthy, 'Wages in Australia, 1891 to 1914', *Australian Economic History Review*, 10/1 (March 1970), quoted in B.K. de Garis, '1890–1900' in F.K. Crowley (ed.), *A New History of Australia* (Melbourne: William Heinemann, 1974), p.225.
40. There were twelve villages founded in Queensland in 1893. See de Garis, '1890–1900', in Crowley (ed.), *New History of Australia*, p.226.
41. There were three village settlements founded in 1893 in New South Wales, the largest of which was at Pitt Town, with two smaller ones at Bega and Wilberforce. See de Garis, op.cit., p.226.
42. Hartley, who died in September 1896, appears to have been a very popular inspector, committed to the development of education in South Australia. A newspaper notice of his death was pasted behind the cover of Davitt's notebook, TCD MS. 9562, and in *Life and Progress* Davitt praised his 'amiable qualities and his singular and efficient devotedness to the best interests of popular education in the colony'. *Life and Progress*, p.75, footnote.
43. Davitt, *Life and Progress*, pp.84–5.
x44. Ibid., p.98.
45. Ibid., p.87.
46. Ibid., p.84.
47. *South Australian Register* (Adelaide), 20 June 1895; reprinted in *Freeman's Journal*, 2 August 1895.
48. Davitt, *Life and Progress*, p.109.
49. Ibid., p.153.
50. de Garis, '1890–1900', in Crowley (ed.), *New History of Australia*, pp.226–7.
51. O'Farrell, *The Irish in Australia*, p.236.
52. Davitt, *Life and Progress*, p.366.
53. Ibid., p.viii.
54. Ibid., p.ix.

14

The Peace Mission of
Archbishop Clune

Michael Hopkinson

Archbishop Joseph Patrick Clune, from 1913 Perth's first archbishop, and head of his diocese between 1910 and his death in 1935, is a somewhat obscure figure in the history of the Australian Catholic Church. A Redemptorist missionary, Clune, who had served in New South Wales and New Zealand, was born in 1864 in Ruane, near Ennis, in County Clare. His episcopal career was chiefly notable for the re-establishment of the finances of the Church in Western Australia, for the building of St Mary's Cathedral in Perth, for grandiloquent sermons, and for his support for First World War conscription. He played a quiet but important role in defending the Catholic Church's position in the anglophile-dominated Western Australian community, while always proclaiming loyalty to the British Crown. In 1916 he was appointed Chaplain-General for the Catholic contingent of the Australian Infantry Forces in Europe. He is, however, still remembered chiefly for his brief role, in December 1920 and January 1921, in trying to bring about a truce and settlement in the Irish War of Independence. This chapter aims to consider how significant Clune's peace mission was, who was to blame for its failure, what its consequences were, and whether it represented a significant missed opportunity.[1] Despite the clandestine nature of Clune's mission to Ireland a considerable amount of documentary evidence in England and Ireland allows these issues to be tackled with some confidence.

In late November 1920 Clune had been in England and Ireland for several months following an *ad limina* visit to Rome. He was due to return to Perth. At that time the Irish War of Independence had reached its darkest and most violent phase. Shortly before the Clune mission, the tit-for-tat killings of Bloody Sunday in Dublin on 21 November, and the Kilmichael ambush of 28 November in west Cork, at which seventeen Auxiliaries were killed, had occurred. Since the summer the hastily recruited support police forces, the Black and Tans and Auxiliaries, had been responsible for widespread reprisals, usually following IRA attacks and ambushes. In less than two weeks, on 10 December, martial law was to be declared for most of Munster and a day after that much of the centre of Cork was to be burnt by Auxiliaries. A range of opinion in Britain and abroad was demanding negotiations to resolve the conflict and placing huge pressure on the British Government. The British administration of Ireland was in a state of collapse and a military solution did not appear either practical or desirable. On 30 November at a farewell dinner for Clune, attended by members of the Irish Parliamentary Party and hosted by the Agent-General for Western Australia, he was prevailed upon by the West Belfast MP Joe Devlin to delay his departure and to meet with Lloyd George, the Coalition's prime minister on 1 December.[ii]

In the preceding five months there had been a series of secret and tortuous peace initiatives between British and Irish intermediaries, some involving the Foreign Office and Dublin Castle. None moved beyond the tentative, preliminary stage. In public Lloyd George continually stressed his commitment to putting down rebellion and appeared to opt for a coercion policy as demonstrated by the swift passage of the Restoration of Order in Ireland Act of August 1920. None the less he did not discourage various informal peace moves involving the prospect of amendment of the Government of Ireland Bill, which made provision for two devolved governments in a partitioned Ireland; the Bill was then completing its slow passage through the British Parliament. At the end of November 1920 Lloyd George had told the writer and mystic George Russell (AE) that the British government 'will not tolerate a Republic but anything short of that'. At that time the British Labour Party Commission on Ireland were investigating the situation in Ireland and were looked upon as possible intermediaries. Lloyd George's approach to Clune, however, was the first time the prime minister himself had become personally and directly involved.

During a long meeting with the archbishop Lloyd George emphasised the critical need for a settlement and asked Clune to travel with a safe conduct to Ireland and to interview the Sinn Féin and IRA leaders in Dublin, including the recently imprisoned Arthur Griffith in Mountjoy Prison: Griffith had been the acting President of the Dáil government. The archbishop agreed to undertake the mission while taking the opportunity to remind the prime minister of the disastrous consequences of police reprisals, which he had recently seen first-hand in Clare. In a letter to the Irish chief secretary, Hamar Greenwood, Lloyd George referred to Clune as 'an Australian Bishop who during the war was chaplain to the Catholics in the Australian Forces. He is thoroughly loyal. His real anxiety is to promote peace and I think he can be trusted.'[3]

Over the next three weeks Clune practised shuttle diplomacy, visiting Dublin several times. He stayed incognito, under the name of Reverend

Doctor Walsh, in the house of the prominent solicitor Sir John O'Connor in Killiney, the most prosperous and scenic of south Dublin suburbs, and regularly reported back to the British government. Initially all went well. The archbishop established good relations with the senior civil servants in Dublin Castle notably Sir John Anderson, the joint under-secretary, Alfred ('Andy') Cope, the assistant under-secretary, and Mark Sturgis, effectively Anderson's deputy, all strong supporters of the offer of Dominion Status to Sinn Féin and the scaling down of the war. With other civil servants they had been seconded from Whitehall in mid 1920 to reform the Dublin executive and to provide a fresh perspective on events. They did much to improve the efficiency of Dublin Castle but did not, however, win acceptance from the government for their advocacy of a conciliation policy, despite all their advice to the prime minister. Cope was often involved in undercover negotiations with prominent advanced nationalists and had been sent over by Lloyd George with that purpose in mind. Sturgis commented on Clune's importance as an intermediary; 'The real one is Clune ... Andy [Cope] says an excellent fellow.'[4]

Cope arranged for the archbishop to be escorted into Mountjoy Prison to meet with Arthur Griffith and Clune was also taken to Dr Robert Farnan's house in Mountjoy Square to see Michael Collins. This latter meeting was organised by Art O'Brien, the main IRA contact in London. The discussions with Collins and Griffith appear to have gone well. Clune told Greenwood that Collins and Mulcahy, the IRA GHQ leaders, 'were much more reasonable than he expected they would be'.[5] Mark Sturgis recorded that Clune 'expressed himself to Andy [Cope] as very confident ... said he was sure that the leaders could stop the gunmen in a moment if they wished to'. Sturgis went on to comment 'I wonder how it is that the Archbishop sees Collins apparently without difficulty in Dublin and our intelligence fails to find him after weeks of search'.[6] Both the British government and Sinn Féin appeared receptive to Clune's proposal which was for an unconditional truce followed by a meeting of Dáil members, plus Church, labour and other independent representatives, to discuss peace terms. Clune proposed that 'if reprisals, hostilities, raids, pursuits etc cease' the Irish should 'undertake to use all possible means at our disposal to stop aggressive acts on our side, provided the Dáil Eireann be allowed to meet and pursue its peaceful activities'. He advocated also that espionage should cease.[7] The British authorities seemed agreeable to this while initially insisting that the IRA leaders Collins and Mulcahy not be involved.

At this delicate stage, between 3 and 5 December, two unhelpful developments occurred in the public arena. First, the Galway County and Urban District Councils passed resolutions which appeared in the national press supporting negotiations for a truce. Second, a telegram by Father

Michael O'Flanagan, the Sinn Féin Vice-President, was widely published in British and Irish newspapers asking Lloyd George to state his peace terms. O'Flanagan declared: 'You state you are willing to make peace at once without waiting till Christmas. Ireland is also willing to make peace. What first step do you propose?'[8] Both these public initiatives appeared to indicate splits in Sinn Féin ranks. Collins was outraged by what he regarded as O'Flanagan's interference; later O'Flanagan admitted that he had deliberately attempted to sabotage Clune's efforts which he held to have been over-influenced by Dublin Castle.[9] These interventions encouraged many within the British political and military establishment to adopt an intransigent line regarding Clune's mission and to argue that the apparent Irish willingness to negotiate implied weakness. In any case the military situation in Ireland made it inconceivable that the military would show any sympathy for peace initiatives. The funerals of British police and military killed on Bloody Sunday and at Kilmichael was hardly an appropriate context for political initiatives.

Miffed at being sidelined at the time of the original invitation to Clune, Hamar Greenwood declared that he was firmly against a truce. Displaying characteristic over-optimism he told the prime minister:

> We are coming to grips, but I feel we must be firm as to terms or any settlement will not be permanent. We are on top, with the House, the Country, and I believe, most Irishmen-wishing us well. Our position and strength is [sic] rapidly improving. The SF Cause and organisation is breaking up. Clune and everyone else admits this ... there is no need of hurry in settlement. We can in due course and on our own and fair terms settle this Irish Question for good.

Greenwood concluded of the IRA leaders; 'In plain English, they want to save their faces and their skins.'[10]

The military and political resistance to any thought of a truce would seem to explain the much harder and pessimistic line the Prime Minister took when he saw Clune again, on 8 December. Griffith then concluded that Lloyd George 'apparently wants peace but is afraid of his Militarists'.[11] By this time Lloyd George apparently was insisting that arms would have to be surrendered prior to a truce and Clune was correctly warning that this would wreck his efforts. The prime minister told the House of Commons on 9 December that the Government 'have no option but to continue and indeed to intensify their campaign'.[12] All this led Art O'Brien to express opposition to the continuation of the mission arguing that a naive Clune had been hoodwinked by Lloyd George.[13] Collins had become less convinced than Griffith of the prime minister's sincerity, telling O'Brien that 'there is far too much a tendency to believe that LG is wishful for Peace, and it is only his own wild men prevent him from accomplishing his desires ... I am not convinced he is the peace-maker'.[14]

There was never a prospect that the Sinn Féin/IRA leadership would agree to the revised terms, and Griffith by this time felt that the British were using the mission for spying purposes. On 14 December Collins told Griffith that 'no additional good result can come from further continuing these discussions' and that Clune should make it clear to Lloyd George that he had gone back on his original position. Sturgis reported Clune saying that 'the Government have jumped a step and are laying down terms of peace whereas what he has been discussing is not that at all, but the terms of an informal truce during which atmosphere can be created and peace discussed'.[15]

Clune unavailingly persisted with his efforts until the end of the month, striving to win agreement for a month's truce over the New Year period during which, with Anderson's help, the surrender of arms demand would be waived. He suggested negotiations should begin between representatives from the Dáil and the British government.[16] At a meeting on 29 December the British cabinet met with military top-brass to review the military and political situation. General Macready, the head of the army in Dublin, warned then of the dangers of IRA reorganisation during a truce and the chief of the imperial general staff, Sir Henry Wilson, affirmed that any halt to the conflict 'would be absolutely fatal'. The Tory majority in the Cabinet prevailed, with the decision taken to reject any thought of truce. The military leadership stated that they required another few months to clean up the situation.

In a meeting with Clune in late December, Philip Kerr, a member of the prime minister's kitchen cabinet, thanked the archbishop for his efforts, and reminded him of the South African precedent at the end of the Boer War for arms decommissioning preparatory to truce and settlement. Clune replied that the Cabinet would regret rejecting his peace terms and stressed that 'they were living in a fool's paradise in hoping that they could crush the people and frighten them'. He rejected Kerr's idea that the Irish Church hierarchy should directly intervene in the situation. Futilely Clune mooted the notion of Archbishop Mannix going with him to join the Catholic leaders in Ireland on a further peace mission, this to be accompanied by a month's ceasefire and a full meeting of the Dáil. Kerr refused to consider the lifting of the ban on Mannix.[17]

In no way mollified, and much to Art O'Brien's annoyance, Clune broke his silence on his peace efforts in an interview in Paris with *La Liberté* in January1921. He then declared that the Irish leaders were not assassins but were, in a well-broadcast phrase, 'the cream of their race'.

The archbishop gave his account of his mission, commenting that the Irish leaders 'made an excellent impression. They seemed to me very moderate in their aims. They accepted the principle of a truce.' Clune still held that Lloyd George had sincerely sought a settlement but had been derailed in his efforts by military and political opposition. When asked for his view of the Irish leadership he replied:

> I admire their gallantry. When during the negotiations, my taxi stopped before their doors, I was exposing them to certain death. I saw no sign of trepidation. I admire the ideal which has caused them to act. When Mr Lloyd George termed them assassins, I was content to reply to him; 'No! Not murderers, but the cream of their race!'

When the questioning moved on to Clune's attitude to the British forces, he commented:

> I must speak without resentment. Let me shortly tell you that they have shot my poor defenceless nephew [Conor Clune, who was shot dead in Dublin Castle on the weekend of Bloody Sunday]. When I detailed the pathetic facts of his death to Mr Lloyd George, he simply said: 'It is awful; tell me no more of that . . . '.[18]

The archbishop concluded, significantly talking of a home rule settlement rather than a republican one: 'I pray that Home Rule may soon be granted to my hapless country similar to that of the Dominions. It is the only way, in my idea, to get peace.'

Clune went on to Rome, where he played an important role in countering British diplomatic pressure on Pope Benedict XV to condemn IRA outrages. Mrs Gavan Duffy, the wife of one of the Sinn Féin representatives in Paris, had heard from various sources that the Pope 'was immensely impressed by Dr Clune, the murder of his young nephew, his admiration for our leaders in particular Mick Collins, his testimony of the religious faith of our republicans'.[19]

As a consequence of Clune's Paris interview, the Western Australian Governor-General, Sir Francis Newdegate, unavailingly urged the British Home Office to delay Clune's return to Australia by detaining him in Britain on the grounds that his presence would exacerbate labour divisions at home. Hardly surprisingly Home Office officials replied that any such move would be counter-productive. This only encouraged the assembling of a large welcoming party in Perth to hear Clune denounce British policy in Ireland, and to compare police atrocities to German ones in Belgium during the First World War.[20]

The Clune mission's failure did not represent the end of peace moves but up to June 1921 it was the most promising effort to achieve the basis for compromise. Following these few weeks of fame Clune, it appears, had little to say publicly about Irish affairs for the rest of his career and, in line with his moderate views, he welcomed the Anglo-Irish Treaty in December 1921. The archbishop, in the month following the Treaty, reportedly commented to an Irish friend: 'Don't you get practically all you would have as a republic?'[21]

Several questions arise. First, why did Lloyd George choose Clune as an intermediary? The choice of any Australian Catholic bishop is surprising. In an embarrassing and widely covered event the British Government had in August 1920 ordered the interception off Penzance, on the coast of Cornwall, of the boat Archbishop Daniel Mannix was returning on after a speaking tour of the US. An ex-President of Maynooth College, Mannix had been Archbishop of Melbourne since 1917 and the highly vocal leader of anti-conscription opinion in Australia. He was prevented from setting foot in Ireland. Mannix had made several speeches denouncing British rule in Ireland during his American stay. A leading English Benedictine, Cardinal Gasquet, had vainly and absurdly suggested Mannix as a potential middle man between Sinn Féin and Britain. Mannix was kept under the watch of Scotland Yard during his stay in London.[22] Clune consulted Mannix in Ireland before his Irish mission. One would have thought that the British Government had had its fill of Australian bishops and would have doubted their potential as peace mediators.

Clune, however, in stark contrast to Mannix, had been pro-conscription during the First World War, was pro-monarchy and a moderate Home Ruler. He had described the Easter Rising as insane and said that those of Irish birth or descent in Australia regarded it with shame. He was to comment on the divisions following the Anglo-Irish Treaty: 'The bickerings and recriminations made us sick.'[23] It is unclear whether the British Government recalled that Clune's nephew, Conor, had been killed in Dublin Castle following his arrest in the centre of the city alongside the IRA Dublin Brigade leaders, Dick McKee and Peadar Clancy, during the Bloody Sunday weekend. Conor was not an IRA man and was in Dublin on a business trip from Clare. The British did know that Archbishop Clune had recently been in his home county at the time of the Rineen ambush, in September, and the associated reprisals. To add to the tension that Clune must have felt, the house of his friend and colleague Bishop Fogarty of Killaloe was raided by Auxiliaries and fears expressed for his life while he was visiting Clune in Dublin. Brigadier Crozier, the head of the Auxiliaries at the time, was to claim that the plan had been to drown Fogarty in the River Shannon. There need have been no surprise, therefore, that Clune's views on the Irish situation had been hardened by his first-hand experience. This would surely have been apparent at Lloyd George's original meeting with the archbishop. On the other hand, overseas Church leaders of moderate political persuasion may have seemed appropriate intermediaries and acceptable to the Irish side; the Bishop of Adelaide, in addition to Clune, was available in England at that time as a potential intermediary. Other likely choices for peace initiatives, and tried at various times, were southern unionists and labour leaders. The use of the Catholic Church overseas had a particular appeal in this connection. Almost all the Catholic hierarchy in Ireland had views more compatible with a Home Rule than a republican settlement and were loath to make public statements on constitutional issues. In December 1920 Collins expressed caution concerning any possibility of asking Church leaders to recognise the Dáil Government. It would not have suited either British or Irish leaders to force the Church in Ireland to become too directly involved in peace initiatives. What is somewhat more surprising is the lack of involvement in such initiatives of American bishops. That may be explained by the fact that most of them, unlike the Australian bishops, were of Irish parentage rather than Irish birth and, therefore, had a less direct relationship with the home country.[24]

Second, how important was the failure of the Clune mission? It had disastrous consequences for Anglo-Irish relations as the war worsened in the aftermath of the mission's failure. In retrospect, the old maverick Parliamentary Party warrior Tim Healy, who had considerable links with Sinn Féin, commented:

> the silly Cabinet turned him (Clune) down, believing they can crush the Shinns, and that their acceptance of a Truce spelled weakness. No worse incident has occurred for 100 years. The Irish have dozens of instances to cite of treachery and breach against the English. They have now been befooled into parley (with) an Australian loyalist, selected not by them, but by LG.

Herbert Asquith, the former prime minister and Liberal Party leader, said that the failure of the mission was a great disappointment to him and he held the insistence on the surrender of arms to be a bad mistake.[25] There is evidence to suggest that the IRA and Sinn Féin were keen to negotiate at this stage and saw a truce as a necessary relief from military and intelligence pressure, as they did seven months later at the time of the actual truce. Given the later divisions over the Anglo-Irish treaty such an attitude was bound to be denied. The IRA had recently come under increasing pressure from the reorganised British intelligence forces. The aftermath of Bloody Sunday from late November saw a vast increase in raids and arrests. Numbers interned rose from 1,478 for the week ending 17 January 1921 to 2,569 for the week ending 21 March and 4,454 for the week ending 16 July.[26] In any move towards negotiation secrecy was paramount both for the IRA and the British. Collins told Griffith, on 2 December, 'My view is that a Truce on the terms specified cannot possibly do us any harm. It appears to me that it is distinctly an advance.'[27] Such calculations were upset by the public Galway Council and O'Flanagan interventions.

From the perspective of Dublin Castle it is clear also that Anderson and Cope invested considerable hope in Clune's mission. Lloyd George's original initiative seemed to indicate that the prime minister was coming round to their way of thinking. Lloyd George, moreover, at this most sensitive of times would surely not have invited Clune to undertake his mission if he had not been in earnest. The most likely explanation for what went wrong is that Lloyd George backed away from interest in a truce when alarmed by the military and the Conservative Party opposition within the Cabinet. Before encouraging the mission he must have been aware of the level of opposition it would provoke once it became known and that general agreement to the decommissioning of arms by the IRA was inconceivable. This was not the first time that Lloyd George had launched an Irish initiative which he was subsequently to regret making.[28] Both at the time and since then, it suited both Irish and British sides to underplay the possibility of a settlement. Republicans were unwilling to admit to any involvement in talks, the prospect of compromise with the enemy and betrayal of weakness. For their part British politicians were averse to accusations of conversing with gunmen and of violating imperial principles. In agreeing to talk both sides showed a flexibility they could not afford to exhibit in public.

Third, was the failure of the mission avoidable? Mark Sturgis was to confirm the accuracy of Sinn Féin claims that the prime minister had imposed terms during the mission that did not exist at the start of the mission. On 3 January 1921, Cope wrote to Sturgis:

Just back from tea with the Archbishop. He wishes to be remembered to you and Jonathan. He is very disappointed . . . he is satisfied that if the business had been left to the three of us in the Castle, a settlement would be a few days off – a final settlement he means. He says he felt sure that Jonathan and himself had arranged a truce commencing Christmas.[29]

During later peace efforts Sinn Féin were frequently to ascribe their unwillingness to trust Lloyd George and begin talks to the experience of the Clune initiative. In March 1921 Sturgis reported while in discussions with Irish labour leaders: 'the Shins regard themselves as tricked and sold over Clune. Clune saw them all and went to London with terms in his pocket and was led on and then turned down...Of course I said "not so" but that's their reading of it.'[30] When the truce did come at the beginning of July 1921, de Valera affirmed that he was willing to abide by the truce terms agreed with Clune.

Welcoming the signing of the Anglo-Irish Treaty in December 1921 Warren Fisher, the head of the British civil service and mentor to Anderson and Cope, commented, 'Better late than never, but I can't get out of mind the unnecessary number of graves.'[31] The months between Clune's departure and the Truce in early July saw the worst casualty figures of the war. The existence of a military stalemate had been apparent in December 1920 with the British army asking for a few months more under partial martial law to defeat the IRA.

Peace efforts did not end with Clune. Sundry initiatives involved, amongst others, labour leaders, southern Unionists and individual British politicians acting as middlemen. In all cases the Dublin Castle junta of Anderson, Cope and Sturgis were involved. At various times Lloyd George appeared willing to compromise on fiscal issues and he backed efforts to bring Edward Carson and de Valera together. Again, however, he displayed a lack of commitment and consistency with regard to peace efforts. In defence of Lloyd George it is frequently argued that the premier was constrained by the Tory majority within his Cabinet. However leading conservatives, notably their leader Austen Chamberlain and the Foreign Secretary Lord Curzon, were sympathetic to conciliation. In contrast to his adept performance during the Treaty negotiations at the end of 1921, Lloyd George made little effort in the last part of the War of Independence to isolate diehard Tory opinion and by his harsh rhetoric on military matters often encouraged it. Both British and Irish sides were reluctant to make the first peace move and demonstrated a mutual distrust. When a direct approach was at last made to the Sinn Féin leadership at the end of June 1921 it was brought about by urgent political realities. At that time, the British Government was faced with a choice between martial law for the whole of the twenty-six counties and crown colony government, or, on the other hand, negotiations with Sinn Féin. Again important elements among the military leadership were opposed to a stoppage in the war at a time when they felt they were getting the situation under control. When the Truce was agreed on 9 July, decommissioning of IRA arms was not insisted on.[32]

The Clune mission was the most substantial missed opportunity for peace in the War of Independence – at no other time did Lloyd George authorise such a direct approach to the IRA and Sinn Féin leadership. In all the other peace efforts Lloyd George remained firmly in the background. Clune had been made to look like an innocent abroad during his mission but his reaction to his treatment by the British authorities did have significance in Ireland and Rome. The archbishop could so easily have achieved a long-term fame. Meanwhile, historians have generally underestimated the potential for some agreement in the second half of 1920. The likely peace terms, frequently mooted in 1920 and the first months of 1921 – safeguards on defence and Ulster, fiscal autonomy for the twenty-six counties and a form of dominion status – were the outline of those eventually agreed in the Anglo-Irish Treaty. The dire security situation had made negotiation a political imperative for both sides as early as the autumn of 1920. The military and political consequences of the breakdown of the Clune initiative were dire.

NOTES

1. For Clune and his mission, see D.F. Bourke, *The History of the Catholic Church in Western Australia, 1829–1979* (Perth: Archdiocese of Perth, 1979); Patrick O'Farrell, *The Irish in Australia 1788 to the Present* (Kensington: University of New South Wales Press, 1986); Patrick O'Farrell, *The Catholic Church and Community. An Australian History* (Kensington: University of New South Wales Press, 1992 [revised third edition]); John T. McMahon, *The Cream of Their Race* (Ennis: n.d.) David W. Miller, *Church, State and Nation in Ireland* (Dublin: Gill and Macmillan, 1973.), pp.473–6; Maureen Mortimer, '"An ordinary commonplace outbreak of everyday dirty bigotry." Walter Dwyer and the St Patrick Day Procession in Perth, 1919', *Australian Journal of Irish Studies*, 5 (2005), pp.81–94; Michael Hopkinson, *The Irish War of Independence* (Dublin: Gill and Macmillan, 2002), pp.182–5. Clune's Papers in the Catholic Church Archives in Perth are thin and unrevealing. For the political background in Western Australia, see Danny Cusack, *With an Olive Branch and a Shillelagh: the Life and Times of Senator Paddy Lynch (1867–1944)* (Perth: Hesperian Press, Murdoch University, 2004).
2. For the War of Independence see Hopkinson, *The Irish War of Independence*; Charles Townshend, *The British Campaign in Ireland, 1919–1921* (Oxford: Oxford University Press, 1975); David Fitzpatrick, *Politics and Irish Life: Provincial Experience of War and Revolution* (Dublin: Gill and Macmillan, 1977); Peter Hart, *The IRA and its Enemies: Violence and Community in Cork, 1916–1923* (Oxford: Oxford University Press, 1998); Tim Pat Coogan, *Michael Collins: A Biography* (London: Hutchinson, 1990). Peter Hart (ed.), *British Intelligence in Ireland, 1920–21. The Final Reports* (Cork: Cork University Press, 2002). For the 30 November and 1 December meetings, see John T. McMahon, Statement to Bureau of Military History, National Library of Ireland, MS 27,730.
3. AE to Philip Kerr, 9 December 1920, Lloyd George Papers, House of Lords Library F/91/7/5. *Report of the Labour Commission to Ireland* (London, 1921). Lloyd George to Greenwood, 2 December 1920, Lloyd George Papers, F/19/2/26.
4. See Michael Hopkinson (ed.), *The Last Days of Dublin Castle: The Diaries of Mark Sturgis* (Dublin: Irish Academic Press, 1999), p.86. Original Sturgis diaries, 7 December 1920, Volume III in National Archives, Kew. Sir J.W. Wheeler-Bennett, *Sir John Anderson, Viscount Waverley* (London: Macmillan, 1962); Eunan O'Halpin, *The Decline of the Union: British Government in Ireland, 1892–1920* (Dublin: Gill and Macmillan, 1987).

5. Greenwood Memorandum, Lloyd George Papers, F/19/2/31.

6. Sturgis diary for 7 December 1920, Volume III. Hopkinson, *The Last Days of Dublin Castle*, pp.86–7.

7. Griffith to Collins, 14 December 1920. National Archives of Ireland (NAI), DE 8430.

8. *Irish Daily Press*, 4–6 December 1920. These developments followed on appeals made by Roger Sweetman, a Sinn Féin TD, and the Archbishop of Tuam. For O'Flanagan's admission see Brian P. Murphy, *Patrick Pearse and the Lost Republican Ideal* (Dublin: James Duffy, 1991). See also Arthur Mitchell, *Revolutionary Government in Ireland: Dáil Eireann 1919–22* (Dublin: Gill and Macmillan, 1974).

9. For Collins' annoyance, see Collins to Art O'Brien, 14 December 1920, NAI, DE 234A. Murphy, *Patrick Pearse*, p.120, quoting Father O'Flanagan in *The Plain People*, 30 April 1922.

10. Greenwood to Lloyd George, Lloyd George Papers, F/19/2/31.

11. Griffith to Michael Collins, 13 and 17 December 1920, NAI, DE 234A and 234B.

12. Parliamentary Debates, Hansard Commons, 9 December 1920, cols 2601–11.

13. Art O'Brien to Michael Collins, 25 December 1920, NAI, DE 234B.

14. Collins to Art O'Brien, 15 December 1920, NAI, DE 234B.

15. Griffith to Collins, 13 December 1920, NAI, DE 234A; Griffith to Collins, 17 December, 1920 NAI, DE 234B; Collins to Griffith, 14 December 1920, ibid. McMahon, Statement to Bureau of Military History. Sturgis diary for 17 December 1920, Volume IV. Hopkinson, *The Last Days of Dublin Castle*, p.94.

16. Piaras Béaslaí, *Michael Collins and the Making of a New Ireland* (Dublin: Phoenix, 1926), Vol.2, p.137.

17. British National Archives (BNA), CAB 79A(20), CAB 23/24. Kerr Memorandum, Lloyd George Papers, F /90/1/29. McMahon, Statement to Bureau of Military History; Miller, *Church, State and Nation*, p.476.

18. McMahon, *The Cream Of Their Race*.

19. Statement of Monsignor Michael. J. Curran, Bureau of Military History Volume 3, NLI , MS 27,728. Mrs Gavan Duffy letter from Rome, 11 February 1921, Art O'Brien Papers, NLI, Box 8429.

20. Newdegate to Secretary of State for Colonies, 12 January 1921, BNA, CO 537/1151. Newdegate to Secretary of State for Colonies, Battye Library, Perth AN395/2. *Western Australian*, 19, 26 February 1921.

21. O'Farrell, *The Irish in Australia*, p.291.

22. Miller, *Church, State and Nation*, pp.472–3.

23. O'Farrell, *The Irish in Australia*, pp.259, 260.

24. McMahon, Statement to Bureau of Military History. *Irish Press*, 13 April 1936. For the Catholic Church's attitude at home and abroad, see Mitchell, *Revolutionary Government*, pp.172–6; Miller, *Church, State and Nation*; Patrick Murray, *Oracles of God. The Roman Catholic Church and Irish Politics, 1922–37* (Dublin: University College Dublin Press, 2000).

25. Healy to Beaverbrook, 23 December 1920, NLI, MS 23628. Sturgis diary for 23 February 1921, Volume IV. Hopkinson, *The Last Days of Dublin Castle*, pp.131–2.

26. Townshend, *The British Campaign in Ireland*, Appendix X11, p.223.

27. Collins to Griffith, 2 December 1920, NAI, DE 234A.

28. In the spring of 1919 Lloyd George gave safe conducts to visit Ireland to the Irish-American delegation to the Paris Peace Conference. He was to put the blame elsewhere when the visit had disastrous political and diplomatic consequences. See Michael Hopkinson, 'President Woodrow Wilson and the Irish Question', *Studia Hibernica*, 27 (1993), pp.89–111.

29. Grant-Sturgis Papers (Privately held), Cope to Mark Sturgis, 3 January 1921.

30. Sturgis diary for 23 March 1921, Volume IV. Hopkinson, *The Last Days of Dublin Castle*, p.146.

31. Grant-Sturgis Papers, Fisher to Mark Sturgis, 17 December 1921.

32. See Hopkinson, *The Irish War of Independence*, pp.186–97. For Curzon and Chamberlain's views, ibid., pp.64–5

15

'A roof-raising affair'?
Éamon de Valera's Tour of
Australia and New Zealand
Rory O'Dwyer

The visit of Éamon de Valera to Australia and New Zealand in 1948 presents a colourful insight into the nature of the Irish community in these countries and, more particularly, reveals the impressive survival skills of an astute veteran of the Irish political scene. The tour, de Valera's only visit to the southern hemisphere, formed part of his 'World Anti-Partition Tour' – one of the most prominent events in the notable, if fruitless, campaign of protest against the continuing partition of Ireland in this period.

Throughout his long political career Éamon de Valera was preoccupied by the enduring partition of Ireland, created by the passing of the Government of Ireland Act in 1920. According to de Valera, the threat of partition in the years before the Act was passed was the principal reason for his involvement in politics. Over the following fifty years, he made literally thousands of speeches containing references to Ulster and his aspiration for Irish unity.[1] In his years in office as head of government from 1932 to 1948 he repeatedly reaffirmed this aspiration, although he failed to pursue any coherent policy to achieve this goal. In practice de Valera sought to maintain his republican credentials in this respect through rhetoric and quiescent idealism rather than action. This approach evidently won the tacit approval of a very significant section of the Irish electorate. De Valera's blend of romantic nationalism was unquestionably a key component of his unique and remarkable political appeal.

In 1948, however, in a surprise election result, de Valera and his party, Fianna Fáil, were ousted from power by an inter-party coalition. After sixteen years of uninterrupted leadership, the loss came as an enormous disappointment to de Valera. Party morale quickly plummeted to an all-time low. Fianna Fáil Teachtaí Dála (TDs) were immediately reminded of how frustrating the opposition benches could be. Their resentment and bitterness were manifest in a number of unedifying parliamentary altercations with members of the new government.[2] De Valera's problems were compounded by notification of his requirement to make a court appearance as a witness in a case relating to Sinn Féin funds in 1924.[3] This appearance was inevitably going to force de Valera to answer questions on his activities during his darkest years from 1922 to 1925, the years of his career for which he had always received the most criticism. The outlook appeared bleak

De Valera's response to these events, however, was immediate and pro-active. Supporting an anti-partition campaign, which had begun in Northern Ireland in 1946 with the founding of the Anti-Partition League, de Valera announced his intention to embark on a tour of America to seek international support for the campaign. He also decided to accept an invitation from the Irish-born Archbishop of Melbourne, Daniel Mannix, to attend the diocesan centenary of the Catholic Church in Melbourne.[4] It was this decision which ultimately transformed de Valera's main contribution to the anti-partition campaign into a world tour.

Accompanied by his party colleague, Frank Aiken, de Valera set off for America, one month after his party's demoralising election loss. During a hectic four-week tour of the US, de Valera and Aiken visited all of the major American cities where, without exception, they were warmly received and entertained by ecclesiastical, state and city authorities. In each city they visited they were accorded at least one opportunity of making an address and were treated with extreme courtesy. In New York, for example, de Valera was greeted by the city's governor and, amid cheering crowds, was driven through the city with an impressive police and military escort to the City Hall, where he was conferred with honorary New York citizenship.[5]

In Washington he had a meeting with the American president, Harry Truman, as well as calling on the secretary of state, George Marshall.[6] These high-profile meetings, together with de Valera's mingling with Hollywood stars while celebrating St Patrick's Day in both San Francisco (where he was Marshal at the parade) and Los Angeles (for an evening celebration), his induction as honorary chief of a native American tribe in Oklahoma,[7] his visit to see the famed 'Liberty Bell' in Independence Hall, Philadelphia,[8] and his address to the National Press Club, all helped ensure constant media interest. The *Irish Times* newspaper reported that over 100,000 people threw showers of green confetti and cheered de Valera as he was paraded through the centre of Boston. He received the greatest ovation from some 13,000 people who packed Boston Garden to hear his address. Following his strong condemnation of the 'travesty of democracy' that was partition, de Valera was presented with the symbolic key to Boston by Mayor James McCurley, who claimed that de Valera had America's support in his efforts to unite Ireland.[9]

On returning to Ireland for eleven days in early April before the major stage of the tour, a special anti-partition rally was organised by Fianna Fáil in College Green, Dublin, where de Valera, the key speaker, reflected on his American trip and on his plans to tour Australia and New Zealand. According to de Valera:

It had to be explained that there were no two distinct nations in this island of ours and that there was nothing at issue except the question of political differences, which should be resolved by the majority vote of the people, as in other democratic countries. The time is ripe for a new national advance to end partition and every one of us can play a part.[10]

The meeting, attended by several thousand people, was preceded by a procession made up of ten bands and about fifty Fianna Fáil cumainn (branches). The fanfare and general hullabaloo obscured the real reason for de Valera's brief return to Ireland. On 20 April, he finally appeared in court in the Sinn Féin funds case. Elaborately prepared, with numerous meticulously crafted statements on his activities in the 1922–5 period, he survived the questioning he received with a series of long-winded answers, often digressing entirely from the question. De Valera's concern with the verdict of history was very apparent.

Putting his somewhat idiosyncratic court appearance quickly behind him, he set off from Shannon, accompanied again by his trusted colleague, Frank Aiken, on 22 April bound for Australia. After very brief stops in New York, Omaha, San Francisco, Honolulu, the Fiji Islands, and Canton they eventually landed in Sydney on 27 April. On arrival de Valera stated that his purpose in coming to Australia was to attend the Melbourne diocese centenary celebrations at the invitation of his 'old friend' Archbishop Mannix, but that he was naturally anxious to see a country in whose modern history Irish people had played such a prominent part. He stated that he had wanted to visit Australia since 1917 when he had received a letter of congratulation from the then Archbishop of Sydney, Michael Kelly, on his election to parliament.[11] De Valera claimed that while in Australia he was willing to discuss the partition of Ireland but that was not the primary purpose of his visit. This was certainly not how he had presented his intentions back in Dublin. Guests of honour at a luncheon given by the Premier of New South Wales on the following day, de Valera and Aiken also met with the Archbishop of Sydney, Cardinal Norman Gilroy, the first of many ecclesiastical figures who would offer a very warm welcome to de Valera on this stage of his tour.

After passing two days in Sydney, de Valera and Aiken flew to the Australian capital, Canberra, where as guests of the Commonwealth government they were invited to sit in the national parliament while it was in session, an honour conferred on only one previous visitor, General Douglas MacArthur. They met with the Australian Prime Minister, Ben Chifley, and his cabinet, including the Minister for External Affairs, Herbert 'Doc' Evatt, a noted expert on Commonwealth history with considerable experience of international affairs. That de Valera and Evatt struck up a bond is very likely as Evatt was happy to meet de Valera again later in Melbourne. Before leaving Canberra, de Valera and Aiken visited the residence of the Irish envoy in Australia, Thomas J. Kiernan, who was appointed by de Valera in 1946. By 1948 Kiernan had already made a favourable impression, having travelled around the country lecturing on Irish history and culture, usually accompanied by his wife, the very popular ballad singer known by her maiden name, Delia Murphy.

Flying on to Melbourne later the same day de Valera finally got to meet his 'old friend' Archbishop Mannix once again. Theirs was indeed a very longstanding friendship. In 1912, as President of Maynooth College, Mannix had interviewed de Valera for a temporary lecturing post at the college.[12] Their acquaintance was more closely established in 1920 when de Valera was touring America and the two men met in Omaha. Mannix became a committed convert to de Valera's political cause, and from that time publicly expressed his support for de Valera on many occasions. The two men maintained a correspondence over the next twenty-eight years. In many ways the tour of Australia was made feasible by Archbishop Mannix. His support and influence helped ensure that it could not be a failure. With his backing they were virtually guaranteed respectable audiences, especially in Victoria.

Some 20,000 people crowded the Melbourne Exhibition Hall the following night to hear de Valera during a special rally in his honour. In his address he quickly raised the issue of partition. After highlighting the unprincipled manner in which the boundary line was drawn in 1920, he elaborated on how the island of Ireland was a natural unit and called upon the Australian people to provide moral support to the campaign to end partition. In reference to Ireland's neutrality in the Second World War (which was strongly criticised by the Australian press) de Valera remarked:

> Had part of our soil not been kept from us by force, our conduct in 1939 might – I repeat might – have been different, but while that cruel injustice persisted there could not be any question of the Irish participating in the war. Don't interpret this as an apology. There is no call for an apology. The Irish people were almost universally behind my government's neutrality. There has been no question of that since the war and I do not fear the verdict of history.[13]

The speech was very well received by the audience, who cheered loudly throughout. In a letter to his wife, Aiken described the meeting as 'a roof-raising affair'.[14]

Over the next week de Valera and Aiken attended the various church ceremonies in Melbourne to celebrate the centenary. The event began with a pontifical High Mass in St Patrick's Cathedral and continued with various meetings, exhibitions, and ceremonies over the following week, culminating with a large pageant (attended by over 100,000 people) and Benediction pronounced by Archbishop Mannix. De Valera stayed on in Melbourne for several days after the celebrations. He addressed students and staff in the University of Melbourne on partition and continued to meet with members of the Irish community. The Australian Minister for Information and Immigration, Arthur Calwell, drove de Valera and Aiken to Ballarat, outside Melbourne, to show them the very impressive Eureka monument and, in particular, the Irish names on the monument to those who died in the stockade clash of 1854 – 'Australia's first fight for freedom'.[15] De Valera, no doubt, would have been aware that Peter Lalor, who was in command of the striking miners, was the younger brother of the highly esteemed Young Irelander, James Fintan Lalor.

After the warmth of their reception in Victoria, de Valera and Aiken must have been a little disappointed at the more subdued nature of their reception in Western Australia. Arriving in Perth on 14 May, they received no official welcome from the Western Australian administration. Indeed the media response in Perth to de Valera's visit was largely hostile. Numerous angry letters were published in the editorial pages of the local press. The Perth *Daily News* published one such letter condemning the public welcome to de Valera given by the Commonwealth government:

> It would be interesting to know whether we are to extend public welcomes to defeated politicians from every tinpot republic, or whether the honour is to be reserved for those who hampered Britain and helped our enemies during the most critical days of our history. It is regrettable that loyal British citizens should extend a public welcome to Mr de Valera. If ever a man was responsible for the deaths of thousands of people in England it was this man.[16]

Another letter was equally scathing:

> I protest against the entertaining of Britain's arch-enemy. I never thought I would live to see the day that the man who left the lights on to show the Germans the way to London would be welcomed here in Australia. Mr de Valera certainly proved himself to be no friend to

England, her dominions or her allies during the war. He should not have been allowed to land in Australia. For the state government to honour an avowed enemy by a public reception is an affront to all loyal subjects of the king. The Premier and his government should be brought to book for insulting the dead seamen and their widows and children and all who suffered through the policy of this man.[17]

Irrespective of the harsh media comment and the indifference of the Western Australian authorities, de Valera could, as on all other occasions on this tour, depend on a hospitable and sympathetic welcome from the Catholic Church.[18] As the local Catholic newspaper, the *Record*, noted:

Of the discourtesy of the state to such a distinguished visitor, it is scarcely necessary to speak, for their omissions contrast, humiliatingly for them, with the receptions accorded to Mr de Valera by both commonwealth and state authorities in Victoria. If the grace of God is in courtesy, we must nonetheless admit that good effects may follow from boorishness. What was lacking in the *savoir faire* of the secular authorities was more than compensated by the genuine warmth and spontaneity of the Catholic and Irish sections of the community. And the slurs of the press, which manifested a remarkable similarity of viewpoint, served de Valera's purpose very well indeed, as they gave him the vantage point of being able to forestall criticism. This was all the more valuable in that both [local] papers served up faithfully all the time worn shibboleths of slander against Ireland's cause, and the Irish leader was able to reduce them to pulp without any apparent difficulty.[19]

While staying in Perth, de Valera made sure to visit Fremantle, which had a large working-class Irish community. Apart from visiting the old prison from which five Irish Fenians had escaped in the famed 'Catalpa Rescue' in 1876, they were invited to a football match at Fremantle, as guests of the Western Australian Football League. De Valera afterwards stressed the similarity with Gaelic football and expressed the conviction that the games were similar enough for international matches to be played between Ireland and Australia 'one of these days'.[20]

Before leaving Perth, de Valera gave an anti-partition address to a crowd of approximately 5,000 in the grounds of the Good Shepherd Convent, following a garden party held in his honour. Enjoying a similarly warm reception in Adelaide during a two-day visit, de Valera evidently became less restrained in his condemnation of partition. Addressing the Catholic Club in Adelaide, he spoke, as usual, of his desire for improved relations between Britain and Ireland, although he later exclaimed in an impassioned moment that 'only a bandit would cut one part of Ireland from another'.[21]

De Valera and Aiken next flew to Hobart in Tasmania, where they were met by representatives of the Tasmanian government and a large crowd of supporters. After an interview with the press they proceeded to the Hotel Fairfield, where they were entertained to supper by the Premier and members of the government, along with the Catholic Archbishop of Hobart, Ernest Tweedy. Later the same evening de Valera gave an address in the town hall. Reflecting the mixed opinion towards de Valera in Hobart,[22] a group of protesters, among the crowds of onlookers outside, sang the British National Anthem and 'Rule Britannia' as de Valera approached the hall. Inside, however, he received rapturous applause and was introduced very cordially by the Premier before he launched into yet another anti-partition address.

On the following day, 21 May, de Valera met with the Premier once again and attended a lunch given in his honour by the government. Afterwards de Valera and Aiken, much to their delight, went on a trip to Derwent Valley where revered Young Irelander, John Mitchel, had resided a hundred years previously. The visit very conveniently took place on the centenary of the 1848 Rebellion in Ireland, an event which had strong associations with Tasmania, as many involved in that rebellion were sentenced to transportation to the island's infamous penal colony. Given de Valera's fervent interest in Irish nationalist history and his virtual obsession with his place in that history, it was an important visit to make, and to be seen to make. We can be sure that de Valera was in his element at this stage, tracing the steps of the Young Irelanders against a stunning scenic backdrop, and visiting places which would have been very familiar to an Irish nationalist audience through popular literature, such as Mitchel's nationalist classic *Jail Journal*. That evening in Hobart they were treated to a special lecture on the 1848 exiles in Tasmania given by Monsignor John Cullen, vicar-general of the archdiocese of Hobart in 1948. A native of County Wicklow, Cullen had many years previously published *Young Ireland in Exile: the Story of the Men of '48* (Dublin, 1928). He had already become acquainted with de Valera, having met him while on an extended leave of absence in Ireland in 1926. Following the lecture, de Valera was presented with a collection of letters written by Young Irelanders such as Thomas Francis Meagher while in Tasmania, and he was asked to ensure their safekeeping in Ireland. This responsibility, as a custodian of Irish nationalist heritage, must have been particularly pleasing to de Valera. It is no surprise that he later referred to the Tasmanian visit as the highlight of the entire tour.[23]

On the following day de Valera visited the old Port Arthur penal colony and saw the cottage in which William Smith O'Brien had resided when he was held within the prison compound. Later that day he travelled to Launceston, where he gave a well-attended anti-partition address and visited other places in that area with 1848 connections. The following morning de Valera and Aiken left Launceston, bound for New Zealand.

Shortly after arrival in Wellington, they were warmly welcomed by the Scottish-born Prime Minister of New Zealand, Peter Fraser. That evening there was a special reception organised for de Valera in the town hall. There, he was given a public welcome by the Prime Minister and the Catholic Archbishop of Wellington. In introducing de Valera as a 'great international statesman', Fraser made reference to a period thirty years previously, when he himself held office in an Irish self- determination league in Wellington. From that moment there was little doubt that this part of the tour was going to be another success.[24]

After a state luncheon on the following day, de Valera and Aiken were afforded a special reception in the social hall of the parliament house. Those invited included all sections of the parliamentary, diplomatic, state, departmental, professional and commercial life of the capital, and representatives of the Catholic Church and the Irish community. Again, in his welcome address Fraser spoke glowingly of de Valera as 'a staunch champion of democracy' and elaborated on his contribution to the League of Nations in the previous decade. Fraser expressed a desire for closer economic bonds between the two countries as well as continued political bonds, stressing his hope that Ireland would remain in the Commonwealth.[25]

In thanking the Prime Minister for the hospitality he had received, de Valera, in a fascinating contrast to his own tragic early life, spoke of a family he had known as a child who emigrated to New Zealand where they ultimately found prosperity and happiness, and how the correspondence from them had stirred his childhood imagination greatly. De Valera spoke further on how he had grown to regard New Zealand as one of the most advanced countries in the world and that he particularly wanted to visit as the New Zealand government was regarded as such a model government. He then admitted that he had sometimes been asked why certain things were not done in Ireland as they were done in New Zealand.[26] De Valera and Aiken evidently struck up a warm bond with Fraser and most of his cabinet. In a letter to his wife, Aiken referred to the Prime Minister and his deputy, Sir Walter Nash, as 'two of the nicest and most intelligent members of a government [he had] ever met'.[27]

The following morning they set off by motor car to the beautiful resort of Rotorua. They were given a special Maori reception there that evening and were treated to demonstrations of various native dances. Aiken, whose wife was a very accomplished musician, was particularly fascinated by some of the native rhythms, as he later related in detail to his wife by letter. Late in the night, he expressed his appreciation of the festivities organised for them, by uncharacteristically singing a rousing Irish ballad, 'Bean an Fir Ruaidh'.[28]

While De Valera and Aiken were relaxing in Rotorua, a controversial situation was created when the British high commissioner in New Zealand, Sir Patrick Duff, unwisely contributed an extensive article to the local press criticising de Valera's anti-partition addresses while going on to provide a standard unionist interpretation of the need for partition, emphasising at length differences between North and South in Ireland. The commissioner's remarks served to fuel media interest in de Valera's next address in Auckland, and helped ensure that the local Irish community would be in mass attendance. Always one to thrive on the type of challenge presented by the British high commissioner, de Valera appeared to pull out all the stops in Auckland. After making references to medieval and early modern Irish history and outlining in detail what he referred to as the 'political manoeuvre of gerrymandering' in recent history, de Valera finally addressed the British high commissioner's central claim that there was no argument in favour of Éire's independence that was not an argument in favour of partition. To an extremely enlivened and supportive audience de Valera remarked: 'The argument in favour of Ireland's independence was that it was an ancient nation. The Six Counties were not. The people of Ireland as a whole should decide what was going to be the government of the land and its relation to other lands. That was self-determination.'[29] The speech was certainly well received by the audience. In a letter to his wife, Aiken expressed his belief that it was the best speech of the entire tour.[30] With the mass local Irish community support in full voice it was yet another highlight.

On returning to Sydney, there was a suggestion of trouble as the *Sydney Morning Herald* newspaper reported that 'Orangemen and Ulstermen' intended to be in the audience of de Valera's planned address at the Rushcutter Bay stadium. Following a meeting called by the federation of British ex-servicemen, about 1,000 people carried a resolution protesting against de Valera's visit to Australia and the recognition accorded to him by politicians. The meeting directed that the resolution be forwarded to the Australian Prime Minister.[31] However, the threatened protest did not in fact materialize. Over 7,000 people attended the event in honour of de Valera and there were no serious disturbances. De Valera spoke for more than an hour and a half without interruption, except from cheering supporters.[32]

During his stay in Sydney, de Valera made what was, for him, another very important pilgrimage. As 1948 marked the 150th anniversary of the 1798 Rebellion in Ireland he had particularly good occasion to visit the great monument in Waverley Cemetery where the famous Wicklow rebel Michael Dwyer and a number of others involved in that rebellion are buried, having all been sentenced to transportation to New South Wales in the early nineteenth century, never to return to Ireland. De Valera met with some of Dwyer's descendents and visited the area where Dwyer had lived.[33] Among the Irish community in Sydney, as well as in Ireland, Dwyer had achieved folk hero status and two months later de Valera was also very prominent in a major Michael Dwyer commemoration ceremony back in County Wicklow.

Leaving Sydney on 3 June, Aiken and de Valera began the long journey home by travelling north up the Queensland coast, stopping for a two-day visit to Brisbane. While there, they were treated to a special luncheon by the acting Premier of Queensland and were also greeted by Archbishop James Duhig, another Irish-born ecclesiastic. De Valera visited a number of schools and convents in the city and assisted Duhig in laying the foundation stone for a Marist Brothers' regional school.[34] De Valera also gave another powerfully worded anti-partition address to the Queensland Irish Association in Brisbane. Over the next few days de Valera and Aiken continued travelling north, stopping in several places with strong Irish associations, namely Cairns, Bowen and the nostalgically titled town of Inisfail. In a final interview before leaving the country via Darwin, on 11 June, de Valera spoke of Australia as a young country with tremendous possibilities and expressed his appreciation for the warm welcome he had received.[35]

After short visits to Singapore; to Burma, where he was well known to the Burmese cabinet due to his association with Irish independence and his external association concept; to India, where he received an extremely warm welcome for the same basic reasons in Delhi, Calcutta and Bombay; and to Cairo, the tour came to a spiritual climax with a final stop in Rome. This included an audience with Pope Pius XII, and reunions with their numerous friends and supporters in the Eternal City.[36]

De Valera and Aiken finally arrived back in Ireland on 21 June. Over 1,000 people crowded the Mansion House in Dublin that night for a special reception to welcome them home. Seán Lemass commented on the rebuilding of the Fianna Fáil organisation which had been taking place while they were away and remarked that the Árd Fheis (Annual Conference), which was specially arranged to start on the following day, would be of outstanding importance in the history of the organisation. 'Fianna Fáil is now stronger than ever,' Lemass claimed, 'not merely in membership but in the vigour and enthusiasm of its members.'[37]

In a brief address to the press de Valera remarked on how the Irish abroad were 'proud of the progress made in Ireland' and that 'this country can no longer be regarded as a small country, for everywhere you may go throughout the world, you will meet Irish men and women'. He lamented the lack of news about Ireland in the Australian press, and strongly encouraged Irish people to correspond with relatives abroad as often as possible. He also eagerly anticipated the establishment of the short-wave radio station.[38]

De Valera also, not surprisingly, paid tribute to the Irish Catholic missionaries who had been so welcoming and generous to himself and Aiken throughout their tour. He noted that in every part of the globe that they visited they found Irish people doing noble work.[39] He noted the pride Irish people felt for the work done by the missionaries in early Christian Ireland, but that there was now work being done of greater magnitude by present-day missionaries. He spoke of the hospitals, schools and colleges being built around the world by the sacrifices of Irish priests, brothers and nuns.[40]

At the beginning of the Árd Fheis the following evening de Valera again received a tumultuous welcome. He told the convention that he had plans for a world-wide effort against partition and had already prepared the ground for campaigns in the United States, Australia and New Zealand, and hoped that similar efforts could also be organised in Canada, South Africa and India. 'We have a splendid case,' he claimed, 'partition is on a rotten foundation and it will totter and end. All we want to do is make up our mind to make the proper assault.'[41]

CONCLUSION

De Valera's six and a half weeks' visit to Australia and New Zealand in 1948 provided the central focus for his world tour. It was also, politically speaking, the riskiest part of the tour. Both de Valera and Aiken were able to avail of their previous experience touring the US to ensure a successful tour there but Australia and New Zealand were uncharted waters, where de Valera had received much hostile press. However, expectations were exceeded, and the tour was a success. The careful use of all friendly contacts, most especially de Valera's friendship with Archbishop Mannix, helped ensure this success. In Australia they assisted in establishing committees of the Australian League for an Undivided Ireland in all the major cities – short-lived though they proved to be – but the tour was about more than partition. Political survival was probably the most important incentive for de Valera at the time and the tour must have delivered a major confidence boost to him. His various public addresses were extremely well attended, and he was afforded courtesies from virtually all important political dignitaries in the various countries they visited. De Valera also, not surprisingly, appeared to enjoy the tour immensely, his pride and interest in Irish influence and achievements around the world was genuine. He had a particularly strong sense of the Irish contribution to the building of modern Australia and he was at ease among the various gatherings of the Irish diaspora. Despite the austere political persona, he frequently impressed on these informal occasions as an earnest and even charming individual.

Given that de Valera was the leader of an opposition party from a small and impoverished country, the extent of his welcome abroad was remarkable. If we follow the conventional wisdom of de Valera as an insular and narrow-minded leader in a period when Ireland was at its most remote and unpopular position in international affairs, then the tour must be seen as a remarkable success. It actually served to confirm de Valera's status as a world figure and internationally recognised statesman. It also demonstrated how he came to embody the Ireland of his time in an extremely unique fashion. Many among the Irish communities who attended his addresses appeared to do so in the understanding that they were witnessing an embodiment of Ireland, albeit idealised by both themselves and de Valera. Among the Irish diaspora in Australia and New Zealand, de Valera provided a focus for nostalgic yearnings.

There is no doubt that the tour served to reinvigorate de Valera and dispelled the rumours of his impending retirement. His and Aiken's return added a charge to the opposition and the positive publicity from the tour contributed to a Fianna Fáil resurgence. In terms of partition, de Valera was seen to be doing something, although he was in fact achieving very little. Raising awareness of partition abroad and attempting to encourage international pressure on Britain from the Commonwealth countries, America and elsewhere to end partition was a good idea in principle, though never very realistic. To de Valera, however, it was essential that he remained 'a custodian of republican virtue',[42] and in terms of his continuing political appeal it was very important that he be seen to maintain the aspiration to Irish unity. That the Australian and New Zealand governments did not put themselves out on a limb for de Valera and a united Ireland could hardly have been a great surprise. But the fact that de Valera nevertheless privately and publicly referred to the tour as a great success illustrates the pragmatism, in the guise of idealism, that was so often a feature of his political actions.

NOTES

1. John Bowman, *De Valera and the Ulster Question 1917–1973* (Oxford: Clarendon Press, 1982), p.5.
2. The Earl of Longford and T.P. O'Neill, *Éamon de Valera* (London: Hutchinson, 1970), p.431

3. *Irish Times,* 21 and 22 April 1948.
4. University College, Dublin, Archives (UCDA), De Valera Papers, P150/2952.
5. *Irish Times,* 10 March 1948.
6. *Irish Press,* 11 March 1948.
7. Ibid, 25 March 1948.
8. Ibid.
9. *Irish Times,* 30 March 1948.
10. Ibid., 8 April 1948.
11. *Daily Telegraph,* 28 April 1948; UCDA, Frank Aiken Papers, P104/4778.
12. Dermot Keogh, 'Mannix, de Valera and Irish Nationalism', in J. O'Brien and P. Travers (eds), *The Irish Emigrant Experience in Australia* (Dublin: Poolbeg Press, 1991), pp.196–225.
13. *Argus,* 1 May 1948; UCDA, Frank Aiken Papers, P104/4778.
14. UCDA, Frank Aiken Papers, P104/4828.
15. *Australian Catholic Newsletter,* 21 June 1948; UCDA, Frank Aiken Papers, P150/2952.
16. *Perth Daily News,* 15 April 1948.
17. Ibid.
18. This included a warm welcome from the Irish-born Archbishop of Perth, Raymond Prenderville.
19. *Record,* Perth, 20 May 1948; UCDA, Frank Aiken Papers, P104/4778.
20. *Daily News,* 15 May 1948; UCDA, Frank Aiken Papers, P104/4778.
21. T.P. Coogan, *Éamon de Valera: Long Fellow, Long Shadow* (London: Hutchinson, 1993), p.639.
22. A member of the Liberal opposition in Tasmania, Athol Townley, had earlier strongly criticized de Valera's tour of Australia.
23. *Irish Press,* 22 June 1948.
24. *Dominia,* 26 April 1948; UCDA, Frank Aiken Papers, P104/4778.
25. *Dominia,* 27 April 1948; UCDA, Frank Aiken Papers, P104/4778.
26. *Dominia,* 26 May 1948; UCDA, Frank Aiken Papers, P104/4778.
27. UCDA, Frank Aiken Papers, P104/4830.
28. Ibid.
29. UCDA, Frank Aiken Papers, P104/4778.
30. UCDA, Frank Aiken Papers, P104/4830.
31. *Sydney Morning Herald,* 31 May 1948, UCDA, Frank Aiken Papers, P104/4778.
32. *Daily Telegraph,* 2 June 1948; UCDA, Frank Aiken Papers, P104/4778.
33. UCDA, Frank Aiken Papers, P104/4778.
34. *Courier,* 6 June 1948; UCDA, Frank Aiken Papers, P104/4778.
35. *Irish Times,* 12 June 1948.
36. Ibid., 22 June 1948.
37. Ibid.
38. Ibid., 23 June 1948.
39. Ibid., 22 June 1948.
40. Ibid.
41. Ibid., 23 June 1948.
42. J. J. Lee and G. Ó Tuathaigh (eds), *The Age of de Valera* (Dublin: Ward River Press, 1982), p.109.

16

The Australian Press and the IRA Border Campaign, 1956–62

Ruán O'Donnell

The Irish Republican Army (IRA) offensive which commenced on 12 December 1956 took the Irish and British authorities by surprise. While acts of sabotage along the border separating the six counties controlled by Westminster from the twenty-six governed by Dublin had flared since 1954, the scale of attacks in late 1956 was of a significantly higher order. Australian newspapers, however, immediately grasped the essential importance of events in Ireland and the centrality of partition to their causation. This attentiveness owed much to the fact that Australian editors had tracked related Irish stories from 1954 and possessed the necessary channels of information to offer reportage and commentary to their readers. Australian public interest had been established in the advent of the campaign and the services of professional press agencies were utilised on an ongoing basis in consequence. In this respect, the Australian media were in step with their international peers who also devoted space to the Irish question. As in North America, bonds forged by shared history, culture and recent migration rendered Irish affairs more relevant than would otherwise have been the case. Common ties to the United Kingdom accentuated this focus in Australia.[1]

Local factors also encouraged coverage of political conflict in Ireland, not least the existence of pro-republican pressure groups in Australia. Although the opinions and general activities of the Australian League for an Undivided Ireland (ALUI), the Irish National Association (INA) and Sinn Féin rarely commanded state-level reports, the occasional controversies incited by Irish-Australian organisations could not be entirely ignored. The role of the Irish-Australians in hosting Éamon de Valera's speaking tour in 1948 was acknowledged, as was the agency of Melbourne-based activists in protesting against a visit by Stormont premier Lord Brookeborough in late 1954 and early 1955. By chance, 1954 was also the year in which controversy arose over the terms of accreditation of the Australian ambassador to Ireland.[2] Ephemeral episodes of this nature leavened features on such familiar and innocuous themes as St Patrick's Day, tourism and sport. Naturally, the oversight of state and national media was supplemented by more detailed accounts published in the papers serving the Irish and Irish-Australian sector. The short-lived *Gaelic Link* (Melbourne) and the *Sydney Gael* catered for those interested in the Gaelic Athletic Association, the Irish National Association, ALUI and other bodies.[3] The *United Irishman*, monthly organ of the Republican movement, was imported and sold in Australia on a regular basis. Its content was deemed suitable for Australian consumption whereas American readers received modified editions.[4] More generally, the *Advocate* (Melbourne) and *Catholic Weekly* (Sydney) addressed perceived religious and secular concerns within Irish-Australia at a time of crisis occasioned by the (ALP)/ Democratic Labor Party (DLP) split.[5]

The context in which news of the 1956 Border Campaign was received had been shaped by a series of unusual precursor stories in 1954. On 14 June 1954 the *Sydney Morning Herald* carried a front-page report of a major IRA raid which had taken place two days earlier at Gough barracks, Armagh. The barracks, simply described as the 'arms depot' of the British army's Royal Irish Fusiliers, was also their regimental headquarters and recruits quarters.[6] Moreover, the operation was the first significant action undertaken by the resurgent IRA since the 1940s and this connected the incident to the long history of armed opposition to the British presence in Ireland. Drawing on information provided by the Australian Associated Press (AAP) service, the *Herald* presented an IRA claim to have secured several hundred firearms alongside a disingenuous British assertion that 'some arms' had been stolen. The IRA had actually acquired at least thirteen Bren light machine guns, thirty Sten submachine guns and 305 Lee Enfield rifles.[7] The *Canberra Times* was less concerned with providing the British viewpoint and acknowledged that the 'audacious raid by 22 uniformed [IRA] men' had been 'made with split second timing'.[8] Peter Kilroy, Irish correspondent of the *Advocate*, went much further in terms of detail and commentary. Drawing on information received in Ireland, Kilroy outlined the positive reaction to the raid by Limerick Corporation and other official bodies. His column was the only regular Irish feature in any Australian paper.[9]

The second harbinger of crisis in Ireland, a raid on Omagh barracks on 16 October 1954, was also front-page news in Sydney. In a piece sub-headed '11 hurt in Ulster gun battle', the *Sydney Morning Herald* of 18 October once again sourced its information from the unreliable Australian Associated Press agency. The item included a factually incorrect reference to the Armagh precedent 'last May [recte June]' and otherwise failed to explain an important armed escalation in a territory within the

Commonwealth.[10] A follow-up story on 19 October fleshed out details of searches, arrests and military casualties in Tyrone, yet singularly failed to highlight the salient political ramifications. No comment from either the disapproving Dublin authorities or supportive Sinn Féin party was deemed newsworthy.[11] This narrow approach seemed to substantiate Irish-Australian suspicions that the *Herald* then pursued an Anglo-centric agenda with scant regard for objectivity.

Unreported and possibly unrealised was the fact that the arms raids were manifestations of a republican revival in which Irish-Australians played a role. This stemmed from a 1948 decision of the IRA's ruling Army Council to prepare for an offensive against the British military in the north of Ireland. Logistic challenges ensured that Australia, unlike America and Canada, was rarely a source of republican weaponry but all other facets of support activity were in evidence. By 1955 Sinn Féin branches had been founded in Sydney and Melbourne and INA events in New South Wales were developing a notably militant character. Irish republicans in Australia forged a connection between reports of IRA activities in Ireland and solidarity events in the southern hemisphere. Sinn Féin's Sheares/Connolly Cumann in Sydney and Tone/Pearse Cumann in Melbourne numbered several former IRA members of organisational ability. There were also prominent Irish-Australians, of whom Gerard Fitzgerald, a close advisor of Labor stalwart Arthur Calwell, was pre-eminent. Fitzgerald was the Australian-born son of a Limerick Irish Republican Brotherhood officer and Cork Land League mother.[12] The new activists quickly supplanted more moderate veteran figures, particularly Dr Albert Dryer of Sydney, who had been interned in Darlinghurst prison for membership of the Irish Republican Brotherhood in 1918. Dryer's control of the INA ebbed away to the newcomers in 1955–6, just as the organisation's Gaelic Club headquarters was being established. Dryer sent confidential reports of this process to the Irish embassy in Canberra and corresponded directly with de Valera, who returned to power in March 1957.[13]

The first clear indication that such matters were in train in Australia were the protests which greeted Lord Brookeborough on his official visit to Melbourne in January 1955. This caught the normally vigilant Commonwealth Investigation Service off guard. Brookeborough had arrived in Fremantle on the liner *Himalaya* in mid-December 1954 and travelled to Victoria via South Australia.[14] By coincidence, reports of the arrival of the 'North Ireland Premier' in Fremantle clashed with another Irish story, the trial of eight men captured in the aftermath of the failed Omagh raid.[15] While Brookeborough claimed he had 'little interest in politics' on page ten of the *West Australian* of 16 December, a bizarre disavowal from a man who served as premier at Stormont for eleven years, page six carried a detailed account of the defiant conduct of the IRA men accused of 'treason felony' in his home jurisdiction. The republicans refused to recognise the Belfast court and initially faced capital charges under legislation introduced to transport John Mitchel, William Smith O'Brien and other Young Ireland leaders to Van Diemen's Land in the late 1840s. On 16 December 1954 Perth readers were informed that IRA defendant Jack McCabe had brazenly challenged the unionist judge. McCabe was quoted as stating: 'We owe allegiance only to God and the people of Ireland. I deny your right to charge me with treason to an alien Queen.' Brookeborough's sojourn in a country bound to the same monarch was subsequently marred by his attempts to avoid serious discussion of partition.[16]

Heckled arriving into Melbourne's Spencer Street station on 2 January 1955, Brookeborough was pursued by republicans who disrupted his press conference in the Menzies Hotel.[17] Two men, John Murray and Joe O'Gorman, posed as Irish journalists but were ejected by hastily augmented security personnel. Neither Murray nor O'Gorman was named in published accounts but both were prominent in the ALUI and Sinn Féin.[18] While Brookeborough attempted to make light of the negative publicity, his banal comments on trade within the empire were relegated to page four of the Melbourne *Age*. Evidence of his unpopularity graced page one.[19] The Victorian edition of the *Sun* noted the visitor's 'embarrassments' and quoted an ALUI member as saying: 'We have a cause to fight for, we are not hooligans.'[20] Out-of-state newspapers, including Brisbane's *Courier Mail*, immediately picked up on the story and, while the predictable soft interviews dictated by diplomacy continued, Brookeborough found it impossible to maintain the pretense of normality in Ireland.[21]

Douglas Wilkie of the *Sun News-Pictorial* attempted to minimize the seriousness of the episode in his syndicated 'As I see it' column. His line of argument, as carried by the *Advertiser* on 4 January, was predicated on a range of profound, albeit common, misconceptions regarding the role of Ireland during the Second World War. Wilkie's experiences as a war correspondent in Singapore and Burma in the 1940s and Korea in the 1950s had confirmed his rightist, pro-British outlook.[22] His credibility on 'Ulster' affairs, however, was undermined by his assertion that Donegal's Field Marshal Bernard Montgomery hailed from the Six Counties.[23] A leading Sinn Féin activist, Maurice Kelly, was sufficiently frustrated by his failure to have a letter opposing Wilkie's pro-unionist bias carried by the *Age* as to call to the paper's premises seeking redress. On stating his business, the Kerry man was reputedly thrown down stairs by two men summoned for the purpose. Kelly's misfortune was untypical and one of the most important results of the Melbourne incident was the flurry of correspondence in the letter pages of the *Age*.[24]

The protests created an ephemeral local news interest in partition and thereby enabled members of Melbourne's ALUI to highlight its origins and nature. A similar opportunity had been grasped by Irish advocates in April/May1948 when harsh statements arising from de Valera's first tour of Australia enabled informed commentators to publish cogent correctives. In early 1955, an Australian platform had been created by a better organised and more assertive Irish republican position.[25] Tipperary man Ken Toomey, General Secretary of the ALUI in Victoria, was unequivocal in describing the north of Ireland as 'a puppet state' that was 'occupied by British forces'.[26] A letter from John Murray, Armagh-born president of the ALUI and a key protagonist in the demonstrations, was also placed on record. Immediate dividends were thus garnered by the reinforcement of direct action in the streets with propaganda in the press. The final city event of Brookeborough's stay in Victoria, a reception at Town Hall on 5 January, was sparsely reported and in negative terms. The subheading 'Guard kept as Ulster head feted' communicated a new and unwelcome sense of unease.[27]

Moreover, reports in the *Advocate* of 13 January 1955 indicated that Stormont was facing further, more rigorous, challenges. The paper reprinted extracts of a major speech by Cardinal D'Alton, Archbishop of Armagh, in which he made an 'appeal to our young men not to have recourse to methods of violence in their eagerness to end the unnatural division of our country'. The clear import of this statement was that such a campaign was deemed to be in the offing. The appearance of similar stories in the Australian media strengthened the hand of the republican support base in the country. Several activists, not least Toomey, wrote from Australia to register their opposition to the Dublin government's handling of the partition controversy.[28]

The long-anticipated IRA campaign of sabotage and cross-border raids commenced on 12 December 1956 and immediately spurred their international networks into action. The earliest reports appeared on 13 December on the front pages of the *Sydney Morning Herald* and *West Australian*. The *Herald* supplemented AAP information with additional facts provided by Reuters to outline news of attacks in Derry city, Armagh, Magherafelt, Newry, Enniskillen, north Antrim and elsewhere. Under the headline 'I.R.A. Raiders Swoop On Northern Ireland', the paper explained that the republicans sought 'to unite Eire and Northern Ireland, by force if necessary'.[29] The *West Australian*, reliant on the same sources, carried this justification in virtually identical language and with a neutral tenor.[30] The Melbourne *Argus*, however, credited the IRA with an 'audacious series of bomb and fire-raising outrages' under the heading, 'Irish raiders slip police net'. Although relegated to page two, the *Argus* version, also based on data collated by AAP/Reuters, was arguably positive in highlighting the achievement of the IRA.[31] This was no subediting slip and a subsequent report on IRA operations described their activities in stirring terms as 'Commando-style raids'. Commentary of this nature reflected the viewpoint of the nationalist *Irish Press* in Dublin and the *Argus* was untypical in covering the campaign from an Irish perspective.[32]

The Melbourne line contrasted sharply with the tone of the story as related by the *Daily Telegraph* and *Sun*. Internal structures and editorial decisions pushed news of the offensive back to pages seven and fifteen respectively. Both papers were linked to British titles of the same name, to which the *Sun* alluded when citing the assistance of 'Special' sources. These associations clearly informed their sensationalist reportage. The *Daily Telegraph* of 13 December 1956 described the attacks in greatly exaggerated terms as an 'invasion' of 'N[or]th[ern] Ireland', as if the six contested counties in Ulster formed part of another country threatened by foreign 'Irish Nationalists'. The IRA were not named and the supposed agenda of the 'invaders' was totally ignored. News of the Royal Ulster Constabulary (RUC) ambush of an IRA party near Torr Head, Antrim, was relayed in perfunctory fashion, along with an unfounded claim that the raiders had 'abandoned a truck loaded with sub-machine guns and ammunition'.[33] Essentially, the Sydney paper's digest of events had been edited to meet the expectations of a reactionary English tabloid readership. The result was a cavalier approach to accuracy of content as well as political context, a story which few Australians could have comprehended if solely informed by such news outlets.

The *Sun*'s Anglocentrism was even more pronounced with its first accounts appearing under a London dateline. The heading, 'U.K. alert, Guard on Royalty' projected the explicitly and specifically English perspective of its authors. The phrase 'terrorist raids' was unusually pejorative *vis-à-vis* the IRA and one which was normally reserved for the far more extreme anti-British activities of the Mau Mau in Kenya and National Organisation of Cypriot Fighters (EOKA) in Cyprus. Australian editors, with rare exceptions, did not bracket the IRA of the 1950s with such contemporary groupings.[34] There were other signs that the *Sun*'s account was imported with little regard for its Australian readership, including the strange emphasis placed on listing Special Branch duties in London. Criticism of the Irish government's security policy, when juxtaposed with opinions emanating from Stormont and Westminster, constituted nakedly biased reportage. An allegation that the Dáil 'continued to afford sanctuary and succour to terrorists' was utterly false, yet was repeated in Australia without commentary from either the Irish government or Foreign Affairs personnel.[35] This interpretation did not accord with that of the Australian diplomatic community. In general, the news stream tapped by the two main Sydney tabloids was unsuitable in virtually every respect as a means of informing Australians of events in Ireland.[36]

Significantly, there is no evidence that the tabloids deliberately sought to encourage an anti-Irish constituency within Australia. If British-orientated reports resonated with vestigial empire loyalism in New South Wales, this usually occurred unconsciously and as a by-product of the paper's news-gathering apparatus. The *Daily Telegraph* of 14 December 1956 was content to carry extracts from an IRA manifesto issued two days previously, even if the preoccupation with a potential 'all-out extremist campaign' in Britain endured. Other than coining the idiosyncratic term 'Sinn Feinnians', a near comical conjunction of 'Sinn Féin' and 'Fenian', the item was not unduly hostile.[37] Curiously, the same day's *Sydney Morning Herald* highlighted an element of the London *Daily Telegraph*'s story on its front page which its city rival had ignored: the alleged role of republican splinter groups in spurring the mainforce IRA into action.[38] In this respect the *Daily Telegraph* of Sydney elected to devote less space to the Irish news than either its British counterpart or its local broadsheet competition. Its target readership, presumably, were more interested in basic outlines and dramatic themes than comprehensive articles.

As before, the *West Australian* followed the unfolding story with diligence and its front page account on 14 December was titled 'I.R.A. put out call for help'. The editor may not have fully realised the importance of carrying the quote issued in Dublin which 'called on all Irishmen to rally to the Republican cause'. This appealed directly to Australia's Sinn Féin supporters, who operated below the radar of the major dailies.[39] The announcement was underscored by a second night of IRA attacks which served to confirm that a major offensive was underway. Lisnaskea barracks, Fermanagh, was severely damaged by explosives and gunfire on the night of 13 December, when nearby Derrylin barracks was also hit. British and unionist frustration at their inability to curb such activities echoed in Australia arising from the AAP/Reuters news channels. Much of the reportage relayed intemperate Stormont and House of Commons statements which wrongly blamed John A. Costello's Fine Gael-led coalition government in Dublin for allowing the IRA freedom of movement. In actuality, the British military had failed to secure the contentious borderlands it sought to maintain in Ireland, whereas the Gardaí on the 'southern' side were prompt in arresting suspected guerrillas whenever they could be found.[40] Much greater balance would have been in evidence had Irish news channels been referenced in the manner favoured on occasion by the *Advocate* and *Argus*. The story, however, was beginning to slip from the headlines. The *Sydney Morning Herald* of 15

December carried its account on page three and the *Canberra Times* provided a diminished level of copy.[41] Against this trend, the populist *Sun* covered the 'Irish street battle' in Lisnaskea on page two, while the *Daily Telegraph* accessed the UP service to augment its sources of information. Wild claims of 1,000 shots being fired by the RUC against '100 terrorists armed with machine-guns and hand grenades' were evidently judged sufficiently exciting to warrant increased attention.[42]

The prolonged stream of violent incidents in Ireland led to modifications in Australian reportage. The *Sydney Morning Herald* obtained additional information from a London-based staff correspondent from 16 December, and the *West Australian* cited 'Reuters' Dublin correspondent' two days later.[43] Greater consideration of the Dáil's position flowed from such connections and at a time when the liberal *Manchester Guardian* and other British papers were endeavouring to more accurately contextualise the IRA campaign. Even the British *Sunday Express* belatedly acknowledged the work of the Irish Special Branch in curbing the militants in the Republic.[44] From an Australian vantage, the reintroduction of the Special Powers Act in the North of Ireland and the mass arrests which ensued were clearly newsworthy. Insurgency and the deployment of regular British soldiers in support of the RUC and B-Specials were extraordinary in an English-speaking sector of the Commonwealth in the 1950s.[45]

Although unarticulated, the commonality of interest between Irish unionists and Australian empire loyalists was a real, if minor and fading, element of the story. The aberrant policy pursued by Canberra in relation to the appointment of an ambassador to Dublin, more stringent than that emanating from Whitehall, was indicative of a residual anti-Irish mentality in certain quarters. Wilkie, furthermore, had seen fit to posit a justification of unionist/empire loyalist empathy in 1955 when faced with proof that politically aware Irish-Australians were far more sympathetic towards the nationalist population of the Six Counties. The border campaign, however, forced Australian opinion-makers to recognise that partition remained a problem and to acknowledge the legitimate position of their Dublin counterparts in Anglo-Irish affairs. Costello's ideological opposition to both partition and political violence was eventually communicated to the Australian public and in terms which shielded him from accusations of political confliction.[46]

The pre-Christmas lull in news reports of the campaign mirrored the reduced scope of IRA operations during the same period. This hiatus was abruptly ended on 31 December 1956, when a second major attack on Derrylin barracks killed RUC Constable John Scally. Accounts of the first fatality of the offensive were closely followed by the raid on the RUC barracks in Brookeborough village where two IRA men were killed on 1 January 1957. The funerals of Seán South and Feargal O'Hanlon unleashed a tide of public sympathy and votes of condolence from numerous county councils. While Scally's death was reported in Australia, much greater publicity surrounded South and O'Hanlon. The Brookeborough incident received front-page attention and was followed by updates on the search for survivors.[47]

The *West Australian* of 4 January 1957 described the IRA as being 'pledged to put an end to the partition of Ireland' and, four days later, as 'fighting for Irish union'.[48] This was precisely the message the Army Council wished to convey to the international community. Under the *nom de guerre* 'J. McGarrity', IRA Chief of Staff Seán Cronin claimed in December 1957:

> The story of Irish Resistance to British aggression began to reach the ears of the world. News correspondents came from the U.S.A., Canada, Australia, many European countries as well as Britain. Some of them search diligently for the facts. Others had preconceived notions about what was happening and had these prejudices strengthened in London, Belfast and Dublin . . . And so what the world was told was most often incorrect.[49]

The sanguine assessment, set down by Cronin in the *Resistance* pamphlet, was born of personal disappointment at the failure of militant republicans to stimulate irresistible dynamism. Being so close to events, Cronin clearly underestimated the mid and long term impact of the publicity generated by the campaign he directed into 1959.

As Cronin feared, much news coverage in Australia did not suit the agenda of the IRA and its sympathisers overseas. A firm denunciation of the campaign by Costello contradicted republican claims to act on behalf of the nation, even if their support base was much larger than politically prudent to acknowledge. Costello's radio speech, when disseminated in Australia, gained a level of prominence in the country's media which his general Dáil duties had rarely elicited.[50] His intervention lent weight to a renewed call by Cardinal D'Alton for the IRA to desist. The *Catholic Weekly* of 10 January 1957 broke a month's self-imposed silence on the IRA's gambit to lead with the Irish Primate's explicit condemnation of 'subversive groups'. The weekly had seemingly stalled, awaiting advice from Maynooth and Armagh before committing itself to an editorial position fashioned for the laity and clergy of Australia.[51] While the Sydney publication was fully aware that the IRA did not pursue sectarian, let alone Catholic, objectives, elements within the Church's hierarchy feared that republican insurgency would facilitate communist infiltration. The

Advocate stressed this angle in its edition of the same day and took its cue from statements made by a junior Dáil minister at an Irish rally in Birmingham, England. Comments attributed to Patrick Lindsay were readily employed to shore up a much broader perception of atheistic threat posed by communists in Hungary and elsewhere.[52]

News of the rebuff of the IRA by both Church and state in Ireland coincided with a spurious charge of Soviet intrigue made by right-wing British pundits. This bizarre theory reached Australia via the Sydney tabloids and enjoyed a short but vivid shelf life. On 7 January 1957 Dr Albert Dryer expressed his dismay at the *Daily Telegraph* to Michael Skentelbery of the Irish embassy in Canberra. Dryer claimed that the paper was

> pursuing its remorseless attack on us (in yesterday's issue) by brazenly linking the Reds with the gravely unwise conduct of those fellows in the Six-counties. These lads are, of course, jeopardising our position, but I know they would certainly not associate with the enemies of civilisation. How we do deplore the absence of a press that would dispense elementary justice to us.[53]

Dryer appreciated that fear of the Left had fuelled the bitter ALP/DLP split and, in the wake of the Petrov spying affair, Australians were acutely sensitised to the notion of communist subversion. In actuality, as Dryer was probably cognisant, the IRA constitution forbade membership of the Communist Party. Such details were unlikely to be published in Australia to either clarify or correct accusations in which persons had not been named. Scope for advocating the moderate republican position of Dryer's Irish National Association was further undermined in mid-January when the *Argus* went out of business in Melbourne.[54]

Tensions between Clann na Poblachta and Fine Gael over the prosecution of IRA activists brought down the government in February 1957. The collapse of the coalition and the subsequent election campaign were covered by the *Advocate* drawing, as before, on Kilroy's detailed features from Dublin.[55] Fianna Fáil returned to power under de Valera in March, a month in which Cardinal D'Alton proposed a settlement under which Ireland would be reunited in federal form and join the Commonwealth. The *Catholic Weekly* noted D'Alton's efforts, which received wider publicity in July when the *West Australian* and others reported the cold reaction of Stormont.[56] More attention, however, was accorded to the decision of de Valera's cabinet to re-introduce internment without trial in early July in order to clamp down on the IRA. Known militants were sent to the Curragh Camp, along with much of the leadership of Sinn Féin which had not been proscribed in the Republic.

Ruairí O'Brádaigh, one of four abstentionist Teachtaí Dála (TDs) elected for Sinn Féin in March, was named in a front page Australian report as being interned.[57] Informed of such incidents, Ken Toomey wrote to de Valera from Melbourne in November 1957, accusing him of 'doing the work of England by interning and jailing Irish patriots in their fight against the British Army of Occupation on Irish soil'.[58]

Internment in both Irish jurisdictions dented the IRA's capacity to fight but paramilitary incidents continued. Very few, however, were sufficiently significant in scale or novel in character as to attract Australian press coverage. The over-arching focus on sabotage operations, moreover, tended to deny the organisation publicity of the level generated by anti-personnel attacks. While the republican *United Irishman* circulated as before, the Australian media as a whole turned their attention to other matters. This undoubtedly suited the Irish government which largely resolved residual tensions with Canberra arising from the ambassador accreditation controversy of 1954–5. Diminished reportage also complimented the long-term British strategy of isolating the IRA from the international support it needed to function. Prime Minister Menzies was loath to voice official commentary on the north of Ireland and in March 1961 sidestepped the divisive apartheid question by describing it as a 'domestic matter' for South Africa.[59] Mindful of Commonwealth unease with Australia's immigration policy, Menzies would not condemn the abuse of civil rights by Stormont. Although internment was abolished in the Republic by March 1959, the momentum of overseas reportage on the IRA which had been building since 1954 had ground to a virtual halt. The final phase of the campaign was distinctly under-reported in Australia, a circumstance which could not be rectified by the then defunct *Argus*, *Sydney Gael* and *Gaelic Link*.

Over-reliance on the British-orientated AAP/Reuters agency ensured that the mainstream Australian press missed stories of potential interest to its readers. In June 1957 Australian Sinn Féin cumainn (branches) sent wreaths to the annual Wolfe Tone commemoration at Bodenstown, Kildare. The event was presided over by Tomás MacCurtain of the Army Council and was addressed by the former IRA commander in north Antrim, Sean Dougan. Bodenstown was the most important event in the republican calendar and the direct input of Irish-Australian groups during an armed campaign warranted coverage that was not forthcoming.[60] Moreover, statements made in Dublin by Daniel Minogue, Federal MP for West Sydney, passed without commentary in Australia. On 28 September 1958 Minogue, a native of Clare and INA member, informed an Irish-Australian Society dinner in the Gresham Hotel that 'Ireland was entitled to demand complete freedom and the abolition of the infamous Border'.

Few would have disagreed but the context and timing of the remarks, as reported by the *Irish Independent*, were significant. Many would have inferred from Minogue's speech, delivered at the height of the campaign and without qualification, that at least one Australian MP openly supported the IRA.[61]

The downgrading of reportage of the border campaign in Australia opened the door to other journalistic anomalies. One arose in March 1961 when five people were arrested in Melbourne as 'alleged supporters of the outlawed Irish Republican Army'.[62] Fodla McKeown, Joe O'Gorman, Michael O'Shea, Christopher O'Kelly and Jack Hartnett were members of the Irish Republican Aid Committee, a front-group of Melbourne Sinn Féin, which collected money for IRA prisoners and dependents. Melbourne's City Court heard on 20 March that the defendants had solicited funds for 'the prisoners in the Belfast Gaol' in an illegal manner. They had also sold copies of the *United Irishman* to St Patrick's Day parade-goers, an event where Sinn Féin had previously encountered difficulties with elements of the crowd.[63] One account specified that the collection tins were decorated with green stickers bearing the words 'Irish Republican Army' and the five declined to reveal how the money was transmitted to Dublin.[64] It was left to the readers, however, to deduce that the case linked local activists to the still ongoing IRA campaign. Writing as 'G Mac Gearailt', the able Gerard Fitzgerald of Sinn Féin succeeded in getting the Melbourne *Herald* to publish an explanatory letter critical of both the Dáil and Stormont.[65]

The Melbourne edition of the *Sun* described the acquittal of the defendants in upbeat terms as a 'Great day for the Irish five'. Indeed, there was no hint of censure in any of the numerous Australian reports.[66] The press was clearly unaware that one of the five had obtained legal advice from a top left-wing lawyer and that many in the Irish community in Victoria believed that the ailing Archbishop Mannix had intervened to have the case thrown out. If known to journalists, it was not revealed that O'Gorman was one of the two men who had attempted to gate-crash Brookeborough's news conference in January 1955.[67] The Melbourne case proved to be the last major story of the campaign. While the *Daily News* had reported the trial for its Perth readership, it ignored the historic February 1962 cessation of the IRA offensive.[68] The *West Australian* had followed events in Ireland with greater stamina than most, yet quoted the 'dump arms' order on page ten of its edition of 28 February 1962. The *Canberra Times* advanced the announcement to page three but limited its coverage to just seven lines in the 'News in Brief' section. Clearly, the Australian media had tired of the campaign and were either unwilling to or incapable of documenting its local reverberations.[69]

Nevertheless, it is likely that the return of chronic unrest in Ireland in 1968–9 was somewhat more explicable to Australian readers due to the coverage devoted to the previous armed effort in 1956–62. Certainly, the Official and Provisional IRA were both actively supported in Australia by late 1970. Politically minded Irish-Australians mobilised with unprecedented ease from 1972, when incidents of international importance unfolded in Ireland.[70]

NOTES

1. For general background to the campaign see Ruán O'Donnell, 'Sean South and the Border Campaign' in *Village*, 21 December 1996, and J. Bowyer Bell, *The Secret Army: The IRA*, revised 3rd edn (Dublin: Poolbeg, 1997).
2. See *Commonwealth of Australia, Parliamentary Debates, Session 1956, House of Representatives* (Canberra, 1956), Volume H, 27 September 1956, p.905, and *Age*, 15 January 1954.
3. *Gaelic Link* did not survive the migration of editor Dick Furniss from Melbourne to Sydney in 1954. The *Sydney Gael*, however, grew from the news sheet format of its August 1953 inception to a monthly tabloid in January 1954. It was edited by Patrick J. O'Malley. See *Sydney Gael*, the official organ of the INA and GAA, January 1954. For information on this milieu see Val Noone, 'Irish migrants in 1950s Melbourne', Unpublished paper for the Melbourne Irish Studies Seminar, Newman College, Melbourne University, 16 April 2002. For a short and strangely negative account of the ALUI see Patrick O'Farrell, 'Irish Australia at an end; the Australian League for an Undivided Ireland, 1948–54' in *Tasmanian Historical Research Association*, Vol. 21, No. 4, December 1972. I am indebted to Val and Mary Noone for facilitating my research trip to Melbourne in 2005.
4. Irish-Australian developments were noted in Dublin. See *United Irishman*, May 1955.
5. *Advocate* columnist Peter E. Kilroy wrote at length on Brookeborough's furious reaction to allegations of 'intolerance' on the part of Stormont. The attack was made on a BBC programme by Bishop Heenan of Leeds. *Advocate*, 19 April 1954.
6. *Sydney Morning Herald*, 14 June 1954.
7. See 'Armed raid on Gough army barracks, Armagh, 12th June, 1954', part one. Unpublished paper, RUC Historical Society.
8. *Canberra Times*, 14 June 1954.
9. See 'Raid on British Army Barracks in Six Counties', *Advocate*, 1 July 1954. Kilroy's information had been posted from Dublin on 15 June. Ibid.
10. *Sydney Morning Herald*, 18 October 1954.
11. Ibid., 19 October 1954.
12. National Library of Australia (NLA), Dryer Papers, Box Eleven, Frank McGregor to Albert Dryer, 18 October 1955; and National Archives of Ireland (NAI), D/T (Department of the Taoiseach), S16209A, Gerard Fitzgerald to Costello, 23 January 1957.
13. De Valera was directly informed of Dryer's difficulties in February 1956 in a letter critical of 'a number of the younger generation of Irishmen and their associates ... who describe themselves as "Sinn Feiners [sic]"'. Dryer explained: 'In Sydney and Melbourne they have organised themselves under this name and have become intolerable nuisances. In attempting to elect an executive of the League some time ago, we discovered that the meeting was almost overwhelmed by these people and a sufficient number was elected to render the rational and efficient working of the League entirely impossible.' NLA, Dryer Papers, Box Ten, Dryer to Eamon de Valera, 5 February 1956.
14. See *Daily News* [Sydney], 15 December 1954.

15. *West Australian*, 16 December 1954. The same issue carried news of the arrest of an IRA recruits class in Armagh and the recovery of firearms presumed to have been stolen by republicans in Liverpool. Ibid. See also *Canberra Times*, 16 December 1954.
16. *West Australian*, 16 December 1954. Subsequent reportage of the trial presented highly specific information sourced in Belfast, *West Australian*, 17 December 1954.
17. bid., 3 January 1955.
18. Information of John Murray, Melbourne, 28 July 2005.
19. *Advertiser*, 3 January 1955.
20. *Sun* [Melbourne edition], 3 January 1955, p.3. The *Sun* emphasised the second 'embarrassment', the fact that Brookeborough wore a nylon shirt when promoting linen imports to Australia, ibid.
21. *Courier Mail*, 3 January 1955.
22. Information of Peter Gifford, Limerick, 5 September 2006. See also *Age*, 18 April 2002 and *Time*, 16 February 1942.
23. *Advertiser*, 4 January 1955. See also *Sun* [Melbourne edition], 4 January 1955, p.4.
24. Information of Maurice Kelly, Melbourne, 26 July 2005.
25. *Age*, 11 and 13 January 1955.
26. K. Toomey to the editor, 12 January 1955 in *Age*, 13 January 1955.
27. *West Australian*, 6 January 1955. Curiously, Brookeborough's public comments on the constitutional position of the Six Counties were notably more trenchant after his arrival in New Zealand on 25 January 1955. Statements on 'Border raids' when in Wellington on 15 February revealed a hard line attitude he had concealed from the Australian press. Brookeborough may have been assured that the patent inaccuracy of his comments on the nature of the Irish crisis would go untested in a more Anglophile country where his public appearances had passed off without protest, *New Zealand Herald*, 16 and 26 February 1955.
28. *Advocate*, 13 January 1955. The *Sydney Gael* positively noted the increased coverage of the IRA and Sinn Féin. See *Sydney Gael*, September 1955.
29. *Sydney Morning Herald*, 13 December 1956.
30. See 'I.R.A. strikes in Ulster again' in *West Australian*, 13 December 1956.
31. *Argus*, 13 December 1956.
32. Ibid., 15 December 1956.
33. *Daily Telegraph*, 13 December 1956.
34. The *Daily Telegraph* of 1 January 1957 detailed how 'Irish Republican Army men' had killed an RUC member in Fermanagh. The same page carried an account of the shooting of an RAF man by 'Cypriot terrorists'.
35. *Sun*, 13 December 1956. Something of the ethos of the paper can be inferred from another article in the same issue entitled 'Swing back to nigger minstrels'. Ibid., p.43. A more detailed account of the verbal attack on the Irish government appeared in the *Canberra Times* of 14 December 1956. This identified the source of the remarks in Westminster as the unionist MP Lawrence Orr, a highly pertinent attribution. Ibid.
36. Ireland, however, opposed Australia on a number of issues at the United Nations in 1956–7. The Irish contingent in New York supported calls for a special investigation of Soviet intervention in Hungary, when Australia abstained, and, unlike Canberra, opposed the British, French and Israeli bloc on their disastrous invasion of Egypt. However, in 1957, Ireland backed Australia in pressing for self-determination in West Irian despite alienating Portugal and Indonesia. Joseph Skelly, *Irish Diplomacy at the United Nations, 1945–1965* (Dublin: Irish Academic Press, 1997), pp.54–8, 139–42.
37. *Daily Telegraph*, 14 December 1956.
38. *Sydney Morning Herald*, 14 December 1956.
39. *West Australian*, 14 December 1956.
40. For a more fair-minded assessment see *Argus*, 17 December 1956.
41. *Sydney Morning Herald* and *Canberra Times*, 15 December 1956.
42. *Sun*, 15 December 1956. See also *Daily Telegraph*, 15 December 1956.
43. *West Australian*, 18 December 1956. See also *Sydney Morning Herald*, 17 December 1956.

44. See *Argus*, 17 December 1956.

45. See *West Australian*, 17 December 1956.

46. Australian magazines rarely tackled the subject. 'Uncabled additions' in *Bulletin* of 29 October 1958, a piece discussing the IRA and EOKA, was lifted from the London *Spectator*.

47. Scally's death was carried on page six of the *Daily Telegraph* of 1 January 1957. South and O'Hanlon were reported on the front pages of the *Sydney Morning Herald* and *West Australian* of 3 January 1957.

48. *West Australian*, 4 and 7 January 1957.

49. J. McGarrity [Sean Cronin], *Resistance, The story of the struggle in British-occupied Ireland* (Dublin: Irish Freedom Press, 1957) new edn, Dublin, 2006, pp.13–14.

50. *Sydney Morning Herald*, 8 January 1957. The article, 'Eire P.M. says raids must end' was accompanied by a photograph of the Taoiseach. A much fuller and frank commentary by Costello, based on a *Sunday Independent* article and a Government Information Bureau release, appeared in the *Advocate* on 17 January 1957. However, this feature by Peter Kilroy had been posted on 26 December 1956 and was consequently superseded in important respects by agency reports of the radio broadcast. Kilroy's follow-up piece was not in print in Australia until the issue of 24 January 1957.

51. *Catholic Weekly*, 10 January 1957.

52. *Advocate*, 10 January 1957. An expatriate in Queensland took offence at Lindsay's comments and wrote to the Taoiseach: 'We regret that the present Government of Ireland's twenty-six counties appears to be a puppet of England; to prove same I am submitting a cutting taken from a Brisbane [*Courier Mail*] paper'. NAI, D/T, S16209A , J. Page to Costello, 15 January 1957.

53. NLA, Dryer Papers, Box Twelve, Dryer to Skentelbery, 7 January 1957. See also *Daily Telegraph*, 6 January 1957. The story seems to have originated with Noel Barber of the [London] *Daily Mail* who had been briefed by Stormont sources. Elsewhere in the Commonwealth, a Montreal paper cited Barber's claims that 'Russian agents in Dublin are in direct contact with the left wing member of the IRA ... the agents are supplying the IRA with large sums of money'. *Gazette*, 4 January 1957.

54. See 'Director explains closing of Argus' in *Daily Telegraph*, 19 January 1957. This compounded the loss of coverage occasioned by the closure of the *Sydney Gael*, a paper 'carried' until June 1956 by the *Advocate*. See *Sydney Gael*, June 1956.

55. See *Advocate*, 21 February 1957.

56. *Catholic Weekly*, 28 March 1957 and *West Australian*, 16 July 1957.

57. *West Australian*, 15 July 1957. See also *Irish Independent*, 15 and 16 July 1957. Internment was prompted by the shooting of RUC man Cecil Gregg near Forkhill, Armagh, *Irish Independent*, 5 July 1957.

58. NAI, D/T, S 16209 B, Toomey to de Valera, 3 November 1957.

59. *West Australian*, 20 March 1961.

60. *Irish Independent*, 24 June 1957.

61. *Irish Independent*, 29 September 1958. The Dublin event was attended by Patricia Williams, Acting Australian Charge d'Affairs and C.V. Kellway, president of the Irish-Australian Society. Ibid. See also *Sydney Gael*, June 1954, p.4.

62. *Sydney Morning Herald*, 20 March 1961.

63. Melbourne *Herald*, 21 March 1961. The *Age* was one of the few papers to ignore the arrests but it followed up with an account of the resultant trial. See *Age*, 20 and 22 March 1961.

64. *West Australian*, 20 March 1961.

65. Melbourne *Herald*, 29 March 1961.

66. *Sun* [Melbourne edition], 22 March 1961.

67. Other Melbourne events, such as the annual republican Easter commemoration at the Carlton grave of Sean McSwiney, were not covered by the mainstream press. The *Advocate* was an exception. See *Advocate*, 30 March 1961. See Ruán O'Donnell, 'Republican support groups in Melbourne in the 1950s and 1960s', unpublished paper delivered to the Melbourne Irish Studies Seminar, University of Melbourne, 26 July 2005.

68. West Australian readers would have been kept informed by the *West Australian* of 28 February 1962.
69. *Canberra Times*, 28 February 1962.
70. See *Civil Rights News Bulletin*, [Melbourne] May 1972 and Mary Lynch, 'Three groups in Melbourne 1969–1975, Responding to the Troubles', in *Tain*, June–July 2002, pp.23–5.

17

Who Fears to Speak of '14–'18? Remembrance in Ireland and Australia[1]

Jeff Kildea

INTRODUCTION

The First World War had a profound effect on Ireland and Australia. Both countries suffered huge losses, killed and wounded, so much so that few families or communities were unaffected. Consequently, it is a period that is etched into the social psyche of each country.[2]

In Australia this is evidenced physically by the profusion of war memorials across the landscape and conceptually by the vitality of the Anzac tradition, which more than ninety years after the landing at Gallipoli 'retains significant emotional power and political utility'.[3] But in Ireland attitudes to the soldiers of the First World War have been deeply divided, more or less along the border that divides North from South. In the North, remembrance is observed with diligence and emotion, much as it is in Australia, though with a sectarian edge, while in the South it has been noteworthy for its near-complete absence, both physically and conceptually.

This chapter explores how the First World War has been commemorated over the years in Ireland and Australia. In particular, it will examine the interrelationship between remembrance and the expression of national identity in each country. Although for the most part remembrance in Australia has been a unifying national influence, it has at times and for a variety of reasons been contentious. Relevantly, in the context of this chapter, there were divisions along sectarian lines lasting into the 1960s. In Ireland, on the other hand, remembrance became a battleground upon which unionists and nationalists, each in their own way, continued the national struggle, particularly in Northern Ireland, long after the guns fell silent.

REMEMBRANCE IN AUSTRALIA

While most of Australia's First World War allies set aside 11 November to commemorate those who fought and died in that war,[4] Australians have chosen to commemorate not the day the killing stopped, but the day on which for them it began – the day widely regarded as the anniversary of their national baptism of fire, the day of the landing at Gallipoli, 25 April 1915. Throughout the country, in cities, towns and suburbs, tens of thousands of Australians turn out to attend commemoration services and to march, or watch others march, in honour of those who fell in all the wars in which Australia has participated. Many Australians take the commemoration one step further and travel more than ten thousand kilometres to Turkey to be on the spot at Gallipoli where the Anzacs landed as dawn breaks on Anzac Day.

But Anzac Day has not always enjoyed the popularity it does today. In the 1950s, Anzac Cove was almost deserted on 25 April, while on the fiftieth anniversary in 1965 the question being asked in the media was whether it would continue to be observed for much longer.[5] In the late 1960s, the anti-Vietnam War movement challenged the assumptions underlying the Anzac tradition, as did the feminist movement in the 1980s: members of the Women Against Rape campaign attempted to join in Anzac Day marches to protest against male violence and rape in war and to criticise the 'male glorification of war' they regarded as inherent in the Anzac legend.[6]

When Anzac Day was first celebrated in 1916, a march of Australian soldiers took place in London, while spontaneous unofficial activities occurred in Egypt, where there were concentrations of Australian soldiers. In Australia, a variety of small-scale events was organised by state governments and community groups. These ceremonies were the product of popular enthusiasm, with a local rather than a national focus, a pattern that continued for some years. Yet from the outset there were high hopes that Anzac Day would become a symbol of national unity.

Before the war Australian society had been divided along religious and ethnic lines with many Irish-Catholics, who made up about a quarter of the population, believing themselves to be a persecuted minority, particularly over the issue of state aid for Catholic schools. When the idea of Anzac Day was first promoted, Catholics enthusiastically endorsed it, seeing it as a portent of a new Australia in which they might find acceptance. A Catholic newspaper the *Freeman's Journal*, in an editorial subtitled 'The birth of a nation', opined effusively:

We were Australian in name, and we had a flag, but we had been taught by our politicians not to trust ourselves – we were constantly admonished by our daily journals to remember that we were nothing better than a joint in the tail of a great Empire...The Empire Day orators had a better hearing than the faithful souls who clung to Australia Day and gave special honour to their own starry banner.

Anzac Day has changed all that. The Australian flag has been brought from the garret and has been hoisted on a lofty tower in the full sight of its own people. No matter how the war may end – and it can only end one way – we are at last a nation, with one heart, one soul, and one thrilling aspiration...Anzac Day and Australia Day, honoured by hundreds of thousands of deeply-stirred people – what a great change this is![7]

But as the editor was penning those words, news of the Easter Rising was beginning to reach Australia. Irish-Australian Catholics initially deplored the rising as misguided and a threat to the promised implementation of Irish home rule. However, following the execution of the leaders and the imposition of martial law, they became quite critical of British rule in Ireland, in turn provoking a Protestant backlash that saw sectarianism in Australia, dormant since the outbreak of war, flare up and intensify, particularly during the conscription debates of 1916 and 1917. By 1920, interdenominational relations in Australia were at flashpoint, even infecting relations between soldiers who a few years before had been serving shoulder to shoulder in the trenches. In November that year, Catholic returned soldiers formed a separate ex-servicemen's organisation because of perceived anti-Catholic bigotry of the Returned Sailors' and Soldiers' Imperial League of Australia (RSSILA).[8]

For years after the war, Catholic ex-servicemen refused to participate in some Anzac Day ceremonies.[9] This was not because they disapproved of remembrance as such, but rather because as Catholics they were forbidden by Church teaching of the time from attending interdenominational religious services of any kind, and the main Anzac Day ceremonies included such a service. In the case of Sydney, for instance, this meant that Catholic ex-servicemen would start out marching with their units but would then proceed to St Mary's Cathedral to attend mass while their Protestant comrades continued to Hyde Park or the Domain for the official ceremony there.[10] The withdrawal of Catholic ex-servicemen from such ceremonies reinforced Protestant impressions of Catholic exclusiveness and raised suspicions as to the reasons for their reservation, while Catholics felt excluded because the organisers insisted on including a combined religious service as part of the commemoration.

Finding an acceptable solution to the problem was not easy. In 1938 Catholic ex-servicemen in Melbourne persuaded the RSSILA to substitute a civic service for the combined religious service. Archbishop Mannix applauded the initiative, but Protestant clergy boycotted the new service, protesting that it was no longer a Christian ceremony. In Sydney, it was not until 1962 that the issue was resolved by a compromise which, though simple, illustrated the absurdity of the stand-off. The ceremony was to include a religious service, but the prayers would be said by leaders of the armed services and the RSSILA, while a religious leader would give the Anzac address, which would be patriotic and not religious.[xi]

But in the decade after the war, provincialism rather than sectarianism posed the greatest threat to Anzac Day becoming a symbol of national unity. Not until 1921 did Prime Minister William Hughes express interest in a national celebration, a suggestion the RSSILA took up and promoted among the states. It was another two years before the states agreed at the 1923 Premiers' Conference that Anzac Day should be Australia's national day of remembrance and that it should be celebrated on 25 April. They also decided that each state should take its own steps to implement the day's observance. In 1919, Western Australia had been the first state to declare Anzac Day a public holiday. In 1923, the Commonwealth government made it a holiday, but only for federal public servants. Not until the end of the decade did all the states pass the necessary legislation to make it a public holiday across the country.

The emerging national focus of Anzac Day was boosted by the inauguration of the Australian War Memorial at Canberra on Anzac Day 1929. However, the project progressed slowly, with the building not being completed and open to the public until 1941. The inauguration ceremony itself sent a mixed message. Prime Minister Stanley Bruce said that the memorial was 'destined to stand as a symbol of Australia's nationhood'. However, Governor-General Lord Stonehaven 'spoke of the spirit of sacrifice displayed by "more than 60,000 Australian soldiers [who] had died to save the institutions and the birthright of all those who inhabited British soil"'.[12] In some people's minds, the link between the nation and the empire was still strong. The Catholic Church was not represented at the ceremony, a fact that historian Joan Beaumont attributes to the legacy of the divisive conscription debates.[13] However, the absence was more likely to have been due to the order of the ceremony, which included prayers and bible readings by Protestant ministers of religion.[14]

In the meantime, local communities had demonstrated their desire to remember those who had fought and died in the Great War by erecting war memorials. The popularity of the movement to erect memorials is evidenced by the presence in almost every city, town and suburb across the country of a memorial as a 'community's statement of bereavement, pride and thanksgiving'.[15] Although there were divisions in Australian society, those divisions related not so much to remembrance itself, but rather to the manner in which people of different ethno-religious backgrounds might participate in the forms of remembrance. Ken Inglis has written: 'The making of the Great War memorials in Australia was a quest for the right way, materially and spiritually, to honour the soldiers.'[16]

Inglis, whose detailed study of Australian war memorials is itself a monumental work, cites many instances where divisiveness impacted on the movement. For instance, in Boorowa, in western New South Wales, where there was a large Irish Catholic population, it was not until 1933 that a memorial was erected because Protestants and Catholics could not find common cause about its meaning. Eventually, the RSSILA stepped in and built a memorial clock tower.[17] In Moruya, on the New South Wales south coast, in a district with a high proportion of Irish Catholics, no standalone public memorial was ever erected, though in 1992 a small memorial was built as part of the memorial hall of the Returned and Services League (the name by which the RSSILA is known today). The town had voted two to one against conscription, and the 1917 referendum campaign had witnessed local violence. Private memorials were erected in the state school and in the Protestant churches, but not in the Catholic churches. Inglis has written: 'Moruya's missing memorial is itself a kind of monument, to wartime division so painful that people unwilling to risk a recurrence tacitly agree not to put the matter on their civic agenda.'[18]

Some towns ended up with two memorials. One example is Wagga Wagga, in south-western New South Wales. Two committees were established, one Protestant and the other Catholic. One committee erected a pillar, the other an arch. The pillar was erected in 1922 and the arch five years later. But by the time of the later ceremony, the rupture had been healed and the chairman of the pillar committee spoke as mayor at the unveiling of the arch.[19]

There were, however, some individuals who disapproved of the remembrance movement itself, and either stayed away from commemorations or remained silent if they were obliged to attend as part of their official duties. An example of the latter is Joseph Lyons, son of Irish-born Catholic parents, who had led the Tasmanian anti-conscription campaign in 1916 and who as Premier of his state sat on platforms at the unveiling of monuments but did not speak.[20] Lyons later became Prime Minister in a non-Labor government during the 1930s. Jack Bailey, a Labor member of parliament and a wartime anticonscriptionist, absented himself from remembrance ceremonies.[21] But opposition of this kind was not united and motives were mixed: some were pacifists, some socialists, some Irish nationalists, while some simply believed the money would be better spent on those who had returned and were now in need.

Such examples are the exceptions that made the rule that Australians tended to look positively on the sacrifice of the soldiers of the Great War. Partly this was because both empire loyalists and Australian nationalists could interpret the war to suit their own preconceptions: it was either a wonderful victory for the British empire or it was an experience out of which the Australian nation emerged. Either way, it was something to be remembered.

REMEMBRANCE IN IRELAND

While the Irish share with Australians a self-irony that often elevates defeat into victory, nationalist Ireland, unlike Australia, does not commemorate Gallipoli even though its soldiers were slaughtered in their thousands in much the same needless fashion as the Anzacs. In *The Irish at the Front*, an exaltation of the Irish contribution to the war effort published in 1916, Michael MacDonagh made the following prediction (wrongly as it turned out): 'Because of those [Irish] dead Gallipoli will ever be to the Irish race a place of glorious pride and sorrow.'[22]

In fact, prior to the mid-1980s, when Irish historians rediscovered the Great War, the popular understanding in the South was that Ireland had played only a minor part in the war. Most people in the twenty-six counties were infinitely more acquainted with the rising in Easter week in which sixty-four rebels and 254 Irish civilians were killed than with the four years of the Great War that claimed the lives of over 35,000 Irishmen. The harsh treatment of the leaders of the rising 'created an atmosphere in which the achievements of Irish soldiers in the Great War was [*sic*] never glorified'.[23] Furthermore, in seeking to establish its own sense of nationhood during the postwar years, a nationhood which, unlike Australia's, claims an ancient heritage predating English occupation, 'the Irish Free State had little use for the memory of Irishmen who served in the British army'.[24]

Far from being honored as returning heroes of the "war for civilization", they were a distinct embarrassment to the governments of the independent Irish state, whose credentials rested on resistance to recruitment and, indeed, outright rebellion against British rule.[25]

It is this point that so clearly distinguishes the Irish and Australian experience.

After federation had united the six Australian colonies the people of this self-governing dominion began searching for a sense of nationhood to go with their new country, and they believed they had found it in the blood sacrifice of Gallipoli and the western front. Although they had fought in the empire's cause, they did so for Australia as members of the Australian Imperial Force (AIF), a force which through the digger legend had developed a sense of identity that was unique and superior. Although Irish soldiers also developed a sense of their superiority as warriors, not unlike that of the Australians, the three Irish divisions did not possess or maintain a distinctive national identity in the same way as did the five Australian divisions. From the start, the 36th (Ulster) Division saw itself as exclusively Protestant and unionist, while the 16th (Irish) Division was 'nationalist and catholic Ireland's most distinctive contribution to the British war effort'.[26] Moreover, both the 16th and the 10th (Irish) Divisions included British units and individuals. As the war progressed, the Irishness of these divisions declined even further as English and Indian reinforcements replaced Irish casualties. After its near-destruction at Gallipoli, the 10th (Irish) Division spent the rest of the war in the backwater of the eastern theatre, eventually becoming an Indian formation in May 1918, while the 16th (Irish) Division suffered the ignominy of annihilation during the German offensive of March 1918.[27] By contrast, the Australian divisions ended the war on a high note with a series of brilliant victories, the most outstanding being the Battle of Hamel on 4 July 1918, which diverted attention from the symptoms of decline, such as mutinies, that were beginning to manifest themselves due to the lack of adequate reinforcements.

Nevertheless, in Ireland, collective amnesia of the war, which F.X. Martin called 'the Great Oblivion', did not set in immediately.[28] Some public memorials were erected and, although not as ubiquitous as in the North or in Australia, they can be seen in towns such as Bray, Cahir, Drogheda, Longford, Sligo, Tullamore, Whitegate and Cork city, as well as Dublin. But often they were dedicated in a manner that emphasised imperial over national sentiment, thus alienating Irish nationalists, who objected to having the Union Jack waved in their faces.[29]

Between the wars, Armistice Day was commemorated in the South, with masses being offered up for the war dead and poppies being sold openly in Dublin, the money usually going to ex-servicemen's charities. Throughout the 1920s, Armistice Day services in Dublin drew large crowds, including an estimated 70,000 in 1924, though a sour note was struck in 1919, when students from Trinity College, singing 'God Save the King', clashed with students from University College, singing the 'Soldier's Song', a nationalist song soon to become the Irish national anthem. Ordinary citizens often found themselves harassed from both sides by aggressive poppy-sellers or poppy-snatchers.

Construction of the National War Memorial at Islandbridge near the Phoenix Park, designed by Sir Edwin Lutyens, an Englishman who had designed the cenotaph in London, began in 1931. Even so, the project was not without controversy. The site was deliberately located on the outskirts of the city rather than in a prominent position nearer the city centre. A bill introduced in the Senate in 1927, proposing to erect it at Merrion Square, had been withdrawn in the face of nationalist opposition. The memorial was completed by ex-servicemen in 1938, but the opening ceremony was postponed indefinitely and did not occur until more than half a century later.

In its efforts to create a national identity, the new Irish state enshrined the Easter Rising as the country's defining historical moment. Public acknowledgement of Ireland's participation in 'England's war' was discouraged, with the result that Armistice Day services in Dublin came to be regarded as an outmoded celebration of Ireland's imperial past. From 1933, no government representative attended the ceremonies. Ireland's part in the Great War was no longer seen as its contribution to the defence of small nations as John Redmond had envisaged; rather it was 'a great mistake, a profound betrayal'.[30] Even in 1992, Terence Denman wrote:

> The fate of tens of thousands of patriotic Irishmen who, in response to the granting of home rule, chose to follow a different path to Irish nationhood by volunteering to serve with the British armed forces rarely attracts more than a passing reference, and that often pejorative.[31]

What might have served as a bridge between Ireland and the empire, even while the fetters on Irish independence were being loosened, was gradually obliterated from public memory. As if to symbolise the dominant mood, the National War Memorial after the Second World War was allowed to fall into a state of dilapidation. In 1986, Jane Leonard described it in these terms:

> Today the Irish National War Memorial is in a sorry state. The memorial records have long since been destroyed by vandals, the fountains are dry, the graffiti seem ineradicable. The most constant visitors are horses grazing and dogs being exercised ... In a sense the bleak granite, decapitated columns, broken-down hedges, rotted pergolas, damaged fountains and empty pavilions are aptly evocative of a long-abandoned battlefield. Neglect verging upon desecration symbolizes the persistent indifference to the War and its legacy of successive administrations, anxious to guard the people from historical awareness lest they remember too much.[32]

It was as if the Irish war dead had once again found themselves in no-man's-land – this time a political no-man's-land. Stephen Gwynn, a poet and Irish Parliamentary Party MP who had fought in the war, wrote:

> We trod our way to the end;
> We were part of victory:
> And in the face of the world
> Ireland disowned us.[33]

In Northern Ireland 'memory of the war soon became an ideological football kicked around for the sake of political expediency'.[34] The Great War was appropriated as another sacred chapter in unionist mythography, with Ulster Protestants commemorating their war dead as defenders of the empire, where 'death on the battlefield is commemorated as some sort of ritualistic act reaffirming Ulster Protestants' covenant with the Union and faith in their preordained political destiny'.[35] This manifest destiny was irreparably linked with the sacrifice of the 36th (Ulster) Division on the first day of the Somme, an event whose significance for unionists is akin to that of Gallipoli for Australians, being remembered not as a disastrous British failure but as a glorious chapter in the quest for communal identity.[36]

Memorial services in the North took on an imperial and sectarian tone, with the Somme becoming as emblematic as the Boyne. Protestant churches installed memorials, while Catholic churches in the main did not. Remembrance Day services employed imperialistic ritual and were often organised by the local Orange Lodge, deterring attendance by nationalists fearful that their participation might be construed as an act of solidarity with unionism. Catholic ex-servicemen formed the Irish Nationalist Veterans Association separate from the Royal British Legion and organised their own church services. The poppy became synonymous with the Orange lily, seen by nationalists as a supremacist emblem commemorating 'their' sacrifices but not 'ours'. It was also regarded, both North and South, as an imperial icon. The identification of remembrance with Protestantism, imperialism and unionism served to reinforce northern nationalists' indifference by deterring their participation, effectively hijacking Irish memory of the war for the unionist cause.[37]

Of the war years, it is 1916 that holds a special place in the memory of the people of Ireland, much as 1915 does for Australians. But, whereas Australians look back to 1915, with its evocation of Gallipoli and the Anzacs, as a source of unity, remembrance of 1916 for the people of Ireland is a source of division. Two major events of that year in Irish history, the Easter Rising and the Battle of the Somme, have become exclusively iconic for nationalists and unionists, respectively. As David Fitzpatrick has pointed out in *The Two Irelands 1912–1939*,[38] both events share a sense of fighting against overwhelming odds, an acceptance of defeat with dignity, the suffering of appalling losses, and the sense of martyrdom for a just cause. According to Fran Brearton in *The Great War in Irish Poetry*:

> The Battle of the Somme and the Easter Rising functioned, in their different ways, as part of the origin myths of Northern Ireland and the Irish Free State respectively. They became events which were held to encapsulate the inherent qualities of the true Ulster Protestant (proud, reticent, unimaginative) or true Irish Catholic (spiritual, voluble, imaginative), oppositional stereotypes used and abused on both sides. But they have this in common: they simplify interpretations of history, and in doing so leave completely out of the equation those Irish soldiers who fought in the Great War and yet were committed to an independent Ireland, or indeed those who fought for no complex political reason at all – those, in other words, whose actions cannot be easily explained in one or other version of events.[39]

By viewing the Easter Rising as part of the Irish experience of the Great War, rather than as an event independent of it, we can begin to understand how it came to displace the memory of the 10th and 16th Divisions, in much the same way as northern remembrance of the Somme has displaced memory of the 36th Division's other battles and obliterated memory of the 10th and 16th Divisions, in which many northerners fought and died. A similar phenomenon has occurred in Australia, where Gallipoli has displaced other battles in which the AIF fought. How many Australians have heard, for instance, of the battle of Hamel, arguably the finest Australian military achievement of the war? The Easter Rising, as it came to be imagined with all the overlays of heroic romanticism and blood sacrifice, provided a memory that was both compelling and effective in bolstering a sense of national identity. Thirty-five thousand Irishmen might have died at Gallipoli and in Flanders and Picardy, but as far as most nationalists were concerned they had been simply in the wrong place at the wrong time.

As he prepared to leave Ireland for the front, Tom Kettle, an Irish Parliamentary Party MP who had been in Dublin during Easter week 1916, referred to the rebels and lamented: 'These men will go down in history as heroes and martyrs, and I will go down – if I go down at all – as a bloody British officer.'[40] He was killed a few weeks later during the 16th Division's attack on Ginchy on 9 September. A memorial to him in St Stephen's Green was erected only after controversy, including objections to the words 'Killed in France' from the Commissioners of Public Works, who, according to historian Keith Jeffery, feared 'possible political repercussions'.[41] Francis Ledwidge, another nationalist soldier-poet, was recovering from wounds received while fighting with the 10th Division when he penned his famous 'Lament for Thomas McDonagh', one of the executed leaders of the Rising. Ledwidge was killed in July 1917 during the Third Battle of Ypres (Passchendaele).

Today, in Northern Ireland, the powerful symbolism of the Easter Rising and the Somme is exploited by the propagandists. Loyalist murals in Belfast depicting scenes of battle during the First World War seek to reinforce tribal identity. Jim Haughey in *The First World War in Irish Poetry* points out that 'Memory of the war has been submerged by the subsequent mythmaking industry of unionism and nationalism...Surely these divergent memories of the Great War have played their part...in maintaining current political divisions in Ireland.'[42]

A Remembrance Sunday ceremony was the occasion for one of the worst atrocities of the recent Troubles. Shortly before 11am on 8 November 1987, as the citizens of Enniskillen in County Fermanagh were assembling at the cenotaph for the remembrance service, a bomb exploded, killing eleven people and injuring sixty-three. The bombing drew immediate condemnation from around the world. Apart from deploring the number killed and injured and the fact that the victims were mostly civilians – men, women and children – many critics of the IRA's tactics on that day, including Irish nationalists, singled out for particular abhorrence the fact that the victims had come to the cenotaph to commemorate their war dead.

THE RHETORIC OF REMEMBRANCE

But remembrance is not simply about honouring the dead. It forms 'a potent element in the endorsement of a particular political culture or the creation of an alternative one'.[43] Its power derives from the fact that it evokes a sense of duty owed by the survivors to those who died 'for us'. But it is a duty without legal or moral force, imagined rather than real. And in the same way that nations derive their power as imagined communities, it is the imagined duty to the dead which empowers remembrance.[44] While the community is exhorted to further the cause for which 'they' died, so that their sacrifice is not in vain, it is those who control the rituals of remembrance who define the cause for which the remembered were 'faithful until death'. And it is they who are in a position to deploy its power to further the interests of a section of the community.

James Loughlin illustrates the phenomenon with the following extract from the *Belfast News Letter published* in 1920:

The war is now, happily, a thing of the past, but we can profit by its lessons, and one of the most important of these is that no community can be deprived of its birthright if it is sufficiently firm in its determination to defend and maintain it. The two minutes of silence was an act of solemn remembrance – remembrance of the men who were faithful until death and recollection of the duty laid upon us, for whom they died, to see that their sacrifice was not in vain.[45]

Because the unionists controlled the rituals of remembrance in Ulster, they were able to use remembrance of the war dead to further the interests of unionism during the critical post-war period when various forms of constitutional arrangement were being considered by the British government, including an all-Ireland parliament. The subtext of the above quotation is that these men died to defend and maintain Ulster as an integral part of the United Kingdom, free from the tyranny that would inevitably flow from the grant of home rule to an all-Ireland parliament. In other words, the duty laid upon 'us', the survivors, is to see that their sacrifice was not in vain, by mobilising to defeat home rule. The political quality of remembrance in post-war Ulster can be seen in stark relief when one considers the thousands of Irishmen from that province who enlisted to further the cause of home rule, as John Redmond and Belfast Nationalist MP Joe Devlin had urged them to do. Is there no duty laid upon the survivors to see that their sacrifice was not in vain? And what of those who enlisted without regard to a cause, but did so out of a sense of adventure or for economic reasons? Are they less worthy of remembrance?

Remembrance in Northern Ireland is not so much unique as polarised: its spectrum of public discourse lacking the shades of grey that moderate differences in most other communities. In Australia, too, remembrance serves a political purpose, but one that accommodates a broader cross-section of the community.

In Ireland in recent years, however, the rituals and rhetoric of remembrance have been changing. This transformation has coincided with a revolution in Irish historiography in which traditional interpretations have given way to a more complex, varied and inclusive narrative of Ireland's past. The change in attitudes to remembrance has been symbolised in the South by the condition of the National War Memorial, which underwent a major restoration in the 1990s. Attempts have been made in the North to bridge the gap between unionist and nationalist attitudes to remembrance and in the South to dispel ignorance of Ireland's part in the First World War. In the 1990s a spate of publications, some by journalist-historians whose work is accessible to a mass readership, raised the awareness of the Irish people to the significant contribution which nationalist Ireland made during the war. These included books by Tom Johnstone, Terence Denman, Tom Dooley and Myles Dungan.[46]

In 1996, plans were announced to build a memorial to commemorate Irish war dead in the form of an Irish round tower at Mesen (formerly Messines) in Belgium, where in June 1917 the 16th (Irish) Division and 36th (Ulster) Division had fought alongside each other. As far back as 1921, a monument had been erected to the 36th Division at Thiepval, where the Ulstermen had suffered so terribly on the first day of the Battle of the Somme. Memorials had also been erected in 1923 to the 10th (Irish) Division at Salonika and in 1926 to the 16th (Irish) Division at Guillemont in France and at Wytschaete in Belgium. But the round tower was to be a memorial to all Irishmen who had served, regardless of politics or religion. On 11 November 1998, the Irish Peace Park at Mesen was dedicated in a ceremony in which the Irish President, Mary McAleese, stood beside Queen Elizabeth. Just a few days earlier President McAleese had been seen wearing a poppy while laying a wreath at London's Cenotaph.[47]

On both sides of the border there have been attempts to find common ground. At Newtownards, a unionist stronghold east of Belfast, the Somme Heritage Museum tells the story not only of the 36th (Ulster) Division, but of the 10th and the 16th Divisions as well. At the 1996 West Belfast Festival, an annual cultural festival organised by the nationalist community, one of the topics discussed was 'on the lessons of 1916 – both the Easter Rising and the Battle of the Somme'. Seamus Breslin, from a nationalist area of Derry, has written numerous articles in the press on the contribution of Derry nationalists in the First World War.[48] However, as yet, he does not participate in the official Remembrance Day ceremony as he considers it totally British in nature; instead, after the service, he and others lay a wreath for 'everybody'.[49]

There is still a long way to go, and, in this highly contested aspect of Irish political and cultural life, mutual ground can be hard to find. In 2002, the Sinn Féin Lord Mayor of Belfast, Alex Maskey, laid a wreath at the cenotaph on the anniversary of the Somme – a gesture that would have been unimaginable a few years before. However, Maskey performed the ritual two hours before the official ceremony. While some unionists accepted the gesture as a step forward, others took it as an insult, arguing that he should have attended the main ceremony, to which Maskey's supporters replied that nationalists might consider doing so if the ceremony were made inclusive. At the same time, many diehard republicans remain opposed to honouring Irishmen killed in the empire's war in the same manner as those who died fighting for Ireland's liberation.[50]

In the South, a number of groups have been formed to promote the memory of the Irish war dead, such as the Royal Dublin Fusiliers

Association and the Fame of Tipperary Group. In recent years, war memorials have been erected: at Bandon, County Cork, in 1996; at Leighlinbridge, County Carlow, in 2002; and at Tipperary town in 2005. In October 2006, Taoiseach Bertie Ahern unveiled a new war memorial at Fermoy, County Cork, saying in the course of his speech:

> As a country, we owe it to the many Irish men who fought and died [in the First World War] to remember the part that they played...Those that survived came back to a very changed Ireland that did not value their sacrifice. Those that died in the battlefield came close to being completely forgotten by the following generations. It is right and proper that in more recent times the memory of these men has been resurrected and proper tribute has been paid to them.[51]

Philip Lecane of Dún Laoghaire has been instrumental in having a memorial erected to remember those who perished in October 1918 on the *RMS Leinster*. There are exhibits on the First World War at the Waterford County Museum, Dungarvan, and the Athy Heritage Centre in County Kildare. In October 2006 the National Museum of Ireland opened an exhibition at the Collins barracks museum in Dublin which includes displays on Irish soldiers in the First World War.

Remembrance Day is commemorated each year in St Patrick's Church of Ireland Cathedral, Dublin, under the auspices of the Royal British Legion, though it has not enjoyed popular support, despite the presence in recent years of President McAleese. However, a number of cities and towns have recently revived remembrance services: in 1999 a remembrance ceremony was held at the Drogheda War Memorial for the first time in thirty years;[52] in 2003, the Sinn Féin mayor of Sligo attended the remembrance service at the town's war memorial;[53] in 2005, Cork's Lord Mayor attended that city's wreath laying ceremony.[54]

In a gesture of inclusiveness, Belvedere College, the Jesuit school in Dublin, unveiled a memorial plaque in 2003, which lists the names of old Belvederians who died in all Irish wars and civil strife. The names include those who fought and died on opposing sides in the Easter Rising and in the Civil War, as well as those from the two world wars.

At a popular level, Sebastian Barry's *A Long Long Way*, a best-selling novel about the Dublin Fusiliers during the war, is informing a new Irish generation of their long-forgotten past.[55] But perhaps the most significant recent development was the Irish government's commemoration of the ninetieth anniversary of the Battle of the Somme, which involved a ceremony in Dublin attended by the President and the Taoiseach, as well as ministerial representation at commemorations in France. It was the first time the Irish state has commemorated that battle, so long the exclusive preserve of unionists.[56] As yet there is no official commemoration in the Republic of Ireland of the Gallipoli campaign in which thousands of Irishmen died. Nevertheless, there is an Anzac Day service in Dublin, organised alternately by the Australian embassy and the New Zealand Irish Association. The ceremony involves a church service and reception. In 2006, the Irish government was represented for the first time by a minister of state, while senior Irish military officers have attended for a number of years, as have members of Irish ex-service associations.

CONCLUSION

In Australia, remembrance on the whole has served to unify the nation, though at times sections of the population have been marginalised. In Ireland, however, it has contributed to the division between unionists and nationalists, North and South, Protestants and Catholics, though in recent years tentative steps have been taken to devise memorials and forms of remembrance that are more inclusive and less contested. Perhaps, as a result, people across Ireland might find sufficient common ground to commemorate together the sacrifice of too many lives cut short or devastated in the conflicts of the past. Whether we can hope for more is hard to say. As President Mary McAleese observed in 1998 in relation to the Irish Peace Park at Messines, 'Its message of reconciliation is clear, but we must not forget that reconciliation is made up of a series of steps – it is a journey, not an event.'[57]

NOTES

1. The chapter title is a reference to 'Who Fears to Speak of '98?', the popular name of John Kells Ingram's poem 'The Memory of the Dead', written in 1843 to commemorate those who died in the rising of 1798. It became a popular nationalist ballad.
2. In relation to remembrance of the war generally, see, for example, Paul Fussell, *The Great War and Modern Memory* (Oxford: Oxford University Press, 1977); Jay Winter and Emmanuel Sivan (eds), *War and Remembrance in the Twentieth Century* (Cambridge: Cambridge University Press, 2000); T.G. Ashplant, Graham Dawson, Michael Roper (eds), *The Politics of War Memory and Commemorations* (London: Routledge, 2000).
3. Joan Beaumont, *Australia's War 1914–18* (Sydney: Allen & Unwin, 1995), p.xvii.
4. This day, variously known as Armistice Day or Remembrance Day, marks the armistice that ended the fighting in 1918. In some places it is observed on the nearest Sunday and referred to as Remembrance Sunday.
5. Jenny Macleod, 'The Fall and Rise of Anzac Day: 1965 and 1990 Compared', *War and Society*, 20 (May 2002), pp.149–68.
6. Alistair Thomson, *Anzac Memories: Living with the Legend* (Oxford: Oxford University Press, 1995), pp.189–90, 200.

7. *Freeman's Journal,* 27 April 1916, p.22.
8. Letter from the General Secretary of the Catholic Returned Soldiers and Sailors Association, published in the *Sydney Morning Herald* and republished in the *Catholic Press,* 22 June 1922, p.15.
9. Joan Beaumont, 'The Politics of a Divided Society', in Beaumont, *Australia's War*, p.56.
10. John Luttrell, 'Cardinal Gilroy's Anzac Day Problem', *Journal of the Royal Australian Historical Society* 85 (June 1999), pp.1–19.
11. Luttrell, 'Cardinal Gilroy's Anzac Day Problem'.
12. Graham Seal, *Inventing Anzac: The Digger and National Mythology* (St Lucia, Queensland: University of Queensland Press, 2004), p.119.
13. Beaumont, 'Politics of a Divided Society', p.56.
14. K.S. Inglis, 'A Sacred Place: The Making of the Australian War Memorial', *War & Society* 3/2 (1985), pp.99–126 at p.109.
15. K.S. Inglis, *Sacred Places: War Memorials in the Australian Landscape* (Carlton, Victoria: Melbourne University Press, 2001), p.124.
16. Ibid., p.128.
17. Ibid., p.227.
18. Ibid., pp.227–8, 384–5
19. Ibid., p.128.
20. Ibid., p.224.
21. Ibid., p.226.
22. (London: Hodder and Stoughton, 1916), p.102.
23. Mark McCarthy (ed.), *Ireland's Heritages: Critical Perspectives on Memory and Identity* (Aldershot: Ashgate Publishing, 2005), p.22.
24. Jim Haughey, *The First World War in Irish Poetry* (Lewisburg: Bucknell University Press, 2002), p.37.
25. Charles Townshend, 'Religion, War, and Identity in Ireland', *The Journal of Modern History* 76/4 (December 2004), pp.882–902, at p. 890.
26. Terence Denman, *Ireland's Unknown Soldiers: The 16th (Irish) Division in the Great War, 1914–1918* (Dublin: Irish Academic Press, 1992), p.17.
27. For a history of the changing national identity of the Irish divisions during the war see Nicholas Perry, 'Nationality in the Irish Infantry Regiments in the First World War', *War & Society* 12/1 (May 1994), pp.65–95.
28. F.X. Martin, '1916 – Myth, Fact and Mystery', *Studia Hibernica*, No. 7, pp.7–124 at p.68.
29. Keith Jeffery, *Ireland and the Great War* (Cambridge: Cambridge University Press, 2000), chapter 4 and David Fitzpatrick, 'Commemoration in the Irish Free State: A Chronicle of Embarrassment', in Ian McBride, *History and Memory in Modern Ireland* (Cambridge: Cambridge University Press, 2001), pp.184–203 discuss forms of remembrance of the First World War in the South. See also Ewan Morris, *Our Own Devices: National Symbols and Political Conflict in Twentieth-Century Ireland* (Dublin: Irish Academic Press, 2005), pp.153–66.
30. D.G. Boyce, '"That Party Politics Should Divide Our Tents": Nationalism, Unionism and the First World War', in Adrian Gregory and Senia Paseta (eds), *Ireland and the Great War: 'A War to Unite Us All'?* (Manchester: Manchester University Press, 2002), pp.190–216, at p.202.
31. Denman, *Ireland's Unknown Soldiers*, p.16.
32. Jane Leonard, 'Lest We Forget' in David Fitzpatrick, *Ireland and the First World War* (Dublin: Trinity History Workshop Publications, 1986), p.67.
33. Quoted in Haughey, *The First World War in Irish Poetry*, p.206.
34. Ibid., p.37.
35. Ibid., p.42.
36. See David Officer, '"For God and for Ulster"': The Ulsterman on the Somme', in McBride, *History and Memory in Modern Ireland*, pp.160–83.
37. James Loughlin, 'Mobilising the Sacred Dead: Ulster Unionism, the Great War and the

Politics of Remembrance', in Gregory and Paseta (eds), *Ireland and the Great War*, pp.133–54.

38. (Oxford: Oxford University Press, 1998), p.61.
39. Fran Brearton, *The Great War in Irish Poetry: W.B. Yeats to Michael Longley* (Oxford: Oxford University Press, 2003), pp.37–8.
40. Quoted in Boyce, 'That Party Politics Should Divide Our Tents', p.201.
41. Jeffery, *Ireland and the Great War*, p.128.
42. Haughey, *The First World War in Irish Poetry*, p.61.
43. P. Travers, 'Our Fenian Dead: Glasnevin Cemetery and the Genesis of the Republican Funeral', in J. Kelly and U. MacGearailt (eds), *Dublin and Dubliners* (Dublin, 1990) p.52, quoted in Nuala C. Johnson, 'The Spectacle of Memory: Ireland's Remembrance of the Great War, 1919', *Journal of Historical Geography* 25/1 (1999), pp.36–56 at p.37.
44. See Benedict Anderson, *Imagined Communities: Reflections on the Origin and Spread of Nationalism* (London: Verso, 1991).
45. Loughlin, 'Mobilising the Sacred Dead', pp.142–3.
46. Tom Johnstone, *Orange, Green and Khaki: The Story of the Irish Regiments in the Great War, 1914–18* (Dublin: Gill and Macmillan, 1992); Denman, *Ireland's Unknown Soldiers*, 1992; Thomas P. Dooley, *Irishmen or English Soldiers?: The Times and World of a Southern Irish Man (1876–1916) Enlisting in the British Army During the First World War* (Liverpool: Liverpool University Press, 1995); Myles Dungan, *Irish Voices from the Great War* (Dublin: Irish Academic Press, 1995); Myles Dungan, *They Shall Grow Not Old: Irish Soldiers and the Great War* (Dublin: Four Courts Press, 1997).
47. Haughey, *The First World War in Irish Poetry*, p.38.
48. See, for example, *Derry Journal*, 12 January 1996, p.17; 23 January 1998, p.22; 3 August 2004, p.17; *Andersonstown News*, 30 October 1999, p.32.
49. Email communications with the author.
50. See reports in the BBC News Archive at <http://news.bbc.co.uk>.
51. <http://www.taoiseach.gov.ie/index.asp?locID=200&docID=2920> [accessed 29 November 2006].
52. <http://community.channel4.com/eve/ubb.x/a/tpc/f/8896096411/m/683608464/p/18> [accessed 10 October 2006].
53. *Sligo Weekender*, 18 November 2003. <http://archives.tcm.ie/sligoweekender/2003/11/18/story15300.asp> [Accessed 10 October 2006].
54. <http://www.corkcorp.ie/news/archive/2005/remembrance_day.shtml> [accessed 10 October 2006].
55. (London: Faber & Faber, 2005). It was shortlisted for the Man Booker Prize for 2005.
56. In 2006, the Taoiseach's website added a page entitled 'Irish Soldiers in the First World War', which includes a reasonably detailed narrative of Ireland's role in the war <http://www.taoiseach.gov.ie/eng/index.asp?docID=2517> [accessed 10 October 2006].
57. Quoted in McCarthy (ed.), *Ireland's Heritages*, p.27.

Index